THE BIRDS OF ANCIENT EGYPT

The BIRDS of ANCIENT EGYPT

Patrick F. Houlihan

With the Collaboration and a Preliminary Checklist to the Birds of Egypt by

STEVEN M. GOODMAN

ARIS & PHILLIPS — WARMINSTER — ENGLAND

ISBN 0 85668 283 7

Printed & Published in England by Aris & Phillips Ltd., Teddington House, Warminster, Wiltshire BA12 8PQ.

CONTENTS

THE CATALOGUE	Fig. Nos.	Page Nos.
1. Ostrich	1-5	1
2. Diver	6	6
3. Cormorant	7-9	7
4. Darter	10	9
5. White or Pink-backed Pelican	11-13	10
6. Dalmatian Pelican	14	12
7. Heron	15-19	13
8. Egret	20-22	16
9. Night Heron	23	18
10. Little Bittern/Bittern	24-26	20
11. Black Stork	27	22
12 Saddlebill Stork	28-30	23
13. Whale-headed Stork (?)	31	25
14. Glossy Ibis	32-33	26
15. Sacred Ibis	34-38	28
16. Hermit Ibis	39-42	31
17. European Spoonbill	43-46	33
18. Greater Flamingo	47-50	35
19. Black Kite	51-54	36
20. Egyptian Vulture	55	39
21. Griffon Vulture	56	40
22. Lappet-faced Vulture	57-58	41
23. Long-legged Buzzard	59	44
24. Lesser Kestrel/Kestrel	60	45
25. "Horus Falcon"	61-65	46
26. Mute Swan	66a-66b	50
27. Whooper or Bewick's Swan	67-71	53
28. Greylag Goose	72-75	54
29. White-fronted Goose	76-82	57
30. Bean Goose	83	60
31. Red-breasted Goose	84	61
32. Egyptian Goose	85-89	62
33. Ruddy Shelduck	90-91	65
34. Common Shelduck	92	66
35. Green-winged Teal	93-95	67
36. European Wigeon	96-97	69
37. Pintail	98-103	71
38. Tufted Duck	104	74
39. Common Quail	105-110	74

SOURCES OF THE FIGURES

All of the photographs were provided by the institutions who own the objects illustrated, except where indicated otherwise. The authors and publishers wish to thank the copyright holders for their kind permission to reproduce the material.

frontispiece: Photograph by P.F. Houlihan.
p. xxx. Reproduced from Steindorff 1913, pl. 113.

1. Egyptian Museum, Cairo.
   Photograph by the Egyptian Expedition, the Metropolitan Museum of Art, New York.
2. Reproduced from Winkler 1938, pl. XX; by courtesy of the Egypt Exploration Society, London.
3. Photograph by the Egyptian Expedition, the Metropolitan Museum of Art, New York.
4. Tempera facsimile reproduced from Davies 1913, pl. XXIII; by courtesy of the Egypt Exploration Society, London.
5. Tempera facsimile reproduced from Davies 1936, pl. XXXVIII; by courtesy of the Oriental Institute, University of Chicago.
6. Photograph by S. M. Goodman.
7. Photograph by S. M. Goodman.
8. Photograph by S. M. Goodman.
9. Tempera facsimile reproduced from Newberry 1900, pl. XI; by courtesy of the Egypt Exploration Society, London.
10. Photograph by P. F. Houlihan.
11. Ägyptisches Museum, East Berlin.
    Reproduced from Wreszinski 1936, pl. 84.
12. Reproduced from Bissing 1956, pl. XVII(a).
13. Photograph by S. M. Goodman.
14. Tempera facsimile reproduced from Davies 1936, pl. XLI; by courtesy of the Oriental Institute, University of Chicago.
15. Photograph courtesy of the Museum of Fine Arts, Boston.
16. Photograph by S. M. Goodman.
17. Photograph courtesy of the Rijksmuseum van Oudheden, Leiden.
18. Photograph by S. M. Goodman.
19. Photograph courtesy of the Musées royaux d'Art et d'Histoire, Brussels.
20. Tempera facsimile reproduced from Davies 1936, pl. XIX; by courtesy of the Oriental Institute, University of Chicago.
21. Photograph courtesy of the Museum of Fine Arts, Boston.
22. Tempera facsimile reproduced from Davies 1936, pl. LIV; by courtesy of the Oriental Institute, University of Chicago.
23. Photograph by S. M. Goodman.
24. Egyptian Museum, Cairo.
    Photograph by S. M. Goodman.
25. Reproduced from Wild 1953, pl. CXXII; by courtesy of the Institut français d'archéologie orientale du Caire.
26. Photograph by S. M. Goodman.
27. Photograph by S. M. Goodman.
28. The Metropolitan Museum of Art, Purchase, Edward S. Harkness Gift, 1926.
29. The Metropolitan Museum of Art, Theodore M. Davis Collection, Bequest of Theodore M. Davis, 1915.
30. Photograph courtesy of the Lowie Museum of Anthropology, University of California, Berkeley.
31. Photograph courtesy of the Institut français d'archéologie orientale du Caire.
32. Photograph by S. M. Goodman.
33. Photograph by S. M. Goodman.
34. Tempera facsimile reproduced from Newberry 1900, pl. IX; by courtesy of the Egypt Exploration Society, London.
35. Photograph by S. M. Goodman.
36. The Brooklyn Museum, Charles Edwin Wilbour Fund.
37. Photograph courtesy of the Walters Art Gallery, Baltimore.
38. Courtesy of the Visitors of the Ashmolean Museum, Oxford.
39. Photograph courtesy of the Rijksmuseum van Oudheden, Leiden.
40. Egyptian Museum, Cairo.
    Reproduced from Hassan 1936, pl. LI.
41. Reproduced from Dunham 1946, p. 24 fig. 1; by courtesy of the Museum of Fine Arts, Boston.
42. Photograph courtesy of the Ägyptisches Museum der Karl-Marx-Universität, Leipzig.
43. Tempera facsimile reproduced from Newberry 1900, pl. X; by courtesy of the Egypt Exploration Society, London.
44. Photograph by S. M. Goodman.
45. Photograph courtesy of the Musées royaux d'Art et d'Histoire, Brussels.

46. The Brooklyn Museum, Gift of Mrs. Lawrence Coolidge and Mrs. Robert Woods Bliss.

47. Ägyptisches Museum, East Berlin.
Photograph courtesy of the Fondation égyptologique Reine Élisabeth, Brussels.

48. Photograph courtesy of the Lowie Museum of Anthropology, University of California, Berkeley.

49. Photograph by S. M. Goodman.

50. Photograph by P. F. Houlihan.

51. Photograph courtesy of the Trustees of the British Museum, London.

52. British Museum, London.
Photograph by P. F. Houlihan.

53. Tempera facsimile courtesy of the Metropolitan Museum of Art, New York, Rogers Fund, 1930.

54. Reproduced from Singer et al. 1954, p. 264, fig. 164. Drawing by N. M. Davies from J. G. Wilkinson MSS.

55. Egyptian Museum, Cairo.
Photograph by P. F. Houlihan.

56. Photograph by P. F. Houlihan.

57. Egyptian Museum, Cairo.
Photograph courtesy of the Griffith Institute, Ashmolean Museum, Oxford.

58. Egyptian Museum, Cairo.
Reproduced from Quibell 1908, pl. V.

59. Tempera facsimile reproduced from Griffith 1898, pl. I, fig. 1; by courtesy of the Egypt Exploration Society, London.

60. Photograph by S. M. Goodman.

61. Tempera facsimile reproduced from Loret 1903, pl. I; by courtesy of the Institut français d'archéologie orientale du Caire.

62. Photograph courtesy of the Staatliche Sammlung Ägyptischer Kunst, Munich.

63. Photograph courtesy of the Musée du Louvre, Paris.

64. Tempera facsimile reproduced from Naville 1897, pl. XXXIX; by courtesy of the Egypt Exploration Society, London.

65. Photograph courtesy of the Detroit Institute of Arts.

66a. Egyptian Museum, Cairo.
Photograph by S. M. Goodman.

66b. Photograph by S. M. Goodman.

67. Photograph by S. M. Goodman.

68. Petrie Museum, University College, London.
Reproduced from Quibell 1900, pl. XVI fig. 4; by courtesy of the Egypt Exploration Society, London.

69. Egyptian Museum, Cairo.
Reproduced from Daressy 1902, pl. LV.

70. Reproduced from Davis 1912, pl. LXXXVII.

71. Reproduced from Abitz 1979, p. 16 fig. 3(a).

72. Ashmolean Museum, Oxford.
Tempera facsimile reproduced from

Frankfort 1929, pl. XI; by courtesy of the Egypt Exploration Society, London.

73. Reproduced from Éperon et al. 1939, pl. XXVIII; by courtesy of the Institut français d'archéologie orientale du Caire.

74. Reproduced from Éperon et al. 1939, pl. XXV; by courtesy of the Institut français d'archéologie orientale du Caire.

75. Photograph courtesy of the Trustees of the British Museum, London.

76. Egyptian Museum, Cairo.
Photograph by S.M. Goodman.

77. Tempera facsimile reproduced from Davies 1946, frontispiece; by courtesy of the Egypt Exploration Society, London.

78. Photograph by S. M. Goodman.

79. Photograph by S. M. Goodman.

80. Tempera facsimile reproduced from Rosellini 1834, pl. XIII fig. 9.

81. Egyptian Museum, Cairo.
Reproduced from Gaillard and Daressy 1905, pl. XLVII.

82. Photograph courtesy of the Trustees of the British Museum, London.

83. Egyptian Museum, Cairo.
Photograph by S. M. Goodman.

84. Photograph by S. M. Goodman.

85. Photograph courtesy of the Trustees of the British Museum, London.

86. Photograph by S. M. Goodman.

87. Photograph by S. M. Goodman.

88. British Museum, London.
Photograph by S. M. Goodman.

89. Photograph courtesy of the Roemer-Pelizaeus-Museum, Hildesheim.

90. Photograph by S. M. Goodman.

91. Photograph by S. M. Goodman.

92. Reproduced from Newberry 1895, pl. XXI; by courtesy of the Egypt Exploration Society, London.

93. Tempera facsimile reproduced from Davies 1930a, pl. XXXI; by courtesy of the Metropolitan Museum of Art, New York.

94. Tempera facsimile courtesy of the Metropolitan Museum of Art, New York, Rogers Fund, 1933.

95. Tempera facsimile reproduced from Rosellini 1834, pl. VII.

96. Photograph by S. M. Goodman.

97. Photograph by S. M. Goodman.

98. Photograph courtesy of the Trustees of the British Museum, London.

99. The Metropolitan Museum of Art, New York, Lent by Norbert Schimmel.

100. The Brooklyn Museum, Charles Edwin Wilbour Fund.

101. Photograph courtesy of the Institut français d'archéologie orientale du Caire.

102. The Metropolitan Museum of Art, New York, Rogers Fund, 1915.

103. Tempera facsimile reproduced from Phillips 1948, fig. 25; by courtesy of the Metropolitan Museum of Art, New York.
104. Reproduced from Wild 1953, pl. CXX; by courtesy of the Institut français d'archéologie orientale du Caire.
105. Reproduced from Wreszinski 1936, pl. 47.
106a. Photograph courtesy of the Staatliche Museen zu Berlin/Hauptstadt der DDR.
106b. Reproduced from Northampton *et.al.* 1908, p. 5 fig. 2.
107. Egyptian Museum, Cairo.
Photograph by P. F. Houlihan.
108. Reproduced from Wreszinski 1923, pl. 191.
109. Photograph by S. M. Goodman.
110. Photograph by S. M. Goodman.
111. British Museum, London.
Photograph by P. F. Houlihan.
112. The Metropolitan Museum of Art, New York, Rogers Fund, 1907.
113. Photograph courtesy of the Staatliche Museen zu Berlin/Hauptstadt der DDR.
114. Reproduced from Lefebvre 1924, pl. XLVII; by courtesy of the Institut français d'archéologie orientale du Caire.
115. Photograph courtesy of the Staatliche Museen zu Berlin/Hauptstadt der DDR.
116. Photograph by S. M. Goodman.
117. Courtesy of the Visitors of the Ashmolean Museum, Oxford.
118. Ägyptisches Museum, East Berlin. Reproduced from Wreszinski 1936, pl. 83(c).
119. Photograph courtesy of the Ny Carlsberg Glyptothek, Copenhagen.
120. Photograph by S. M. Goodman.
121. Photograph by S. M. Goodman.
122. Photograph of a cast courtesy of the Royal Ontario Museum, Toronto, Canada.
123. Photograph courtesy of the Rijksmuseum van Oudheden, Leiden.
124. Photograph courtesy of the Institut français d'archéologie orientale du Caire.
125. Photograph by S. M. Goodman.
126. Egyptian Museum, Cairo.
Photograph by S. M. Goodman.
127. Tempera facsimile reproduced from Rosellini 1834, pl. IX fig. 8.
128. Photograph by S. M. Goodman.
129. Photograph by S. M. Goodman.
130. Photograph by S. M. Goodman.
131. Photograph by S. M. Goodman.
132. Photograph by S. M. Goodman.
133. Ashmolean Museum, Oxford.
Reproduced from Gardiner 1961, p. 403.
134. Egyptian Museum, Cairo.
Photograph by S. M. Goodman.
135. Photograph courtesy of the Ägyptisches Museum Berlin SMPK.

136. The Cleveland Museum of Art, Gift of Hanna Fund.
137. Tempera facsimile reproduced from Davies 1936, pl. XIX; by courtesy of the Oriental Institute, University of Chicago.
138. Photograph by S. M. Goodman.
139. Photograph courtesy of the Institut français d'archéologie orientale du Caire.
140. Photograph courtesy of the Institut français d'archéologie orientale du Caire.
141. Photograph by S. M. Goodman.
142. Photograph by S. M. Goodman.
143. Photograph courtesy of the Institut français d'archéologie orientale du Caire.
144. Reproduced from Newberry 1895, pl. XXIII; by courtesy of the Egypt Exploration Society, London.
145. Photograph by S. M. Goodman.
146. British Museum, London.
Tempera facsimile reproduced from Frankfort 1929, pl. V; by courtesy of the Egypt Exploration Society, London.
147. Tempera facsimile reproduced from Davies 1936, pl. XLIX; by courtesy of the Oriental Institute, University of Chicago.
148. Photograph courtesy of the Trustees of the British Museum, London.
149. Tempera facsimile reproduced from Davies 1936, pl. CI; by courtesy of the Oriental Institute, University of Chicago.
150. Photograph courtesy of the Museum of Fine Arts, Boston.
151. Reproduced from Éperon *et al.* 1939, pl. XXV; by courtesy of the Institut français d'archéologie orientale du Caire.
152. Reproduced from Wild 1953, pl. CIX; by courtesy of the Institut français d'archéologie orientale du Caire.
153. Photograph courtesy of the Museum of Fine Arts, Boston.
154. Tempera facsimile reproduced from Newberry 1900, frontispiece; by courtesy of the Egypt Exploration Society, London.
155. Photograph by S. M. Goodman.
156. Photograph by P. F. Houlihan.
157. Photograph courtesy of the Musée du Louvre, Paris.
158. Courtesy of the Oriental Institute, University of Chicago.
159. Egyptian Museum, Cairo.
Photograph by S. M. Goodman.
160. Photograph by S. M. Goodman.
161. Tempera facsimile reproduced from Rosellini 1834, pl. X fig. 9.
162. Egyptian Museum, Cairo.
Photograph by S. M. Goodman.
163. Egyptian Museum, Cairo.
Tempera facsimile reproduced from Davies 1936, pl. LXXVI; by courtesey of the Oriental Institute, University of Chicago.

164. Egyptian Museum, Cairo.
Photograph by S. M. Goodman.
165. Photograph courtesy of the Rijksmuseum van Oudheden, Leiden.
166. Photograph by S. M. Goodman.
167. Tempera facsimile reproduced from Davies 1936, pl. IX; by courtesy of the Oriental Institute, University of Chicago.
168. Photograph courtesy of the Museum of Fine Arts, Boston.
169. Egyptian Museum, Cairo.
Photograph by S. M. Goodman.
170. Photograph by S. M. Goodman.
171. Photograph by S. M. Goodman.
172. Egyptian Museum, Cairo.
Photograph by S. M. Goodman.
173. Egyptian Museum, Cairo.
Photograph by S. M. Goodman.
174. Egyptian Museum, Cairo.
Reproduced from Piankoff 1957, pl.2.
175. Photograph courtesy of the Trustees of the British Museum, London.
176. Museo Egizio, Turin.
Reproduced from Maspero 1897, p. 536.
177. Egyptian Museum, Cairo.
Photograph by S. M. Goodman.
178. British Museum, London.
Photograph by S. M. Goodman.
179. Tempera facsimile reproduced from Davies 1936, pl. IX; by courtesy of the Oriental Institute, University of Chicago.
180. Tempera facsimile reproduced from Davies 1936, pl. IX; by courtesy of the Oriental Institute, University of Chicago.
181. Photograph by S. M. Goodman.

182. Photograph by S. M. Goodman.
183. Photograph courtesy of the Musée du Louvre, Paris.
184. Egyptian Museum, Cairo.
Reproduced from Wreszinski 1936, pl. 105(b).
185. Photograph by S. M. Goodman.
186. Courtesy of the Visitors of the Ashmolean Museum, Oxford.
187. Reproduced from Vandier d'Abbadie 1936b, pl. II; by courtesy of the Institut français d'archéologie orientale du Caire.
188. Photograph courtesy of the Medelhavsmuseet, Stockholm.
189. Museo Egizio, Turin.
Reproduced from Brunner-Traut 1955, pl. III.
190. British Museum, London.
Photograph by S. M. Goodman.
191. Photograph courtesy of the Museum of Art and Archaeology, University of Missouri-Columbia. Gift of Mr. and Mrs. Donald N. Wilber. Drawing by John Huffstot.
192. The Manchester Museum, England.
193. Tempera facsimile reproduced from Davies 1936, pl. IX; by courtesy of the Oriental Institute, University of Chicago.
194. Reproduced from Mekhitarian 1954, p. 137; by courtesy of Rizzoli International Publications, Inc., New York.
195. Egyptian Museum, Cairo.
Photograph by S. M. Goodman.
196. Photograph by S. M. Goodman.
197. Photograph by S. M. Goodman.
198. Photograph by S. M. Goodman.
199. Reproduced from Price 1893, p. 344.

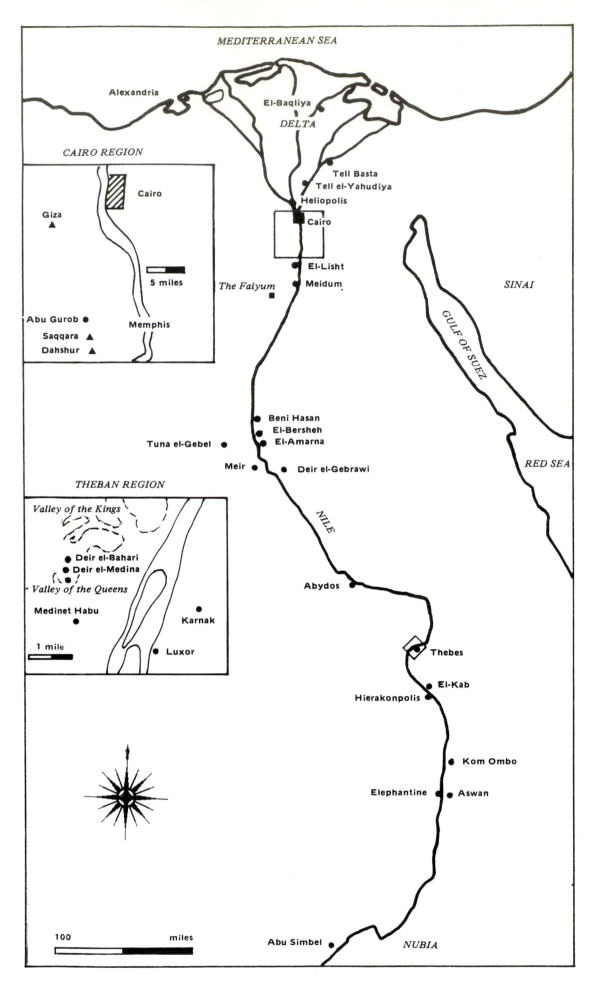

Ancient Egypt and the principal sites mentioned in the text

PREFACE

It has aptly been observed that "nowhere in the world have animals been drawn, painted or otherwise represented so frequently and in such variety as in Egyptian art."[1] This is particularly true for birds. In both secular and religious contexts, from predynastic times through the Ptolemaic Period, depictions of birds abound in all mediums. They are also very commonly figured in the hieroglyphic script. In Sir Alan Gardiner's Sign List, sixty-three standard hieroglyphs are listed which deal with birds and parts of birds.[2] Birds played more than just a minor role in the culture of ancient Egypt.

Egypt lies on a major migratory route for birds of the Palearctic region. Twice each year, during the spring and fall, great numbers of birds pass through the country while on their journey between Europe and central and southern Africa. Egypt also serves as an important wintering area for migratory birds from nearly the entire Palearctic region. After their long flights of passage across the Mediterranean Sea or sands of the Sahara, the birds arrive in Egypt in a much exhausted state and can be trapped with relative ease. These migrant birds, together with the resident species, were an abundant and easily exploited source of food for the ancient Egyptians. We can be reasonably confident that throughout the long course of Egyptian history birds were always readily consumed, and probably by all strata of society. There is some evidence to show that birds were sold very cheaply in ancient Egypt.[3] However, the specially raised and force-fed table birds we view in tomb scenes were more than likely reserved for those who could afford them. Even when certain species of fowl were domestically bred in captivity, birds were doubtless still taken from the wild to meet the high demand for them.

The Egyptians visualized the next world as a mirror image of the life they knew here. When they carved or painted scenes of everyday life on the walls of their tombs it was a way of magically ensuring that this life was to continue in the beyond. Much space was devoted to scenes in tombs which were designed to ensure the deceased with an endless supply of victuals throughout eternity. Among some of the most popular themes are those of poultry yards, aviaries, bird hunting and trapping, and almost always, great processions of offering bearers bringing gifts of fowl. It is the birds which appear in these scenes, those regarded as a potential article of food, which are most often represented in art and from which we learn the most about the birds of ancient Egypt. Numerous birds also had religious associations and appear in countless scenes which reflect their various roles.

The aim of this study is easy to define: to provide a systematic survey of all the bird life depicted by the ancient Egyptians in art and hieroglyphic writing, to sketch the birds' role in secular and religious spheres, and to attempt to compare their present-day distribution range with that in the time of the Pharaohs, based on the most current Egyptological and ornithological knowledge. It is also hoped that the Checklist (Appendix II) to the birds of modern Egypt will fill a long need to give bird enthusiasts an accurate and concise list. It must be noted that the present study does not cover the ancient Egyptian names for the respective species of birds. A new work by Dimitri Meeks investigates the birds identified in this book from a lexicographical point of view.[4]

Patrick F. Houlihan
Ann Arbor, 1985

---

1. te Velde 1980, p. 76.
2. Gardiner 1957, pp. 467-74.
3. Janssen 1975, p. 178.
4. Meeks (forthcoming).

ACKNOWLEDGEMENTS

I wish to express my heartiest thanks to Mr. William H. Peck for his encouragement and assistance over the years that this book has been in preparation, and for reading the manuscript in draft and making many useful observations and suggestions. For the prompt supply of photographs and kind permission to use them in this book, I am most grateful to Dr. J. C. Biers of the Museum of Art and Archaeology, University of Missouri-Columbia; Dr. E. Blumenthal of the Ägyptisches Museum der Karl-Marx-Universität, Leipzig; Dr. J.-L. de Cenival of the Musée du Louvre, Paris; Dr. A. David of the Manchester Museum; Dr. A. Eggebrecht of the Roemer-Pelizaeus-Museum, Hildesheim; Mr. R. A. Fazzini of the Brooklyn Museum; Mr. M. Jørgensen of the Ny Carlsberg Glyptothek, Copenhagen; Dr. J. S. Karig of the Ägyptisches Museum, West Berlin; Dr. A. P. Kozloff of the Cleveland Museum of Art; Mr. J. A. Larson of the Oriental Institute, the University of Chicago; Dr. C. Lilyquist of the Metropolitan Museum of Art, New York; Mr. L. Limme of the Musées royaux d'Art et d'Histoire, Brussels; Mr. A. Mekhitarian of the Fondation Égyptologique Reine Élisabeth, Brussels; Dr. N. B. Millet of the Royal Ontario Museum, Toronto; Dr. F. A. Norick of the Lowie Museum of Anthropology, University of California, Berkeley; Mr. W. H. Peck of the Detroit Institute of Arts; Dr. B. E. J. Peterson of the Medelhavsmuseet, Stockholm; Prof. P. Posener-Kriéger of the Institut français d'archéologie orientale du Caire; Dr. K.-H. Priese of the Ägyptisches Museum, East Berlin; Dr. H. D. Schneider of the Rijksmuseum van Oudheden, Leiden; Dr. S. Schoske of the Staatliche Sammlung Ägyptischer Kunst, Munich; Prof. W. K. Simpson of the Museum of Fine Arts, Boston; Dr. A. J. Spencer of the British Museum, London; Miss F. Strachan of the Griffith Institute, Ashmolean Museum, Oxford; Dr. H. Whitehouse of the Ashmolean Museum, Oxford; Dr. E. R. Williams of the Walters Art Gallery, Baltimore. I also wish to thank Dr. J. Lipińska for allowing me to photograph and publish material from the temple of Tuthmosis III at Deir el-Bahari excavated by the Polish Centre of Archaeology. My thanks are also due to Dr. R. A. Caminos and Dr. H. te Velde for kindly granting me permission to quote directly passages from their respective works in this book.

This book is a work of collaboration. I owe a special debt of gratitude to Mr. Steven M. Goodman who from drawing on his extensive knowledge of the Egyptian avifauna has been of immense assistance in this study. He is also responsible for many of the photographs which appear and has contributed the Checklist to the birds of modern Egypt (Appendix II). Jointly we wish to express our warm thanks to Dr. Robert W. Storer for all of his help. We also wish to thank the officials of the Egyptian Museum, Cairo, and the Egyptian Antiquities Organization for their friendly co-operation. For the preparation of many of the illustrations for this book, our thanks go to Bill and Pat Pelletier of Photo Services, Ann Arbor. We must also record the assistance and co-operation we have received over the years from the staff of the Harlan Hatcher Graduate Library, The University of Michigan, Ann Arbor.

I would also like to thank Mr. Adrian Phillips of Aris & Phillips Ltd for including this study in their Modern Egyptology series. Last, but by no means least of all, my very special thanks go to Laurie J. Stedman who typed the final manuscript and has given me much assistance during the period of its preparation.

ABBREVIATIONS AND REFERENCES CITED

AJA   *American Journal of Archaeology*, Baltimore and Norwood.

AJSL   *American Journal of Semitic Languages and Literatures*, Chicago.

AMHNL *Archives du Muséum d'Histoire naturelle de Lyon*, Lyon.

ASAE   *Annales du Service des Antiquités de l'Égypte*, Cairo.

BBOC   *Bulletin of the British Ornithologists' Club*, London.

BIFAO   *Bulletin de l'Institut français d'archéologie orientale du Caire*, Cairo.

BMFA   *Bulletin of the Museum of Fine Arts*, Boston.

BMMA   *Bulletin of the Metropolitan Museum of Art*, New York.

BZSE   *Bulletin of the Zoological Society of Egypt*, Cairo.

CdE   *Chronique d'Égypte*, Brussels.

ETM   *Egypt Travel Magazine*, Cairo.

JEA   *Journal of Egyptian Archaeology*, London.

LÄ   *Lexikon der Ägyptologie*, Wiesbaden.

PZSL   *Proceedings of the Zoological Society of London*, London.

RdE   *Revue d'Égyptologie*, Cairo & Paris.

RecTrav *Recueil de travaux relatifs à la philologie et à l'archéologie égyptiennes et assyriennes*, Paris.

ZÄS   *Zeitschrift für ägyptische Sprache und Altertumskunde*, Leipzig and Berlin.

Abitz 1979. F. Abitz. *Statuetten in Schreinen als Grabbeigaben in den ägyptischen Königsgräbern der 18. und 19. Dynastie.* Wiesbaden, 1979.

Abu-Bakr 1953. A.-M. Abu-Bakr. *Excavations at Gîza 1949-1950.* Cairo, 1953.

Adams 1870. A. L. Adams. *Notes of a Naturalist in the Nile Valley and Malta.* Edinburgh, 1870.

Aldred 1971. C. Aldred. *Jewels of the Pharaohs.* London, 1971.

Aldred 1972. C. Aldred. *New Kingdom Art in Ancient Egypt during the Eighteenth Dynasty.* 2nd edition. London, 1972.

Aldred 1973. C. Aldred. *Akhenaten and Nefertiti.* Brooklyn, 1973.

Aldred 1980. C. Aldred. *Egyptian Art in the Days of the Pharaohs.* New York, 1980.

Aldred et al. 1980. C. Aldred, F. Daumas, C. Desroches-Noblecourt and J. Leclant. *L'Égypte du crépuscule.* Paris, 1980.

Aldrovandi 1599. U. Aldrovandi. *Ulyssis Aldrovandi Historia Naturalis: Ornithologiae.* Vol. 1. Bologna, 1599.

Ali and Hafez 1976. A. M. Ali and H. A. Hafez. "Wildlife and Vertebrate Pests in Egypt," in *Proceedings Seventh Vertebrate Pest Conference* (1976), pp. 277-278.

Al-Hussaini 1938a. A. H. Al-Hussaini. "Some Birds Observed in Ghardaqa (Hurghada), Red Sea Coast," in *Ibis* (1938), pp. 541-544.

Al-Hussaini 1938b. A. H. Al-Hussaini. "The Avifauna of the Bahariya Oasis in Winter," in *Ibis* (1938), pp. 544-547.

Al-Hussaini 1939. A. H. Al-Hussaini. "Further Notes on the Birds of Ghardaqa (Hurghada), Red Sea," in *Ibis* (1939), pp. 343-347.

Al-Hussaini 1954. A. H. Al-Hussaini. *Egyptian Birds.* Cairo, 1954 (in Arabic).

Al-Hussaini 1959. A. H. Al-Hussaini. "The Avifauna of Al-Wadi al-Gadid in the Libyan Desert," in *BZSE* 14 (1959), pp. 1-14.

Allen 1939. G. M. Allen. *Bats.* Cambridge, 1939.

Altenmüller 1974. H. Altenmüller. "Bemerkungen zur Kreiselscheibe Nr. 310 aus dem Grab des Hemaka in Saqqara," in *Göttinger Miszellen* 9 (1974), pp. 13-18.

Altenmüller 1977. H. Altenmüller. "Falke," in *LÄ* 2 (1977), pp. 94-97.

Anderson 1902. J. Anderson. *Zoology of Egypt: Mammalia.* London, 1902.

Anonymous 1941. Anonymous. "List of Birds of Egypt," in *BZSE*, Supplement 3 (1941), pp. 1-38.

Anonymous 1944. Anonymous. "The Bird and Animal Artist of 4000 Years Ago and the Present Day," in *Illustrated London News* (Christmas number, 1944), pp. 31-34.

Anonymous 1959. Anonymous. "The Incubators of Upper Egypt," in *ETM* 54 (1959), pp. 29-33.

Anonymous 1960. Anonymous. "What about the Picturesque?," in *ETM* 68 (1960), pp. 22-28.

Anonymous 1981. Anonymous. "Recent Egyptian Reports," in *Bulletin Ornithological Society Middle East* 6 (1981), pp. 12-13.

Archibald 1974. G. W. Archibald. "Methods for Breeding and Rearing Cranes in Captivity," in *International Zoo Yearbook* 14 (1974), pp. 147-155.

Archibald and Viess 1979. G. W. Archibald and D. L. Viess. "Captive Propagation at the International Crane Foundation 1973-78," in J. C. Lewis (ed.). *Proceedings 1978 Crane Workshop.* pp. 51-73. Fort Collins, 1979.

Arnold 1962. P. Arnold. *Birds of Israel.* Haifa, 1962.

Asselberghs 1961. H. Asselberghs. *Chaos en Beheersing.* Leiden, 1961.

Badaway 1976. A. Badaway. *The Tombs of Iteti, Sekhem 'ankh-Ptah, and Kaemnofert at Giza.* Berkeley, 1976.

Bagnold 1935. R. A. Bagnold. *Libyan Sands. Travel in a Dead World.* London, 1935.

Baha el Din and Saleh 1983. S. M. Baha el Din and M. A. Saleh. *Report on the Ornithological Results of the Egyptian Red Sea Pollution Expedition.* Cairo, 1983.

Baines and Málek 1980. J. Baines and J. Málek. *Atlas of Ancient Egypt.* New York, 1980.

Baker 1913. E. C. S. Baker. *Indian Pigeons and Doves.* London, 1913.

Baker 1921. E. C. S. Baker. *The Game-Birds of India, Burma and Ceylon.* Vol. 2. London, 1921.

Ballmann 1980. P. Ballmann. "Report on the Avian Remains from Sites in Egyptian Nubia, Upper Egypt and the Fayum," in F. Wendorf and R. Schild (ed. by A. E. Close). *Loaves and Fishes: The Prehistory of Wadi Kubbaniya.* pp. 307-310. Dallas, 1980.

Balsac and Mayaud 1962. H. Heim de Balsac and N. Mayaud. *Les oiseaux du nord-ouest de l'Afrique.* Paris, 1962.

Bannerman 1930. D. A. Bannerman. *The Birds of Tropical West Africa.* Vol. 1. London, 1930.

Bannerman 1971. D. A. Bannerman. *Handbook of the Birds of Cyprus and Migrants of the Middle East.* Edinburgh, 1971.

Barrett-Hamilton 1897. G. E. H. Barrett-Hamilton. (untitled paper) in *Ibis* (1897), p. 486.

Belzoni 1820. G. Belzoni. *Narrative of the Operations and Recent Discoveries within the Pyramids, Temples, Tombs, and Excavations in Egypt and Nubia.* London, 1820.

Bénédite 1909. G. Bénédite. "Faucon ou épervier, à propos d'une recénte acquisition du Musée égyptien du Louvre," in *Académie des inscriptions et belles-lettres. Monuments et mémoires* 17 (1909), pp. 5-28.

Bénédite 1918. G. Bénédite. "The Carnarvon Ivory," in *JEA* 5 (1918), pp. 1-15 and 225-241.

Berlandini 1982. J. Berlandini. "Varia Memphitica V," in *BIFAO* 82 (1982), pp. 85-103.

Bijlsma 1982. R. G. Bijlsma. "De Trek van Roofvogels over Suez (Egypte) in het Najaar van 1981," in *Vogeljaar* 30 (1982), pp. 141-151.

Bijlsma and de Roder 1982. R. G. Bijlsma and F. E. de Roder. "Goliath Herons in Egypt 1981," in *Dutch Birding* 4 (1982), pp. 82-84.

Bissing 1905. F. W. von Bissing. *Die Mastaba des Gem-ni-kai.* Vol. 1. Berlin, 1905.

Bissing 1941. F. W. von Bissing. *Der Fussboden aus dem Palaste des Königs Amenophis IV zu El Hawata im Museum zu Kairo.* Munich, 1941.

Bissing 1956. F. W. von Bissing. "La chambre des trois saisons du sanctuaire solaire du roi Rathourès (V dynastie) à Abousir," in *ASAE* 53 (1956), pp. 319-338.

Blackman 1914. A. M. Blackman. *The Rock Tombs of Meir.* Vol. 1. London, 1914.

Blackman 1924. A. M. Blackman. *The Rock Tombs of Meir.* Vol. 4. London, 1924.

Blackman and Apted 1953a. A. M. Blackman and M. R. Apted. *The Rock Tombs of Meir.* Vol. 5. London, 1953.

Blackman and Apted 1953b. A. M. Blackman and M. R. Apted. *The Rock Tombs of Meir.* Vol. 6. London, 1953.

Blanford 1898. W. T. Blanford. *The Fauna of British India.* Vol. 4. London, 1898.

Bleeker 1958. C. J. Bleeker. "Isis and Nephthys as Wailing Women," in *Numen* 5 (1958), pp. 1-17.

Bleeker 1973. C. J. Bleeker. *Hathor and Thoth.* Leiden, 1973.

Bodenham 1945. K. L. Bodenham. "Some Notes on Birds at R.A.F. Station Aboukir," in *BZSE* 7 (1945), pp. 14-20.

Bodenheimer 1972. F. S. Bodenheimer. *Animal and Man in Bible Lands.* Vol. 2. Leiden, 1972.

Boessneck 1953. J. Boesssneck. "Die Haustiere in Altägypten," in *Veröffentlichungen der Zoologischen Staatssammlung München* 3 (1953), pp. 1-50.

Boessneck 1960. J. Boesssneck. "Zur Gänsehaltung im alten Ägypten," in *Festschrift der Wiener Tierärztlichen Monatsschrift Herrn Professor Dr. Josef Schreiber zum 70.* pp. 192-206. Vienna, 1960.

Boessneck 1962. J. Boessneck. "Die Domestikation der Graugans im alten Aegypten," in *Zeitschrift für Tierzüchtung und Züchtungsbiologie* 76 (1962), pp. 356-357.

Boessneck 1981. J. Boessneck. *Gemeinsame Anliegen von Ägyptologie und Zoologie aus der Sicht des Zooarchäologen.* Munich, 1981.

Boessneck and von den Driesch 1982. J. Boessneck and A. von den Driesch. *Studien an subfossilen Tierknochen aus Ägypten.* Munich, 1982.

Bonnet 1952. H. Bonnet. *Reallexikon der ägyptischen Religionsgeschichte.* Berlin, 1952.

Booth 1961. B. D. McD. Booth. "Breeding of the Sooty Falcon in the Libyan Desert," in *Ibis* (1961), pp. 129-130.

Borchardt 1928. L. Borchardt. "Ein Bildhauermodell aus dem frühen alten Reich," in *ASAE* 28 (1928), pp. 43-50.

Boreux 1925. C. Boreux. *Études de nautique égyptienne.* Cairo, 1925.

Borman 1929. F. W. Borman. "An Ornithological Trip in the Gulf of Suez and Red Sea," in *Ibis* (1929), pp. 639-650.

Bothmer and Keith 1974. B. V. Bothmer and J. L. Keith. *Brief Guide to the Department of Egyptian and Classical Art. Brooklyn Museum.* Brooklyn, 1974.

Botti and Romanelli 1951. G. Botti and P. Romanelli. *Le sculture del Museo Gregoriano Egizio.* Vatican, 1951.

Boylan 1922. P. Boylan. *Thoth. The Hermes of Egypt.* London, 1922.

Bourriau 1981. J. Bourriau. *Umm el-Ga'ab. Pottery from the Nile Valley before the Arab Conquest.* Cambridge, 1981.

Boussac 1904. H. Boussac. "Les anséridés dans l'Égypte pharaonique" in *Naturaliste* 26 (1904), pp. 209-211.

Boussac 1905a. H. Boussac. "L'hirondelle dans les mythes égyptiens," in *Cosmos* (1905), pp. 661-665.

Boussac 1905b. H. Boussac. "Le Héron cendré et la légende du Phénix," in *Naturaliste* 27 (1905), pp. 41-44.

Boussac 1907. H. Boussac. "La chauve-souris dans l'Égypte pharaonique," in *Naturaliste* 29 (1907), pp. 211-212.

Boussac 1908. H. Boussac. "Identification de quelques oiseaux représentés sur le monuments pharaoniques," in *Naturaliste* 30 (1908), pp. 105-107, 122-123, 179-181, 230-231, 242-243, 252-254, 276-277, 285.

Boussac 1909. H. Boussac. "Le pigeon dans l'ancienne Égypte," in *La Nature* 37 (1909), pp. 264-267.

Boussac 1910a. H. Boussac. "La spatule blanche (*Platalea leucorodia, Linné*)," in *RecTrav* 32 (1910), pp. 50-52.

Boussac 1910b. H. Boussac. "Oiseaux de l'Afrique tropicale représentés sur les monuments égyptiens. Le baléniceps roi (*Balaeniceps rex*, Gould)," in *Revue française d'ornithologie* 1 (1910), pp. 309 and 312.

Boussac 1912. H. Boussac. "Le baléniceps roi (*Balaeniceps rex*, Gould)," in *RecTrav* 34 (1912), pp. 163-165.

Brack and Brack 1977. A. Brack and A. Brack. *Das Grab des Tjanuni. Theben Nr. 74.* Mainz, 1977.

Brack and Brack 1980. A. Brack and A. Brack. *Das Grab des Haremheb. Theben Nr. 78.* Mainz, 1980.

Breasted 1906. J. H. Breasted. *Ancient Records of Egypt.* Vol. 2. Chicago, 1906.

British Museum 1975. *A General Introductory Guide to the Egyptian Collections in the British Museum.* London, 1975.

Brooklyn Museum 1956. *Five Years of Collecting Egyptian Art 1951-1956. Catalogue of an Exhibition held at the Brooklyn Museum.* Brooklyn, 1956.

Brooksbank 1925. F. H. Brooksbank. *Egyptian Birds.* London, 1925.

Brunner-Traut 1955. E. Brunner-Traut. "Ägyptische Tiermärchen," in *ZÄS* 80 (1955), pp. 12-32.

Brunner-Traut 1975. E. Brunner-Traut. "Affe," in *LÄ* 1 (1975), pp. 83-85.

Brunner-Traut 1977a. E. Brunner-Traut. *Altägyptische Tiergeschichte und Fabel.* 5th edition. Darmstadt, 1977.

Brunner-Traut 1977b. E. Brunner-Traut. "Geier," in *LÄ* 2 (1977), pp. 513-515.

Brunner-Traut 1979. E. Brunner-Traut. *Egyptian Artists' Sketches.* Leiden, 1979.

Brunner-Traut 1980. E. Brunner-Traut. "Huhn," in *LÄ* 3 (1980), pp. 70-72.

Bruyère 1928. B. Bruyère. *Rapport sur les fouilles de Deir el Médineh (1927).* Cairo, 1928.

Bruyère 1933. B. Bruyère. *Rapport sur les fouilles de Deir el Médineh (1930).* Cairo, 1933.

Bruyère 1952. B. Bruyère. *Rapport sur les fouilles de Deir el Médineh (1935-1940).* Fasc. 3. Cairo, 1952.

Bruyère 1959. B. Bruyère. *La tombe n⁰ 1 de Sen-nedjem à Deir el Médineh.* Cairo, 1959.

Bulman 1944. J. F. H. Bulman. "Notes on the Birds of Safaga," in *Ibis* (1944), pp. 480-492.

Burgess and Arkell 1958. E. M. Burgess and A. J. Arkell. "The Reconstruction of the Hathor Bowl," in *JEA* 44 (1958), pp. 6-11.

Burlington Fine Arts Club 1922. Burlington Fine Arts Club. *Catalogue of an Exhibition of Ancient Egyptian Art*. London, 1922.

Burton 1972. A. Burton. *Diodorus Siculus Book I. A Commentary*. Leiden, 1972.

Butzer 1959. K. W. Butzer. "Environment and Human Ecology in Egypt during Predynastic and Early Dynastic Times," in *Bulletin de la Société de Géographie d'Égypte* 32 (1959), pp. 43-87.

Butzer 1976. K. W. Butzer. *Early Hydraulic Civilization in Egypt*. Chicago, 1976.

Butzer 1980. K. W. Butzer. "Klima," in *LÄ* 3 (1980), pp. 455-457.

Calverley 1958. A. M. Calverley. *The Temple of King Sethos I at Abydos*. Vol. 4. (ed. by A. H. Gardiner). London, 1958.

Caminos 1954. R. A. Caminos. *Late-Egyptian Miscellanies*. London, 1954.

Caminos 1975. R. A. Caminos. "Ei," in *LÄ* 1 (1975), pp. 1185-1188.

Capart 1905. J. Capart. *Primitive Art in Egypt*. Philadelphia, 1905.

Capart 1907. J. Capart. *Une rue de tombeaux à Saqqarah*. Brussels, 1907.

Capart 1927. J. Capart. *Documents pour servir à l'étude de l'art égyptien*. Vol. 1. Paris, 1927.

Capart 1930. J. Capart. "Falconry in Ancient Egypt," in *Isis* 14 (1930), p. 222.

Capart 1931. J. Capart. *Documents pour servir à l'étude de l'art égyptien*. Vol. 2. Paris, 1931.

Capart 1940. J. Capart. "Un cercueil de vautour d'el Kab," in *CdE* 15 (1940), pp. 30-37.

Capart 1941. J. Capart. "Les poussins au tombeau de Ti," in *CdE* 16 (1941), pp. 208-212.

Capart and Werbrouck 1926. J. Capart and M. Werbrouck. *Thebes. The Glory of a Great Past*. New York, 1926.

Carter 1923. H. Carter. "An Ostracon Depicting a Red Jungle-fowl. (The Earliest Known Drawing of the Domestic Cock.)," in *JEA* 9 (1923), pp. 1-4.

Carter 1927. H. Carter. *The Tomb of Tut-ankh-Amen*. Vol. 2. New York, 1927.

Carter and Newberry 1904. H. Carter and P. E. Newberry. *The Tomb on Thoutmôsis IV*. Westminster, 1904.

Cecil 1904. Lady William Cecil. *Bird Notes from the Nile*. Westminster, 1904.

Černý 1952. J. Černý. *Ancient Egyptian Religion*. London, 1952.

Chapman 1930. A. Chapman. *Memories of Fourscore Years less Two 1851-1929*. Edinburgh, 1930.

Chevrier 1930. H. Chevrier. "Rapport sur les travaux de Karnak (1929-1930)," in *ASAE* 30 (1930), pp. 159-173.

Cholmley 1897. A. J. Cholmley. "Notes on the Birds of the Western Coast of the Red Sea," in *Ibis* (1897), pp. 196-209.

Churcher 1972. C. S. Churcher. *Late Pleistocene Vertebrates from Archaeological Sites in the Plain of Kom Ombo, Upper Egypt*. Toronto, 1972.

Clark 1955. C. R. Clark. "The Sacred Ibis," in *BMMA* 13 (1955), pp. 181-184.

Clarke 1817. E. D. Clarke. *Travels in Various Countries of Europe, Asia and Africa*. Vol. 5. 4th Edition. London, 1817.

Coltherd 1966. J. B. Coltherd. "The Domestic Fowl in Ancient Egypt," in *Ibis* (1966), pp. 217-223.

Cooney 1965. J. D. Cooney. *Amarna Reliefs from Hermopolis in American Collections*. Brooklyn, 1965.

Cott 1947. H. B. Cott. "The Edibility of Birds," in *PZSL* 116 (1947), pp. 371-524.

Cott 1954. H. B. Cott. "The Palatability of the Eggs of Birds: Mainly Based Upon Observations of an Egg Panel," in *PZSL* 124 (1954), pp. 335-463.

Cottevieille-Giraudet 1931. R. Cottevieille-Giraudet. *Rapport sur les fouilles de Médamoud (1930). La verrerie—les graffiti*. Cairo, 1931.

Cramp and Simmons 1977. S. Cramp and K. E. L. Simmons (eds.). *The Birds of the Western Palearctic*. Vol. 1. London, 1977.

Cramp and Simmons 1980. S. Cramp and K. E. L. Simmons (eds.). *The Birds of the Western Palearctic*. Vol. 2. London, 1980.

Dam 1927. C. H. Dam. "The Tomb Chapel of Ra-Ka-pou, a Court Official of 2650 B.C.," in *University of Pennsylvania Museum Journal* 18 (1927), pp. 188-200.

Darby et al. 1977. W. J. Darby, P. Ghalioungui and L. Grivetti. *Food: The Gift of Osiris*. London, 1977.

Daressy 1902. G. Daressy. *Fouilles de la Vallée des Rois (1898-1899)*. Cairo, 1902.

Darwin 1898. C. Darwin. *The Variation of Animals and Plants under Domestication*. Vol. 1. New York, 1898.

David 1980. R. David. *The Macclesfield Collection of Egyptian Antiquities*. Warminster, 1980.

Davies 1900. N. de G. Davies. *The Mastaba of Ptahhetep and Akhethetep at Saqqareh*. Vol. 1. London, 1900.

Davies 1901. N. de G. Davies. *The Mastaba of Ptahhetep and Akhethetep at Saqqareh*. Vol. 2. London, 1901.

Davies 1902. N. de Garis Davies. *The Rock Tombs of Deir el Gebrâwi.* Vols. 1-2. London, 1902.

Davies 1905. N. de Garis Davies. *The Rock Tombs of El Amarna.* Vol. 2. London, 1905.

Davies 1908. N. de Garis Davies. *The Rock Tombs of El Amarna.* Vol. 6. London, 1908.

Davies 1913. N. de Garis Davies. *Five Theban Tombs.* London, 1913.

Davies 1917a. N. de Garis Davies. *The Tomb of Nakht at Thebes.* New York, 1917.

Davies 1917b. N. de Garis Davies. "Egyptian Drawings on Limestone Flakes," in *JEA* 4 (1917), pp. 234-240.

Davies 1920. N. de Garis Davies. *The Tomb of Antefoker.* London, 1920.

Davies 1922. N. de Garis Davies. *The Tomb of Puyemrê at Thebes.* Vol. 1. New York, 1922.

Davies 1923. N. de Garis Davies. *The Tomb of Puyemrê at Thebes.* Vol. 2. New York, 1923.

Davies 1927. N. de Garis Davies. *Two Ramesside Tombs at Thebes.* New York, 1927.

Davies 1930a. N. de Garis Davies. *The Tomb of Ken-Amūn at Thebes.* New York, 1930.

Davies 1930b. N. de Garis Davies. "The Work of the Graphic Branch of the Expedition," in *The Egyptian Expedition 1929-1930. BMMA Supplement* (Dec., 1930), pp. 29-42.

Davies 1936. N. M. Davies. *Ancient Egyptian Paintings.* (ed. by A. H. Gardiner). Chicago, 1936.

Davies 1940. N. M. Davies. "Some Notes on the *nḫ*-Bird," in *JEA* 26 (1940), pp. 79-81.

Davies 1941. N. de Garis Davies. *The Tomb of the Vizier Ramose.* London, 1941.

Davies 1942. N. M. Davies. "Nubians in the Tomb of Amunedjeh," in *JEA* 28 (1942), pp. 50-52.

Davies 1943. N. de Garis Davies. *The Tomb of Rekh-mi-Rē' at Thebes.* New York, 1943.

Davies 1946. N. M. Davies. In *JEA* 32 (1946), frontispiece.

Davies 1949. N. M. Davies. "Birds and Bats at Beni Hasan," in *JEA* 35 (1949), pp. 13-20.

Davies 1958. N. M. Davies. *Picture Writing in Ancient Egypt.* London, 1958.

Davies 1963. N. M. Davies. *Scenes from some Theban Tombs.* Oxford, 1963.

Davies and Davies 1933. N. M. Davies and N. de Garis Davies. *The Tombs of Menkheperrasonb, Amenmosĕ, and Another (nos. 86, 112, 42, 226).* London, 1933.

Davies and Davies 1940. N. M. Davies and N. de Garis Davies. "The Tomb of Amenmosĕ (no. 89) at Thebes," in *JEA* 26 (1940), pp. 131-136.

Davies and Gardiner 1915. N. M. Davies and A. H. Gardiner. *The Tomb of Amenemḥēt (no. 82).* London, 1915.

Davies and Gardiner 1926. N. M. Davies and A. H. Gardiner. *The Tomb of Huy.* London, 1926.

Davies and Gardiner 1962. N. M. Davies and A. H. Gardiner. *Tutankhamun's Painted Box.* Oxford, 1962.

Davis 1908a. T. M. Davis. *The Tomb of Siphtah.* London, 1908.

Davis 1908b. T. M. Davis. *The Funerary Papyrus of Iouiya.* London, 1908.

Davis 1912. T. M. Davis. *The Tombs of Harmhabi and Touatânkhamanou.* London, 1912.

Davis 1968. G. Davis. "God's Little Poultry," in *Avicultural Magazine* 74, (1968), pp. 91-94.

Dawson 1925. W. R. Dawson. "The Bee-eater (*Merops apiaster*) from the Earliest Times, and a further Note on the Hoopoe," in *Ibis* (1925), pp. 590-594.

Day 1938. J. W. Day. *Sport in Egypt.* London, 1938.

Delacour 1951. J. Delacour. *The Pheasants of the World.* London, 1951.

Delacour 1954. J. Delacour. *The Waterfowl of the World.* Vol. 1. London, 1954.

Delacour 1956. J. Delacour. *The Waterfowl of the World.* Vol. 2. London, 1956.

Delacour 1959. J. Delacour. *The Waterfowl of the World.* Vol. 3. London, 1959.

de Morgan 1903. J. de Morgan. *Fouilles à Dahchour en 1894-1895.* Vienna, 1903.

de Rachewiltz 1960. B. de Rachewiltz. *Egyptian art. An Introduction.* London, 1960.

Derchain 1975. P. Derchain. "La perruque et le cristal," in *Studien zur altägyptischen Kultur* 2 (1975), pp. 55-74.

Derchain 1976. P. Derchain. "Symbols and Metaphors in Literature and Representations of Private Life," in *Royal Anthropological Institute News* (Aug., 1976), pp. 7-10.

Dechambre 1951. E. Dechambre. "Discussion de l'interprétation de figurations animales anciennes," in *Terre et la Vie* 98 (1951), pp. 105-115.

Desroches-Noblecourt 1976. C. Desroches-Noblecourt. *Ramsès le grand.* Paris, 1976.

Diener 1973. L. Diener. "A Human-Masked and Doll-Shaped Hawk-Mummy," in *CdE* 48 (1973), pp. 60-65.

Dondelinger 1979. E. Dondelinger. *Papyrus Ani (BM 10.470).* Graz, 1979.

Dresser 1884-1886. H. E. Dresser. *A Monograph of the Meropidae.* London, 1884-1886.

Duell 1939. P. Duell. *The Mastaba of Mereruka.* Chicago, 1938.

Dunham 1937. D. Dunham. "Two Parallels to Ancient Egyptian Scenes," in *BMFA* 35 (1937), pp. 50-54.

Dunham 1946. D. Dunham. "An Egyptian Diadem of the Old Kingdom," in *BMFA* 44 (1946), pp. 23-29.

Dunham 1955. D. Dunham. *Nuri.* Boston, 1955.

Dunham and Smith 1949. D. Dunham and W. S. Smith. "A Middle Kingdom Painted Coffin from Deir el Bersheh," in *Studi in memoria di Ippolito Rossellini.* Vol. 1. pp. 261-268. Pisa, 1949.

Edel 1961. E. Edel. "Zu den Inschriften auf den Jahreszeitenreliefs der 'Weltkammer' aus dem Sonnenheiligtum des Niuserre," in *Nachrichten der Akademie der Wissenschaften in Göttingen. I. Philologisch-Historische Klasse.* (1961), pp. 209-255.

Edel 1963. E. Edel. "Zu den Inschriften auf den Jahreszeitenreliefs der 'Weltkammer' aus dem Sonnenheiligtum des Niuserre," in *Nachrichten der Akademie der Wissenschaften in Göttingen. I. Philologisch-Historische Klasse.* (1963), pp. 87-217.

Edgar 1906. C. C. Edgar. *Sculptors' Studies and Unfinished Works.* Cairo, 1906.

Edwards 1955. I. E. S. Edwards. "An Egyptian Bestiary of 5000 Years Ago," in *Illustrated London News* 227 (Dec., 1955), p. 1061.

Edwards 1976a. I. E. S. Edwards. *Treasures of Tutankhamun.* New York, 1976.

Edwards 1976b. I. E. S. Edwards. *Tutankhamun's Jewelry.* New York, 1976.

Edwards 1979. I. E. S. Edwards. "Zoomorphic Anomalies in Tutankhamun's Treasures," in *AJA* 83 (1979), pp. 205-206.

Elliott and Monk 1952. H. F. I. Elliott and J. F. Monk. "Land-bird Migration over the Suez Route to East Africa," in *Ibis* (1952), pp. 528-530.

El Negumi 1949. A. El Negumi. "List of, Desert Animals Seen or Collected during the Periods Shown," in *BZSE* 8 (1949), pp. 20-21.

El Negumi et al. 1950. A. El Negumi, H. F. Zain El Din, M. A. El Monery and M. K. Fayed. *Birds of Egypt.* 2nd edition. Cairo, 1950 (in Arabic).

Emery 1938. W. B. Emery. *The Tomb of Hemaka.* Cairo, 1938.

Emery 1962. W. B. Emery. *A Funerary Repast in an Egyptian Tomb of the Archaic Period.* Leiden, 1962.

Engelbach 1915. R. Engelbach. *Riqqeh and MemphisVI.* London, 1915.

Épron et al. 1939. L. Épron, F. Daumas, G. Goyon and P. Montet. *Le tombeau de Ti.* Fasc. 1 Cairo, 1939.

Etchécopar and Hüe 1964. R. D. Etchécopar and F. Hüe. *Les oiseaux du nord de l'Afrique.* Paris, 1964.

Etchécopar and Hüe 1967. R. D. Etchécopar and F. Hüe. *The Birds of North Africa from the Canary Islands to the Red Sea.* Edinburgh, 1967.

Faulkner 1972. R. O. Faulkner. *The Book of the Dead.* New York, 1972.

Fazzini 1975. R. Fazzini. *Images for Eternity. Egyptian Art from Berkeley and Brooklyn.* Brooklyn, 1975.

Firth 1927. C. M. Firth. *The Archaeological Survey of Nubia. Report for 1910-1911.* Cairo, 1927.

Firth 1929. C. M. Firth. "Excavations of the Department of Antiquities at Saqqara (October 1928 to March 1929)," in *ASAE* 29 (1929), pp. 64-70.

Firth and Gunn 1926. C. M. Firth and B. Gunn. *Teti Pyramid Cemeteries.* Cairo, 1926.

Firth and Quibell 1935. C. M. Firth and J. E. Quibell. *The Step Pyramid.* Cairo, 1935.

Fischer 1963. W. Fischer. "Vogelbeobachtungen in Tropischen Häfen und am Suezkanal," in *Ornithologische Mitteilungen* 15 (1963), pp. 99-102.

Fischer 1968. H. G. Fischer. *Ancient Egyptian Representations of Turtles.* New York, 1968.

Fischer 1978. H. G. Fischer. "Five Inscriptions of the Old Kingdom," in *ZÄS* 105 (1978), pp. 42-59.

Fischer 1979. H. G. Fischer. *Ancient Egyptian Calligraphy.* New York, 1979.

Fitzgibbon 1976. T. Fitzgibbon 1976. *The Food of the Western World.* New York, 1976.

Flower 1932. S. S. Flower. "Notes on the recent Mammals of Egypt, with a List of the Species Recorded from that Kingdom," in *PZSL* (1932), pp. 376-386.

Flower 1933. S. S. Flower. "Notes on some Birds in Egypt," in *Ibis* (1933), pp. 34-46.

Forbes 1909-1910. H. O. Forbes. "The Identity of Certain Large Birds on Egyptian Vases," in *Nature* 82 (1909-1910), p. 38.

Forbes 1955. R. J. Forbes. *Studies in Ancient Technology.* Vol. 3. Leiden, 1955.

Forman and Kischkewitz 1972. W. Forman and H. Kischkewitz. *Egyptian Drawings.* London, 1972.

Frankfort 1929. H. Frankfort (ed.). *The Mural Paintings of El-'Amarneh.* London, 1929.

Friedmann 1964a. H. Friedmann. *Evolutionary Trends in the Avian Genus Clamator.* Washington, D. C., 1964.

Friedmann 1964b. H. Friedmann. "The History of our Knowledge of Avian Brood Parasitism," in *Centaurus* 10 (1964), pp. 282-304.

Gabra 1941. S. Gabra. *Rapport sur les fouilles d'Hermoupolis Ouest (Touna el-Gebel).* Cairo, 1941.

Gaillard 1907. C. Gaillard. "Les oies de Meidoum," in *Revue égyptologique* 12 (1907), pp. 212-215.

Gaillard 1929. C. Gaillard. "Sur deux oiseaux figurés dans les tombeaux de Béni-Hassan," in *Kêmi 2* (1929), pp. 19-40.

Gaillard 1931. C. Gaillard. "Quelques représentations du martin-pêcheur pie (*Ceryle rudis*), sur les monuments de l'Égypte ancienne," in *BIFAO* 30 (1931), pp. 249-271.

Gaillard 1933. C. Gaillard. "Identification de l'oiseau *amâ* figuré dans un tombe de Béni-Hassan," in *BIFAO* 33 (1933), pp. 169-190.

Gaillard 1934. C. Gaillard. "Sur une figuration coloriée du pluvier armé relevée dans une tombe de Béni-Hassan," in *AMHNL* 14 (1934), pp. 1-14.

Gaillard and Daressy 1905. C. Gaillard and G. Daressy. *La faune momifiée de l'antique Égypte*. Cairo, 1905.

Gaisler *et al.* 1972. J. Gaisler, G. Madkour and J. Pelikán. "On the Bats (Chiroptera) of Egypt," in *Acta scientiarum naturalium Academiae scientiarum bohemoslovacae-Brno* 6 (1972), pp. 1-40.

Galal El Din 1959. H. Galal El Din. "The Sooty Falcon, *Falco concolor* Temm," in *BZSE* 14 (1959), pp. 52-53.

Gardiner 1947. A. H. Gardiner. *Ancient Egyptian Onomastica*. Vol. 1. Oxford, 1947.

Gardiner 1957. A. H. Gardiner. *Egyptian Grammar*. 3rd edition. London, 1957.

Gardiner 1961. A. H. Gardiner. *Egypt of the Pharaohs*. Oxford, 1961.

Gauthier 1908. H. Gauthier. "Rapport sur une campagne de fouilles à Drah abou'l Neggah en 1906," in *BIFAO* 6 (1908), pp. 121-171.

Ghabbour 1976. S. I. Ghabbour. "The Ecology and Pest Status of Sparrows (*Passer*) in Egypt," in *International Studies on Sparrows* 9 (1976), pp. 17-29.

Glanville 1926. S. R. K. Glanville. "Egyptian Theriomorphic Vessels in the British Museum," in *JEA* 12 (1926), pp. 52-69.

Goelet 1983. O. Goelet. "The Migratory Geese of Meidum and some Egyptian Words for 'Migratory Bird'," in *Bulletin of the Egyptological Seminar* 5 (1983), pp. 41-60.

Goodman 1982. S. M. Goodman. "The Introduction and Subspecies of the Rose-ringed Parakeet *Psittacula krameri* in Egypt," in *BBOC* 102 (1982), pp. 16-18.

Goodman 1984a. S. M. Goodman. "Report on Two Small Bird Collections from the Gebel Elba Region, Southeastern Egypt," in *Bonner Zoologische Beiträge* (1984), forthcoming.

Goodman 1984b. S. M. Goodman. "The Validity and Relationships of *Prinia gracilis natronensis* (Aves:Sylviidae)," in *Proceedings Biological Society of Washington* 97 (1984), pp. 1-11.

Goodman and Houlihan 1981. S. M. Goodman and P. F. Houlihan. "The Collared Turtle Dove *Streptopelia decaocto* in Egypt," in *BBOC* 101 (1981), pp. 334-336.

Goodman and Ames 1983. S. M. Goodman and P. L. Ames. "A Contribution to the Ornithology of the Siwa Oasis and Qattara Depression, Egypt," in *Sandgrouse* 5 (1983), pp. 82-96.

Goodman and Tewfik 1983. S. M. Goodman and S. Tewfik. "A Specimen Record of the Firecrest, *Regulus ignicapillus*, from North-western Egypt," in *Gerfaut* 73 (1983), pp. 201-204.

Goodman and Sabry 1984. S. M. Goodman and H. Sabry. "A Specimen Record of Hume's Tawny Owl *Strix butleri* from Egypt," in *BBOC* 104 (1984), pp. 79-84.

Goodman and Watson 1983. S. M. Goodman and G. E. Watson. "Bird Specimen Records of some Uncommon or Previously Unrecorded Forms in Egypt," in *BBOC* 103 (1983), pp. 101-106.

Goodman and Watson 1984. S. M. Goodman and G. E. Watson. "Records of Palearctic Thrushes (*Turdus* spp.) in Egypt and Northeastern Africa," in *Gerfaut* (1984), forthcoming.

Goodman *et al.* 1984. S. M. Goodman, P. F. Houlihan and I. Helmy. "Recent Records of the Ostrich *Struthio camelus* in Egypt," in *BBOC* 104 (1984), pp. 39-44.

Goodman and Mowla Atta 1985. S. M. Goodman and G. A. Mowla Atta. "The Birds of Southeastern Egypt," in *Gerfaut* (1985), forthcoming.

Goodman and Storer 1985. S. M. Goodman and R. W. Storer. "The Seabirds of the Egyptian Red Sea and Adjacent Waters, with Notes on Selected Ciconiiformes," in *Gerfaut* (1985), forthcoming.

Goodwin 1949. D. Goodwin. "Notes on the Migration of Birds of Prey over Suez," in *Ibis* (1949), pp. 59-63.

Goodwin 1955. D. Goodwin. "Notes on European Wild Pigeons," in *Avicultural Magazine* 61 (1955), pp. 54-85.

Goodwin 1967. D. Goodwin. *Pigeons of the World*. London, 1967.

Grdseloff 1938. B. Grdseloff. "Zum Vogelfang im alten Reich," in *ZÄS* 74 (1938), pp. 136-139.

Greaves 1939. R. H. Greaves. "Notes from Egypt," in *Oologists' Record* 19 (1939), pp. 49-51.

Greaves 1943. R. H. Greaves. *Sixty Common Birds of the Nile Delta*. Cairo, 1943.

Griffith 1896. F. L. Griffith. *Beni Hasan*. Vol. 3. London, 1896.

Griffith 1898. F. L. Griffith. *A Collection of Hieroglyphs*. London, 1898.

Griffiths 1966. J. G. Griffiths. *The Origins of Osiris*. Berlin, 1966.

Grossman and Hamlet 1964. M. L. Grossman and J. Hamlet. *Birds of Prey of the World*. New York, 1964.

Guilmant 1907. F. Guilmant. *Le Tombeau de Ramsès IX.* Cairo, 1907.

Gunn 1926. B. Gunn. "Inscriptions from the Step Pyramid Site," in *ASAE* 26 (1926), pp. 177-202.

Gurney 1876. J. H. Gurney. *Rambles of a Naturalist in Egypt and other Countries.* London, 1876.

Haensel 1980. J. Haensel. "Ornithologische Eindrücke während eines weiteren Studienaufenthalts in Ägypten im Herbst und Früwinter 1972," in *Beiträge zur Vogelkunde* 26 (1980), pp. 19-29.

Hafez 1978. H. Hafez. *List of Birds of Egypt.* Cairo, 1978.

Halland and Moreau 1970. B. P. Halland and R. E. Moreau. *An Atlas of Speciation in African Passerine Birds.* London, 1970.

Haller 1954. A. Haller. *Die Gräber und Grüfte von Assur.* Berlin, 1954.

Hanzák 1977. J. Hanzák. "Egyptian Mummies of Animals in Czechoslovak Collections," in *ZÄS* 104 (1977), pp. 86-88.

Hartert 1919-20. E. Hartert. *Die Vögel der Paläarktischen Fauna.* Vol. 3. Berlin, 1919-1920.

Hassan 1936. S. Hassan. *Excavations at Gîza.* Vol. 2. Cairo, 1936.

Hassan 1943. S. Hassan. *Excavations at Gîza.* Vol. 4. Cairo, 1943.

Hasselquist 1766. F. Hasselquist. *Voyages and Travels in the Levant; in the Years 1749, 50, 51, 52.* London, 1766.

Hayes 1937. W. C. Hayes. *Glazed Tiles from a Palace of Ramesses II at Kantîr.* New York, 1937.

Hayes 1953. W. C. Hayes. *The Scepter of Egypt.* Vol. 1. New York, 1953.

Hayes 1959. W. C. Hayes. *The Scepter of Egypt.* Vol. 2. Cambridge, 1959.

Hayes 1965. W. C. Hayes. *Most Ancient Egypt.* (ed. by K. C. Seele). Chicago, 1965.

Heimpel and Calmeyer 1972-1975. W. Heimpel and P. Calmeyer. "Huhn," in D. O. Edzard (ed.). *Reallexikon der Assyriologie und Vorderas atischen Archäologie.* Vol. 4. pp. 487-488. Berlin, 1972-1975.

Heinzel et al. 1977. H. Heinzel, R. Fitter and J. Parslow. *The Birds of Britain and Europe with North Africa and the Middle East.* 3rd edition. London, 1977.

Hermann 1932. A. Hermann. "Das Motiv der Ente mit zurückgewendetem Kopfe im ägyptischen Kunstgewerbe," in *ZÄS* 68 (1932), pp. 86-105.

Heuglin 1869. M. T. von Heuglin. *Ornithologie Nordost-Afrika's, der Nilquellen-und Küsten-Gebiete des Rothen Meeres und des Nördlichen Somal-landes.* Vol. 1, part 1. Cassel, 1869.

Heuglin 1873. M. T. von Heuglin. *Ornithologie Nordost-Afrika's, der Nilquellen-und Küsten-Gebiete des Rothen Meeres und des Nordlichen Somal-lands.* Vol. 2, pt. 2. Cassel, 1873.

Hodjash and Berlev 1982. S. Hodjash and O. Berlev. *The Egyptian Reliefs and Stelae in the Pushkin Museum of Fine Arts, Moscow.* Leningrad, 1982.

Hölscher 1951. U. Hölscher. *The Mortuary Temple of Ramses III.* Vol. 2. Chicago, 1951.

Holwerda et al. 1908. A. E. J. Holwerda, P. A. A. Boeser and J. H. Holwerda. *Beschreibung der aegyptischen Sammlung des niederländischen Reichsmuseums der Altertümer in Leiden. Die Denkmäler des alten Reiches.* Vol. 1. Atlas. The Hague, 1908.

Hoogstraal 1962. H. Hoogstraal. "A Brief Review of the Contemporary Land Mammals of Egypt (including Sinai). 1. Insectivora and Chiroptera," in *Journal Egyptian Public Health Association* 37 (1962), pp. 143-162.

Hornblower 1935. G. D. Hornblower. "The Barndoor Fowl in Egyptian Art," in *Ancient Egypt and the East* (1935), p. 82.

Hornell 1937. J. Hornell. "Traps and Snares from Upper Egypt," in *Ethnos* 2 (1937), pp. 65-73.

Hornell 1947. J. Hornell. "Egyptian and Medieval Pigeon-houses," in *Antiquity* 21 (1947), pp.182-185.

Hornung 1971. E. Hornung. *Das Grab des Haremhab im Tal der Könige.* Bern, 1971.

Hornung 1982. E. Hornung. *Tal der Könige.* Zurich, 1982.

Horváth 1959. L. Horváth. "The Results of the Zoological Collecting Trip to Egypt in 1957, of the Natural History Museum, Budapest," in *Annales Historico-Naturales Musei Nationalis Hungarici* 51 (1959), pp. 451-481.

Houlihan and Goodman 1979. P. F. Houlihan and S. M. Goodman. "Comments on the Identification of Birds Depicted on Tutankhamun's Embossed Gold Fan," in *Society for the Study of Egyptian Antiquities Journal* 9 (1979), pp. 219-225.

Howell 1979. T. R. Howell. *Breeding Biology of the Egyptian Plover, Pluvianus aegyptius.* Berkeley, 1979.

Hubbard and Seymour 1968. J. P. Hubbard and C. Seymour. "Some Notable Bird Records from Egypt," in *Ibis* (1968), pp. 575-578.

Hudson 1975. R. Hudson (ed.). *Threatened Birds of Europe.* London, 1975.

Husselman 1953. E. M. Husselman. "The Dovecotes of Karanis," in *Transactions and Proceedings of the American Philological Association* 84 (1953), pp. 81-91.

Hutson 1944. H. P. W. Hutson. "Spring Migration-Egypt-1943," in *BZSE* 6 (1944), pp. 5-12.

Jackson 1938. F. J. Jackson. *The Birds of Kenya Colony and the Uganda Protectorate.* Vol. 1. London, 1938.

James 1982. T. G. H. James (ed.). *Excavating in Egypt.* Chicago, 1982.

Janssen 1975. J. J. Janssen. *Commodity Prices from the Ramessid Period.* Leiden, 1975.

Jarvis 1932. C. S. Jarvis. *Yesterday and To-day in Sinai.* Boston, 1932.

Jéquier 1918. G. Jéquier. "Quelques objets appartenant au rituel funéraire sous le Moyen Empire," in *BIFAO* 15 (1918), pp. 153-164.

Jéquier 1921. G. Jéquier. *Les frises d'objets des sarcophages du Moyen Empire.* Cairo, 1921.

Johnson and West 1949. A. C. Johnson and L. C. West. *Byzantine Egypt: Economic Studies.* Princeton, 1949.

Jourdain and Lynes 1936. F. C. R. Jourdain and H. Lynes. "Notes on Egyptian Birds, 1935," in *Ibis* (1936), pp. 39-47.

Junker 1938. H. Junker. *Gîza.* Vol. 3. Vienna, 1938.

Junker 1940. H. Junker. *Gîza.* Vol. 4. Vienna, 1940.

Junker 1943. H. Junker. *Gîza.* Vol. 6. Vienna, 1943.

Kadry 1942. I. Kadry. "The Economic Importance of the Buff-backed Egret (*Ardea ibis*, L.) to Egyptian Agriculture," in *BZSE* 4 (1942), pp. 20-26.

Kaiser 1890. A. Kaiser. "Beiträge zur Ornithologie von Aegypten," in *Ornis* 6 (1890), pp. 455-546.

Kaiser 1967. W. Kaiser. *Ägyptisches Museum Berlin.* Berlin, 1967.

Kákosy 1982. L. Kákosy. "Phönix," in *LÄ* 4 (1982), pp. 1030-1039.

Kamil and Sallamah 1967. S. Kamil and R. Sallamah. *The Birds of the Arab World.* Cairo, 1967 (in Arabic).

Kantor 1948. H. J. Kantor. "A Predynastic Ostrich Egg with Incised Decoration," in *Journal of Near Eastern Studies* 7 (1948), pp. 46-51.

Kaplony 1977. P. Kaplony. "Eule," in *LÄ* 2 (1977), pp. 39-40.

Kayser 1958. H. Kayser. "Die Gänse des Amon (Eine Neuerwerbung des Pelizaeus-Museums)," in *Mitteilungen des Deutschen Archäologischen Instituts Abteilung Kairo* 16 (1958), p. 193.

Keel 1977. O. Keel. *Vögel als Boten.* Fribourg, 1977.

Kees 1939. H. Kees. "Darstellung eines Geflügelhofes der Ramessidenzeit," in *ZÄS* 75 (1939), pp. 85-89.

Kees 1961. H. Kees. *Ancient Egypt. A Cultural Topography.* (ed. by T. G. H. James). London, 1961.

Keimer 1925. L. Keimer. "Egyptian Formal Bouquets (*bouquets montés*)," in *AJSL* 41 (1925), pp. 145-161.

Keimer 1926. L. Keimer. "Agriculture in Ancient Egypt," in *AJSL* 42 (1926), pp. 283-288.

Keimer 1927. L. Keimer. "A Note on the Hieroglyphs 𓄿 and 𓄿," in *AJSL* 43 (1927), pp. 226-231.

Keimer 1930a. L. Keimer. "Quelques hiéroglyphes représentant des oiseaux," in *ASAE* 30 (1930), pp. 1-26.

Keimer 1930b. L. Keimer. "Quelques remarques sur la huppe (*Upupa epops*) dans l'Égypte ancienne," in *BIFAO* 30 (1930), pp. 305-331.

Keimer 1936. L. Keimer. "Sur quelques représentations de caméléon de l'ancienne Égypte ," in *BIFAO* 36 (1936), pp. 85-95.

Keimer 1938. L. Keimer. "Sur l'identification de l'hiéroglyphe *nḥ* 𓃂 ," in *ASAE* 38 (1938), pp. 253-263.

Keimer 1940. L. Keimer. "Sur un monument égyptien du Musée de Louvre. Contribution à l'histoire de l'égyptologie," in *RdE* 4 (1940), pp. 45-65.

Keimer 1942. L. Keimer. "Quelques nouvelles remarques au sujet de l'hiéroglyphe *nḥ* 𓃂 ," in *ASAE* 41 (1942), pp. 325-332.

Keimer 1947. L. Keimer. *Histoires de serpents dans l'Égypte ancienne et moderne.* Cairo, 1947.

Keimer 1950. L. Keimer. "Falconry in Ancient Egypt," in *Isis* 41 (1950), p. 52.

Keimer 1951. L. Keimer. "Les Hiboux constituant les prototypes de la lettre M de l'alphabet égyptien," in *Annals of the Faculty of Arts, Ibrahim Pasha University* 1 (1951), pp. 73-83.

Keimer 1954a. L. Keimer. "Interprétation de plusieurs représentations anciennes d'ibis," in *CdE* 29 (1954), pp. 237-250.

Keimer 1954b. L. Keimer. "Jardins zoologiques d'Égypte," in *Cahiers d'histoire égyptienne* 6 (1954), pp. 81-159.

Keimer 1955. L. Keimer. "The Egyptian Ibis," in *ETM* 16 (1955), pp. 16-19.

Keimer 1956a. L. Keimer. "Chanticleer in Ancient Egypt," in *ETM* 27 (1956), pp. 6-11.

Keimer 1956b. L. Keimer. "The Pigeons & Pigeon Cotes of Egypt," in *ETM* 20 (1956), pp. 24-29.

Keimer 1957a. L. Keimer. "Notes de lecture (*suite*)," in *BIFAO* 56 (1957), pp. 97-117.

Keimer 1957b. L. Keimer. A review of E. Brunner-Traut's, *Die altägyptischen Scherbenbilder (Bildostraka) der Deutschen Museen und Sammlungen.* in *Bibliotheca Orientalis* 14 (1957), pp. 148-151.

Kerrn 1959. E. E. Kerrn. "The Development of the Ornamental 'Boatman's Fillet' in Old and Middle Kingdom in Egypt;" in *Acta Orientalia* 24 (1959), pp. 161-188.

Kitchen 1971. K. A. Kitchen. "Punt and How to Get There," in *Orientalia* 40 (1971), pp. 184-207.

Klebs 1934. L. Klebs. *Die Reliefs und Malereien des neuen Reiches*. Heidelberg, 1934.

Koenig 1926. A. Koenig. "Die Ergebnisse meiner zweiten Forschungsreise in das Gebiet der Quellflüsse des Nils," in *Journal für Ornithologie* 74 (1926), pp. 315-361.

Koenig 1928. A. Koenig. "Fortsetzung und Schluss der Watvögel (Grallatores) Aegyptens," in *Journal für Ornithologie*, Sonderheft 76 (1928), pp. 1-311.

Koenig 1932. A. Koenig. "Die Schwimmvögel (Natatores) Aegyptens," in *Journal für Ornithologie*, Sonderheft 80 (1932), pp. 1-191.

Kuentz 1924. C. Kuentz. "La danse des autruches," in *BIFAO* 23 (1924), pp. 85-88.

Kuentz 1926. C. Kuentz. "L'oie du Nil (*Chenalopex aegyptiaca*) dans l'antique Égypte," in *AMHNL* 14 (1926), pp. 1-60.

Kueny and Yoyotte 1979. G. Kueny and J. Yoyotte. *Grenoble, Musée des Beaux-Arts. Collection égyptienne*. Paris, 1979.

Kuhlmann and Schenkel 1983. K. P. Kuhlmann and W. Schenkel. *Das Grab des Ibi, Obergutsverwalter der Gottesgemahlin des Amun*. Vol. 1. Mainz, 1983.

Kumerloeve 1962. H. Kumerloeve. "Basstöpel (*Sula Bassana*) und Zwergmöwen (*Larus minutus*) vor der Libanesischen Küste," in *Vogelwarte* 21 (1962), pp. 221-222.

Kumerloeve 1967. H. Kumerloeve. "Recherches sur l'avifaune de la République arabe syrienne. Essai d'une aperçu," in *Alauda* 35 (1967), pp. 243-266.

Kumerloeve 1977. H. Kumerloeve. "Waldrapp, *Geronticus eremita* (Linnaeus, 1758), und Glattnackenrapp, *Geronticus calvus* (Boddaert, 1783): Zur Geschichte ihrer Erforschung und zur gegenwärtigen Bestandssituation," in *Annalen des Naturhistorischen Museums in Wien* 81 (1977), pp. 319-349.

Kumerloeve 1983. H. Kumerloeve. "Zur Kenntnis altägyptischer Ibis-Darstellungen, unter besonderer Berücksichtigung des Waldrapps, *Geronticus eremita* (Linnaeus, 1758)," in *Bonner Zoologische Beiträge* 34 (1983), pp. 197-234.

Lacau and Chevrier 1969. P. Lacau and H. Chevrier. *Un chapelle de Sésostris Ier à Karnak*. Plates. Cairo, 1969.

Lane 1860. E. W. Lane. *An Account of the Manners and Customs of the Modern Egyptians*. 5th edition. London, 1860.

Lange and Hirmer 1968. K. Lange and M. Hirmer. *Egypt: Architecture, Sculpture, Painting in Three Thousand Years*. 4th Edition. London, 1968.

Lauer 1976. J. -P. Lauer. *Saqqara. The Royal Cemetery of Memphis*. New York, 1976.

Laufer 1926. B. Laufer. *Ostrich Egg-Shell Cups of Mesopotamia and the Ostrich in Ancient and Modern Times*. Chicago, 1926.

Lefebvre 1924. G. Lefebvre. *Le tombeau de Petosiris*. Vol. 3. Cairo, 1924.

Legge 1909. F. Legge. "The Carved Slates and this Season's Discoveries," in *Proceedings of the Society of Biblical Archaeology* 31 (1909), pp. 204-211 and 297-310.

Lhote and Hassia 1954. A. Lhote and Hassia. *Les chefs-d'oeuvre de la peinture égyptienne*. Paris, 1954.

Lloyd 1976. A. B. Lloyd. *Herodotus Book II. Commentary 1-98*. Leiden, 1976.

Loret 1901. V. Loret. "Les publications coloriées," in *Sphnix* 5 (1901), pp. 226-233.

Loret 1903. V. Loret. "Horus-le-faucon," in *BIFAO* 3 (1903), pp. 1-24.

Lortet and Gaillard 1903. L. Lortet and C. Gaillard. "La faune momifiée de l'ancienne Égypte," (série 1). in *AMHNL* 8 (1903), pp. i-viii and 1-205.

Lortet and Gaillard 1905. L. Lortet and C. Gaillard. "La faune momifiée de l'ancienne Égypte," (série 2). in *AMHNL* 9 (1905), pp. i-xiv and 1-130.

Lortet and Gaillard 1907. L. Lortet and C. Gaillard. "La faune momifiée de l'ancienne Égypte," (série 3). in *AMHNL* 10 (1907), pp. 1-104.

Lortet and Gaillard 1908. L. Lortet and C. Gaillard. "La faune momifiée de l'ancienne Égypte," (série 4). in *AMHNL* 10 (1908), pp. 105-224.

Lortet and Gaillard 1909. L. Lortet and C. Gaillard. "La faune momifiée de l'ancienne Égypte," (série 5). in *AMHNL* 10 (1909), pp. 225-336.

Lucas 1962. A. Lucas. *Ancient Egyptian Materials and Industries*. 4th edition (by J. R. Harris). London, 1962.

Mackay et al. 1929. E. Mackay, L. Harding and W. M. F. Petrie. *Bahrein and Hemamieh*. London, 1929.

Mackworth-Praed and Grant 1952. C. W. Mackworth-Praed and C. H. B. Grant. *Birds of Eastern and North Eastern Africa*. Vol. 1. London, 1952.

Maclaren 1949. P. I. R. Maclaren. "Bird Notes of the Arabian and Red Seas," in *Journal Bombay Natural History Society* 46 (1949), pp. 543-545.

Macpherson 1897. H. A. Macpherson. *A History of Fowling.* Edinburgh, 1897.

Macramallah 1935. R. Macramallah. *Le mastaba d'Idout.* Cairo, 1935.

Madkour 1977. C. Madkour. "*Rousettus aegyptiacus* (Megachiroptera) as a Fruit Eating Bat in A. R. Egypt," in *Agricultural Research Review* 55 (1977), pp. 167-172.

Maspero 1897. G. Maspero. *Histoire ancienne des peuples de l'Orient classique. Les premières mêlées.* Paris, 1897.

Mastaba of Ptahshepses 1976. *Preliminary Report on Czechoslovak Excavations in the Mastaba of Ptahshepses at Abusir.* Prague, 1976.

Marchant 1941. S. Marchant. "Notes on the Birds of the Gulf of Suez," in *Ibis* (1941), pp. 265-295, 378-396.

Mariette 1876. A. Mariette. *Les papyrus égyptiens du Musée de Boulaq.* Vol. 3. Paris, 1876.

Marietti 1933. G. Marietti. "Notizie Sommarie su Alcuni Uccelli Osservati durante un Breve Viaggio in Oriente (Egitto, Palestina e Siria)," in *Rivista Italiana di Ornitologia* 3 (1933). pp. 162-170.

Markham 1621. G. Markham. *Hungers Preuention: or, The Whole Arte of Fowling by Water and Land.* London, 1621.

Martin 1891. A. Martin. *Home Life on an Ostrich Farm.* New York, 1891.

Martin 1979. G. T. Martin. *The Tomb of Ḥetepka.* London, 1979.

Martin 1981. G. T. Martin. *The Sacred Animal Necropolis at North Saqqâra.* London, 1981.

Mayr and Cottrell 1979. E. Mayr and G. W. Cottrell (eds.). *Check-list of Birds of the World.* Vol. 1. 2nd edition. Cambridge, 1979.

Meeks (forthcoming). D. Meeks. *Les oiseaux de l'Égypte ancienne. Étude d'un champ lexical.* (forthcoming).

Meiklejohn 1944. M. F. M. Meiklejohn. "Bird Notes from Egypt, Autumn 1943," in *BZSE* 6 (1944), pp. 16-18.

Meinertzhagen 1930. R. Meinertzhagen. *Nicoll's Birds of Egypt.* London, 1930.

Meinertzhagen 1954. R. Meinertzhagen. *Birds of Arabia.* Edinburgh, 1954.

Meininger and Dielissen 1979. P. L. Meininger and B. Dielissen. "Ornitologische Waarnemingen in Egypte in 1977 en 1978," in *Veldornitologisch Tijdschrift* 2 (1979), pp. 78-86.

Meininger *et al.* 1979. P. L. Meininger, W. C. Mullié, J. van der Kamp and B. Spaans. *Report of the Netherlands Ornithological Expedition to Egypt in January and February 1979.* Middleburg, 1979.

Meininger *et al.* 1980. P. L. Meininger, W. C. Mullié and B. Brunn. "The Spread of the House Crow, *Corvus splendens*, with Special Reference to the Occurrence in Egypt," in *Gerfaut* 70 (1980), pp. 245-250.

Meininger and Mullié 1981a. P. L. Meininger and W. C. Mullié. "Some Interesting Ornithological Records from Egypt," in *Bulletin Ornithological Society Middle East* 6 (1981), pp. 2-5.

Meininger and Mullié 1981b. P. L. Meininger and W. C. Mullié. "Egyptian Wetlands as Threatened Wintering Areas for Waterbirds," in *Sandgrouse* 3 (1981), pp. 62-77.

Meininger and Sørensen 1984. P. L. Meininger and U. G. Sørensen. "Streaked Weaver *Ploceus manyar* Breeding in Egypt," in *BBOC* 104 (1984), pp. 54-57.

Meininger and Sørensen 1985. P. L. Meininger and U. G. Sørensen. "Skuas (Stercoraridae) in the Middle East and the Eastern Mediterranean, with Special Reference to Egypt and Adjacent Waters," (1985), forthcoming.

Mekhitarian 1954. A. Mekhitarian. *Egyptian Painting.* Geneva, 1954.

Mercer 1942. S. A. B. Mercer. *Horus, Royal God of Egypt.* Grafton, 1942.

Michalowski 1968. K. Michalowski. *L'art de l'ancienne Égypte.* Paris, 1968.

Misonne 1974. X. Misonne. "Les oiseaux de Kufra et du Jebel Uweinat," in *Gerfaut* 64 (1974), pp. 41-73.

Mörzer Bruyns and Voous 1965. W. F. J. Mörzer Bruyns and K. H. Voous. "Great Skuas (*Stercorarius skua*) in Northern Indian Ocean," in *Ardea* 53 (1965), pp. 80-81.

Mogensen 1921. M. Mogensen. *Le mastaba égyptien de la Glyptothèque Ny Carlsberg.* Copenhagen, 1921.

Mogensen 1930. M. Mogensen. *La Glyptothèque Ny Carlsberg. La collection égyptienne.* Copenhagen, 1930.

Mohr 1943. H. T. Mohr. *The Mastaba of Hetep-her-Akhti.* Leiden, 1943.

Montet 1942. P. Montet. "La nécropole des rois tanites," in *Kêmi* 9 (1942), pp. 1-96.

Moorey 1970. P. R. S. Moorey. *Ancient Egypt. Ashmolean Museum.* Oxford, 1970.

Moreau 1927-1928. R. E. Moreau. "Quail," in *BZSE* 1 (1927-1928), pp. 6-13.

Moreau 1928. R. E. Moreau. "Some Further Notes from the Egyptian Deserts," in *Ibis* (1928), pp. 453-475.

Moreau 1930. R. E. Moreau. "The Birds of Ancient Egypt," in R. Meinertzhagen. *Nicoll's Birds of Egypt*. pp. 58-77. London, 1930.

Moreau 1934. R. E. Moreau. "A Contribution to the Ornithology of the Libyan Desert," in *Ibis* (1934), pp. 595-632.

Moreau 1966. R.E. Moreau. *The Bird Faunas of Africa and its Islands*. New York, 1966.

Morris 1895. B. R. Morris. *British Game Birds and Wildfowl*. Vol. 2. (revised by W. B. Tegetmeier), London, 1895.

Moussa and Altenmüller 1971. A. M. Moussa and H. Altenmüller. *The Tomb of Nefer and Ka-hay*. Mainz, 1971.

Moussa and Altenmüller 1977. A. M. Moussa and H. Altenmüller. *Das Grab des Nianchchnum und Chnumhotep*. Mainz, 1977.

Müller 1940. H. W. Müller. *Die Felsengräber der Fürsten von Elephantine*. Glückstadt, 1940.

Müller 1959a. H. W. Müller. *Alt-ägyptische Malerei*. Berlin, 1959.

Müller 1959b. H. W. Müller. "Ein neues Fragment einer reliefgeschmückten Schminkpalette aus Abydos," in *ZÄS* 84 (1959), pp. 68-70.

Müller 1964. H. W. Müller. *Ägyptische Kunstwerke, Kleinfunde und Glas in der Sammlung E. und M. Kofler-Truniger, Luzern*. Berlin, 1964.

Murray 1905. M. A. Murray. *Saqqara Mastabas*. Vol. 1. London, 1905.

Murray 1937. M. A. Murray. *Saqqara Mastabas*. Vol. 2. London, 1937.

National Geographic Society 1978. The National Geographic Society. *Ancient Egypt. Discovering its Splendors*. Washington, D. C., 1978.

Naville 1897. E. Naville. *The Temple of Deir el Bahari*. Vol. 2. London, 1897.

Naville 1898. E. Naville. *The Temple of Deir el Bahari*. Vol. 3. London, 1898.

Naville 1901. E. Naville. *The Temple of Deir el Bahari*. Vol. 4. London, 1901.

Naville 1908. E. Naville. *The Temple of Deir el Bahari*. Vol. 6. London, 1908.

Newberry 1893a. P. E. Newberry. *Beni Hasan*. Vol. 1. London, 1893.

Newberry 1893b. P. E. Newberry. *Beni Hasan*. Vol. 2. London, 1893.

Newberry 1895. P. E. Newberry. *El Bersheh*. Vol. 1. London, 1895.

Newberry 1900. P. E. Newberry. *Beni Hasan*. Vol. 4. London, 1900.

Newberry 1951. P. E. Newberry. "The Owls in Ancient Egypt," in *JEA* 37 (1951), pp. 72-74.

Nicoll 1911. M. J. Nicoll. "Exhibition of Some Birds New to the Avifauna of Egypt," in *BBOC* 27 (1911), pp. 91-92.

Nicoll 1919. M. J. Nicoll. *Handlist of the Birds of Egypt*. Cairo, 1919.

Northampton et al. 1908. The Marquis of Northampton, W. Spiegelberg and P. E. Newberry. *Report on some Excavations in the Theban Necropolis during the Winter of 1898-9*. London, 1908.

Omlin 1973. J. A. Omlin. *Der Papyrus 55001 und seine Satirisch-erotischen Zeichnungen und Inschriften*. Turin, 1973.

Osborn and Helmy 1980. D. J. Osborn and I. Helmy. *The Contemporary Land Mammals of Egypt (Including Sinai)*. Chicago, 1980.

Otto 1968. E. Otto. *Egyptian Art and the Cults of Osiris and Amon*. London, 1968.

Page 1983. A. Page. *Ancient Egyptian Figured Ostraca in the Petrie Collection*. Warminster, 1983.

Paran 1980. Y. Paran. "Some Notes on Waterbirds Observed in Egypt and North Sinai-1978/79," in *Ornithological Society of the Middle East Bulletin* 4 (1980), pp. 2-4.

Peck and Ross 1978. W. H. Peck and J. G. Ross. *Egyptian Drawings*. New York, 1978.

Pegge 1773. Rev. Mr. Pegge. "A Dissertation on the Crane, as a Dish served up at Great Tables in England," in *Archaeologia* 2 (1773), pp.171-176.

Peterson 1973. B. E. J. Peterson. *Zeichnungen aus einer Totenstadt*. Stockholm, 1973.

Petrie 1890. W. M. F. Petrie. *Kahun, Gurob, and Hawara*. London, 1890.

Petrie 1892. W. M. F. Petrie. *Medum*. London, 1892.

Petrie 1914. W. M. F. Petrie. *Amulets*. London, 1914.

Petrie 1921. W. M. F. Petrie. *Corpus of Prehistoric Pottery and Palettes*. London, 1921.

Petrie 1927. H. F. Petrie. *Egyptian Hieroglyphs of the First and Second Dynasties*. London, 1927.

Petrie 1953. W. M. F. Petrie. *Ceremonial Slate Palettes*. London, 1953.

Phillips 1948. D. W. Phillips. *Ancient Egyptian Animals*. New York, 1948.

Piankoff 1954. A. Piankoff. *The Tomb of Ramesses VI* (ed. by N. Rambova). New York, 1954.

Piankoff 1957. A. Piankoff. *Mythological Papyri*. (ed. by N. Rambova). New York, 1957.

Piankoff and Jacquet-Gordon 1974. A. Piankoff and H. Jacquet-Gordon. *The Wandering of the Soul*. Princeton, 1974.

Posener 1959. G. Posener. *Dictionary of Egyptian Civilization*. New York, 1959.

Price 1893. F. G. H. Price. "Notes upon some Egyptian Antiquities in my collection," in *Transactions of the Society of Biblical Archaeology* 9 (1893), pp. 333-354.

Prideaux 1978. T. Prideaux. "Was Botany Born at Karnak?," in *Horticulture* 56 (1978), pp. 22-25.

Quibell 1900. J. E. Quibell. *Hierakonpolis.* Vol. 1. London, 1900.

Quibell 1908. J. E. Quibell. *Tomb of Yuaa and Thuiu.* Cairo, 1908.

Quibell and Green 1902. J. E. Quibell and F. W. Green. *Hierakonpolis.* Vol. 2. London, 1902.

Quibell *et al*. 1898. J. E. Quibell, R. F. E. Paget and A. A. Pirie. *The Ramesseum and the Tomb of Ptah-hetep.* London, 1898.

Randall-Maciver and Woolley 1911. D. Randall-Maciver and C. L. Woolley. *Buhen.* Philadelphia, 1911.

Reisner 1907. G. A. Reisner. *Amulets.* Vol. 1. Cairo, 1907.

Rice 1983. E. E. Rice. *The Grand Procession of Ptolemy Philadelphus.* Oxford, 1983.

Rich 1974. P. V. Rich. "Significance of the Tertiary Avifaunas from Africa (with Emphasis on a Mid to Late Miocene Avifauna from Southern Tunisia)," in *Annals of the Geological Survey of Egypt* 4 (1974), pp. 167-210.

Ricke *et al*. 1967. H. Ricke, G. R. Hughes and E. F. Wente. *The Beit el-Wali Temple of Ramesses II.* Chicago, 1967.

Riddell 1943. W. H. Riddell. "The Domestic Goose," in *Antiquity* 17 (1943), pp. 148-155.

Ripley 1963. S. D. Ripley. "Brief Bird Observations in Nubia," in *Ibis* (1963), pp. 108-109.

Risdon 1971. D. H. S. Risdon. "Breeding the Sacred Ibis and the Scarlet Ibis *Threskiornis aethiopica* and *Eudocimus ruber* at the Tropical Bird Gardens, Rode," in *International Zoo Yearbook* 11 (1971), pp. 131-132.

Roeder 1956. G. Roeder. *Ägyptische Bronzefiguren.* Berlin, 1956.

Roemer- und Pelizaeus-Museum 1979. Roemer- und Pelizaeus-Museum, Hildesheim. *Götter und Pharaonen.* Hildesheim, 1979.

Rosellini 1834. I. Rosellini. *I monumenti dell'Egitto e della Nubia. Monumenti civili.* Atlas. Pisa, 1834.

Rosen 1961. B. von Rosen. "Träskostork i Fornegypten," in *Fauna och Flora* (1961), pp. 174-178.

Rossiter 1979. E. Rossiter. *The Book of the Dead. Papyri of Ani, Hunefer, Anhaï.* Fribourg, 1979.

Rowntree 1943. M. H. Rowntree. "Some Notes on Libyan and Egyptian Birds," in *BZSE* 5 (1943), pp. 18-32.

Russell 1835. M. Russell. *View of Ancient and Modern Egypt; with an Outline of its Natural History.* New York, 1835.

Saleh 1984. M. Saleh. *Das Totenbuch in den Thebanischen Beamtengräbern des neuen Reiches.* Mainz, 1984.

Safriel 1975. U. N. Safriel. "Reoccurrence of the Red Avadavat *Amandava amandava* (L.) (Aves:Estrildidae) in Egypt," in *Israel Journal Zoology* 24 (1975), p. 79.

Safriel 1980. U. N. Safriel. "Notes on the Extinct Population of the Bald Ibis *Geronticus eremita* in the Syrian Desert," in *Ibis* (1980), pp. 82-88.

Salonen 1973. A. Salonen. *Vögel und Vogelfang im alten Mesopotamien.* Helsinki, 1973.

Sandborn and Hoogstraal 1955. C. C. Sandborn and H. Hoogstraal. "The Identification of Egyptian Bats," in *Journal Egyptian Public Health Association* 30 (1955), pp. 103-119.

Sauneron 1969. S. Sauneron. *Le temple d'Esna.* Vol. 4(I). Cairo, 1969.

Säve-Söderbergh 1957. T. Säve-Söderbergh. *Four Eighteenth Dynasty Tombs.* Oxford, 1957.

Savigny 1805. J. -C. Savigny. *Histoire naturelle et mythologique de l'ibis.* Paris, 1805.

Schäfer 1974. H. Schäfer. *Principles of Egyptian Art.* (ed. by E. Brunner-Traut and J. Baines). Oxford, 1974.

Schrader 1892. G. Schrader. "Ornithologische Beobachtungen auf meinen Sammelreisen. V. Aegypten," in *Ornithologisches Jahrbuch* 3 (1892), pp. 41-54.

Schüz 1966. E. Schüz. "Über Stelzvögel (Ciconiiformes und Gruidae) im alten Ägypten," in *Vogelwarte* 23 (1966), pp. 263-283.

Schüz and König 1983. E. Schüz and C. König. "Old World Vultures and Man," in S. R. Wilbur and J. A. Jackson (eds.). *Vulture Biology and Management.* pp. 461-469. Berkeley, 1983.

Schweinfurth 1919. G. Schweinfurth. "Pflanzenbilder im Tempel von Karnak (Theben)," in *Botanische Jahrbücher* 55 (1919), pp. 464-480.

Sclater 1878. P. L. Sclater. "Note on the Breeding of the Sacred Ibis in the Zoological Society's Gardens," in *Ibis* (1878), pp. 449-451.

Sclater 1895. P. L. Sclater. (untitled paper) in *PZSL* (1895), pp. 400-401.

Scott 1940. N. E. Scott. "An Egyptian Bird Trap," in *BMMA* 35 (1940), pp. 163-164.

Scott 1973. N. E. Scott. "The Daily Life of the Ancient Egyptians," in *BMMA* 31 (1973), pp. 121-172.

Seele 1959. K. C. Seele. *The Tomb of Tjanefer at Thebes.* Chicago, 1959.

Sethe 1916. K. Sethe. "Die älteste Erwähnung des Haushuhns in einem ägyptischen Texte," in *Festschrift für Friedrich Carl Andreas*. pp. 109-116. Leipzig, 1916.

Shelley 1872. G. E. Shelley. *A Handbook to the Birds of Egypt*. London, 1872.

Short and Horne 1981. L. L. Short and J. F. M. Horne. "Bird Observations along the Egyptian Nile," in *Sandgrouse* 3 (1981), pp. 43-61.

Simon 1952. A. L. Simon. *A Concise Encyclopaedia of Gastronomy*. London, 1952.

Simpson 1959. W. K. Simpson. "The Vessels with Engraved Designs and the Repoussé Bowl from the Tell Basta Treasure," in *AJA* 63 (1959), pp. 29-45.

Simpson 1976. W.K. Simpson. *The Offering Chapel of Sekhem-ankh-Ptah in the Museum of Fine Arts, Boston*. Boston, 1976.

Simpson 1978. W. K. Simpson. *The Mastabas of Kawab, Khafkhufu I and II*. Boston, 1978.

Simpson 1980. W. K. Simpson. *Mastabas of the Western Cemetery: Part I*. Boston, 1980.

Singer *et al*. 1954. C. Singer, E. J. Holmyard and A. R. Hall (eds.). *A History of Technology*. Vol. 1. Oxford, 1954.

Sluys and van den Berg 1982. R. Sluys and M. van den Berg. "On the Specific Status of the Cyprus Pied Wheatear *Oenanthe cypriaca*," in *Ornis Scandinavica* 13 (1982), pp. 123-128.

Smith 1937. W. S. Smith. "The Paintings of the Chapel of Atet at Mēdūm," in *JEA* 23 (1937), pp. 17-26.

Smith 1946. W. S. Smith. *A History of Egyptian Sculpture and Painting in the Old Kingdom*. London, 1946.

Smith 1960. W. S. Smith. *Ancient Egypt as Represented in the Museum of Fine Arts, Boston*. 4th edition. Boston, 1960.

Smith 1964. W. S. Smith. "Some Recent Accessions: Birds and Insects," in *BMFA* 62 (1964), p. 145.

Smith 1965a. W. S. Smith. *The Art and Architecture of Ancient Egypt*. Baltimore, 1965.

Smith 1965b. W. S. Smith. *Interconnections in the Ancient Near East*. New Haven, 1965.

Smith 1970. K. D. Smith. "The Waldrapp *Geronticus eremita* (L.)," in *BBOC* 90 (1970), pp. 18-24.

Smith 1974. H. S. Smith. *A Visit to Ancient Egypt. Life at Memphis & Saqqara (c. 500-30 BC)*. Warminster, 1974.

Smith and Redford 1976. R. W. Smith and D. B. Redford. *The Akhenaten Temple Project*. Vol. 1. Warminster, 1976.

Snow 1978. D. W. Snow. *An Atlas of Speciation in African Non-Passerine Birds*. London, 1978.

Sonnini 1800. C. S. Sonnini. *Travels in Upper and Lower Egypt*. London, 1800.

Speleers 1917. L. Speleers. *Le papyrus de Nefer Renpet. Un Livre des morts de la XVIII dynastie aux Musées royaux du Cinquantenaire à Bruxelles*. Brussels, 1917.

Spencer 1980. A. J. Spencer. *Early Dynastic Objects*. London, 1980.

Steindorff 1913. G. Steindorff. *Das Grab des Ti*. Leipzig, 1913.

Steindorff 1946. G. Steindorff. *Catalogue of the Egyptian Sculpture in the Walters Art Gallery*. Baltimore, 1946.

Sterbetz 1978. É. Sterbetz. "Documents dans les arts plastiques pour l'étude de la migration des bernaches à cou roux," in *Bulletin du Musée Hongrois des Beaux-Arts* 50 (1978), pp. 73-78.

Störk 1977a. L. Störk. "Fauna," in *LÄ* 2 (1977), pp. 128-138.

Störk 1977b. L. Störk. "Fledermaus," in *LÄ* 2 (1977), pp. 263-264.

Störk 1977c. L. Störk. "Gans," in *LÄ* 2 (1977), pp. 373-375.

Störk 1980. L. Störk. "Kormoran," in *LÄ* 3 (1980), pp. 741-742.

Störk 1982. L. Störk. "Pelikan," in *LÄ* 4 (1982), pp. 923-924.

Stricker 1957. B. H. Stricker. "Die heilige uil," in *Oudheidkundige Mededelingen uit het Rijksmuseum van Oudheden te Leiden* 38 (1957), pp. 1-14.

Strzygowski 1904. J. Strzygowski. *Koptische Kunst*. Vienna, 1904.

Stubbs and Rowe 1912. F. J. Stubbs and A. J. Rowe. "The Prehistoric Origin of the Common Fowl," in *Zoologist* 16 (1912), pp. 1-14.

Taylor 1891. E. C. Taylor. (untitled paper) in *Ibis* (1891), pp. 473-475.

Taylor 1896. E. C. Taylor. "A Few Notes on Birds of Egypt, from Observations Made at Cairo in the Months of January and February, 1896," in *Ibis* (1896), pp. 477-482.

Terrace 1967. E. L. B. Terrace. *Egyptian Paintings of the Middle Kingdom*. New York, 1967.

Terrace and Fischer 1970. E. L. B. Terrace and H. G. Fischer. *Treasures of the Cairo Museum*. London, 1970.

te Velde 1972. H. te Velde. "The Swallow as Herald of the Dawn in Ancient Egypt," in *Ex Orbe Religionum*. Vol. 1. pp. 26-31. Leiden, 1972.

te Velde 1980. H. te Velde. "A few Remarks upon the Religious Significance of Animals in Ancient Egypt," in *Numen* 27 (1980), pp. 76-82.

Thausing and Goedicke 1971. G. Thausing and H. Goedicke. *Nofretari. A Documentation of her Tomb and its Decoration.* Graz, 1971.

Thompson 1966. D'Arcy W. Thompson. *A Glossary of Greek Birds.* Hildesheim, 1966.

Thomson 1965. A. L. Thomson. "Orthography of the Name *Ammoperdix heyi* (Temminck)," in *BBOC* 85 (1965), pp. 117-119.

Thomson 1976. A. L. Thomson. "The Name of Eleonora's Falcon," in *BBOC* 96 (1976), p. 112.

Ticehurst 1912. C. B. Ticehurst. "The Birds of Lower Egypt," in *Zoologist* (1912), pp. 41-59.

Ticehurst 1931. C. B. Ticehurst. "Notes on Egyptian Birds," in *Ibis* (1931), pp. 575-578.

Tosi and Roccati 1972. M. Tosi and A. Roccati. *Stele e altre epigrafi Deir el Medina n. 50001-n. 50262.* Turin, 1972.

Toynbee 1973. J. M. C. Toynbee. *Animals in Roman Life and Art.* Ithaca, 1973.

Tregenza 1951. L. A. Tregenza. "Observations on the Birds of the S. E. Desert of Egypt," in *BZSE* 9 (1951), pp. 1-18.

Tregenza 1958. L. A. Tregenza. *Egyptian Years.* London, 1958.

University of Chicago, Oriental Institute 1934. University of Chicago, Oriental Institute. *Medinet Habu.* Vol. 3. Chicago, 1934.

University of Chicago, Oriental Institute 1940. University of Chicago, Oriental Institute. *Medinet Habu.* Vol. 4. Chicago, 1940.

University of Chicago, Oriental Institute 1980. University of Chicago, Oriental Institute. *The Tomb of Kheruef. Theban Tomb 192.* Chicago, 1980.

van den Broek 1972. R. van den Broek. *The Myth of the Phoenix According to Classical and Early Christian Traditions.* Leiden, 1972.

Vandersleyen 1975. C. Vandersleyen. *Das alte Ägypten.* Berlin, 1975.

van de Walle 1978. B. van de Walle. *La Chapelle funéraire de Neferirtenef.* Brussels, 1978.

van de Walle 1984. B. van de Walle. "Schwan," in *LÄ* 5 (Lieferung 5, 1984), pp. 755-757.

Vandier 1935. J. Vandier. *La tombe de Nefer-abou.* Cairo, 1935.

Vandier 1950. J. Vandier. "Une statue d'ibis," in *RdE* 7 (1950), pp. 33-35.

Vandier 1952. J. Vandier. *Manuel d'archéologie égyptienne.* Vol. 1. Paris, 1952.

Vandier 1954. J. Vandier. *Egypt. Paintings from Tombs and Temples.* Greenwich, 1954.

Vandier 1969. J. Vandier. *Manuel d'archéologie égyptienne.* Vol. 5. Paris, 1969.

Vandier 1971. J. Vandier. "L'oie d'Amon. A propos d'une récente acquisition du Musée du Louvre," in *Académie des inscriptions et belles-lettres. Monuments et mémoires* 57 (1971), pp. 5-41.

Vandier 1973. J. Vandier. *Musée du Louvre. Le départment des antiquités égyptiennes. Guide sommaire.* 5th edition. Paris, 1973.

Vandier d'Abbadie 1936a. J. Vandier d'Abbadie. "A propos d'une chauve-souris sur un ostracon du Musée du Caire," in *BIFAO* 36 (1936), pp. 117-123.

Vandier d'Abbadie 1936b. J. Vandier d'Abbadie. *Catalogue des ostraca figurés de Deir el Médineh.* Fasc. 1. Cairo, 1936.

Vandier d'Abbadie 1937. J. Vandier d'Abbadie. *Catalogue des ostraca figurés de Deir el Médineh.* Fasc. 2. Cairo, 1937.

Vandier d'Abbadie 1946. J. Vandier d'Abbadie. *Catalogue des ostraca figurés de Deir el Médineh.* Fasc. 3. Cairo, 1946.

Vandier d'Abbadie 1959. J. Vandier d'Abbadie. *Catalogue des ostraca figurés de Deir el Médineh.* Fasc. 4. Cairo, 1959.

Vandier d'Abbadie 1973. J. Vandier d'Abbadie. "Le cygne dans l'Égypte ancienne," in *RdE* 25 (1973), pp. 35-49.

Varille 1938. A. Varille. *La tombe de Ni-ankh-Pepi à Zâouyet el-Meyetîn.* Cairo, 1938.

Vaurie 1959. C. Vaurie. *The Birds of the Palaearctic Fauna. Passerines.* London, 1959.

Vaurie 1965. C. Vaurie. *The Birds of the Palearctic Fauna. Non-passeriformes.* London, 1965.

Vercoutter 1956. J. Vercoutter. *L'Égypte et le monde égéen préhellénique.* Cairo, 1956.

Vigneau 1935. A. Vigneau (photographer). *Encyclopédie photographique de l'art. Les antiquités égyptiennes du Musée du Louvre.* Vol. 1. Paris, 1935.

Voous 1973. K. H. Voous. "List of Recent Holarctic Bird Species, Non-passerines," in *Ibis* (1973), pp. 612-638.

Voous 1977. K. H. Voous. "List of Recent Holarctic Bird Species, Passerines," in *Ibis* (1977), pp. 223-250, 376-406.

Walter 1979. H. Walter. *Eleonora's Falcon.* Chicago, 1979.

Wassermann 1984. R. Wassermann. "Schwalbe," in *LÄ* 5 (Lieferung 5, 1984), pp. 754-755.

Weigall 1906. A. E. P. Weigall. "A Report on the Excavation of the Funeral Temple of Thoutmosis III at Gurneh," in *ASAE* 7 (1906), pp. 121-141.

Werbrouck 1934a. M. Werbrouck. *Musées royaux d'Art et Histoire, Bruxelles. Département égyptien. Album.* Brussels, 1934.

Werbrouck 1934b. M. Werbrouck. "L'oiseau dans les tombes thébaines," in *Mélanges Maspero.* Vol. 1. pp. 21-25. Cairo, 1934.

Werbrouck 1938. M. Werbrouck. "Deux bas-reliefs d'Ancien Empire," in *Bulletin des Musées royaux d'Art et d'Histoire* 10 (1938), pp. 137-141.

Whymper 1909. C. Whymper. *Egyptian Birds for the most part seen in the Nile Valley.* London, 1909.

Wilber 1960. D. N. Wilber. "The Off-beat in Egyptian Art," in *Archaeology* 13 (1960), pp. 259-266.

Wild 1953. H. Wild. *Le tombeau de Ti.* Fasc. 2. Cairo, 1953.

Wild 1966. H. Wild. *Le tombeau de Ti.* Fasc. 3. Cairo, 1966.

Wilkinson 1878. J. G. Wilkinson. *The Manners and Customs of the Ancient Egyptians.* Vols. 1-3. (rev. by S. Birch). London, 1878.

Wilkinson 1983. C. K. Wilkinson. *Egyptian Wall Paintings. The Metropolitan Museum of Art's Collection of Facsimiles.* New York, 1983.

Williams 1932. C. R. Williams. *The Decoration of the Tomb of Per-nēb.* New York, 1932.

Williams 1955. J. G. Williams. "A Systematic Revision and Natural History of the Shining Sunbird of Africa," in *Condor* 57 (1955), pp. 249-262.

Wilson-Yang and Burns 1982. K. M. Wilson-Yang and G. Burns. "Chemical and Physical Aspects of the Beni Hasan Tombs," in *Journal of the American Research Center in Egypt* 19 (1982), pp. 115-117.

Wimpfheimer *et al.* 1983. D. Wimpfheimer, B. Bruun, S. M. Baha el Din and M. C. Jennings. *The Migration of Birds of Prey in the Northern Red Sea Area.* New York, 1983.

Winkler 1938. H. A. Winkler. *Rock-Drawings of Southern Upper Egypt.* Vol. 1. London, 1938.

Winlock 1941. H. E. Winlock. *Materials used at the Embalming of King Tūt-ʿankh-Amūn.* New York, 1941.

Winlock 1945. H. E. Winlock. *The Slain Soldiers of Neb-hepet-Rēʿ Mentu-hotpe.* New York, 1945.

Winlock 1948. H. E. Winlock. *The Treasures of Three Egyptian Princesses.* New York, 1948.

Winlock 1955. H. E. Winlock. *Models of Daily Life in Ancient Egypt from the Tomb of Meket-Rēʿ at Thebes.* Cambridge, 1955.

Witherby 1938. H. F. Witherby (ed.). *The Handbook of British Birds.* Vol. 2. London, 1938.

Witherby *et al.* 1940. H. F. Witherby, F. C. R. Jourdain, N. F. Ticehurst and B. W. Tucker. *The Handbook of British Birds.* Vol. 4. London, 1940.

Woldhek 1979. S. Woldhek. *Bird Killing in the Mediterranean.* Zeist, 1979.

Wreszinski 1923. W. Wreszinski. *Atlas zur altägyptischen Kulturgeschichte.* Vol. 1. Leipzig, 1923.

Wreszinski 1935. W. Wreszinski. *Atlas zur altägyptischen Kulturgeschichte.* Vol. 2. Leipzig, 1935.

Wreszinski 1936. W. Wreszinski. *Atlas zur altägyptischen Kulturgeschichte.* Vol. 3. Leipzig, 1936.

Yapp 1981. B. Yapp. *Birds in Medieval Manuscripts.* London, 1981.

Yoyotte 1968. J. Yoyotte. *Treasures of the Pharaohs.* Geneva, 1968.

Zivie 1980. A.-P. Zivie. "Ibis," in *LÄ* 3 (1980), pp. 115-121.

Zeuner 1963. F. E. Zeuner. *A History of Domesticated Animals.* London, 1963.

The great swampland scene in the mastaba of Ti (No. 60), Saqqara, showing a Hippopotamus hunt, with variegated bird life above. Dynasty V.

XXX

CATALOGUE OF THE BIRDS IDENTIFIED

1. Ostrich (*Struthio camelus*)

Identification: The diagnostic proportions, the long neck and legs, the small wings, and the feathered neck are the unmistakable features of a juvenile Ostrich.

Distribution: The bird breeds in select parts of the Middle East,[1] and Africa. The Ostrich has long been thought to be extinct from its former range in Egypt since the middle of the nineteenth century,[2] predominantly due to excessive hunting pressures by man.[3] However, in 1935 an Ostrich was reported to have been killed in the Western Desert between the Dakhla and Kharga Oases,[4] while in 1967, an adult male, a nestling and a pair of unhatched fresh eggs were collected in the Eastern Desert near Gebel Elba in the extreme southeastern corner of the country. This latter record, and even more recent observations, have not only confirmed its presence in the Eastern Desert, but its breeding there as well.[5] Whether the species has re-established itself in its former haunts in Egypt as the result of the movement of populations from the south (i.e. the Sudan), or continuously existed from antiquity until recent times in small isolated pocket populations which have gone unnoticed in the intervening years is impossible to determine. If the birds did indeed come from the south, after a long interval when they were no longer sought after by man, which seems the most likely explanation, they would have had to colonize at least twice, as the 1935 and the 1967 records are from opposite sides of the Nile (assuming of course that Ostriches do not swim across the Nile).

Comments: Ostriches are regularly represented in Egyptian art; they are very rare as hieroglyphs,[6] but the Ostrich feather is a common sign. From the Dynasty XVIII royal tomb of Tutankhamun (No. 62) in the Valley of the Kings, came a fan (fig. 1) made of wood sheathed with sheet gold. When found, the debris of thirty alternating brown and white

Ostrich plumes was associated with it, a few of the stumps still fixed in the holes on the outer edges of the palm.[7] The feathers, according to an inscription engraved on the handle of the fan, were obtained "by His Majesty when hunting in the desert east of Heliopolis."[8] Embossed on each face of the fan are scenes of the young Pharaoh hunting the birds for feathers for the fan. On this side, Tutankhamun is pictured riding in a horse-drawn chariot, the reins of which are secured around his body, freeing his hands, allowing him to draw his bow down on his quarry, a pair of juvenile Ostriches.[9] His Saluki hound (*Canis familiaris*), in full pursuit, is ready to pounce on the already wounded birds, to finish them off. The king wears a short Nubian wig with two streamers at the back, a leopard skin corselet, a pleated kilt, and a decorative apron. Taking up the space behind the chariot is an anthropomorphized hieroglyphic sign for "life" (*ankh*), which carries a fan resembling the one seen here. The reverse side portrays the triumphal return of the hunt, with two attendants walking in front of the chariot, carrying the slain Ostriches slung over their shoulders.[10] Although only juveniles (we estimate no more than four months old), these flightless birds would certainly have been able to provide the king with ample sport, as even month-old Ostrich chicks can evade danger by running at speeds reaching 50 km/h.[11] It is to be noted that these young birds have reduced tail-plumes in comparison with the large ornamental type of an adult, as can be seen attached on top of the headstalls of the horses' bridles. As is sometimes the case with illustrations of the Ostrich in Egyptian art, here the artist has rendered the birds as possessing three toes on each foot (fig. 4), a spurious feature, as the species has but two.[12]

The Ostrich is the first species of bird for which we have pictorial evidence from Egypt. Its distinctive form can be recognized from the oldest series of rock drawings carved by

Fig. 1. Tutankhamun depicted hunting Ostriches on an embossed gold fan from his tomb, (No. 62), Valley of the Kings. Dynasty XVIII.

2

hunters on cliffs along the edge of the Nile Valley and in the deserts of Upper Egypt and Lower Nubia, which apparently date from Badarian or Amratian (Naqada I) times.[13] Rock drawings of Ostrich are fairly common during predynastic times. Probably the most outstanding example is preserved on a rock wall near Silwa Bahari (fig. 2), where a man is depicted hunting an Ostrich with bow and arrow. Also note in this spirited scene the presence of a rhinoceros (*Diceros* sp.) and an African Bush Elephant (*Loxodonta africana*).

believe, as they lay their eggs in simple depressions in the ground. The abnormality only slightly detracts from this interesting relief detail.

Beginning with the Dynasty XI tomb of Baket III (No. 15) at Beni Hasan,[17] and continuing through Dynasty XVIII, Ostriches can frequently be observed amongst the desert fauna corralled together in large fenced-off enclosures which served as "reserves" for the hunting pleasures of noblemen and courtiers. Numerous compositions depict tomb owners or

Fig. 2. A rock drawing of an Ostrich and other animals being hunted, near Silwa Bahari. Predynastic.

Another beautiful instance of this early hunting of the Ostrich can be viewed on a fragment of the Hunters' Palette dating from the Late Predynastic Period, now in the British Museum, London.[14] The swift-footed bird is being given chase by a party of huntsmen, who surround it and a horde of other wild game. Ostriches are not very often shown in Old Kingdom art,[15] but one charming depiction is especially worth our attention as no parallel exists for it. On a fragment from the Dynasty V sun temple of Niuserre at Abu Gurob, now in the Egyptian Museum, Cairo, an Ostrich is pictured nesting and tending its clutch of eggs.[16] Ostriches, however, do not build structural nests as the artist would have us

their huntsmen standing either outside or inside the walls of the stockades, shooting their arrows at the multitude of fleeing game: White Oryxes (*Oryx dammah*), gazelles (*Gazella* sp.), Ibexes (*Capra ibex*), wild bulls (family Bovidae), Striped Hyenas (*Hyaena hyaena*), Hares (*Lepus capensis*), hedgehogs (family Erinaceidae), etc., while their dogs give chase.[18] This type of hunting scene is well shown in the Dynasty XVIII tomb of Amenemhet (No. 53) at Thebes (fig. 3), and where the diversity of the game is great. Upon having secured the desired take, the trophies of the hunt were then presented to the owner for his inspection. Sometimes the bag included live adult Ostriches, which are shown being led by

3

Fig. 3. Relief of hunting scene in the tomb of Amenemhet (No. 53), Thebes, showing the deceased drawing his bow on a mass of game, including Ostriches, enclosed in a stockade of nets. Dynasty XVIII.

attendants in a most effortless manner,[19] and who employ little or no restraints on the animal (fig. 4). To some writers this suggests that the Egyptians domesticated the Ostrich,[20] because an adult wild bird could not be so confidently managed and could easily lash out with its powerful legs and inflict serious, if not fatal, wounds to its handler. These scenes, however, should probably not be interpreted quite so literally, as they may be less a record of reality than an expression of an ideal. On the other hand, Ostriches are similarly handled in scenes which show them being brought as tribute.[21] Another notable example of the species occurs in the decoration of a late Dynasty XIX or early Dynasty XX silver bowl from Tell Basta (fig. 112). Three birds, two adult and one juvenile, are shown in a scene which takes place along the desert margin. These Ostriches may perhaps be tame ones, as has been suggested,[22] since they appear to be under the charge of a keeper (he is only partly visible in our photograph). There is also some textual evidence to support the domestication of the Ostrich.[23] The bird was surely domesticated during the

Ptolemaic Period, as eight pairs of Ostriches are said to have walked in harness in Ptolemy II's procession.[24] Whether any of the Ostrich bagged in the above mentioned hunting episodes ever found their way onto the table is not known. But as Ostrich flesh is considered edible,[25] the potential for its consumption was at least there. It was clearly for its plumes and eggs that the Ostrich was most valued (fig. 5). Ostrich eggs make delicious eating, and they are so large that a single egg is said to be capable of providing a good meal for as many as eight people.[26] Once emptied (or blown) of their contents, Ostrich egg-shells were sometimes used as vessels.[27] In fact, Ostrich egg-shells are amongst the earliest objects of any kind from ancient Egypt, as are small ornaments made from them.[28] The demand for Ostrich plumes and eggs was such that additional supplies of them were imported and brought as tribute. They are figured amongst the products carried by bearers from Libya,[29] Punt,[30] Syria,[31] and especially from Nubia.[32]

In a text from the New Kingdom, the Ostrich is said to greet the dawn by "dancing" in the

Fig. 4. An Ostrich captured in the hunt is brought before the deceased by an attendant, from the tomb of User (No. 21), Thebes. Dynasty XVIII.

Fig. 5. Painting of an offering bearer with an Ibex, a Hare, and Ostrich eggs and plumes, from the tomb of Haremhab (No. 78), Thebes. Dynasty XVIII.

wadis in honor of the sun. Ostriches have actually been observed in the wild at sunrise running around, spinning and flapping their wings, an activity which could indeed remind one of a kind of dance. There are at least two scenes in art in which Ostriches are shown "dancing" in this manner.[33]

There is some evidence to suggest that during the Byzantine Period in Egypt, Ostriches were raised on special farms,[34] apparently for their ornamental tail-plumes. We again hear of an Ostrich farm in Egypt from travelers who visited one located near Heliopolis late in the last century. Here as many as 1,400 birds were kept at one time, and again it was their plumes which were the desired product.[35] The actual hunting of wild Ostriches in Egypt continued on a sizeable scale at least up until the late eighteenth century. The hunters were content to pluck the plumes and remove the fat from the carcass (the fat was used for cooking and medicine), the flesh of the birds was not eaten.[36] Also, at this same time, Ostrich eggs were still rather common in the markets of Egypt. The long tradition of utilizing the Ostrich in Egypt may still continue to this very day. Rashaida tribesmen living in the Gebel Elba region are thought to consume Ostrich,[37] and perhaps eggs as well, but this awaits conclusive documentation.

5

2. Diver (*Gavia* sp.)

Fig. 6. Diver from the "Botanical Garden" in the Festival Hall of Tuthmosis III, Karnak. Dynasty XVIII.

Identification: The distinctive posture, the short tail, the comparatively long, thin pointed bill, the large feet, and the diagnostic position of the legs set far to the rear on the underside of the body are features of a diver.

Distribution: There are four species of diver in the western Palearctic. Of them only the Black-throated Diver (*G. arctica*) has tentatively been reported in modern Egypt.[38] The bird breeds in parts of northern Europe and Asia. It winters along parts of the Atlantic coast of Europe, in the Mediterranean, Black and Caspian Seas, and along the Pacific coast of Asia. In modern Egypt, the Black-throated Diver is thought to be an accidental winter visitor along the Mediterranean coast.[39]

Comments: This is the only example of a diver that we have been able to positively identify in Egyptian art and hieroglyphs (fig. 6). With the military success Egypt experienced under the leadership of Tuthmosis III, her Western Asiatic empire at its zenith stretched to the banks of the Euphrates River in northern Syria. Like his immediate predecessor and aunt Queen Hatshepsut, whose mortuary temple at Deir el-Bahari is decorated in part with reliefs commemorating her trading expedition to the distant land of Punt (see under bird No. 61), so too was Tuthmosis III fascinated by exotica. In two chambers set to the rear of his Festival Hall at Karnak, and conveniently referred to by Egyptologists as the "Botanical Garden", we are informed that in the twenty-fifth year of his reign he had carved upon their walls "all plants that grow, all flowers that are in God's Land which were found by His Majesty when His Majesty proceeded to Upper Retenu [Palestine and Syria]" in order to "put them before my father Amun, in this great temple of Amun, as a memorial for ever and ever."[40] The flora, which is also intermixed with a collection of fauna, is thought to have been gathered by naturalists who accompanied the king on his military campaigns into Western Asia.[41] Approximately 275 plant specimens[42] and 52 animals, of which 38 are birds, can be discerned on the extant walls of the chambers. To the layperson these strange plant and flower repre-

6

sentations may look entirely authentic, but, unfortunately, the vast majority of them have defied the attempts of modern botanists at identification, and not one of the plants can be proven to be of Syrian origin. According to Ludwig Keimer, almost all of the plants at the "Botanical Garden" are "purely fantastic forms that might just as well have come out of Australia", and they "served only to indicate something as foreign as possible."[43] So too must we regard a portion of the fauna as totally fanciful, as it includes such obvious flights of the imagination as two-tailed and three-horned bovines. Many of the birds, at least in what can be determined in the absence of pigment, are strikingly similar to those species traditionally pictured in Egyptian art for centuries. In a few instances, however, the forms depicted cannot be recalled from any other occurrence. One such example is that of the diver we exhibit here. The bird has been executed in a manner which suggests that it is swimming. This is in full accord with their behavior, as divers, except when nesting, are rarely seen out of the water. The features of the bird have been superbly observed, and this is particularly true of its legs, which are properly shown attached to the extreme posterior of the body. Since the majority of divers exclusively confine their winter movements to sheltered coastal marine environments,[44] and as divers have never been known to occur south of the Mediterranean Sea,[45] the artist who delineated this picture could only have observed or collected it near that body of water. Whether this has any direct bearing on the Syrian travels of Tuthmosis III is impossible to say. It is to be remembered that the Black-throated Diver is thought to be an accidental visitor to modern Egypt, and therefore the bird which served as the model for this illustration could have been obtained or viewed in Egypt proper and would not have had to be an exotic. Because this portrayal is completely devoid of color, and as there are several other varieties of diver which frequent the northern and northeastern region of the Mediterranean Sea, the identification of the exact species is not possible.

3. Cormorant (*Phalacrocorax* sp.)

Identification: The characteristic posture, the long squared tail, the elongated body, and the rather long neck (which is held here slightly retracted) are features of a cormorant.

Distribution: There are three species of cormorant that have been reported in modern Egypt. The Great Cormorant (*P. carbo*) is a winter visitor in the Nile Valley and Delta, the Faiyum, along the Mediterranean Sea coast, and in the general vicinity of the Suez Canal. The Shag (*P. aristotelis*) is an uncommon migrant along the Mediterranean Sea coast. The Long-tailed Cormorant (*P. africanus*) is now extinct from its former breeding range in Egypt, where it was known to breed in the Faiyum, and perhaps in the Nile Delta, until late in the last century.[46]

Comments: Cormorants are commonly represented in both Egyptian art and hieroglyphs.[47] This handsome picture of a cormorant (fig. 7), from the Dynasty VI mastaba of Mereruka at Saqqara, is shown facing toward the right, with its left leg placed forward of the right, roosting on top of a Papyrus (*Cyperus papyrus*) umbel in a swamp which is teeming with other wild life.[48] The pattern of papyrus stems, which is composed of a series of vertically cut lines of relief, serves as the background to the figure, and indicates that the bird is to be thought of as completely surrounded by papyrus in the thicket. The placement of it in this type of environment is in keeping with the nature of the bird, as cormorants do indeed haunt similar aquatic habitats. Cormorants, however, do not and could not perch on papyrus blossoms, and this aspect to the illustration is purely conventional. Throughout Egyptian art birds are routinely shown roosting on and even nesting on top of papyrus umbels in swamp scenes. Because the sheer weight of most of the birds involved makes it impossible for them to actually do so, it is clear that the artists' intention was to convey the idea of their general location, that is amid papyrus, rather than on the plant itself. Exceptionally imitative of the living bird is its upright stance, and note that the neck is partially drawn back and that the head is angled slightly upward, all typical of cormorant posture. Due to a small chip in the

Fig. 7. (above) Cormorant from a swamp scene in the mastaba of Mereruka, Saqqara. Dynasty VI.

Fig. 8. (top right) Relief of a cormorant eating a fish, from the mastaba of Mereruka, Saqqara. Dynasty VI.

Fig. 9. (bottom right) Cormorant roosting on top of a papyrus umbel, from the tomb of Khnumhotep III (No. 3), Beni Hasan. Dynasty XII.

relief, it is impossible to determine whether the bird was rendered with a hook-tipped bill or not. This detail of the cormorant, however, was in fact frequently overlooked by the Egyptian artist. The absence of any distinguishing plumage characteristics in this portrayal inhibits our identification of it to the species level.

The earliest extant representation of a cormorant is from Dynasty IV. Beginning with the Dynasty IV tomb of Nebemakhet (LG 86) at Giza,[49] cormorants can regularly be observed in swamp scenes, roosting in the thick vegetation along with other types of waterside birds.[50] Another fine depiction of a cormorant in the mastaba of Mereruka (fig. 8), shows it fishing near the water's edge. We view the bird after it has made a catch and is attempting to swallow the fish whole. This activity is quite befitting of a cormorant, as they are voracious fish eaters. Perhaps the best known occurrence

of a cormorant in art, and one which retains much of its coloring, appears in the Dynasty XII tomb of Khnumhotep III (No. 3) at Beni Hasan, where it appears having come to rest on a stand of papyrus in a swamp (fig. 9). It has been most handsomely painted,[51] and while its coloring approaches that of a living cormorant, the bird cannot be identified to the species level. During the New Kingdom the cormorant hieroglyph is very often executed in a manner that immediately reminds one of another member of the family Phalacro-coracidae.[52] They are portrayed with excessively long and strongly curved necks,[53] as though the artists had been influenced by the Darter (*Anhinga rufa*), see bird No. 4. However, this remains uncertain, as it is not possible to determine whether this irregularity was due to stylization of the sign, or because of actual familiarity with the form of the Darter.

4. Darter (*Anhinga rufa*)

Fig. 10. *Darter from the "Botanical Garden" in the Festival Hall of Tuthmosis III, Karnak. Dynasty XVIII.*

Identification: The extremely long serpentine neck, the long slender pointed bill, and the very long tail are the diagnostic features of a Darter.

Distribution: The bird breeds in parts of Turkey,[54] southern Iraq, and sub-Saharan Africa. It winters in parts of the Middle East and sub-Saharan Africa. The occurrence of the Darter has never been documented in modern Egypt.[55]

Comments: This is the only representation of a Darter that we have been able to identify confidently in Egyptian art and hieroglyphs (fig. 10). Carved in crisp relief, this portrayal of the species appears on a wall in the "Botanical Garden" at Karnak, see under bird No. 2. The artist has deftly captured all of the bird's arresting features, most notably that of its extremely attenuated neck with its characteristic kink, with total fidelity. The precision of the detail, even in the absence of pigment, successfully conveys the essence of the Darter. As the bird is depicted in the "Botanical Garden", it was intended to be thought of as an exotic and not a native species. Today the Darter is an accidental migrant in Syria[56] and Israel,[57] and therefore it was at least feasible for Tuthmosis III to have observed or collected a specimen while on his Asiatic campaigns.

Although the Darter has never been documented in modern Egypt, R. E. Moreau has stated that it is virtually certain that the bird lived in the country in the not too distant past.[58] Only recently bone remains of it have been identified from a probable predynastic site in the Faiyum,[59] and from dynastic levels at Elephantine.[60] Thus, the bird rendered at the "Botanical Garden" could very well have been a resident species, and not necessarily an exotic. That being the case, it is rather unusual that such an interesting animal as the Darter would have only been pictured in art on one occasion. Surely the Egyptians would have been fascinated by the species' curious habit of swimming with its body entirely submerged underwater, only with its head and neck above the surface, with which it makes snakelike movements as it swims along. There are other representations which at least recall the Darter, but specific identification of them as such is impossible (see under bird No. 3).

9

5. White or Pink-backed Pelican (*Pelecanus onocrotalus* and *P. rufescens*)

Identification: The marked posture and proportions, the enormous bill with its distended gular pouch, and the apparent absence of a coarse or "shaggy" plumage are features of a White or Pink-backed Pelican.

Distribution: The White Pelican breeds in select parts of eastern Europe, Asia, Turkey and sub-Saharan Africa. It winters in parts of southern Europe, Asia, the Middle East and Africa. In modern Egypt, the White Pelican is a winter visitor in the Nile Valley and Delta, the Faiyum, in the general vicinity of the Suez Canal, and along the Red Sea coast. The Pink-backed Pelican breeds in parts of the Middle East and Africa. In modern Egypt, the Pink-backed Pelican is an uncommon winter visitor in the Upper Nile Valley.[61]

Comments: White or Pink-backed Pelicans are infrequently depicted in Egyptian art. The birds portrayed here appear on a block of relief from a room in the Dynasty V sun temple of Niuserre at Abu Gurob (fig. 11), the so-called "Chamber of the Seasons" (*Weltkammer*). The walls of this room were decorated with scenes illustrating the various agricultural activities, natural history events, etc., which took place during the *akhet* season (inundation) and the *shemu* season (harvest). A considerable amount of space was devoted to recording the yearly cycles of a large collection of fauna and flora, which was labeled with detailed explanatory hieroglyphic captions.[62] The avifauna in particular received a good deal of attention, and many of the accompanying inscriptions not only identify the birds by name, but provide us with insights into what the Egyptians perceived the mode of the individual species to be, such as if it were thought of as a migrant. Unfortunately, only fragments of the scenes survive today, but they can be of great value in studying the animals of ancient Egypt. The White or Pink-backed Pelicans shown here were displayed in the *shemu* season.[63] They are executed walking toward the right in a manner which suggests the typical slow clumsy gait of pelicans. The birds' handlers, who all wear wigs and short kilts, are identified in the inscription as priests.[64] They follow behind the pelicans with their arms outstretched, touching the birds' backs, apparently to help guide them along. The pelicans appear to be very well adjusted to captivity. They were probably domestic birds,[65] and were kept at the sun temple for religious reasons. In comparison to the men, the birds may seem to be excessively large, particularly the one furthest to the left; however, the relative sizes of the figures are more or less accurate, as an adult White Pelican stands about 140 cm tall. The features of the pelican have been penetratingly observed in this relief. Their huge pouched-bills and the general awkward appearance of them is especially noteworthy. Because the birds do not exhibit what we would consider as obvious plumage features (see below), we feel that these three birds were probably intended to represent either White or Pink-backed Pelicans.

The pelican can first be identified on an ivory wand from the Late Predynastic Period, now in the Ägyptisches Museum, West Berlin, where a number of the birds appear.[66] The characteristic features of the pelican make for easy recognition. The three pelicans discussed above are not the only occurrence of the bird in the "Chamber of the Seasons." On another relief fragment a keen awareness of the behavior of these large aquatic birds is revealed. A single pelican is depicted swimming in a canal amid a large school of fish which is being caught by fishermen using basket-traps (fig. 12). The bird has been drawn to the fishermen's activities by the great congregation of fish. This animated behavior is characteristic of pelicans, who without showing timidity, often become used to the routine of fishermen and faithfully follow them in hope of obtaining an easy meal. This same detail is partly paralleled in a scene in the Dynasty V mastaba of Niankhkhnum and Khnumhotep at Saqqara,[67] and in the Dynasty VI mastaba of Mereruka at Saqqara (fig. 13). Still yet another relief fragment from the chamber shows three White or Pink-backed Pelicans nesting and sitting on their respective clutches of eggs.[68] This scene, however tempting, cannot be used to demonstrate that the Egyptians were successful in breeding pelicans, as it is not possible to determine whether the birds are thought to be in captivity or in the wild. But what is does suggest is that while neither the White nor the Pink-backed Pelican breed today in modern

Fig. 11. (top) Priests bringing White or Pink-backed Pelicans, from the "Chamber of the Seasons" in the sun temple of Niuserre, Abu Gurob. Dynasty V.

Fig. 12. (center) Drawing of a relief showing a White or Pink-backed Pelican swimming near men fishing, from the "Chamber of the Seasons", in the sun temple of Niuserre, Abu Gurob. Dynasty V.

Fig. 13. (bottom) White or Pink-backed Pelican, from the mastaba of Mereruka, Saqqara. Dynasty VI.

11

Egypt, at least one of them appears to have in antiquity.

Every representation of a pelican in art lacks the plumage features needed for an identification of the species, the one exception being an exquisitely painted group of Dalmatian Pelicans (*P. crispus*), bird No. 6, where the coarse "shaggy" plumage of the living bird has been nicely expressed. It appears that the Egyptians pictured two types of pelicans, those without pronounced plumage characteristics or "non-shaggy" (White or Pink-backed Pelicans), and on this one occasion at least with distinctly formulated plumage features or "shaggy" (Dalmatian Pelican). Since there seems to have been no attempt to show the "shaggy" plumage of the Dalmatian Pelican on the other depictions of pelicans, we feel that there is a good possibility that the artists were trying to render a pelican of the "non-shaggy" variety, namely a White or Pink-backed Pelican. Thus, for our purposes, we have distinguished between them on the basis of the presence or absence of this plumage character. We cannot be certain which "non-shaggy" pelican(s) the Egyptians meant to portray, but it was certainly either the White or the Pink-backed Pelican, or both.

6. Dalmatian Pelican (*Pelecanus crispus*)

Fig. 14. Painting showing a small flock of captured Dalmatian Pelicans, from the tomb of Haremhab (No. 78), Thebes. Dynasty XVIII.

Identification: The customary posture, the massive bill, and the diagnostic elongated white feathers which give the plumage a rather "shaggy" appearance are features of a Dalmatian Pelican.

Distribution: The bird breeds in parts of eastern Europe, Asia, and Turkey. It winters in parts of southeastern Europe, Asia, the Middle East, and North Africa. In modern Egypt, the Dalmatian Pelican is a winter visitor in the Nile Delta, the Faiyum, and in the general vicinity of the Suez Canal.

Comments: These are the only representations of the Dalmatian Pelican that we have identified in Egyptian art and hieroglyphs (fig. 14). From a scene in the Dynasty XVIII tomb of Haremhab (No. 78) at Thebes which illustrates fowlers at work with a clap-net in the swamplands,[69] these five Dalmatian Pelicans are shown amongst the fruits of the trappers' efforts.[70] The birds have a particularly charming naturalism to them. They are depicted grouped together, and two of them appear to be preening themselves or perhaps engaged in some type of social interaction. The painter's skillful brushwork has well captured the species' conspicuous and diagnostic loose "shaggy" plumage. The vivacity of this group and the close attention to detail, right down to the nail of the bill (on the bird furthest to the left), makes this little picture remarkably pleasing to the eye (sadly, these birds have quite recently undergone serious mutilation). Rather than having been caught in the fowlers' net, the pelicans were probably obtained from a breeding colony the trappers discovered amongst the aquatic vegetation along the periphery of the swamp. Their eggs, which have been gathered and neatly stacked in ceramic vessels and covered with grass on top and bottom to protect them during transport, were the result of a successful raid upon their nests. The purpose of collecting their eggs is not known, but one would suspect that they were to be eaten. The pelicans too, it would seem, were intended for the table.[71] Based on modern Western standards, pelican[72] and pelican eggs[73] possess an extremely low level of palatability, both having a strong fishy flavor. Their use as a food source has historically been associated with those of humble station. It is interesting to note that Horapollo (fourth century A.D.) states that while Egyptian priests were supposed to abstain from pelican, it was consumed by other Egyptians.[74] The eating of pelicans has also been reported in modern Egypt,[75] but to what extent is uncertain. The Dalmatian Pelican does not breed today in Egypt, but the inference from this painting suggests that the species may have in ancient times. For further remarks on pelicans, see bird No. 5.

---

7. Heron (*Ardea* sp.)

Identification: The distinguishing long legs, bill and neck (which is held here drawn back), and the diagnostic elongated ornamental crest which protrudes from behind the head are features of an adult heron.

Distribution: There are three species of *Ardea* herons that have been reported in modern Egypt. The Grey Heron (*A. cinerea*) is a breeding resident in the Nile Delta, and along the Red Sea coast. It winters throughout the Nile Valley and Delta, along the Red Sea coast, and in the Dakhla, Kharga and Siwa Oases. The Goliath Heron (*A. goliath*) is an uncommon winter visitor along the Red Sea coast.[76] The Purple Heron (*A. purpurea*) is a winter visitor in the Nile Valley and Delta, the Faiyum, and the Dakhla and Kharga Oases.

Comments: Herons are abundantly pictured in both Egyptian art and hieroglyphs. This relief fragment (fig. 15) from the Dynasty IV mastaba of Kawab (G 7110-7120) at Giza, portrays a man with a partly balding head, wearing a short kilt leaning to the right on a long staff on board a raft, in what may have been his return home after an exhausting day spent fowling in the swamplands.[77] Directly behind him is a heron, apparently domesticated, who sits attentively on top of two cages filled with ducks, which were a portion of the day's catch. Fashioned in an attitude of repose, the artist has accurately perceived and acknowledged the mode of a living heron at rest. The sharp silhouette of the bird is characterized by its retracted head and large neck (which creates a bulge), and produces a wholly convincing image. The piece may originally have been painted, but the absence of color today prohibits a positive identification to the species level. However, based on the numerous other examples of herons in art in which pigment is still extant, the bird is probably a Grey Heron.

The heron is certainly one of the most commonly represented birds in Egyptian art, appearing in both secular and religious scenes. They can be first recognized during Dynasty IV. Like the example we discussed above, herons were frequently rendered near or associated with the activities of fowlers, and their close relationship with these professional trappers clearly shows that they were domesticated for use as decoys. There is scarcely a scene in Egyptian art picturing the pursuit of the fowlers in the swamps that does not include

Fig. 15. Man in a boat returning from trapping birds, with a tame heron on top of the filled cages, from the mastaba of Kawab (G 7110-7120), Giza. Dynasty IV.

Fig. 16. (bottom) A scene from the mastaba of Ptahhotep II (D 64), Saqqara, showing two groups of fowlers trapping water-fowl with clap-nets in the swamp-lands, and using a tame heron as a decoy to attract them. The 'look-out' man signals to his companions that the nets are filled and to heave on the draw-ropes by standing up and spreading a stripe of cloth across the back of his shoulders. Dynasty V.

Fig. 17. Hieroglyph of a heron with a fish, from the mastaba of Hetepherakhti (D 60), Saqqara. Dynasty V.

Fig. 18. (right) Heron roosting on a papyrus umbel in a swamp, from the mastaba of Mereruka, Saqqara. Dynasty VI.

at least one of these tamed aquatic birds wading in the shallows alongside of their clapnets (figs. 16 and 121) which have been stretched across the surface of the water.[78] The birds were acting as decoys so as to lure the desired quarry into the open traps. It seems that these clever fowlers realized a relationship between the haunt of wild herons and the gathering of waterfowl, and employed domesticated herons to entice various species of ducks, geese and cranes into their nets. As wild herons are generally cautious and wary of the ways of man, they tend to be quite selective of the areas they chose to frequent, and it is probably for this reason that other birds seeking a place of refuge are attracted into their immediate environment. Of all the different species of long-legged birds that the Egyptian fowler used as decoys, the heron was by far the most popular. Although modern ornithology has yet to support scientifically the symbiotic behavior between water birds and herons, the practice of using herons to draw birds in this manner has been reported from several other cultures as well.[79] For instance, Gervase Markham in his book on the methods of fowling (1621) states that a fowler who wishes to obtain a multitude of waterfowl with a net need only utilize a decoy heron: ". . . if you shall closse by your

Nett stake downe a live *Heron* (formerly taken) for a Stale [decoy], and to entice the Fowle within your danger it will be better making her now and then to flutter her wings."[80] This same hunting technique, though using tame birds, was used by the Egyptian fowler some four thousand years earlier. Even more remarkable is that in recent times live herons (and wooden models of them) continue to be regularly used as decoys by Egyptian fowlers in the Delta when trapping wildfowl with nets.[81] Herons are great fishing birds. In keeping with the nature of the bird, a standard hieroglyphic sign depicts a heron with a fish in its bill (fig. 17) and about to consume it. The bird is also regularly shown in art in a wild state, inhabiting the dense vegetation of the swamplands (fig. 18), one of their common haunts.[82] They are occasionally depicted nesting there too.[83] Many of these figures still retain traces of color, which allows for a more precise identification of them. In most cases the plumage features more or less correspond to those of the Grey Heron.

The heron played a role in mythology, where it was involved with the theology surrounding the creation of the world. According to legend, the heron or, to give its Egyptian name, the *benu* bird, and better known in the classical

Fig. 19. A pair of phoenixes represented in a vignette which accompanies a spell (Chapter 115) on a papyrus copy of the "Book of the Dead" prepared for Neferrenpet, from Thebes. Dynasty XIX.

world as the phoenix, represented the earthly manifestation of the god Atum, when he emerged from the waters of chaos and first revealed himself on the primeval earth.[84] As a solar bird, the phoenix was identified with Re, the sun god, at the rising sun, and with Osiris, god of the underworld, at sunset. The phoenix came to symbolize not only the rebirth of the sun every morning, but man's resurgence from death. The association of the heron with the phoenix resulted in making the bird the subject of a great many mythological scenes. They are often figured in vignettes which accompany certain spells on funerary papyri,[85] and are

shown decorating the walls of a number of Theban tombs of Ramesside date.[86] Many of the birds portrayed in these scenes have plumage features and markings which are not entirely authentic. The example we illustrate here (fig. 19) from the Dynasty XIX papyrus "Book of the Dead" of Neferrenpet for instance, the birds are painted completely blue,[87] a color which was commonly chosen for the phoenix. However, there are enough depictions in which the plumage characteristics follow those of the Grey Heron for us to be reasonably certain that it was the principal model for the phoenix.[88]

---

8. Egret (*Egretta* sp.)

Identification: The distinctive proportions, the long slender neck, the long pointed bill, and the unmistakable wholly white plumage are features of an egret.

Distribution: There are four species of egrets that have been reported in modern Egypt. The

Great Egret (*E. alba*) is a winter visitor in the Nile Delta, the Faiyum, in the general vicinity of the Suez Canal, and along the Red Sea coast. The Cattle Egret (*E. ibis*) is a common permanent breeding resident in the Nile Valley and Delta, the Faiyum, and the Kharga Oasis. The Little Egret (*E. garzetta*) is a breeding

16

resident in the Nile Valley and Delta, and the Faiyum. It winters in the Nile Valley and Delta, the Faiyum, and the Siwa Oasis. The Western Reef Heron (*E. gularis*) is a permanent breeding resident along the Red Sea coast.

Comments: Egrets are commonly represented in Egyptian art.[89] One of the most handsome examples of an egret that has come down to us, and one which retains its full coloring, is this small picture (fig. 20) from an almost completely destroyed wall painting in the Dynasty XVIII tomb of Amenemhet (No. 82) at Thebes, which illustrates a traditional hunting and fowling in the swamp scene. All that remains of the fowling composition are several beautifully

Fig. 20. (top) Egret in a swamp scene in the tomb of Amenemhet (No 82), Thebes. Dynasty XVIII.

Fig. 21. (center) Egret on the wing above a papyrus thicket, from the mastaba of Kaemnofret (No. 57), Saqqara. Dynasty V.

Fig. 22. (bottom) A pair of egrets being used as decoys, from the tomb of Menna (No. 69), Thebes. Dynasty XVIII.

painted birds on the wing over a stand of papyrus.[90] We view the egret rising from concealment within the dense vegetation and flying with its long neck outstretched. It was doubtlessly startled by the approach of Amenemhet in his raft, who would have been about to hurl his throwsticks at the flock. Although only partially extant, and unfortunately its entire posterior has perished, the strong features that are present leave no doubts as to this bird's identity. The placement of an egret in this type of aquatic environment is concordant with their mode in nature, as egrets frequent marshes, edges of rivers and the like. Despite the clear features rendered here, each species of egret displays a variety of different bill, leg, feet, etc., colorations which are subject to change during particular seasons of the year. Because of these easily confusable characteristics, which even tend to trouble the modern bird observer, specific identification of this example as one or the other species of egret

17

seems highly inappropriate. This holds true of every egret in art.

Egrets can first be met with during Dynasty V. They are frequently encountered in scenes which display the appropriate swampland habitat, where they are shown perched amongst the vegetation or more regularly, like our illustrations (figs. 20-21), flying above it.[91] One unusual example appears in the Dynasty V mastaba of Ti (No. 60) at Saqqara, where an egret is exhibited nesting in the thick papyrus. We can see three of its fledglings standing in the nest, while the parent bird is flying nearby.[92] Although this detail is strongly conventionalized, egrets in fact choose to breed in similar surroundings. Even in examples such as the one in the tomb of Ti and fig. 21 where no trace of pigment adheres to the relief, the bird is so well rendered and distinguishable from the other species of long-legged water birds as to make identification of it quite straightforward. Perhaps the most interesting occurrences of egrets in Egyptian art are those where they are shown being deployed as decoys. In the exact same manner as herons (see bird No. 7), egrets were seemingly tamed and employed by fowlers for use as decoys. The practice occurs on a number of occasions,[93] but nowhere has it been better preserved than in the Dynasty XVIII tomb of Userhet (No. 56) at Thebes. Two egrets stand flanking a large clap-net which is crammed full of waterfowl, which the egrets by their presence have lured into the immediate area.[94] The egrets have been nicely expressed, particularly with regard to their posture and immaculate white plumage. As decoys they apparently worked exceedingly well. The domestication of egrets is also known from more recent times,[95] as is the use of them as decoys,[96] even in modern Egypt.[97] Egrets were sometimes used as decoys in another manner. When the deceased tomb owner is shown fowling in the marshes, he frequently holds high in one hand two or more decoy birds, which during the New Kingdom are usually herons, and hurls his throwsticks with the other (see fig. 85). In the Dynasty XVIII tomb of Menna (No. 69) at Thebes, the decoy birds Menna holds onto are egrets (fig. 22).

The most common egret today of the Egyptian countryside is the Cattle Egret, which is popularly known by the vernacular name "Abuu Qurdaan." The species has justly earned the affectionate title "friend of the farmer." These highly sociable birds are indifferent to human disturbance.[98] They can often be observed in cultivated lands following the farmers' plough or hoe with their comical ducklike gait, devouring the exposed insects which the cutting blade has turned up. One study conducted has shown that over 75% of the Cattle Egret's diet in Egypt is composed of insects which are potentially harmful to crops,[99] thereby confirming its distinction as a true friend indeed. The naturalists who visited Egypt in the eighteenth century came to the erroneous conclusion that the Cattle Egret with whom they met throughout the country must have been the famous ibis of the ancient Egyptians referred to by the classical authors.[100] To this day in Egypt, it is still not uncommon to hear the uninformed layperson call this ubiquitous egret an ibis, confusing it with the Sacred Ibis (*Threskiornis aethiopicus*), see bird No. 15, which is now extinct from its former range in Egypt.

---

9. Night Heron (*Nycticorax nycticorax*)

Identification: The habitual hunched attitude, the relatively long legs, the stout black bill, and the diagnostic black crown and back markings are features of an adult Night Heron.

Distribution: The bird breeds in parts of Europe, Asia, the Middle East, and Africa. It winters in parts of southern Asia, the Middle East, and Africa. In modern Egypt, the Night Heron is a breeding resident in the Nile Valley (between Cairo and Beni Suef and further south between Luxor and Aswan) and Delta, and the Faiyum. It winters in the Nile Valley and Delta, and the Faiyum.

Comments: Night Herons are extremely rare in Egyptian art. This superbly executed portrait of a Night Heron (fig. 23) is from the Dynasty XI tomb of Baket III (No. 15) at Beni Hasan. Not all of the species' morphological features

18

Fig. 23. Night Heron from the collection of birds in the tomb of Baket III (No. 15), Beni Hasan. Dynasty XI.

have been preserved here, though the black bill, and the distinctive black crown and back markings are clearly visible. There is no trace of its grey and white body plumage, nor the white head plumes, and it is not impossible to determine whether they were ever included or not. Only a small section of the bird's feathering is now extant. The form of the bird has been confidently drawn, and its stance is very suggestive of the hunched posture of this marsh dwelling species. The picture has sadly been disfigured by a crude red ink graffito, scrawled by a hermit who inhabited the tomb more than two thousand years after it was hewn. Of interesting detail, the bird is painted with a red iris and a black pupil, which is exactly like that of the living bird. However, the red legs are a noticeable error; they should be yellow. Also note that instead of depicting the bird with the proper hind toes of a Night Heron, the artist has chosen to portray the bird with a curious small spur attached to the lower portion of each leg. This same abnormality is repeated on many of the birds figured in the scene in which this heron appears.[101]

The bird is part of a composition in the tomb of Baket III which exhibits a fascinating collection of twenty-nine different bird species,[102] most of which are identified by an accompanying hieroglyphic caption.[103] Also illustrated are three bats (order Chiroptera), see under entry No. 73, which are drawn with much exactness. The entire group of birds and bats is shown neatly arranged into a series of registers, and no attempt was made to display them in any particular setting or environment.[104] It seems, however, that a conscious effort was made by the artist to order them according to the habitat they most often frequent, as the land birds (including the bats which are rendered side by side) have been placed on the left, while the waterside birds are grouped to the right. Their presentation on the wall in this manner is reminiscent of something one might find in a natural history museum display case. Although the hand of this artist cannot be said to compare with the finest animaliers of the Old Kingdom, many of the birds that he has captured are not only unique in Egyptian art, but are exceedingly accurate as well. Unfortunately, the whole collection is veiled beneath a naturally occurring greyish film of lime, which has seeped from the surface of the plastered walls.[105] This coating has obscured the paintings so that they have to be examined with a discerning eye. The fact that the tomb was used as a hermitage during the early Christian era has also worsened the condition of the scene. Being within easy reach, the anchorites have left their mark in the form of unsightly ink dabbles, scratch marks, and Coptic graffiti (most of it religious in nature) across the greater portion of the figures. The coloring of the birds is rapidly deteriorating; some which survive at present in outline only, were reported to retain their pigment, or traces of it, when copyists worked in the tomb during the nineteenth century. Scenes featuring large numbers of birds grouped together and individually labeled are not uncommon in Egyptian art, and frequently appear in private tombs of Old Kingdom date (fig. 101). A slightly expanded version of the practice is on a wall of the Dynasty V-VI mastaba of Manefer (LS 17) from Saqqara, now in the Ägyptisches Museum, East Berlin. Here a group of thirty-five birds of twelve varieties, mainly consisting of ducks and geese, have been carved and identified with regard to their type.[106] Through the power which lies dormant in picture and word, the purpose of these birds was to provide the deceased magically with provisions of fowl that he could draw upon throughout eternity. What makes the birds in the collection of Baket III so unusual is that they were not included in the decoration of the tomb for the purpose of serving magically as victuals in the beyond, as they are largely made up of species that were probably considered undesirable for consumption (e.g. Night Heron, bats, etc.).

19

Not included are the large numbers of fatted doves, cranes, ducks, and geese which the dead traditionally wished to have on their tables. Rather, it is as if the artist has tried to compile a small catalogue of the land and water birds of his surroundings. The scene suggests to us that Baket III may have been something of a bird-fancier, who enjoyed the intrinsic beauty of birds in life and wished to continue to enjoy them in death. The collection constitutes an important record for the birds of ancient Egypt, and we will have much cause to refer back to it.

The only other example of a Night Heron that we have been able to identify positively appears in the Dynasty VI mastaba of Kagemni (LS 10) at Saqqara.[107] The bird is pictured along with several other species of long-legged birds stationed near a large fowlers' clap-net in the swamps, where it was being used as a decoy. The Night Heron is without color, but the features of the species are well defined in the relief, and its back patch marking is quite clear. Other representations in art were probably intended to depict the Night Heron, but in the absence of specific plumage characteristics, we cannot recognize them as such.

---

10. Little Bittern or Bittern (*Ixobrychus minutus* and *Botaurus stellaris*)

Identification: The familiar hunched stance, the comparatively long bill, legs and toes, the small tuft of elongated feathers on the lower breast, and the general stocky build are features of a bittern.

Distribution: The Little Bittern breeds in parts of Europe, Asia, the Middle East, and Africa. It winters in parts of Asia, the Middle East, and Africa. In modern Egypt, the Little Bittern is a permanent breeding resident in the Nile Delta,

Fig. 24. (left) Little Bittern or Bittern depicted on a block relief, from the mortuary temple of Userkaf, Saqqara. Dynasty V.

Fig. 25. (center right) Drawing of a relief showing a fowler with a tethered bittern, from the mastaba of Ti (No. 60), Saqqara. Dynasty V.

Fig. 26. (far right) Bittern from the collection of birds in the tomb of Baket III (No. 15), Beni Hasan. Dynasty XI.

and the Faiyum. The Bittern breeds in parts of Europe, Asia, Algeria, and southern Africa. It winters in parts of Europe, Asia, the Middle East, and Africa. In modern Egypt, the Bittern is a winter visitor in the Nile Delta, the Faiyum, and in the vicinity of the Suez Canal.

Comments: Bitterns routinely appear in Egyptian art. This crisply carved relief portrait of a bittern (fig. 24) appears on a surviving block from the Dynasty V mortuary temple of Userkaf at Saqqara, now destroyed. The fragment pictures several varieties of birds beautifully arranged amid the stems and umbels of a dense papyrus swamp.[108] They are amongst the most memorable of all the birds captured by the Egyptian sculptors' chisel. In these highly naturalistic figures the artist evinces a great familiarity with his subjects, and has presented their forms with admirable clarity. Fashioned in an attitude of repose and turned to the left, the bittern is executed roosting on top of a papyrus blossom in the thicket, a favorite haunt of their kind. The artist's care for realism, as shown in the incised modelling of the facial features, the well defined elongated breast feathers, and the correct bearing of the bird is quite remarkable. The absence of extant pigment, however, prevents our identification of the bird as one or the other species of bittern.

Bitterns can first be recognized in Egyptian art during Dynasty V. Like other species of long-legged birds, bitterns too were occasionally employed by fowlers for use as decoy birds in the trapping of waterfowl with nets.[109] In the Dynasty V mastaba of Ti (No. 60) at Saqqara for example, a scene illustrates a bittern and a heron (see bird No. 7) serving as decoys by a large clap-net which is filled with ducks and is about to be pulled shut.[110] Included in the same composition, though located away from the net and near a fowler who is busy with a catch of birds already taken, another bittern is pictured and it is tethered by a rope to a stake implanted in the ground (fig. 25). The bird was probably a decoy which was not being used at that moment, and to prevent any attempt of escaping was tethered. This is the only instance we are aware of where a bird is restrained in this manner. Bitterns are regularly shown, much like the representation above, as part of the bird life inhabiting the vegetation of the swamps,[111] and are sometimes rendered nesting there as well.[112] To what degree bitterns enjoyed a close relationship with man is displayed in the Dynasty XII tomb of Ukhhotep III (C No. 1) at Meir. In a scene in which the tomb owner is engaged in harpooning fish from a papyrus raft in the swamplands, the painter has included perching on the bow of the vessel what is apparently a domesticated bittern.[113] The bird may have been a pet,[114] and if Ukhhotep were to do any fowling, the bittern could have served as his decoy bird. In all of the aforementioned examples, it is impossible to determine with accuracy which species of bittern had been intended. A bittern (fig. 26) in the famous collection of birds in the Dynasty XI tomb of Baket III (No. 15) at Beni Hasan, however, can without hesitation be called the Bittern.[115] The bird's body plumage is colored red, this being used to suggest the species' brown plumage. The bill, legs and feet are painted with a greenish hue, which is not very far from that of a living Bittern.

21

11. Black Stork (*Ciconia nigra*)

Fig. 27. Black Stork from the collection of birds in the tomb of Baket III (No. 15), Beni Hasan. Dynasty XI.

Identification: The customary stance, the long legs, the long thick tapering bill, the long neck (which is held here greatly drawn back), and the plumage which is almost entirely black are features of a Black Stork.

Distribution: The bird breeds in parts of Europe, Asia, and southern Africa. It winters in parts of Spain, southern Asia, the Arabian Peninsula, and sub-Saharan Africa. In modern Egypt, the Black Stork is an uncommon migrant in the Nile Valley and Delta, in the general vicinity of the Suez Canal, and along the Red Sea coast.

Comments: This is the only representation of a Black Stork (fig. 27) that we have been able to identify in Egyptian art and hieroglyphs.[116] The portrait is amongst the collection of birds in the Dynasty XI tomb of Baket III (No. 15) at Beni Hasan, see under bird No. 9. Though poorly preserved, we cannot help but admire this fine rendering, one which surely began with a close study of the Black Stork in nature. Perhaps the most striking feature of the bird here is the wonderfully conveyed carriage. The Black Stork could not be more realistically fashioned. The artist has captured the very indifferent spirit of the species at rest, which is told by its deeply retracted neck and with its bill lying flat against the base of its slightly bulged foreneck, so characteristic of a Black Stork during repose.[117] Subtle as this true to life feature may be, it points to a firsthand knowledge of this extremely shy and retiring stork. There is unfortunately no trace of the species' red bill, as the bill is completely unpainted, and it is not known whether it was ever colored or not. Some black pigment still adheres to the legs, which makes it highly improbable that they were depicted red like those of the living bird. Nor is there any hint of the white underside, it having been painted black like the upper parts. In general, the coloring of the bird's black plumage has suffered severely with time. Some areas appear to have faded, while other sections of it are today beginning to scale and gradually flake away from the plastered wall surface (this is especially true on its head), revealing the draftsman's preliminary drawing in red underneath. On the shoulder of the figure (upper back and upper wing coverts), no trace of pigment is extant today, except for the artist's outline denoting details of the feathering. Whether this bare area was ever painted or left unfinished cannot be ascertained. An actual Black Stork's plumage on its upper parts is black, with a strong purple and greenish metallic gloss to it. This iridescent quality is most intense in the area on the shoulder of the bird. It is attractive to speculate, therefore, that the painter may have intended to distinguish this plumage feature on the picture by leaving it unpainted, or with the application of another hue, which has long since disappeared. While admittedly this cannot be proven, it would certainly account for this bare region.[118]

12. Saddlebill Stork[119] (*Ephippiorhynchus senegalensis*)

Fig. 28. A file of Saddlebill Storks depicted on the Carnarvon ivory knife handle. Late Predynastic Period.

Identification: The upright stance, the long bill, neck and legs, the short squared tail, the protruding lappet at the base of the upper mandible, and the diagnostic wattle drooping from the articulation of the lower mandible are features of an adult Saddlebill Stork.

Distribution: The bird is a permanent breeding resident of sub-Saharan Africa. The Saddlebill Stork has never been reported in modern Egypt.

Comments: Saddlebill Storks are only occasionally depicted in Egyptian art; they are frequently rendered as hieroglyphs. Fashioned from a single piece of elephant or hippopotamus ivory,[120] the Carnarvon knife handle, which dates from the Late Predynastic Period, is the work of a master craftsman.[121] The delicately carved relief decoration on the convex side of the handle (fig. 28) consists of three parallel rows of animals which are all shown facing to the right. These miniature figures have been executed with great care and fidelity, and demonstrate that even at this early period the Egyptian artists' talent cannot be underestimated. The first register is composed of eight Saddlebill Storks. Between the first and second birds is a Giraffe (*Giraffa camelopardalis*), its head, like the first stork's, now lost. The final two birds in the file can only be identified as long-legged birds. In the second register, an African Bush Elephant is pictured treading on a pair of intertwined serpents,

whose heads are upraised; their identity has been postulated as Pythons (*Python sebae*), a supposed enemy of the elephant.[122] This is followed by what appear to be three Lions (*Leo leo*). The third register is made up of three horned oxen (family Bovidae), while taking up the rear is another Lion. Originally a curved flint cutting blade whose surfaces had been pressure flaked was fixed to the handle.[123] The creative power of this object is particularly noticeable in the carver's flawless handling of the eight Saddlebill Storks in the top register. The close attention focused on detail, from the posture to the minute features of the head and bill, are all exceptionally imitative of the living species. It is rather unusual to see so many of the birds gathered together in one place, as Saddlebill Storks in nature are usually not considered gregarious, and this aspect was probably the result of artistic preference.[124]

The earliest extant representation of the Saddlebill Stork are those dating from the Late Predynastic Period. The species' positive recognition in art is uniquely confined to their depiction on objects all of very early date. The superbly preserved Davis ivory comb handle (fig. 29), which also dates from Late Predynastic times, exhibits four Saddlebill Storks in carved relief on either side of the handle which bear close similarities to those on the Carnarvon knife handle, and are every bit as good. Saddlebill Storks are probably also to be recognized on two other Late Predynastic knife handles, the Pitt-Rivers handle, now in

23

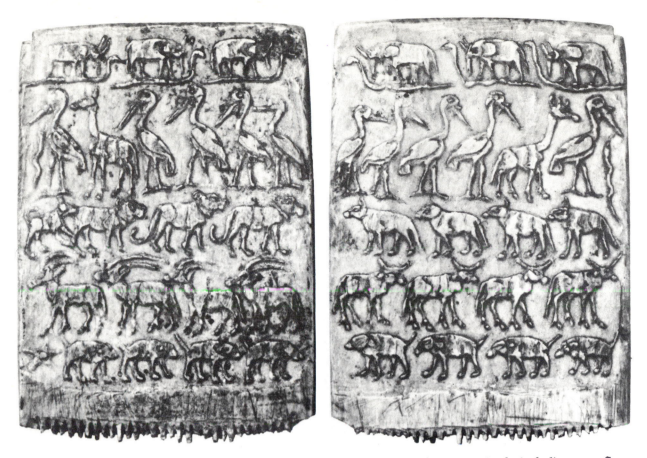

Fig. 29. Both sides of the carved top of the Davis ivory comb showing rows of various animals, including some fine Saddlebill Storks. Late Predynastic Period.

the British Museum, London,[125] and one in the Brooklyn Museum from Abu Zeidan.[126] The birds figured on these handles, however, and another example depicted on a Late Predynastic/Dynasty I gold mace handle from Nubia,[127] lack the necessary detail to enable us to make an entirely certain identification. Another notable occurrence of a Saddlebill Stork appears as a hieroglyph on a fragment of a Dynasty I porphyry bowl from Hierakonpolis,[128] now in the Ashmolean Museum, Oxford. Only the head and neck of the bird have survived, but what is present has been extremely well rendered, and its features are slightly less exaggerated than those of the earlier examples. Following this date, the Saddlebill Stork vanishes as quickly as it first became recognizable. Near the close of Dynasty III and the rise of Dynasty IV, however, a hieroglyph emerges which although highly conventionalized, bears elements which are strongly reminiscent of the Saddlebill Stork. Often depicted in a group of three overlapping figures,[129] an excellent painted relief example is executed on the Dynasty IV slab-

stela of Wepemnofret (G 1201) from Giza (fig. 30). These birds can safely be labeled as Saddlebill Storks, but gone, however, is the accurate morphological featuring achieved by the earlier artists. The bill and legs are a little too short, the wattle is no longer shown attached in the proper position, and the attitude is wanting. The coloring of the birds' plumage, though, is quite close to that of the living species[130] and when combined with the other characteristics, proclaims their true identity. The inaccuracy of this and other representations[131] can be traced back to the Late Predynastic prototypes.[132] Occasionally a hieroglyph of the bird is depicted with more or less correct plumage hues, but the very same figure can also be shown without such diagnostic features as the wattle or frontal saddle.[133] Because of the lack of one entirely precise example of a Saddlebill Stork following Dynasty I, it has been postulated that the bird may have become totally extinct in Egypt fairly early on,[134] probably during the Early Dynastic Period.

The disappearance of the Saddlebill Stork

Fig. 30. Hieroglyph of three Saddlebill Storks from the slab-stela of Wepemnofret (G 1201), Giza. Dynasty IV.

from Egypt is not easy to explain. Today the species is solely confined to tropical Africa where it is basically a bird of the marshes, lake shores, and banks of large rivers.[135] It is still to this day rather common along the upper reaches of the Nile in the Sudan. Its apparent extinction from its haunts in Egypt during antiquity is probably linked to some of the factors which led to the disappearance of other animals such as the elephant, rhinoceros, Giraffe, and Gerenuk (*Lithocranius walleri*) from the Nile Valley north of Aswan between the end of Dynasty I and the beginning of Dynasty IV.[136] This was largely due to human disturbances and hunting pressures, but also related to the increasing desiccation of Egypt after 3000 B.C.[137] To what extent the environmental factor played a part in the extinction of the Saddlebill Stork in Egypt remains unclear, as favorable habitats, though perhaps reduced by a change in climate, would have still existed in the country. Since these storks are extremely shy, they would more likely seem to have been adversely affected by human encroachment or persecution, perhaps to the degree where the local population was completely eradicated.

13. Whale-headed Stork(?) (*Balaeniceps rex*)

Identification: The customary upright stance, the rounded head, the relatively short neck, the short squared tail, the long legs, and the enormous blunt bill are features of the Whale-headed Stork(?)

Distribution: The bird is a permanent breeding resident of sub-Saharan Africa, mainly occupying a belt from the southern Sudan to northern Zambia.[138] The Whale-headed Stork has never been reported in modern Egypt.

Comments: This is the only representation (fig. 31) in Egyptian art and hieroglyphs that can be regarded as possibly depicting a Whale-headed Stork.[139] It appears in the Dynasty V mastaba of Ti (No. 60) at Saqqara. Executed in relief, the bird is handsomely pictured roosting on top of an umbel where it is nestled in amongst the dense aquatic vegetation of a papyrus swamp,[140] the natural haunt of the species. The identification of this figure with the Whale-headed Stork has been espoused by a large number of previous investigators.[141] It is mainly by taking into consideration all these past advocates, rather than due to any certain features in the depiction, that we have elected to include the bird here. For in spite of its distinguished body of supporters, we remain quite skeptical of an identification of this bird as the Whale-headed Stork.

Rather, it appears to display features which, though slightly modified, look more like those of a European Spoonbill (*Platalea leucorodia*), see bird No. 17, a common stock figure of swamp scenes in Old Kingdom art, and frequently portrayed in repose in a like manner. The bird here illustrated just does not contain the necessary detail, especially in regard to the bill, to allow us to call it a Whale-headed Stork. However, we have decided to include the bird here so as to allow the reader to draw his or her own conclusions.

The keen interest in the occurrence of a Whale-headed Stork in Egyptian art over the years has been in part prompted by the fact that probably no single other species of bird can best serve as a biological indicator of permanent papyrus than can this stork, as its modern distribution is virtually confined to the extensive papyrus swamps of sub-Saharan Africa. The existence of this very specialized tropical bird in ancient Egypt would show that this type of habitat must also have existed in Egypt during antiquity.

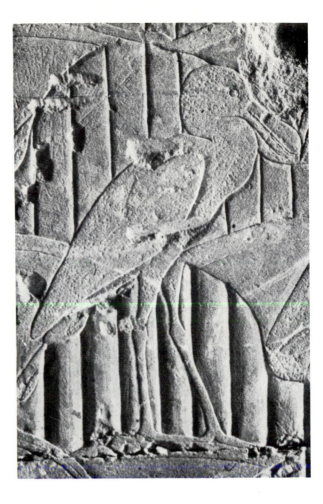

Fig. 31. A possible Whale-headed Stork roosting on a papyrus umbel in a swamp scene, from the mastaba of Ti (No. 60), Saqqara. Dynasty V.

14. Glossy Ibis (*Plegadis falcinellus*)

Identification: The immediately apparent long slender sickle-shaped bill, the long legs and slightly curved neck, and the diagnostic delineation of the iridescent gloss on the "shoulder" (upper back and upper wing coverts) are features of a Glossy Ibis.

Fig. 32. Hieroglyph of a Glossy Ibis in sunk relief, from the mastaba of Kagemni (LS 10), Saqqara. Dynasty VI.

Distribution: The bird breeds in parts of Europe, Asia, the Middle East, and sub-Saharan Africa. It winters in southern Europe, Asia, the Middle East, Morocco, Tunisia, and sub-Saharan Africa. In modern Egypt, the Glossy Ibis is a migrant in the Nile Valley and Delta,[142] the Faiyum, along the Red Sea coast, and the Kharga and Siwa Oases.

Comments: Glossy Ibises are frequently represented as Egyptian hieroglyphs; they are extremely rare in art. Carved in sunk relief, this hieroglyph of a Glossy Ibis (fig. 32) is from the inscription on the exterior false door stela of the Dynasty VI mastaba of Kagemni (LS 10) at Saqqara.[143] The bird is pictured advancing to the left, with the characteristic hunched carriage of an ibis. As previously noted by other writers,[144] this particular hieroglyph has been rendered with an exceptional degree of detail. This is especially evident in the incised interior feather patternings on its upper parts. It is largely due to this important feature that we have been able to distinguish the bird specifically as a Glossy Ibis, despite the absence of pigment. The minute circular feathers on the bird's "shoulder" was probably a device used by the artist in an attempt to differentiate this area from the rest of its plumage, as it is in this region that the Glossy Ibis's rich metallic plumage hue is most intense. The presence of this detailing has enabled others to identify this bird as a Glossy Ibis,[145] an identification with which we concur.

The Glossy Ibis can first be positively recognized during Dynasty VI.[146] The single identification of the species in art which we have been able to establish firmly appears in the Dynasty VI mastaba of Kaemankh (G 4561) at Giza. The bird is figured in a dense papyrus thicket, where it is shown ambling along on top of the umbels (fig. 33). Aiding in this identification is the inclusion of two Sacred Ibises (*Threskiornis aethiopicus*), see bird No. 15, in the swamp, which are painted with the species' unmistakable black and white plumage.[147] This is in deep contrast to the Glossy Ibis, which is displayed with entirely black plumage features. Thus, our identification is confirmed by its comparison to the pied plumage of the Sacred Ibis. The Glossy Ibis probably occurs elsewhere in art, but in the absence of extant plumage details or color, we have been unable to identify them as such. For example, there are several instances where ibises are portrayed feeding in the vicinity of fowlers' clap-nets, where they were probably serving as their decoys in the trapping of waterfowl.[148] But as the figures are rather general in form, it is impossible to determine whether the birds are to be thought of as Glossy or Sacred Ibises. A number of Glossy Ibis hieroglyphs carefully painted on the faces of a wooden coffin of First Intermediate Period date belonging to Gemni-emhet (HMK. 30) from Saqqara,[149] and now in the Ny Carlsberg Glyptothek, Copenhagen, are worth noting as they have been colored entirely black, confirming the identification.

In a text from the Ramesside era, the Glossy Ibis is said to break up cucumber beds.[150] According to Herodotus (mid-fifth century B.C.), the Glossy Ibis, which he describes as being "all deep black, with legs like a crane's, and a beak strongly hooked; its size is that of a landrail,"[151] fights with winged serpents.[152]

Fig. 33. Glossy Ibis frequenting a papyrus swamp, from the mastaba of Kaemankh (G 4561), Giza. Dynasty VI.

15. Sacred Ibis (*Threskiornis aethiopicus*)

Identification: The distinctive upright posture, the pure white body plumage, the long dark sickle-shaped bill, and the diagnostic black neck, legs and upper hind region (wing tips) are features of an adult Sacred Ibis.

Distribution: This bird breeds in parts of Iraq, and sub-Saharan Africa. It winters in parts of the Middle East, and sub-Saharan Africa. The Sacred Ibis was apparently quite common in modern Egypt up until 1800, but by 1850 it had all but completely disappeared from the country.[153] The species has not been documented in Egypt since 1877, when a specimen was collected near Damietta in the Nile Delta.[154]

Fig. 34. Painting of a Sacred Ibis in a papyrus swamp, from the tomb of Khnumhotep III (No. 3), Beni Hasan. Dynasty XII.

Comments: Sacred Ibises are frequently portrayed in both Egyptian art and hieroglyphs.[155] This handsomely painted picture of the species (fig. 34), from the Dynasty XII tomb of Khnumhotep III (No. 3) at Beni Hasan, appears in a scene in which the tomb owner is shown harpooning fish from a papyrus raft in the swamplands.[156] The ibis is displayed as part of the bird life of the thicket, where it has alighted upon a large papyrus umbel. It is rendered with its head and neck slightly elevated, its wings folded at the side, and with one foot placed in front of the other, as if it were about to take a step to the left. This is not only an attractive painting, but a very faithful representation of a Sacred Ibis, one that stands up to close scrutiny. Although there are several areas where the pigment is now lost (most noticeably on the forehead), the bird is on the whole well preserved and is one of the finer examples of a Sacred Ibis in this medium to have come down to us. The species' features and conspicuous black and white plumage have been carefully observed and near faultlessly executed here. The single error is bluish color of the bill,[157] whereas it should be black, the same color of its featherless head and neck. One might also note that as with every other rendering of a Sacred Ibis the artist was satisfied here simply to depict the bird's rump black, and no attempt was made to show the ornamental plumes which extend well beyond the tail of the living bird.

The earliest extant representation of a Sacred Ibis dates from Dynasty IV, when the bird can be clearly recognized as a hieroglyph.[158] The Sacred Ibis is fairly well adapted to a variety of wetland habitats,[159] but in spite of this, when the bird is depicted in art in a wild state it is invariably associated with a papyrus swamp. There the species can often be observed, much like the example above, roosting in the dense aquatic vegetation,[160] and even nesting there too.[161] This latter activity is illustrated on several occasions, a very nice occurrence being in the Dynasty VI mastaba of Idut at Saqqara (fig. 35). Here a Sacred Ibis is pictured in a nest and sitting on its clutch of eggs, where it has been beautifully carved and painted with respect to its species. The Sacred Ibis was venerated as a manifestation of Thoth, the moon god and god of wisdom and learning.[162] It is because of the bird's sanctity to the god that it today bears the vernacular name Sacred Ibis. Representations of the Sacred Ibis in Egyptian art appear in many different forms, but by far the most frequent are the multitude of effigies which were used as votive offerings to Thoth, and which were placed at centers where the god was specially worshipped. Many splendid and highly naturalistic portrayals of the bird are the result of this practice, and there is scarcely a major museum housing Egyptian

Fig. 35. (top left) Sacred Ibis nesting on a papyrus umbel in a swamp, from the mastaba of Idut, Saqqara. Dynasty VI. Fig. 36. (bottom) Gilded wood and silver statue of a Sacred Ibis, which served as a sarcophagus for a mummified ibis, from Tuna el-Gebel. Ptolemaic Period. Fig. 37. (top right) Faience amulet of a Sacred Ibis. Late Dynastic-Ptolemaic Period.

29

antiquities which does not hold in its collections at least one example. They can be fashioned as elegant near life-size statues (fig. 36) of wood and bronze or other metals,[163] small figurines in bronze,[164] etc. Also plentiful are faience amulets (fig. 37) in the shape of the Sacred Ibis.[165] Nearly all of these objects are from a very late date of Egyptian history, at which time the killing of an ibis, even unintentionally, was, according to Herodotus, a crime punishable by death.[166] This was during the Late Dynastic and Greco-Roman Periods, an era in which the Egyptians established large cemeteries for the mass burial of ibises and their eggs, as well as for other sacred animals, in what was a phenomenon unique to this age. The ibises were bred on a massive scale in large sanctuaries which were connected with the temples of Thoth's cult.[167] These centers were situated in various parts of the country: Abydos, Tuna el-Gebel, Kom Ombo, Saqqara, El-Baqliya, etc.,[168] and all contained sizeable burial grounds for the birds. The Sacred Ibis was principally the focus of attention, with the Glossy Ibis (see bird No. 14) occurring only very occasionally.[169] After being put to death, the birds were often then elaborately wrapped in linen bandages, and some of the mummies were also decorated with appliqué figures of Thoth (fig. 38) and other deities. The ibis mummies were usually then placed in ceramic pots and were probably interred in the cemeteries by priests on behalf of the pious pilgrims who had purchased them wishing to petition the god. The excavations conducted in recent years by the Egypt Exploration Society at the northern edge of the Saqqara necropolis have revealed the presence of two vast subterranean galleries or catacombs for the burial of ibises.[170] A conservative estimate places the number of mummified ibises in them at well over 1.5 million,[171] a staggering figure! The rearing of this many Sacred Ibises must have been a monumental task, and it is to be remembered that Saqqara is just one of a number of sites where this activity was carried out. However, it was biologically feasible, as under the proper conditions, Sacred Ibises are known to breed readily in captivity.[172] It is thought that the Egyptians may have artificially incubated the ibis eggs in large ovens.[173] A block of relief now in the Museo Archeologico, Florence, and probably from a late Dynasty XVIII or Ramesside Period tomb at Saqqara, depicts on it a poultry yard and a storehouse.[174] Among the birds shown feeding in the yard are two or three ibises. Although it is impossible to say whether they are Glossy or Sacred Ibises, and the reason for them being with table birds is unclear, it shows that at least small numbers of ibises were kept as early as the New Kingdom. What long term effects, if any, all this had on the wild Sacred Ibis population in the country is not possible to determine accurately, but as the textual and archaeological evidence from Saqqara, as well as from other sites, indicates that the birds were domestically bred, rather than exclusively taken from the wild, the impact on them was probably minimal. Hence, the disappearance of the Sacred Ibis from modern Egypt cannot be correlated to the events of more than two thousand years ago as some have suggested. This indeed would seem to be the case, as the species was reportedly still common in Egypt up until 1800. The real cause for its extinction, in what was a relatively short span of time, remains largely unknown,[175] but it was probably linked to the increasing loss of its **prime swamp habitat and human disturbance.**

Fig. 38. Ibis mummy with appliqué decoration representing the god Thoth, from Saqqara. Late Dynastic-Ptolemaic Period.

16. Hermit Ibis (*Geronticus eremita*)

Identification: The characteristic proportions, the rather long neck and legs, the long sickle-shaped bill, and the diagnostic elongated hackles which form a ruff are features of an adult Hermit Ibis.

Distribution: The bird breeds in parts of Turkey and Morocco. It winters in select parts of the Middle East, and Africa north of the equator.[176] In modern Egypt, the Hermit Ibis is an accidental migrant, having only been recorded once in 1921 a short distance from the pyramid field of Giza.[177]

Comments: The Hermit Ibis routinely appears as an Egyptian hieroglyph;[178] it occurs only occasionally in art. It is impossible to make a sharp distinction between Egyptian art and the ornamental hieroglyphic script, as the latter is really a miniature form of art in its own right and serves as a complementary part of an overall artistic composition.[179] Each character of Egyptian hieroglyphs, when carefully executed, can stand alone and possess its own individuality and charm, and in detail can often compare with that of any large-scale representation. This is readily apparent in this first-rate hieroglyph of a Hermit Ibis (fig. 39) from the Dynasty V mastaba of Hetepherakhti (D 60) at Saqqara, where the fine likeness of this distinctive species has been successfully caught. Carved in relief and facing to the right, the sign has been well-made and it still retains traces of pigment: red for the head, bill, legs

Fig. 39. Hieroglyph of a Hermit Ibis from the mastaba of Hetepherakhti (D 60), Saqqara. Dynasty V.

and feet, and blue for the wing, tail, and the rest of the body plumage.[180] This coloring corresponds in part to that of a living Hermit Ibis, as it exhibits the same red features. The projecting neck ruff of feathers on the figure is shown somewhat accentuated compared to its form in nature, and this generally holds true for every depiction of the bird. The artist was simply emphasizing one of the species' most salient morphological characters, one which immediately identifies it as a Hermit Ibis at a glance. The Hermit Ibis has a hind toe on each foot, but here they have been rather poorly executed and appear more like small pointed spurs, rather than actual toes.

The first evidence for the Hermit Ibis is from a Gerzean Period (Naqada II) schist palette now in the Musées royaux d'Art et d'Histoire, Brussels.[181] Although it is heavily damaged, we can be reasonably confident that the two birds carved on it were intended to depict Hermit Ibises. Another early example of the species is preserved on a rectangular ivory panel from Hierakonpolis (fig. 68), which dates from the Late Predynastic or Early Dynastic Periods. The species is conspicuously absent from scenes in art which illustrate aquatic environments. This is no doubt due to the fact that the Hermit Ibis really cannot be considered a waterside bird, as is, for example, the Sacred Ibis (see bird No. 15), since it prefers a more arid type of haunt.[182] However, there is one exception to this. On a wall of the Dynasty V mastaba of Kaemnofret (No. 57) from Saqqara, and now in the Museum of Fine Arts, Boston, a Hermit Ibis has been rendered roosting on top of an umbel in a papyrus swamp.[183] Not only is this the single delineated example of the bird frequenting a watery habitat, but it is a marvelous little picture of it as well. The Hermit Ibis also appears as a decorative motif on a small number of diadems from the Old Kingdom.[184] The most celebrated of these, and one that was probably worn during life, is a lovely specimen in gold (fig. 40) from a Dynasty IV mastaba of a woman at Giza (Tomb of shaft 294). The jewel consists of a band which is ornamented with three roundels of gold with carnelian inlay. The central disc bears a chased floral design. The two discs on the sides are identical, and are composed of two opposed papyrus umbels with a small Hermit Ibis perched on top of each of the

Fig. 42. Detail showing the central ornament of a diadem, with two Hermit Ibises between an ankh-sign, *from from Giza. Dynasty V.*

Fig. 40. (top) Gold diadem from the tomb of a princess (Shaft 294), Giza, with four Hermit Ibises on papyrus umbels. Dynasty IV.

Fig. 41. (center) A drawing of the central ornament of a plaster and copper diadem from the tomb of a woman (G 7143), Giza, with two Hermit Ibises between an ankh-sign. *Dynasty V.*

blossoms, which are facing away from each other. Two more of these diadems (figs. 41-2), also from Giza but dating from Dynasty V, were made from materials that could not have withstood daily use. They were probably made for funerary use only. On all three, there is no difficulty in identifying the Hermit Ibis.

If the number of representations of the Hermit Ibis in Egyptian art and hieroglyphs is indicative of its frequency in the country during antiquity, then the bird must have been far less rare than it is today. The Hermit Ibis's disappearance from Egypt is by no means exceptional, but is part of a pattern of world decline, which has seen its extinction from many places where it at one time occurred. For example, the species is known to have bred formerly in parts of Europe up until the sixteenth or seventeenth century,[185] and in Algeria[186] and Syria[187] until this century. The Hermit Ibis is today on the brink of total extinction, with a world breeding population of only about 275 pairs in the wild.[188] The causes for its dramatic decline in numbers, even within our own century, have yet to be fully elucidated.[189] Undoubtedly though, human interference in one way or another has probably worked and continues still to work against the two existing Hermit Ibis breeding populations in Turkey and Morocco.

17. European Spoonbill (*Platalea leucorodia*)

Fig. 43. European Spoonbill about to alight in a papyrus swamp, from the tomb of Khnumhotep III (No. 3), Beni Hasan. Dynasty XII.

Identification: The notable profile, the long legs and neck, the entirely white body plumage, and the diagnostic long, broad spoon-shaped bill are features of a European Spoonbill.

Distribution: The bird breeds in parts of Europe, Asia, the Middle East, Mauritania, and Somalia. It winters in parts of southern Europe, Asia, the Middle East, and Africa north of the equator. In modern Egypt, the European Spoonbill is a breeding resident along the Red Sea coast.[190] It winters in the Nile Valley and Delta, the Faiyum, and along the Red Sea coast.

Comments: European Spoonbills are rather commonly figured in Egyptian art; the head of the spoonbill appears as a rare hieroglyph.[191] In artistic achievement, this portrayal of the species (fig. 43) from the Dynasty XII tomb of Khnumhotep III (No. 3) at Beni Hasan is unsurpassed.[192] It has been well preserved, in spite of the fact that there are several areas

where the pigment is now lost. The bird is part of a painting in which the tomb owner is pictured harpooning fish from a papyrus raft while in the swamplands.[193] Here we view the spoonbill gracefully gliding downward, where it is about to alight upon an umbel in the dense papyrus thicket. The bird's form and the general white plumage are accurately expressed, but there are two immediately noticeable problems with the picture. The bill and legs have been painted yellow,[194] while on an adult living European Spoonbill these are black. On the juvenile bird, though, the bill and legs are a pinkish-flesh color, and perhaps a young bird was intended here. Nevertheless, the possibility of a mistake on the part of the artist cannot be ruled out. There is, however, no error in his fine rendering of the spoonbill's remarkable long spatulate bill, and he has even included the deep lines of furrowing on it. Because the spoon-shaped bill is not always easy to see, especially when the bird is airborne, the artist while having depicted the bird's head

and body in profile, has shown the bill not from the side as we would expect, but as if we were viewing it from above. It was executed in this manner so as to enable the observer to see the most characteristic feature of a spoonbill better, thereby allowing for the bird's instant identification without the slightest chance of ambiguity. This method of illustrating the species' bill is not unique to this example, but is a convention followed for every appearance of the bird in relief and painting.

The European Spoonbill can first be recognized in art during Dynasty V. They appear on a number of occasions in scenes which feature a swamp habitat, where they are depicted as part of the bird life of the thicket.[195] A good example of this is in the Dynasty VI mastaba of Kaemankh (G 4561) at Giza, where in a composition illustrating the traditional theme of hunting and fowling in the swamps, a spoonbill (fig. 44), easily told by its distinctive bill, can be spotted roosting amongst the vegetation. The European Spoonbill, it seems, was another favorite long-legged bird which the Egyptian fowlers tamed for use as decoys when trapping waterfowl with nets. Several scenes display these birds feeding (fig. 45) or standing in the shallow water alongside large clap-nets jam-packed with ducks and the like which they were successful in attracting into the area.[196] Probably the most remarkable example of the bird to have come down to us is a small painted wooden figure from the Dynasty XVIII palace of Amenhotep III at Thebes (fig. 46). The spoonbill is depicted at rest, standing on one leg, just as the living bird does in the wild, pointing to a first-hand knowledge of the species. It is thought that this object may have served as a child's plaything. The Metropolitan Museum of Art, New York, possesses a small ivory spring-trap, used for netting birds but probably only a toy, from the New Kingdom, in which the central element of the trap is fashioned in the form of the head of a spoonbill.[197] The European Spoonbill apparently played a minor role in Egyptian religion. A fragment of painted relief from the Late Dynastic Period, now in the Musées royaux d'Art et d'Histoire, Brussels, shows on it an unknown deity with the head of a spoonbill.[198]

Fig. 44. (top) Relief of a European Spoonbill roosting on an umbel in a papyrus swamp, from the mastaba of Kaemankh (G 4561), Giza. Dynasty VI. Fig. 45. (center) A European Spoonbill feeding alongside a clap-net in a swamp, where it was probably serving as a decoy, from the mastaba of Neferirtenef (D 55), Saqqara. Dynasty V. Fig. 46. (bottom) Painted wooden figure of a European Spoonbill, from the palace of Amenhotep III, Thebes. Dynasty XVIII.

18. Greater Flamingo (*Phoenicopterus ruber*)

Identification: The characteristic posture, the robust bill, and the diagnostic extremely long legs and neck are features of a Greater Flamingo.

Distribution: The bird breeds in select parts of southern Europe, Asia, Turkey, the Sinai, and Africa. It winters in parts of southern Europe, Asia, the Middle East, and Africa. In modern Egypt, the Greater Flamingo bred in the Nile Delta up until the end of the nineteenth century,[199] but by 1909 the bird had ceased to be a breeding resident.[200] Nowadays, the species is only a winter visitor in the Nile Delta, the Faiyum, the vicinity of the Suez Canal, along the Red Sea coast, and the Siwa Oasis.

Comments: The Greater Flamingo is frequently portrayed as a hieroglyph;[201] its appearance in art is very limited. This ornamental hieroglyph (fig. 47), which is depicted on a fragment of the Dynasty IV mastaba of Rahotep at Meidum,[202] stands out for its fine execution and faithfulness to the living bird. Carved in relief, the flamingo is pictured facing to the right in an attitude of repose, with its very long neck drawn in and held in a graceful U-shaped curve, and with its head strongly sloping downward. The figure still retains traces of pigment; the body plumage is painted completely white, the outlines and details of feathering on the wing are red, and it has a terminal black bill tip.[203] This coloring is quite realistic, and closely follows that of a Greater Flamingo, right down to the black tip of the bill. Note, however, that the bird's bill is not sharply bent like that of a flamingo, but is only slightly curved.

The earliest flamingo representations are those preserved on a large number of decorated predynastic ceramic vessels (fig. 48) dating from the Gerzean Period (Naqada II). Freely painted with a deep red hue on a buff-colored ground, well defined flocks of flamingoes,[204] sometimes with as many as twenty individuals, are shown in neat rows embellishing these pottery vessels.[205] The birds are generally depicted in what is suggestive of a watery

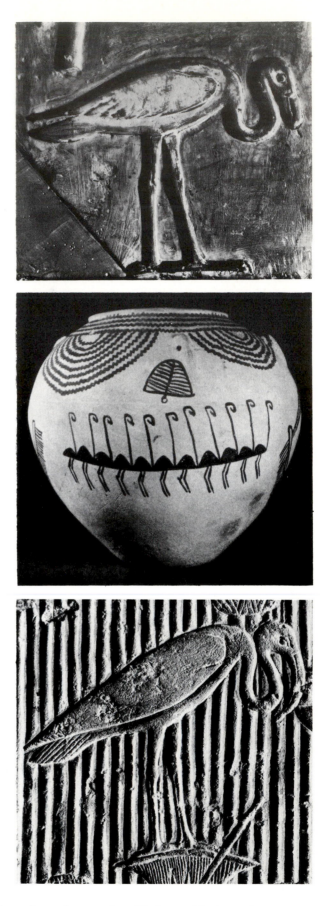

Fig. 47. (top) Ornamental hieroglyph of a Greater Flamingo, from the mastaba of Rahotep, Meidum. Dynasty IV. Fig. 48. (center) Painted pottery vessel, with a file of flamingoes, from Naga el-Deir. Gerzean Period (Naqada II). Fig. 49. (bottom) Greater Flamingo from a swamp scene in the mastaba of Mereruka, Saqqara. Dynasty VI.

35

habitat. The form of the flamingo is characterized by truthful proportions and by the pronounced exaggeration of its uniquely shaped bill. Executed in silhouette only, it is as if the artists had intended to display these highly gregarious birds as they so often appear in nature, grouped together and forming what seems at a distance to be a pinkish line of tall figures on the horizon. This decorative motif disappears at the beginning of the Dynastic era, and with this the flamingo all but vanishes from Egyptian art, only to survive as one of the standard hieroglyphic signs. The single occurrence of a Greater Flamingo in art following this date appears in the Dynasty VI mastaba of Mereruka at Saqqara (fig. 49). Here the bird is pictured inhabiting a papyrus swamp environ-ment, where it is roosting in the typical posture on top of an umbel. The species' features have been well carved, but there is one character which is poorly reproduced, and it detracts from the fidelity of the representation. The bill is far too long, and looks more like the sickle-shaped bill of an ibis, rather than that of a flamingo. Regardless of this error, however, the bird should be identified as a flamingo, as other writers have also suggested.[206] The Egyptian artist always had trouble in getting the distinctive hooked bill of the Greater Flamingo just right. Another example of the flamingo sign (fig. 50), from the Dynasty XVIII temple of Tuthmosis III at Deir el-Bahari, shows only the tip of the bill curved.

Fig. 50 Painted relief hieroglyph of a Greater Flamingo, from the temple of Tuthmosis III, Deir el-Bahari. Dynasty XVIII.

19. Black Kite (*Milvus migrans*)

Identification: The erect raptorial posture, the hooked bill, the general dark coloring of the plumage on the upper parts, with a somewhat paler head and breast which are finely streaked with dark are features of a Black Kite.

Distribution: The bird breeds in parts of Europe, Asia, the Middle East, and Africa. It winters in parts of Asia, the Middle East, and Africa. In modern Egypt, the Black Kite is a permanent breeding resident in the Nile Valley

Fig. 51. (top) Scene showing the goddesses Isis and Nephthys as Black Kites, from the papyrus "Book of the Dead" of Ani. Dynasty XIX.

1.

Fig. 52. (center left) Detail of a vignette from the papyrus "Book of the Dead" of Queen Nodjmet, Deir el-Bahari, showing the goddess Nephthys as a Black Kite. Dynasty XXI.

Fig. 53. (center right) A painting in the tomb of Ipuy (No. 217), Thebes, showing a butcher at work with a Black Kite on a post above. Dynasty XIX.

Fig. 54. (bottom) Drawing of a painting showing a boat with gutted fish hung up to dry and a Black Kite perched on the mast-head, from the tomb of Haremheb (No. 78), Thebes. Dynasty XVIII.

and Delta, the Faiyum, and in the vicinity of the Suez Canal.

Comments: Black Kites are occasionally rendered in Egyptian art. This splendidly painted vignette (fig. 51), from a papyrus copy of the "Book of the Dead" prepared for the scribe Ani,[207] illustrates a detail from a spell (Chapter 17) of that work in which the two sister goddesses Isis (on the left) and Nephthys (on the right) are depicted having assumed the form of Black Kites, in their role as divine mourners for the dead. Here the deceased is identified with Osiris, god of the underworld, who according to tradition after being murdered was mourned by two kites.[208] The shrouded mummy of Ani is pictured lying on a funerary bier within an ornate kiosk. Beneath the bed are objects of daily use to be deposited in the tomb, and included is the tool of Ani's profession, a scribe's wooden palette-and-pencase. At the head and foot of the corpse the two Black Kites are perched, ready and alert, guarding over the mummy. Each bird wears on its head the respective hieroglyph for the goddess's name. Although rather idealized, the kites are the successful product of the artist's close look at nature. His concern to distinguish the different color and textural qualities of the head and breast feathering is lifelike. The black plumage markings on the legs are, however, a spurious feature, one that is frequently met with on birds portrayed in Egyptian mythological scenes (fig. 61). The overall treatment of the figures leaves no room for doubt that they are birds of prey from top to bottom. Isis and Nephthys as wailing women also occur as Black Kites in a similar scene on the Dynasty XXI papyrus "Book of the Dead" of Queen Nodjmet and Herihor from Deir el-Bahari (fig. 52); but the goddesses are pictured more commonly as mourners in the shape of kestrels (see bird No. 24).

A block of relief in the Musées royaux d'Art et d'Histoire, Brussels, said to be from the Old Kingdom, but perhaps of much later date, shows on it birds flying above and roosting in a papyrus swamp. Perched on one of the umbels is the unmistakable profile of a Black Kite.[209] The Black Kite is a very sociable and versatile scavenger, possessing a bold demeanor, and is often associated with dense human habitation.

For example, the visitor to modern Cairo is often struck by the numbers of them flying overhead. To this day the bird provides a valuable service in cleaning the streets of refuse. It is clear that the ancient Egyptians also knew the ways of this cunning species quite well. This is admirably shown in the Dynasty XIX tomb of Ipuy (No. 217) at Thebes, where waiting for an opportunity to strike from its roost on top of a post, a Black Kite is depicted in a scene watching a man who with knife in hand is busily eviscerating a catch of fowl (fig. 53). Hung to dry on lines stretched between two wooden posts, the plucked carcasses would be a prize catch for the bird. The artist, by placing the kite in this situation, shows that he was more than just a little familiar with the habits of this bird, as marauding Black Kites have been known to swoop down and snatch food from market stalls in a like manner,[210] right from under the vendor's nose. A somewhat similar detail as this appears in a now largely destroyed painting of a fishing scene in the Dynasty XVIII tomb of Haremhab (No. 78) at Thebes. Attracted by the scent of fresh offal, a kite is pictured having come to rest on the mast-head of a fishing vessel (fig. 54). Stretched along the length of the boat are lines from which hang gutted fish, drying in the sun and breeze. It is not difficult to imagine this determined hunter suddenly pouncing down from atop its perch to seize a fish, or to retrieve the entrails the fishermen would have discarded into the Nile. This easily overlooked detail is actually the result of careful observation, as the bird could not be more naturally portrayed. For Black Kites in Egypt are known to favor especially the masts of Nile boats for roosting spots,[211] where they can obtain a commanding view over their hunting grounds and can keep close tabs on the activities of fishermen.

That the Egyptians knew the kite well is further shown by a didactic text from the Ramesside era, in which all callings are said to be bad except that of the scribe: "The sandal maker mixes tan; his odor is conspicuous; his hands are red with madder like one who is smeared with his own blood and looks behind him for the kite, even as a wounded man whose live flesh is exposed."[212]

20. Egyptian Vulture (*Neophron percnopterus*)

Fig. 55. Hieroglyph of an Egyptian Vulture, from the mastaba of Atet, Meidum. Dynasty IV.

Identification: The upright carriage, the entirely pure white body plumage, the long thin hooked bill, the bare skin on the head, the black flight feathers, the long wedge-shaped tail, and the diagnostic shaggy occipital ruff are features of an adult Egyptian Vulture.

Distribution: The bird breeds in parts of southern Europe, Asia, the Middle East, and Africa north of the equator. It winters in parts of southern Asia, the Middle East, and Africa. In modern Egypt, the Egyptian Vulture is a breeding resident in the Upper Nile Valley and in the extreme southeast of the country. However, during the nonbreeding season, it wanders throughout much of Egypt.

Comments: The Egyptian Vulture appears as a hieroglyph;[213] it is extremely rare in art. This painted ornamental hieroglyph of an Egyptian Vulture (fig. 55), executed on a fragment of wall painting from the Dynasty IV mastaba of Atet at Meidum,[214] exhibits the highest standard of artistic quality of the decorative hieroglyphic script. Justly famous, this little picture, like the other well-known bird representations from Atet's tomb (see under bird No. 29), survives in a particularly good state of preservation and displays a brilliant freshness after forty-five centuries. The artist has accurately perceived and acknowledged in this painting all the features of this distinctive vulture. Great accuracy of plumage color and morphological characteristics has been achieved in this portrayal, in what is a veritable masterpiece of the Egyptian artists' talent for animal portrayal. There are, however, several minor discrepancies between this figure and the living bird. The shaggy ruff of the bird is only suggested on the illustration by six short strokes, whereas in nature the ruff is a good deal more prominent than this. Also, an Egyptian Vulture does not possess a black bar marking on its tail as is indicated on this hieroglyph, but is completely white. One of the most striking features of an Egyptian Vulture when it is seen at close quarters is its facial appearance, and anyone who has observed the species in this manner would agree that a fine likeness of that face has been caught here. When viewed in color,[215] the bird's body plumage is painted wholly white, the bare skin on the head is yellow, as is the bill, legs and feet. The markings on the wing and tail, tip of the bill and talons are black, with some additional feather detailing along the edge of the wing in rather broad strokes of a reddish-brown hue, tinged with light blue.

The Egyptian Vulture is first met with during Dynasty III, when the bird can be recognized as a hieroglyph.[216] This species is perhaps the most loathsome of all the scavenging birds, often relying on human excrement and refuse for subsistence. They are regularly associated with areas of human settlement, some becoming almost tame residents of rubbish dumps, even within towns and villages.[217] They play an important role, though far more so before the development of modern waste disposal techniques, in cleaning up filthy and potentially disease carrying organic matter from the land. This was especially true in Egypt, as we have numerous accounts of early travelers to the country who refer to large flocks of "Pharaoh's hens" (the species' white plumage and its general indifference toward man calling into mind the domestic *Gallus* hen) which could be seen daily feeding on carrion and offal around towns and villages.[218] We can be sure that the ancients knew this scavenger quite well and would have had much opportunity for close observation. The many splendid examples of the bird that have come down to us attest to their close familiarity with it. The Egyptian Vulture is normally not thought of as a waterside bird, but a unique occurrence of the vulture in the Dynasty XVIII tomb of Senemioh (No. 127) at Thebes shows it roosting on top of an umbel in a papyrus swamp.[219] Easily told by its characteristic silhouette, this is the only rendering of an Egyptian Vulture in art that we are aware of.[220]

21. Griffon Vulture (*Gyps fulvus*)

Identification: The distinctive proportions, the completely white head, neck and collar, the long and widely separated outer primary feathers, the short tail, and the diagnostic highly contrasting light colored wing coverts and dark flight feathers are features of a Griffon Vulture.

Distribution: The bird breeds and winters in parts of southern Europe, Asia, the Middle East, and North Africa. In modern Egypt, the Griffon Vulture is a breeding resident mainly in the eastern half of the country.[221] However, migrating Griffon Vultures pass through other parts of Egypt.

Fig. 56. *Painted relief of the goddess Nekhbet as a Griffon Vulture, from the mortuary temple of Queen Hatshepsut, Deir el-Bahari. Dynasty XVIII.*

Comments: Griffon Vultures frequently appear in Egyptian art. From the Dynasty XVIII mortuary temple of Queen Hatshepsut at Deir el-Bahari, this striking painted relief picture (fig. 56) of a Griffon Vulture can best be appreciated for its decorative qualities, rather than for the artist's embrace of nature in its execution. The vulture has been vastly conventionalized, but enough of the species' features are present for us to establish clearly that it was predominantly from the Griffon Vulture that the artist took inspiration for the figure.[222] The bird represents the vulture goddess Nekhbet of El-Kab, the tutelary deity of Upper Egypt,[223] who is shown with her long protective wings outstretched hovering above and guarding over what was an illustration of Hatshepsut presenting offerings to the god Amun, though the image of the queen has been expunged by the agents of Tuthmosis III.[224] The portrait survives in comparatively good shape, only the tip of the bill having perished. The vulture grasps in its talons the hieroglyphic sign for "infinity" (*shen*). Except for the white plumage on its head, neck and collar, the bird's bright red, blue and green colored plumage bears very little reality to that of a living Griffon Vulture.[225] However, the painter has correctly distinguished on the bird's long, broad wings the light colored wing coverts and the dark flight feathers of the Griffon Vulture, thereby clinching its identification.

It is extremely difficult to establish firmly when the Griffon Vulture first appears. Large thick-billed vulture forms, such as the Griffon Vulture, occur in Egyptian art during the Late Predynastic Period. Several of them are figured preying on the bodies of men that have fallen in battle on the Battlefield Palette, now in the British Museum, London.[226] The vultures depicted on the palette may represent Griffon Vultures, but positive identification is not possible owing to the absence of specific characters. The common hieroglyphic sign ⳡ, which appears at an early date, has generally been taken to represent the Griffon Vulture.[227] This vulture sign is always rendered in a highly conventionalized manner and a good deal of variation appears in its markings, making identification of it impossible to determine accurately. In some cases the plumage pattern and other features of the bird are suggestive of a large thick-billed vulture other than the Griffon Vulture, such as the Rüppell's Vulture (*Gyps rueppellii*)[228] and the giant Lappet-faced Vulture (*Aegypius tracheliotus*), see bird No. 22. Hence, it is best not to try to label firmly from what species of vulture the sign is derived, as it was probably not influenced by any one bird, but by several species of large vulture.[229] From the New Kingdom there are a considerable number of representations in which the Griffon Vulture in particular was the main element of influence.[230] They are regularly depicted in art as a decorative motif, just like the example we illustrate here, with wings spread and guarding over the king, representing a deity (usually Nekhbet) who has assumed the form of a vulture. The coloring of these figures is often quite imaginative indeed, but nevertheless it can suggest the plumage of a Griffon Vulture. In many of these portrayals, though, the artist's familiarity with other species of vulture is also apparent. Often the body and wings are those of the Griffon Vulture, while the head, although painted white, bears the characteristics of a Lappet-faced Vulture.

---

22. Lappet-faced Vulture (*Aegypius tracheliotus*)

Identification: The characteristic proportions, the large wings, the enormous dark, hooked bill, the featherless head and neck, and the easily distinguishable folds of skin (lappets) hanging from the sides of the head and neck are the features of the Lappet-faced Vulture.

Distribution: The bird breeds in Israel, and parts of Africa. It winters in Israel, Jordan, the Arabian Peninsula, and Africa. In modern Egypt, the Lappet-faced Vulture is a breeding resident in the Upper Nile Valley and in the mountains of the Eastern Desert. It is irregularly observed throughout the year in various parts of the country.

Comments: The Lappet-faced Vulture is frequently met with in Egyptian art. From the Dynasty XVIII tomb of King Tutankhamun (No. 62) in the Valley of the Kings, this handsome jewel (fig. 57), fashioned of solid gold, is surely the most beautiful and truthful rendering of a Lappet-faced Vulture[231] that has come down to us from ancient Egypt. The pectoral may have been worn by the young Pharaoh during his lifetime, as it was uncovered close to the royal person, having been placed between the eleventh or twelfth layers of bandages on his mummy. Like the preceding illustration (see bird No. 21), this piece also represents the Upper Egyptian vulture goddess Nekhbet. The bird is shown clutching in its talons the hieroglyphic sign for "infinity" (*shen*). The terminals of its flexible suspending straps are in the form of two stylized falcons (not illustrated), and serve as the necklace's clasp. We view the pectoral from its reverse side, which enables us to see more clearly all of the species' features. The front side of the vulture was crafted much more differently than the back; there the feathering of its body and wings is indicated by the use of colored glass.[232] One of the most arresting characters of a Lappet-faced Vulture when it is seen at close range is its head. Executed here in profile, the head is well told by the massive lapis lazuli bill, the obsidian eye, and the extraordinary moulded sagging folds of bare skin which encompass the head and neck. The lappets in particular are very realistically portrayed, and even the ear is indicated. The bird is displayed with its wings partially outstretched, and with its long primary feathers folded and drooping downward at the side. This impressive posture was not accidental, but suggests the attitude that several of the large vulture species adopt when they are either threatened or showing their dominance over other birds.[233] The figure's naturalism and attractiveness is further enhanced by the goldsmith's fine chasing denoting the various sizes, shapes and layers of feathering of the vulture's underside. Also, note the charming inclusion of a miniature pectoral hanging from the neck of the bird, which identifies its owner with the inscribed cartouche of Tutankhamun.

The earliest evidence we have for the Lappet-faced Vulture is from Dynasty V, when the species' influence on the common hieroglyphic sign is apparent.[234] The bird is well established in the artistic tradition from Dynasty XII onward. One of the first instances of the vulture in art is an exquisitely carved example on the Dynasty XII *sed*-festival shrine of Sesostris I at Karnak.[235] Here the occipital folds of skin are obvious, thus confirming that inspiration, at least in part, came from the Lappet-faced Vulture. Another very outstanding example of the vulture is depicted on the innermost coffin of Yuia (fig. 58) from his Dynasty XVIII tomb (No. 46) in the Valley of the Kings. The lid of the coffin is decorated with a large figure of a Lappet-faced Vulture in gold inlaid with colored glass, representing the sky goddess Nut. With her wings spread across the abdominal region, she served to provide the deceased with magical protection. Beginning with Dynasty XVIII depictions of the species are far more numerous, and there are many fine and deftly executed images of the bird.[236] It is not unusual, however, for the features of this bird (especially the lappets) to be combined with those of the Griffon Vulture (bird No. 21), the result of which is a composite figure of these two vultures.[237] The Lappet-faced Vulture is one of the largest birds in Africa, with a wing span of up to 290 cm. This giant raptorial bird is a very dominant and aggressive hunter. At the kill site other carrion feeding birds give way to the vulture's powerful and robust bill, which is capable of tearing open the hides of the biggest game animals: elephant, Hippopotamus and rhinoceros.[238] We can be confident that the Egyptians were well aware of the Lappet-faced Vulture's awesome power, and frequently chose it to represent the goddess Nekhbet, and sometimes other deities as well, with sure knowledge of that power.

Fig. 57. Necklace with a Lappet-faced Vulture pectoral representing the goddess Nekhbet, from the tomb of Tutankhamun (No 62), Valley of the Kings. Dynasty XVIII.

Fig. 58. The goddess Nut as a Lappet-faced Vulture on the innermost coffin of Yuia, from his tomb (No. 46), Valley of the Kings. Dynasty XVIII.

23. Long-legged Buzzard (*Buteo rufinus*)

Identification: The distinctive upright carriage, the heavy dark hooked upper bill, the black primary feathers, the general dark body plumage, the light colored cere, legs and feet, and the unbarred tail are features of an adult Long-legged Buzzard.

Distribution: The bird breeds in parts of southeastern Europe, Asia, the Middle East, and North Africa. It winters in Asia, the Middle East, and Africa north of the equator. In modern Egypt, the Long-legged Buzzard is a breeding resident throughout most of the country, except in an area of the Western Desert.[239]

Comments: The Long-legged Buzzard is a commonly represented Egyptian hieroglyph.[240] This ornamental hieroglyph (fig. 59) is from the Dynasty XVIII mortuary temple of Queen Hatshepsut at Deir el-Bahari. Care has been taken here to depict most of the species'

morphological characteristics in detail. The bird is pictured at rest, facing to the right in an erect posture. When the sign is viewed in color,[241] the buzzard's plumage and tail are a brownish-red hue, while the cere, legs and feet are brownish-yellow, and the upper bill, talons and primary feathers are in black, with some additional feathering on the wing in dark brown. Although the features of the species are admirably presented, identification of this figure as a Long-legged Buzzard can only be made certain when its coloring is considered.

The Long-legged Buzzard can first be recognized during Dynasty IV from carefully painted examples of the sign.[242] It should be noted that the Egyptian artist/scribe did not always clearly distinguish between the Long-legged Buzzard hieroglyph and that of the Egyptian Vulture (see bird No. 20). Often only the shape of their occiputs and tails separate the two signs.[243]

Fig. 59. Painted relief hieroglyph of a Long-legged Buzzard, from the mortuary temple of Queen Hatshepsut, Deir el-Bahari. Dynasty XVIII.

44

24. Lesser Kestrel or Kestrel (*Falco naumanni* and *F. tinnunculus*)

Identification: The familiar posture and proportions, the black "toothed" and sharply hooked upper bill, the fringed "boots", and the diagnostic dark markings on the back, upper wing coverts and the barred tail are features of a female kestrel.

Distribution: The Lesser Kestrel breeds in parts of Europe, Asia, the Middle East, and North Africa. It winters in Spain, parts of Asia, Turkey, and Africa. In modern Egypt, the Lesser Kestrel is a common migrant in the Nile Valley and Delta, and the Faiyum.[244] The Kestrel breeds and winters in parts of Europe, Asia, the Middle East, and Africa. In modern Egypt, the Kestrel is a common permanent breeding resident in the Nile Valley and Delta, the Faiyum, in the vicinity of the Suez Canal, and the Dakhla, Kharga, and Siwa Oases.[245]

Comments: Kestrels are occasionally pictured in Egyptian art. This very handsome portrayal (fig. 60) is from the Dynasty XIX tomb of Sennedjem (No. 1) at Deir el-Medina. The bird represents the goddess Isis in the guise of a falcon, whose emblem, a throne, rests on top of her head. It is part of a wall painting illustrating a vignette that accompanies a spell (Chapter 17) of the "Book of the Dead." The scene is an enlarged version of exactly the same one in which the Black Kites appear in the papyrus of Ani (see under bird No. 19). However, here the two sister goddesses, Isis and Nephthys, have assumed the form of kestrels rather than kites in their role as divine mourners for the dead. The pair is shown perched next to and guarding over the shrouded mummy of Sennedjem, one on either side, which lies on a lion-shaped bier within a kiosk.[246] The beauty and salient morphological features of a kestrel are fully acknowledged in

Fig. 60. Detail from a scene in the tomb of Sennedjem (No. 1), Deir el-Medina, showing the goddess Isis in the form of a kestrel. Dynasty XIX.

this rendering. The bird's plumage is painted a light brown, with a reddish tint to it, suggesting the brownish-red plumage so characteristic of female kestrels. The markings on its upper parts and the barring on the tail are in dark brown. The falcon is not without a few inaccuracies in its details; the tail should have a terminal black band, the primary feathers are not black, and it is shown with two cloacae, a feature that sometimes turns up on birds figured in mythological contexts. These minor criticisms aside, the falcon has been handled with a considerable degree of sensitivity. The differences between the females of the two species of kestrel are very subtle, and because of this it is not possible to identify the bird as one or the other species.

By far the most commonly depicted falcon in Egyptian art is a type that was selected to represent the falcon deity Horus (see bird No. 25). The form and coloring of the so-called "Horus Falcon", with only slight modification, remained remarkably constant for the entire course of Egyptian history. The identity of the "Horus Falcon" is not to be found in any one particular species, as it was almost certainly influenced by several varieties of large falcon, all possessing similar markings and plumage features. During the Ramesside Period, however, artists portrayed a kind of falcon that was clearly different from the traditional falcon form used to illustrate the bird of Horus. This falcon, we believe, was modeled on a kestrel, or more precisely, from either the female Lesser Kestrel or Kestrel, or both. They are easily distinguished from the "Horus Falcon" as their plumage characteristics, coloring, and facial markings differ vastly. The ancient Egyptians were surely very familiar with kestrels, since not only is the Kestrel the most abundant species of falcon in Egypt,[247] but also the Kestrel seems to have been the most frequently mummified falcon.[248] When kestrels are pictured they are invariably shown in mythological scenes in which the goddesses Isis and Nephthys have assumed the appearance of falcons. Positive identification of them is confined to their occurrence in a number of Dynasty XIX and XX tombs at Thebes,[249] and from funerary papyri of this same period.[250] Deserving of mention are outstanding examples in the Dynasty XIX tomb of Queen Nefertari (No. 66) in the Valley of the Queens.[251] The falcons have been well executed and painted, and although they are highly idealized, they call to mind living female kestrels.

25. "Horus Falcon" (*Falco* sp.)

Identification: The customary upright stance, the black "toothed" and hooked upper bill, the dark back and wing, the still darker cap and nape, the white underside, and the diagnostic broad black moustachial streak which stands out against the white cheek are features of the "Horus Falcon."

Distribution: There are four species of falcon that occur in modern Egypt which exhibit similar features as those of the "Horus Falcon." The Eleonora's Falcon (*F. eleonorae*) is a rare migrant.[252] The Hobby (*F. subbuteo*) is an uncommon migrant in the Nile Valley and Delta. The Lanner Falcon (*F. biarmicus*) is a permanent breeding resident in the Nile Valley and Delta, and parts of the Western and Eastern Deserts. The Peregrine Falcon (*F. peregrinus*) is a permanent breeding resident in the Nile Valley north of Luxor, the Delta, and the Faiyum.[253]

Comments: The "Horus Falcon" is abundantly pictured in both Egyptian art and hieroglyphs.[254] Executed facing to the left, this ornamental hieroglyph (fig. 61), from the Dynasty XX tomb of Ramesses IX (No. 6) in the Valleys of the Kings, is shown in an entirely traditional manner. The bird is portrayed at repose, with its wings folded at the side, the head and body in profile, and its tail in such a position that it seems as if we are viewing it from above. A wide range of color was used for the falcon.[255] The back and wing are painted green, the cap and nape slate blue, the legs, the cere and eye yellow, the underside white, the bill, the moustachial streak and feather markings black, and the tail black and green checked, with a terminal red band. When carefully executed, the image of the "Horus Falcon" is always characterized by a strong facial pattern, featuring a well pronounced moustachial streak, exactly as it is indicated

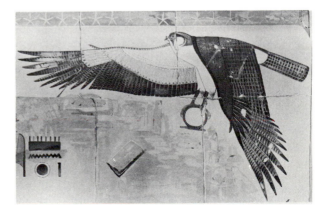

Fig. 61. (top left) Hieroglyph of the "Horus Falcon", from the tomb of Ramesses IX (No. 6), Valley of the Kings. Dynasty XX.

Fig. 62. (top right) Black syenite statue of the god Horus as a falcon-headed man. Dynasty XIX.

Fig. 63. (center left) "Horus Falcon" depicted on the limestone funerary stela of Djet (Uadji), from Abydos. Dynasty I.

Fig. 64. (bottom) Painted relief of a hovering "Horus Falcon", from the mortuary temple of Queen Hatshepsut, Deir el-Bahari. Dynasty XVIII.

47

here. Curiously, there is no trace of the sharp talons that are usually figured on representations of this bird of prey. Also, note the three horizontal bars on the feathers above each leg, a spurious feature, and one that we have already met with on the Black Kite (see bird No. 19). The bird represents the falcon deity, Horus, the sky god, the son of Osiris, with whom the living king was closely identified.[256] If the Egyptians had a national bird, the "Horus Falcon" would doubtless have been it. The name Horus probably means "the superior or lofty one", referring to the capability of the falcon for flying high in the air.[257] Horus is always depicted as a falcon or as a man with a falcon's head (fig. 62). Other gods regularly appear with the same falcon form (e.g., Re-Harakhty, Mont),[258] but it is with Horus that this falcon is most closely associated. Perhaps no single other bird occurs more frequently in art and hieroglyphs than does the "Horus Falcon." Over the years the identification of the bird has been a matter of some dispute. Several early investigators first suggested that it was inspired by the Sparrowhawk (*Accipiter nisus*).[259] While others, after having correctly established that the bird was indeed a falcon, have sought to identify it with virtually every species of large falcon that frequents Egypt,[260] the Peregrine Falcon being the most commonly named bird.[261] From its earliest appearance, the falcon of Horus is always rendered in a highly conventionalized manner. The artists' emphasis clearly lay on the symbolic and decorative qualities of the falcon, and not on an adherence to nature. Our example of the bird from the tomb of King Ramesses IX shows the kind of stylization that often occurs. Little ornithological expertise is needed to know that falcons of any kind do not have black and green check patterned tails, nor do they have black tips on their "boots." Whether in art or as a hieroglyphic sign, the "Horus Falcon" cannot be said to conform exactly to any one particular species. Rather, there are four species of large falcon in Egypt, listed above, which all possess more or less similar markings and plumage characteristics as those of the "Horus Falcon", and could have served as the model for it. Hence, we believe that it is not possible to specify which species of falcon the bird of Horus was derived from,[262] as it was probably influenced by several varieties of large falcon occurring in Egypt.

The earliest evidence for the falcon of Horus comes from the Late Predynastic Period, when for instance, the birds can be recognized mounted on top of standards on slate palettes and a mace-head.[263] On the famous Dynasty I Narmer Palette from Hierakonpolis, now in the Egyptian Museum, Cairo, there is a splendid depiction of the "Horus Falcon."[264] However, it is not until later in Dynasty I that we first see the moustachial streak that came to be such an important feature of the "Horus Falcon." This is well illustrated on the Dynasty I funerary stela of Djet (Uadji) from Abydos (fig. 63). A wealth of representational material exists for the emblem of Horus, ranging from predynastic times through the Greco-Roman Period. In addition to the many fine pictures figured on the walls of tombs[265] and temples (fig. 64), "Horus Falcons" also frequently appear, for example, as part of the design on pieces of ornamental jewelery,[266] as small amulets,[267] and quite often during the Late Dynastic Period and Greco-Roman times, as handsome statuettes (fig. 65) fashioned from bronze or in stone.[268] These latter objects were evidently used as votive offerings to the god, and some of them are of outstanding workmanship. It was during this era that falcons, like the Sacred Ibis (see bird No. 15), were subject to mass burial. As a sacred bird, according to Herodotus, it was a crime to kill a "hawk", even unwittingly, and it was punishable by death.[269] Falcons were mummified by the hundreds of thousands and buried in large cemeteries at a number of sites in the country.[270] The birds were often elaborately and decoratively wrapped, and sometimes were given cartonnage masks or placed in coffins.[271] It is possible that some of these falcons may have been bred in captivity especially for this purpose.[272] Species of large falcon, the types which we believe served to influence the form of the "Horus Falcon", have been identified from mummies.[273] It should also be noted here, that there is some evidence, though very limited, for the practice of falconry in ancient Egypt.[274] See under bird No. 24 for more on falcons.

Fig. 65. Bronze statuette of the "Horus Falcon" wearing the Double Crown of Upper and Lower Egypt. Dynasty XXVI or later.

49

26. Mute Swan (*Cygnus olor*)

Identification: The customary posture, the comparatively short legs, the massive body, the extremely long curved neck, and the diagnostic basal knob on the upper mandible are features of an adult Mute Swan.

Distribution: The bird breeds in parts of Europe, Asia, Turkey, and southern Africa.[275] It winters in parts of Europe, Western Asia, the Middle East, and Africa. In modern Egypt, the Mute Swan is an uncommon winter visitor in the Nile Delta.[276]

Comments: This is the only depiction of a Mute Swan (fig. 66 a-b) that we have been able to identify positively in Egyptian art and hieroglyphs.[277] The statue was found by the archaeologist Jacques de Morgan in the offering chamber of the Dynasty XII tomb of princess Itiwert at Dahshur in 1894-5.[278] Apart from the eyes, which are fashioned of quartz and set in copper sockets, the entire composition,

including the pedestal on which it is mounted, is made of wood. The figure is approximately two-thirds the size of that of a living adult Mute Swan.[279] The legs have been seriously damaged, and as a result the bird can no longer stand without support. A number of pieces of wood were used in the construction of the swan, and most of the joins are evident. The long graceful S-shaped neck and head are formed of three individual pieces fitted together, as are each of the legs and webbed feet, and are attached to the body by means of small wooden pegs. The lower portion of the bird's body is carved from a single block of wood, and is hollow inside. The upper part (back and wings) consists of one or more pieces, and fits on the lower portion much like a cover. The bird is remarkably naturalistic, and is surely the work of a master craftsman. Great care has been taken to duplicate all the morphological features of a Mute Swan. The attitude of the head and neck, the heavy body,

Fig. 66a. Wooden statue of a Mute Swan, from the tomb of the princess Itiwert, from Dahshur. Dynasty XII

and the details of the bill seem to be the product of direct observation. It will be noticed that the swan is displayed with its left leg placed slightly in advance of the right, as if it was about to take a step. However, this leg is damaged, and has been positioned incorrectly in modern times; originally, the legs were together.[280] Very few details, unfortunately, were noted about the piece at the time of its discovery. Several writers have referred to the object as a box;[281] however, this seems unlikely. Along the edges of the "cover" there are a number of regularly spaced small holes, which suggests to us that the upper part was joined to the lower body, probably with pegs, and could not have served as a box, at least in a conventional sense. At Dahshur, de Morgan also found a similar wooden statue of a swan in the tombs of two other Dynasty XII princesses, those of Khnemt and Sit-Hathor-meret.[282] It is not known whether these examples were in the shape of Mute Swans or not, as no description

of them was given, but it seems not improbable. Although not fully understood, it is clear that the swan must have possessed some religious significance[283] which prompted statues of them being deposited in the tombs of these three Dynasty XII princesses. During the New Kingdom, representations of swans were included in other royal burials as well, see under bird No. 27.

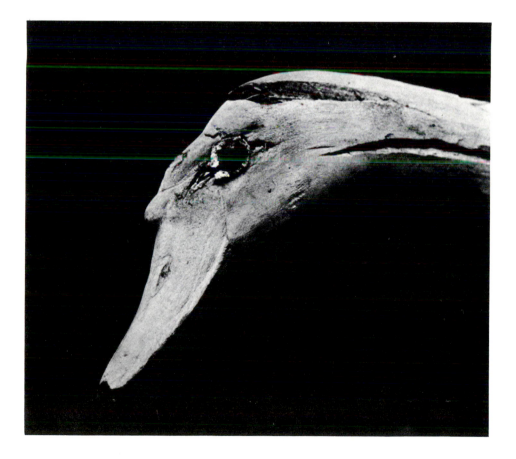

Fig. 66b. Detail showing the characteristic basal knob.

Fig. 67. (top left) Relief of a Whooper or Bewick's Swan, from the mastaba of Ptahhotep II (D 64), Saqqara. Dynasty V.

Fig. 68. (top right) Drawing of a carved rectangular panel of ivory with rows of various animals, including a swan and a Hermit Ibis, from Hierakonpolis. Late Predynastic - Early Dynastic Period.

Fig. 69. (center left above) Wooden statuette of a swan, from the tomb of Tuthmosis III (No. 34), Valley of the Kings. Dynasty XVIII.

Fig. 70. (center left below) Wooden statuette of a swan, from the tomb of Haremhab (No. 57), Valley of the Kings. Dynasty XVIII.

Fig. 71. (bottom) Drawing of a painting showing a statuette of a swan, from the tomb of Seti II (No. 15), Valley of the Kings. Dynasty XIX.

27. Whooper or Bewick's Swan (*Cygnus cygnus* and *C. bewickii*)

Identification: The characteristic profile, the relatively short legs, the rather large, heavy body, the long slender neck, and the knobless bill are features of a Whooper or Bewick's Swan.

Distribution: The Whooper Swan breeds in parts of northern Europe and Asia. It winters in parts of Europe, Asia, the Middle East, and occasionally North Africa. In modern Egypt, the Whooper Swan is an uncommon winter visitor.[284] The Bewick's Swan breeds and winters in the same areas, but has never been reported in modern Egypt.

Comments: Representations of Whooper or Bewick's Swans are only occasionally met with in Egyptian art. Carved in relief, this top-flight portrait of a swan (fig. 67), from the Dynasty V mastaba of Ptahhotep II (D 64) at Saqqara, appears in a scene in which the tomb owner is pictured viewing the processions of animal offerings brought from his estates, and others taken from the wild. Included amongst them is a variety of domestic birds from his aviaries: cranes, geese, ducks, doves, and a single swan.[285] They are arranged into small groups according to their type, with hieroglyphic captions above each giving their numbers. The swan is executed facing toward the right, standing with one leg forward, and with a strongly curved neck.[286] The accompanying inscription, if it is to be believed, informs us that Ptahhotep II possessed 1,225 swans. They might well have been his prize from hunting, as this is the only pictorial evidence to suggest that the Egyptians kept swans or that they were consumed.[287] Both Whooper and Bewick's Swans do well in captivity and are known to breed,[288] and we can safely assume that the ancient Egyptian aviculturalists would have experienced similar success with them. Swan flesh is also reported to be quite palatable,[289] and given these factors, it is curious that they do not show up more often in scenes displaying poultry. Their absence might be a reflection of their rarity in the country, or perhaps they were simply considered a second-class table bird. This illustration is generally taken to represent the Whooper Swan,[290] because the species' present distribution does, as noted, include Egypt. However, one cannot rule out the possibility that Bewick's Swan may also have been known to the Egyptians. Thus, the exact identity of this figure remains uncertain, but would surely have been modeled on one or both of these two species of knobless swan.

The first time the Whooper or Bewick's Swan can be identified is on a rectangular ivory panel from Hierakonpolis, dating from the Late Predynastic or Early Dynastic Periods (fig. 68). As we have already seen under bird No. 26, the swan played a role in Egyptian mythology which caused images of the bird to be placed in tombs. Further evidence of this practice comes from its appearance in the *frise d'objets* painted on the Dynasty XII coffin of Sauazet from El-Riqqa.[291] Both its shape and coloring are exactly like that of a swan. It is, however, from the Dynasty XVIII and XIX tombs of kings in the Valley of the Kings which provides us with the most examples. Small statues in the shape of swans, part of the royal funerary equipment, have been found in the tombs of Tuthmosis III (No. 34) (fig. 69), Tuthmosis IV (No. 43),[292] Tutankhamun (No. 62),[293] and that of Haremhab (No. 57) (fig. 70), while in the tomb of Seti II (No. 15), a statuette of a swan, housed in its shrine, is painted on a wall in the tomb (fig. 71). Similar to the model of the Mute Swan from the Dynasty XII tomb of Itiwert (see bird No. 26), these are not quite life-size, and originally would have stood mounted on pedestals. The example from the tomb of Tutankhamun is the only complete specimen. Like all of these swan figures, it too was covered with a black resin varnish, probably to increase its magical power. It was identified by Howard Carter as an Egyptian Goose (*Alopochen aegyptiaca*), see bird No. 32, but even he did not fail to remark upon the bird's strong swanlike character.[294] Although these figures are usually called swans by Egyptologists,[295] some have expressed serious doubt with this identification, preferring to see them as geese.[296] In our view, they are clearly swans. This is especially evident in the full, heavy body, and the extreme length of the birds' neck, which eliminates every other species of waterfowl except a swan. The absence of a basal knob on any of these representations indicates that a Whooper or Bewick's swan was intended.

The depositing of swan statues in New

Kingdom royal burials seems then to have been part of a continuing tradition of placing depictions of the bird in tombs which apparently began during the Middle Kingdom.

28. Greylag Goose (*Anser anser*)

Fig. 72. Painting of a Greylag Goose, from the North Palace of Akhenaten, El-Amarna. Dynasty XVIII.

Identification: The characteristic proportions, the wholly pink bill, legs and feet, the ash-brown anterior plumage (see Comments), the dark posterior back feathering which is edged with white forming a transverse pattern, and the white underside with irregularly spaced black markings are features of an adult Greylag Goose.

Distribution: The bird breeds in parts of Europe, Asia, Turkey, Iraq, and Algeria.[297] It winters in parts of Europe, Asia, the Middle East, and North Africa. In modern Egypt, the wild Greylag Goose is an accidental winter visitor having only been recorded once in January 1942, when a group of six were observed on Lake Maryiut.[298]

Comments: This is the only example of a Greylag Goose (fig. 72) that we have been able to identify positively in Egyptian art and hieroglyphs.[299] Painted against a deep yellow background, this attractive representation of the goose, which dates from Dynasty XVIII, is from the North Palace of King Akhenaten at

El-Amarna. It appeared in one of the many small chambers which surrounded a large court that had a sunken water garden in its middle. This entire area of the palace was thought by its excavators to have been used for the keeping of domestic poultry.[300] A wall of the chamber was decorated with a scene depicting various kinds of birds being fed, a theme which apparently reflected the actual activities of the court. Attendants are pictured dispensing grain from large vessels to the eagerly awaiting birds.[301] Only portions of the painting were preserved. This fragment shows a Greylag Goose facing to the right, bent low in a feeding posture, pecking at the red dots of grain covering the ground. Above and in front of the goose, on separate ground lines, are traces of two other birds, a crane(?) and a duck(?), which presumably are joining in the meal. This fat Greylag Goose has been executed with special care. The detailing of the bird's plumage, its texturing and subtle hues, down to the small curly neck feathers, is exceedingly lifelike. The goose can be best appreciated, and its identification can only be made certain, when it is

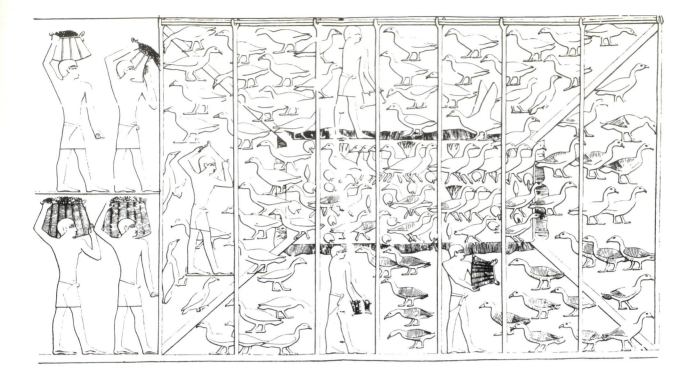

Fig. 73. (top) Drawing of a relief showing men distributing grain from baskets to geese inside a large aviary which has a pool in its middle, from the mastaba of Ti (No. 60), Saqqara. Dynasty V.

Fig. 74. (bottom) Detail of a group of Anser geese from an aviary in the same tomb as above.

viewed in color.[302] The species' pink bill, legs and feet, and ash-brown anterior plumage has been correctly observed. Although it is incomplete, this figure ranks with the most accomplished bird illustrations from ancient Egypt.

The Greylag Goose is a very sociable bird, one that is easily accustomed to captivity and will in a short time become domesticated. Once tame, they will breed without much difficulty. The Greylag Goose is the wild ancestral form of our own domestic farmyard goose.[303] The portrayal of the bird from the palace of Akhenaten would seem to indicate that the Egyptians also domesticated this species, probably for the table. Although we are only aware of one sure representation of the goose, other evidence shows that the goose was fairly well known in ancient Egypt. Remains of Greylag Geese have been identified from the queens' burial chambers in the Dynasty XII pyramid of Amenemhat III at Dahshur,[304] and from a New Kingdom tomb in the Valley of the Queens,[305] where they had been placed as food offerings for the dead.

Throughout Egyptian art depictions of geese abound. As a means of magically ensuring an endless supply of food in the beyond, geese are very commonly shown in the scenes of everyday life rendered on the walls of tombs, particularly during the Old and Middle King-doms. Here large numbers of geese are pictured, for example, in aviaries and poultry yards (figs. 73-4) feeding or being crammed by hand,[306] being herded in flocks (fig. 75) by men wielding long sticks,[307] carried by bearers in processions,[308] being trapped in the swamps with clap-nets, or simply lined up with other fowl and their hieroglyphic name given above (fig. 101). Considering their abundance in art, it is something of a rarity when it is possible to determine to the species level what type of goose was being portrayed. Geese were usually treated by artists in a most summary fashion. They were carved or painted with just enough detail so as to establish that they were to be taken as geese. Quite often when little detail is present or if poorly executed, it is impossible to decide whether a figure should be regarded as a goose or a duck.[309] The birds in these scenes can usually only be called *Anser* geese. The only goose that can be identified with any degree of regularity in art is the White-fronted Goose (*Anser albifrons*), see bird No. 29. It is possible that the Greylag Goose may have been intended to be recognized in some of these scenes, but in the absence of specific plumage features and color, which are needed for certain identification, its occurrence cannot be confirmed other than in the one scene here illustrated.

Fig. 75. Fragment of wall painting showing the bringing of geese for inspection and the recording of their numbers, from the unlocated tomb of Nebamun, Thebes. Dynasty XVIII.

29. White-fronted Goose (*Anser albifrons*)

Identification: The familiar posture and proportions, the grey head and neck, the dark back and wing, the black and grey barring on the underside, and the diagnostic white band surrounding the base of the bill are features of an adult White-fronted Goose.

Distribution: The bird breeds in parts of northern Europe and Asia. It winters in parts of Europe, Asia, the Middle East, and North Africa. In modern Egypt, the White-fronted Goose is a common winter visitor in the Nile Delta.

Fig. 76. Pair of White-fronted Geese, from the mastaba of Atet, Meidum. Dynasty IV.

Comments: The White-fronted Goose only occasionally appears in Egyptian art; it is very rare as a hieroglyphic sign. This pair of White-fronted Geese (fig. 76) is pictured on a fragment of wall painting from the Dynasty IV mastaba of Atet at Meidum,[310] which formed a subregister to a greater scene illustrating Atet's sons trapping waterfowl with a clap-net in the swamplands.[311] Remarkably well preserved and often reproduced, this famous panel, which is 162 cm long and 24 cm high, and known as the "Geese of Meidum", exhibits a group of six geese, three facing toward the right and three to the left. The goose on either end of the frieze is depicted bending in a feeding posture. This painting is one of the great masterpieces of the Egyptian animal genre. The birds comprise three different species, and two of each variety are shown, consisting of White-fronted Geese, Bean Geese (*A. fabalis*), see bird No. 30, and Red-breasted Geese (*Branta ruficollis*), see bird No. 31. They are situated near the water's edge, on a mud flat which is sparsely covered with green plant life, precisely the kind of habitat geese often frequent. The appearance of the three forms together is also quite realistic as geese are known to winter regularly in mixed flocks. Each species is represented with clear individualism and displays a close fidelity to nature. Although they are conventionally rendered, their morphological characteristics and bright coloring are strikingly like those of living geese. To all intents and purposes, the White-fronted Geese are identical to one another. Partly overlapping, they are portrayed standing erect, advancing toward the left, each with its right leg placed in front of the left. The detailing of the geese is exceptional; note the fine rendering of the conspicuous and diagnostic white band at the base of their bills,

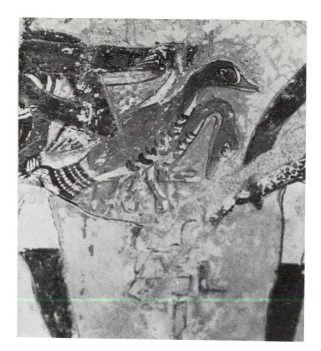

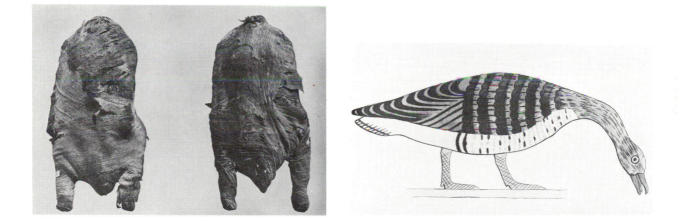

Fig. 77. (top left) Painting of a white-fronted goose, from the mastaba of Kaemankh (G 4561), Giza. Dynasty VI.

Fig. 78. (top right) An offering of white-fronted geese for the tomb owner, from the mastaba of Mehu, Saqqara. Dynasty VI.

Fig. 79. (center left) A dispatched white-fronted goose amongst the offerings laid before the deceased, from the mastaba of Mehu, Saqqara. Dynasty VI.

Fig. 80. (bottom right) White-fronted goose, from the tomb of Khnumhotep III (No. 3), Beni Hasan. Dynasty XII.

Fig. 81. (bottom left) Offering of mummified geese for Tuthmosis IV, from his tomb (No. 43), Valley of the Kings. This pair is thought to be White-fronted Geese. Dynasty XVIII.

58

Fig. 82. Hieroglyph of a white-fronted goose, from the wooden coffin of Seni, El-Bersheh. Dynasty XII.

and the feather patternings on their neck, underside and back. The species' grey-brown plumage, and bright orange bill, legs and feet are well captured.[312] Some have suggested that the Lesser White-fronted Goose (*A. erythropus*) may have been intended here.[313] However, this seems unlikely, as the geese are painted with orange, not pink bills.

The White-fronted Goose is the only species of goose that can be confidently identified from art on more than one occasion. This is largely because it has a distinctive white patch at the base of its bill, which makes this species easy to differentiate from other geese. The White-fronted Goose is in modern Egypt a frequent winter visitor in the Delta, and it was probably even more common in ancient times. In the Dynasty VI mastaba of Kaemankh (G 4561) at Giza, two handsomely painted examples of white-fronted geese are shown (fig. 77), complete with their name written above them, on a wall of the tomb along with other geese, ducks, and doves.[314] Here they were intended to serve as provisions in the beyond. The detailing of the pair is insufficient for us to determine accurately what species of white-fronted goose they represent, but the White-fronted Goose is the more probable. From the Dynasty VI mastaba of Mehu at Saqqara come further examples of this goose. Bearers are shown bringing offerings of white-fronted geese to the deceased (fig. 78). Having had their necks wrung by the bearers, they are depicted amid the piles of offerings heaped before the tomb owner (fig. 79). The geese have been nicely painted, and in particular the white band at the base of the bill is prominently displayed. In the Dynasty XII tomb of Khnumhotep III (No. 3) at Beni Hasan, a white-fronted goose is painted in a scene (fig. 80)

feeding along with other varieties of domestic birds.[315] Here again, the white patch makes it easy to identify the goose. It cannot be said with certainty that white-fronted geese occur elsewhere in art, due to the lack of preserved examples with the necessary coloring and details, but it seems likely to us that others were surely meant to be depicted. In captivity the White-fronted Goose has shown itself to be a sociable and peaceful bird,[316] and because of this would have made an excellent goose for the Egyptian aviculturalists to have kept and domesticated. White-fronted Geese are also very good eating birds, and it appears that the ancient Egyptians looked upon them as one of the more desirable table geese. Remains of them have been found in the queens' burial chambers in the Dynasty XII pyramid of Amenemhat III at Dahshur,[317] and in five New Kingdom tombs at Thebes,[318] where they had been placed as food offerings (fig. 81). A small rock pit discovered 110 m from the Dynasty XVIII tomb of Tutankhamun (No. 62) in the Valley of the Kings contained embalming materials and objects from the king's funerary meal. Among the refuse of the banqueters were the remains of several species of waterfowl, including the bones of a single White-fronted Goose.[319]

The standard hieroglyphic sign 🦢, a goose, is generally taken to represent the White-fronted Goose.[320] Even when carefully executed and painted, this sign can usually only be identified as an *Anser* goose.[321] However, an unusually well detailed example of the sign painted on a face of the Dynasty XII wooden coffin of Seni from El-Bersheh (fig. 82), can at a glance be called a white-fronted goose.

30. Bean Goose (*Anser fabalis*)

Identification: The characteristic proportions, the uniformly colored brown head and neck, the dark greyish-brown back and wing, the black primary feathers, the black tipped upper mandible, and the diagnostic orange bill, legs and feet (see Comments) are features of a Bean Goose.

Distribution: The bird breeds in parts of northern Europe and Asia. It winters in parts of Europe, Asia, Turkey, Iran, and occasionally North Africa. In modern Egypt, the Bean Goose is an uncommon winter visitor in the Nile Delta.[322]

Fig. 83. Painting of a Bean Goose, from the mastaba of Atet, Meidum. Dynasty IV.

Comments: The Bean Goose is extremely rare in Egyptian art. Pictured on a fragment of a wall painting from the Dynasty IV mastaba of Atet at Meidum, which is known today as the "Geese of Meidum" (see under bird No. 29), this representation of a Bean Goose (fig. 83), and a near duplicate of it located on the opposite extremity of the panel,[323] are the only illustrations of the species that we have been able to identify confidently in Egyptian art.[324] Executed facing toward the right, the goose is shown with its neck bent downward, bill opened wide and its left leg in advance of the right, grazing on green vegetation growing along the edge of the water. The likeness of a Bean Goose has been consummately achieved in this portrait. Note, for example, the very realistic rendering of the large bill, with its black tip, and the lamellae "teeth" along the inner edge of the upper mandible. The coloring of the goose, its plumage and bare parts, is of great importance for its identification as a Bean Goose.[325] All of it closely follows that of the living goose, and clinching the identification is the diagnostic orange bill, legs and feet. Of the three species of geese painted on the fragment, in nature the Bean Goose is by far the largest, and interestingly enough, the two Bean Geese are shown considerably larger than the other two varieties in the frieze. Although we know of only these two sure depictions of the bird, there are a tremendous number of geese in art which can only be called *Anser* geese (see under birds Nos. 28-9), and some may have been intended to represent Bean Geese.[326] The Bean Goose is a choice bird for the table. Evidence for its consumption comes from Dynasty XVIII. The remains of two Bean Geese were found amongst the refuse of King Tutankhamun's funerary meal.[327]

31. Red-breasted Goose (*Branta ruficollis*)

Identification: The immediately striking plumage pattern, the rather short, thick neck, the very small bill, the black facial marking, crown, hindneck and lower breast, and the diagnostic russet cheek patch and upper breast (see Comments) are the unmistakable features of a Red-breasted Goose.

Distribution: The bird breeds in select parts of western Siberia. It winters in parts of southeastern and southern Europe, Western Asia, Turkey, Iraq, and occasionally North Africa. In modern Egypt, the Red-breasted Goose is a rare visitor having only been reported on two occasions, once in 1874 near Alexandria,[328] and at Damietta in 1882.[329]

Fig. 84. Pair of Red-breasted Geese, from the mastaba of Atet, Meidum. Dynasty IV.

Comments: These are the only examples of Red-breasted Geese that we have been able to identify in Egyptian art and hieroglyphs. Portrayed on a fragment of wall painting from the Dynasty IV mastaba of Atet at Meidum, which is known today as the "Geese of Meidum" (see under bird No. 29), this pair of Red-breasted Geese (fig. 84) is surely the single most widely known representation of birds from ancient Egypt. Standing erect and partly overlapping, the geese are depicted ambling toward the right, each with its left leg placed forward of the right. At first sight they appear to be identical to one another, but upon closer inspection there is some variation in detail between the two figures. For instance, the russet upper breast area of the bird on the right extends further up the neck than it does on its companion, and the same individual has four white lines running through the lower breast, while the goose on the left has three white bars on its wing. The Red-breasted Goose is regarded as one of the most handsome and ornamental species of waterfowl, and the painter has truly conveyed the beauty of the bird in these renderings. The arresting color and boldly patterned plumage of the living goose is splendidly suggested.[330] The russet hue used for the upper breast and cheek patch is exceptionally imitative of nature. The form of the Red-breasted Goose has also been well defined, and such morphological features as the rather short, thick looking neck, and the extremely small bill have not escaped the eye of the artist. Juvenile geese may have served as the model for these illustrations,[331] as the stippling on the upper breast, and the three white bars on the wing (an adult has but two) seem to indicate inspiration from young birds. Although there are some problems with the

61

total correctness of birds' features, the grey bill, legs and feet being several noticeable errors (they should all be colored black, even on juveniles), their overall characters are those of Red-breasted Geese through and through.

Although this is the only representation of a *Branta* goose appearing in Egyptian art that we are aware of, there is evidence for the knowledge of another member of this genus. The remains of a Brent Goose (*B. bernicla*) were found amongst the refuse of Tutankhamun's funerary meal.[332] While probably never common, the Red-breasted Goose may have occurred more frequently in Egypt during antiquity than it does at the present.[333] The Red-breasted Goose has experienced a disturbing decline in numbers within the last two hundred years, predominantly due to human exploitation and prime habitat loss.[334] This has reduced their total population, as well as their distributional range. These same factors, in varying degrees, also apply to other species of waterfowl which may have been more regularly met with in ancient Egypt (e.g., swan, Bean Goose, Greylag Goose), but today are only rare visitors to the country.

---

32. Egyptian Goose[335] (*Alopochen aegyptiaca*)

Identification: The upright stance, the dark back plumage, the white underside, the lightish colored upper wing coverts which are crossed by two black bars, and the diagnostic black patch on the breast are features of an adult Egyptian Goose.

Distribution: The bird breeds and winters in parts of England[336] and Africa.[337] In modern Egypt, the Egyptian Goose is a breeding resident in the Upper Nile Valley.[338] It winters throughout the Nile Valley, though mainly in the southern portion.[339]

Comments: Egyptian Geese are regularly represented in Egyptian art. One of the finest examples of the traditional scene illustrating the tomb owner fowling in the swamplands is preserved on a fragment of wall painting (fig. 85), from the unlocated Dynasty XVIII tomb of Nebamun at Thebes. Standing on a papyrus raft, and accompanied by his wife and daughter, Nebamun is pictured in the act of hurling his throwstick (a boomerang-like sporting weapon) at a throng of birds which are roosting on and rising in flight from a stand of dense papyrus. His trained cat (*Felis catus*) is depicted busily retrieving the birds that he has already felled. Posed on the bow of the vessel is his tame Egyptian Goose (fig. 86). Executed facing to the left, the bird is standing with its right leg placed in advance of the left, its body erect, neck stretched slightly forward, and bill open, as though uttering its strident "kek-kek" cry. The bird was probably a domestic family pet, which was allowed to join the group on their outing as much for affectionate reasons as for its potential in serving as a decoy,[340] so as to attract birds within the range of Nebamun's throwstick. It is also quite possible that in addition to this function, the figure may have had symbolic significance, perhaps of an erotic nature.[341] Gooselike birds are commonly shown, standing on the front of papyrus rafts in this manner,[342] but only in several instances can they specifically be said to be Egyptian Geese.[343] The diagnostic features of the species have been described with considerable care in this portrayal. When it is viewed in color,[344] the head, neck and upper parts are painted reddish-brown, the throat and under parts are white, the bill, legs and feet are reddish, the primary feathers, tail, breast patch and barring on the wing are black, and the upper wing coverts are light blue. That the artist has well captured the likeness and spirit of a living Egyptian Goose, none can gainsay.

The Egyptian Goose has justly earned for itself the reputation of possessing a vicious temperament and a belligerent attitude,[345] both to animals and humans alike. In modern Egypt, Egyptian Geese often spend much of the daylight hours sunning and loafing on mud flats or sandbanks along the edge of the Nile. In the evening flocks of these aggressive birds sometimes invade grain fields, where they have been known to cause damage to crops.[346] The habits of birds change very little, and as one would expect, the passing of many centuries has done nothing to alter those of the Egyptian Goose. A short didactic text dating from the Ramesside Period, intended to assist in the

Fig. 85. (top) Fragment of wall painting showing Nebamun fowling in the swamplands, from his unlocated tomb, Thebes. Dynasty XVIII. Fig. 86. (bottom left) Close up of Nebamun's Egyptian Goose standing in the boat. Fig. 87. (bottom right) Egyptian Goose nesting in a papyrus swamp, from the mastaba of Mehu, Saqqara. Dynasty VI.

Fig. 88. An Egyptian Goose represented in a vignette on the papyrus "Book of the Dead" of the scribe User-het, from Thebes. Dynasty XVIII.

preparation of young men for the scribal profession, compares the worth of an idle scribe to that of a useless animal: "You are worse than the Egyptian Goose of the river bank, that abounds in mischief. It spends the summer in destroying the dates, and the winter in destroying the emmer. It spends its free time of the year pursuing the cultivators, and allows not the seed to be thrown to the ground before it has got wind of it. It cannot be caught by snaring, nor is it offered up at the temple, that evil bird of piercing sight that does no work."[347] Amusing as this passage may be, the text not only informs us that the ancients knew the ways of the Egyptian Goose extremely well, but that they too experienced some of the same problems with them that farmers in Egypt face nowadays.

The first time this gooselike duck can positively be identified is from a painted relief in the Dynasty VI mastaba of Mehu at Saqqara. The bird is depicted nesting amid the stems and umbels of a papyrus swamp (fig. 87). The coloring of the figure has largely been preserved, which allows for its certain identification. Even the species' dark patch around the eye and the narrow collar are indicated. Nesting birds very similar in form to this one are a stock item of swamp scenes during the Old Kingdom.[348] The absence of extant pigment on them has, up until now, prevented

their identification. On the basis of the example from Mehu, they can probably be considered Egyptian Geese. The bird still remains in Egypt today a breeding resident species. In poultry yard and other related scenes during the Old Kingdom, birds are sometimes rendered which, because of their hieroglyphic labels, though not on the grounds of their morphological characteristics or coloring, can be said to represent Egyptian Geese.[349] Already in the time of the Old Kingdom, therefore, the Egyptian Goose was being kept along with other poultry, and was apparently domesticated for the table,[350] but it is not until Dynasty XVIII that the Egyptian Goose can regularly be identified from an ornithological point of view. Like the picture of the bird from the tomb of Nebamun, Egyptian Geese often appear in scenes in close proximity to humans. It was probably the Egyptian Goose which is so often displayed during Dynasty XVIII sitting in a favored spot beneath the tomb owner's chair.[351] Unfortunately, nearly all of these illustrations have suffered severely and their identification is based more upon circumstantial evidence than on their preserved features. In Egyptian mythology, the Egyptian Goose was held sacred to Amun, the great god of Thebes.[352] Agents of King Akhenaten wishing to obliterate all images and references to Amun and other gods from the monuments, in their wave of persecution destroyed a great many depictions of the Egyptian Goose, due to its association with Amun. The many gooselike birds which appear as pets under tomb owners' chairs,[353] some only barely visible and others completely erased, may well have been Egyptian Geese, but they can no longer be recognized for what they once were. The sacredness of the bird to Amun was probably the stimulus for noblemen to keep them as pets. Because of its religious significance, the Egyptian Goose is often figured in mythological scenes. It appears in vignettes (fig. 88) which accompany certain spells on funerary papyri,[354] in the decoration of tombs at Thebes dating from the Ramesside era,[355] and commonly on votive stelae.[356] A particularly noteworthy example of the species is in the form of a Dynasty XIX votive limestone statuette from Deir el-Medina (fig. 89). This charming piece is composed of a group of nine birds, of three sizes, which are sitting in two rows on the ground at rest, with a dedicatory inscription on the base, which refers to the geese of Amun.[357] There is no difficulty whatsoever in determining exactly what bird the sculptor intended to show, as the diagnostic black breast patch of the Egyptian Goose is clear on them. There is evidence for the consumption of this bird during the New Kingdom, in spite of its being a symbol of Amun and "is not offered up at the temple."[358] In the Dynasty XVIII tomb of Amunemopet (No. 276) at Thebes, the Egyptian Goose is included amongst the food offerings presented to the deceased.[359] The palatability of this species is debated, though most tend to regard its flesh as coarse, and therefore a poor bird for the table.[360] We have already mentioned that the Egyptian Goose appears now and then in scenes with other poultry in the Old Kingdom, but owing to the bird's bad temper and extreme pugnacity, and its need for large amounts of space,[361] it seems unlikely to us that the Egyptian aviculturalists would have relied very heavily upon the Egyptian Goose, when more manageable and better eating birds were readily available to them.[362] In the foundation deposits of the Dynasty XVIII mortuary temple of Tuthmosis III at Thebes, remains of five Egyptian Geese were uncovered.[363] The birds had been placed there after having been ritually sacrificed at the laying out of the temple plan.

Fig. 89. White limestone statuette of nine Egyptian Geese, from Deir el-Medina. Dynasty XIX.

33. Ruddy Shelduck (*Tadorna ferruginea*)

Identification: The uniformly darkish body plumage, the paler head and neck, the conspicuous white wing patch, and the black bill, legs and feet, wing tips, tail, and narrow collar are the unmistakable features of the male Ruddy Shelduck.

Distribution: The bird breeds and winters in parts of eastern Europe, Asia, northwest Africa, and Ethiopia. In modern Egypt, the Ruddy Shelduck is a winter visitor to the Nile Valley (Lower and Middle) and Delta, the Faiyum, and the vicinity of the Suez Canal.[364]

Fig. 90. (top) Painted relief of a Ruddy Shelduck, from the mastaba of Mehu, Saqqara. Dynasty VI.

Fig. 91. (bottom) An offering of Ruddy Shelducks for the tomb owner, from the mastaba of Mehu, Saqqara. Dynasty VI.

Comments: Representations of the Ruddy Shelduck are extremely rare in Egyptian art. The only entirely certain examples of this species known to us are pictured in the Dynasty VI mastaba of the vizier Mehu at Saqqara.[365] Owing to the fine state of preservation of the wall reliefs in many parts of this tomb, we can admire a great number of the birds and other animals portrayed there with much of their bright coloring still extant, whereas in many tombs of the Old Kingdom, as might be expected, the paint has faded or has long since disappeared from the walls—or they were simply left uncolored. It is because of the preserved hues that we can easily spot the Ruddy Shelduck. The bird is figured many times in the tomb. This gooselike duck is depicted in one scene (fig. 90) in a procession along with other domestic poultry, but it is most often shown being carried in bunches (fig. 91) by offering bearers who present them to the deceased. The coloring of the birds is remarkably close to nature. The body plumage is painted a deep reddish-brown, with a paler head and neck, a striking white wing patch, and a black bill, legs and feet, wing tips and tail.[366] We can be certain that the drake of the species was intended, as they are all figured with the narrow black collar of the male. Their appearance here suggests that the Ruddy Shelduck was another bird that the Egyptian aviculturalist kept. As a table bird, the species has received rather low marks for its palatability.[367] However, the Ruddy Shelduck is still consumed today in modern Egypt,[368] and we have seen fowlers selling them at bird markets in the Delta.

34. Common Shelduck (*Tadorna tadorna*)

Identification: The general white body plumage, the dark head, neck, back and wing tips, and the diagnostic broad dark breastband which continues up on the back are features of an adult Common Shelduck.

Distribution: The bird breeds in parts of Europe, Asia, Turkey, Iran, and Tunisia. It winters in parts of Europe, Asia, the Middle East, and North Africa. In modern Egypt, the Common Shelduck is a winter visitor in the Nile Delta, and the Faiyum.

Comments: These are the only representations of the Common Shelduck that we have been able to identify in Egyptian art and hieroglyphs. This drawing (fig. 92) shows a detail of a bird trapping scene from the Dynasty XII tomb of Djehutyhotep (No. 2) at El-Bersheh.[369] Caught beneath the meshing of the clap-net which has been pulled shut by the tomb owner and his son is a great concourse of waterfowl.[370] Included amongst their haul is a party of about twenty-two Common Shelducks (only some are illustrated here). Although the figures

66

Fig. 92. Detail from a drawing of a wall painting showing Common Shelducks caught in a clap-net, from the tomb of Djehutyhotep (No. 2), El-Bersheh. Dynasty XII.

are small, the main characteristics of the species are unmistakably depicted. Note the diagnostic breast band on them. Several of them exhibit what seems to be a suggestion of a basal knob on the bill, which would indicate that they are drakes. Being part of the catch, these shelducks would probably have been prepared for the table of the deceased. As an article of food, the flesh of the Common Shelduck is poorly thought of, and today most regard the duck as a second-class game bird.[371] In modern Egypt, Common Shelducks are still consumed and they occasionally appear in the bird markets.[372]

---

35. Green-winged Teal (*Anas crecca*)

Identification: The rather dark head, the well distinguished speculum, and the diagnostic comma-shaped eye patch which is outlined by a narrow white line are features of an adult male Green-winged Teal.

Distribution: The bird breeds in parts of Europe, Asia, and Turkey. It winters in parts of Europe, the Middle East, and Africa north of the equator. In modern Egypt, the Green-winged Teal is a common winter visitor in the Nile Valley and Delta, the Faiyum, and the Dakhla and Siwa Oases.

Comments: The Green-winged Teal is only rarely depicted in Egyptian art. From the Dynasty XVIII tomb of Kenamun (No. 93) at Thebes, this handsomely painted group of ducks (fig. 93), three sitting facing toward the left and four to the right, appears in a scene in which the tomb owner is pictured viewing the recording of produce from the Delta estates.[373] The yield includes such food items as honey, fish, fruit, cattle, cranes, etc. The ducks may have been trapped by fowlers using clap-nets on the lakes of the Delta. The four Green-winged Teal, shown to the right, have been

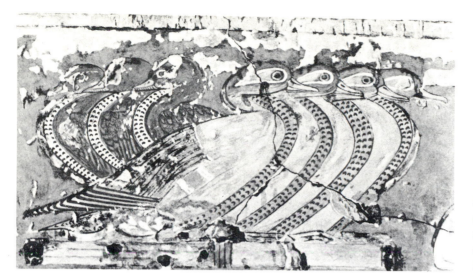

Fig. 93. Green-winged Teal depicted amongst the produce of the Delta, from the tomb of Kenamun (No. 93), Thebes. Dynasty XVIII.

quite beautifully expressed. The artist, though, has taken certain liberties in his reproduction of the species' characteristics, this being especially evident in their coloring. However, the figures totally translate as Green-winged Teal, as the most arresting feature of the duck, the very distinctive eye patch of the drake, has been correctly executed. When these teal are viewed in color,[374] the head, breast, underside, primary feathers, and a portion of the speculum are reddish-pink. The upper back, wing, feet, bill, and the interior of the eye patch are light blue, while the lower back region, tail, and the iris are yellow. The three birds to the left are painted wholly red except for their breasts which are white and are marked with neat rows of small dark red dots, as are the ducks on the right. The true identity of these three is not certain; they may perhaps represent female Green-winged Teal, who unlike the male of the species, do not possess bright plumage but have a rather somber brown appearance without diagnostic plumage patterns. Identification of these birds as female teal is, to be sure, only little more than guesswork.

The earliest extant portrayal of this attractive bird is preserved in the Dynasty XII tomb of Khnumhotep III (No. 3) at Beni Hasan.[375] In one scene, under the cover of a blind (fig. 94), the tomb owner is shown in the act of trapping a large number of brightly painted ducks on a pool with a clap-net.[376] Swimming near the net are three Green-winged Teal, while in the net is a group of four about to be taken. The drakes' colorful plumage and prominent comma-

Fig. 94. Wall painting showing Khnumhotep III netting various species of waterfowl with a clap-net, from his tomb (No. 3), Beni Hasan. Dynasty XII.

Fig. 95. Netting scene from the tomb of Khnumhotep III (No. 3), Beni Hasan, showing Green-winged Teal and other waterfowl trapped in clap-nets. Dynasty XII.

shaped eye patch makes for an easy and accurate identification. Elsewhere in the same tomb, in another fowling scene, three more teal have also been caught in a clap-net along with other ducks (fig. 95). Other examples of them also appear in the tomb.[377] Green-winged Teal are considered excellent birds for the table, and some have described its flesh as superior in flavor to all other waterfowl.[378] The ancient Egyptians too, it would seem, held the duck in high regard, as the representations of them from the tombs of Kenamun and Khnumhotep III suggest. Remains of Green-winged Teal as an item of food have been identified on several occasions,[379] including three from a queen's burial chamber in the Dynasty XII pyramid of Amenemhat III at Dahshur,[380] and four which were found amongst the refuse of King Tutankhamun's funerary banquet.[381] The species is still consumed today in modern Egypt, and they can regularly be found in the bird markets.[382]

---

36. European Wigeon (*Anas penelope*)

Identification: The darkish head, neck, upper breast, back and flank, the white belly, and the diagnostic white forehead and band on the wing are features of an adult male European Wigeon.

Distribution: The bird breeds in parts of Europe and Asia. It winters in parts of Europe, Asia, the Middle East, and Africa north of the equator. In modern Egypt, the European Wigeon is a common winter visitor in the Nile Valley and Delta, the Faiyum, and the Dakhla, Kharga and Siwa Oases.[383]

Comments: The European Wigeon is not commonly represented in Egyptian art and hieroglyphs. Executed facing toward the left, with its right leg placed forward of the left, this painted ornamental hieroglyph of a European Wigeon (fig. 96), from the Dynasty XII tomb of Amenemhat (No. 2) at Beni Hasan, is a splendid delineation of a drake at rest. The very distinctive features of the male have been well observed and are shown with considerable fidelity. The head, neck, upper breast and the primary feathers on the figure are painted reddish-brown, while the back, flank, feet and the bill are green. The forehead, belly and the band on the wing are white, and there is a blackish terminal band on the tail.[384] The coloring of the sign certainly suggests the living bird. However, it is not entirely accurate. A green hue has been substituted on the duck for the grey upper parts of a male European

69

Fig. 96. Hieroglyph of a European Wigeon, from the tomb of Amenemhat (No. 2), Beni Hasan. Dynasty XII.

Fig. 97. European Wigeon brought as an offering to Khnumhotep III, from his tomb (No. 3), Beni Hasan. Dynasty XII.

Wigeon in nature. Also note that the bird is depicted with a much distended crop as though it had just eaten its fill.

The positive identification of this species is limited to its occurrences in the painted decoration and as a common hieroglyphic sign[385] in the Middle Kingdom tombs at Beni Hasan. In the Dynasty XII tomb of Khnumhotep III (No. 3) at the site, the famous fowling scene of the tomb owner trapping waterfowl with a clap-net (fig. 94) shows a party of three drake wigeons about to be caught, while in another scene in the same tomb, a bearer is depicted bringing an offering of a European Wigeon in a cage (fig. 97). The European Wigeon is probably one of the many kinds of ducks which are figured in art during the Old Kingdom, but because of the lack of preserved coloring their identification remains uncertain.[386] The species is today very highly thought of as an article of food,[387] and we can be sure that the examples of them in the tomb of Khnumhotep III would have provided him with a good meal. The European Wigeon is also known to be eaten in modern Egypt, and they routinely appear in the bird markets.[388]

70

37. Pintail (*Anas acuta*)

Identification: The slender build, the long and rather thin neck, the comparatively short legs, and the diagnostic long, pointed central tail feathers are features of an adult male Pintail.

Distribution: The bird breeds in parts of Europe, Asia, Turkey, Morocco, and Tunisia. It winters in parts of Europe, Asia, the Middle East, and Africa north of the equator. In modern Egypt, the Pintail is a common winter visitor in the Nile Valley and Delta, the Faiyum, in the vicinity of the Suez Canal, and the Dakhla and Kharga Oases.

Fig. 98. (top) Painted hieroglyph of a Pintail, from the wooden coffin of Seni, El-Bersheh. Dynasty XII.
Fig. 99. (bottom) Akhenaten making an offering of a Pintail to the Aten, from El-Amarna (found at Hermopolis). Dynasty XVIII.

Comments: Pintails are abundantly pictured in both Egyptian art and hieroglyphs (fig. 98). Carved in sunk relief, this fragment (fig. 99) from an edifice of Akhenaten at El-Amarna portrays the king in the act of wringing the neck of a Pintail and offering it to his god, the Aten, god of the sun disk.[389] Executed in profile and looking toward the right, the king is shown wearing the *khat* headdress, a baglike kerchief. The Aten's rays of light stream down and terminate in small hands, and one holds the hieroglyphic sign for "life" (*ankh*) to the nostrils of the king. The tiny cartouches on the king's upraised arms are the Aten's. With his left hand, the king grasps the outstretched wings of the struggling duck above its back, and with his right he forcibly twists on the neck in order to wring it. The bird's bill is partly open, perhaps uttering a final quack, and the legs appear to be kicking. This method of dispatching fowl is commonly represented in Egyptian art. For example, offering bearers bringing birds to the deceased on the walls of tombs are often shown wringing the necks of the birds they carry (fig. 100). This scene, however, which illustrates the king doing so, is believed to be unique in royal iconography.[390] Although the form of the bird has been rather summarily treated, identification of it as a drake Pintail is certain, as the characteristic elongated central tail feathers of the duck are clearly evident.

The Pintail is by far the most frequently represented species of waterfowl in Egyptian art and hieroglyphs. This easily distinguishable duck can be recognized in a variety of

71

situations. The earliest extant picture of the bird known to us is a hieroglyph on a Dynasty II niche-stela from Saqqara.[391] Pintails appear in a number of scenes inside aviaries, where they are occasionally depicted being force-fed by attendants who cram food pellets down their gullets.[392] Once in captivity, Pintails soon become tame and in time will readily breed.[393] Presumably the Egyptian aviculturalists experienced similar success with them. They are also regularly figured in the wild, being trapped by fowlers (figs. 16, 94, 95, 104) using large clap-nets,[394] and as a favorite quarry of tomb owners who hurl their throwsticks at flocks of them as they rise in flight from the swamp vegetation.[395] Processions of attendants carrying food offerings rendered on tomb and temple walls (fig. 100) nearly always present a generous number of Pintails,[396] and after having their necks wrung, the birds are shown in the piles of offerings heaped before the deceased.[397] The duck is often displayed in tombs, particularly during the Old Kingdom, grouped together with other varieties of domestic poultry, each type neatly labeled with hieroglyphic captions giving their respective name (fig. 101), where they were intended to serve as provisions for the beyond.[398] An especially outstanding example of this is in the Dynasty VI mastaba of Kaemankh (G 4561) at Giza, where amongst the different kinds of fowl, two beautifully painted drake Pintails appear.[399] Several scenes show men plucking the feathers from dead Pintails, then hanging

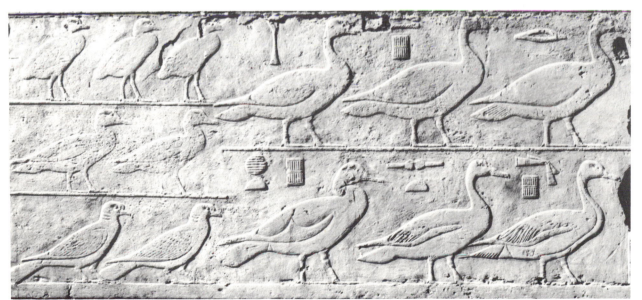

Fig 100. (top) Relief of offering bearer with Pintails in hand and in cages below, from El-Lisht. Dynasty XII.
Fig. 101. (bottom) A procession of domestic fowl, from the mastaba of Ti (No. 60), Saqqara. Dynasty V.

72

the featherless carcasses up to dry in preparation for cooking. This is perhaps nowhere as nicely illustrated than on a fragment of relief from a Dynasty XII mastaba at El-Lisht (fig. 102). Here a man seated on the ground is removing the feathers from a Pintail, and next to him a cook is roasting a duck (Pintail?) on a spit over charcoal which he keeps burning with a small wicker fan. This large body of evidence indicates that the species was regarded as a very desirable bird for the table. As an article of food, the Pintail has received extremely high marks,[400] and the flesh of this game bird is still widely sought after to this day. Remains of Pintails have been identified from the queens' burial chambers in the Dynasty XII pyramid of Amenemhat III at Dahshur,[401] and from a New Kingdom tomb in the Valley of the Queens,[402] where they had been placed as food offerings. The duck is also consumed today in modern Egypt, and can be found in the bird markets.[403] Domestication of the Pintail in ancient Egypt seems to have been so complete that the bird was sometimes kept as a pet (fig. 103). In the Dynasty XVIII tomb of Anen (No. 120) at Thebes, Queen Tiye is portrayed in a scene seated upon her throne and beneath it are her pets, a monkey (family Cercopithecidae), a cat, and a Pintail. The artist has added a bit of humor to this already charming little group of animals by showing the cat with its leg wrapped around the back

of the duck, while the monkey leaps over both of them.

Ducks, sometimes referable to as Pintails, were regularly used in Egyptian art as a decorative motif.[404] Patterns of ducks in flight were painted on the ceilings of tombs and on the floor of a palace in the New Kingdom.[405] The duck could also have subtle erotic associations.[406]

Fig. 102. (below) Relief showing men cooking and plucking Pintails, from El-Lisht. Dynasty XII.

Fig. 103. (above) Pintail under Queen Tiye's throne, from the tomb of Anen (No. 120), Thebes. Dynasty XVIII.

38. Tufted Duck (*Aythya fuligula*)

Fig. 104. Drawing of a relief showing Tufted Ducks trapped in a clap-net, from the mastaba of Ti (No. 60), Saqqara. Dynasty V.

Identification: The general proportions, and the diagnostic comparatively long, drooping crest on the back of the head are features of an adult Tufted Duck.

Distribution: The bird breeds in parts of Europe, and Asia. It winters in parts of Europe, Asia, the Middle East, and Africa north of the equator. In modern Egypt, the Tufted Duck is a common winter visitor in the Nile Valley (near Luxor) and Delta, and the Faiyum.

Comments: These are the only examples of Tufted Ducks (fig. 104) that we have been able to identify in Egyptian art and hieroglyphs.

"Small but unmistakable" is how R. E. Moreau described these three Tufted Ducks,[407] which appear in the upper left hand corner of this drawing of a clap-net filled with waterfowl from a fowling scene in the Dynasty V mastaba of Ti (No. 60) at Saqqara.[408] Although the birds display very little in the way of detail, the drooping crest at the back of their heads is a diagnostic feature of the Tufted Duck. As part of the catch, it is quite likely that these ducks were bound for the table. This species, however, is generally thought to make for rather poor eating.[409] But Tufted Ducks are still consumed today in Egypt, and can sometimes be found in the bird markets.[410]

39. Common Quail (*Coturnix coturnix*)

Identification: The short neck and tail, the small bill, the short legs, the broad, pointed wings, and the rotund body are diagnostic features of a Common Quail.

Distribution: The bird breeds and winters in parts of Europe, Asia, the Middle East, and Africa. In modern Egypt, the Common Quail is a breeding resident in the Nile Delta, and in the general vicinity of Bahig.[411] However, migrating Common Quails pass through the Nile Valley and Delta, the Faiyum, along the Mediterranean Sea coast west of Alexandria, along the Red Sea coast, and in the Dakhla, Kharga and Siwa Oases.

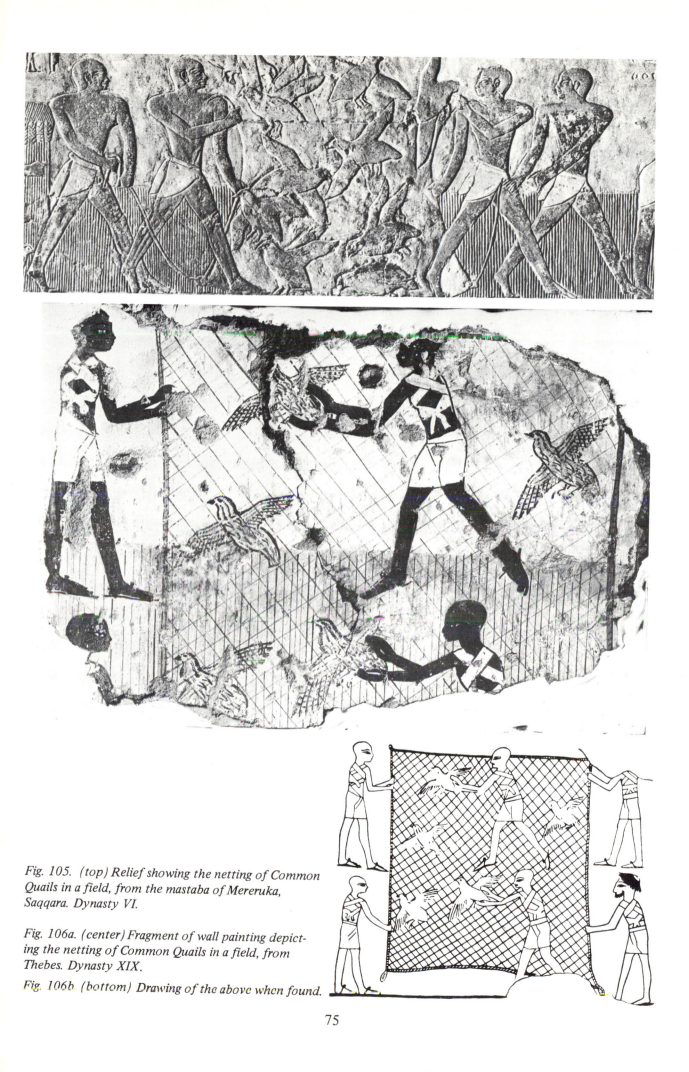

Fig. 105. (top) Relief showing the netting of Common Quails in a field, from the mastaba of Mereruka, Saqqara. Dynasty VI.

Fig. 106a. (center) Fragment of wall painting depicting the netting of Common Quails in a field, from Thebes. Dynasty XIX.

Fig. 106b (bottom) Drawing of the above when found.

75

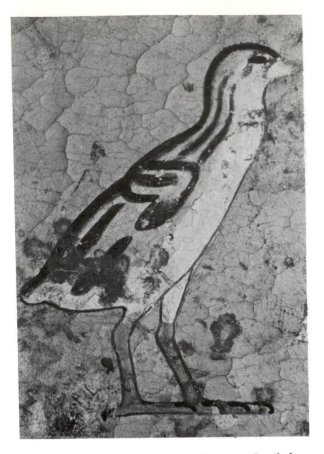

Fig. 107. Hieroglyph of a young Common Quail, from the mastaba of Atet, Meidum. Dynasty IV.

Comments: Common Quails are frequently represented in both Egyptian art and hieroglyphs.[412] From the Dynasty VI mastaba of Mereruka at Saqqara, this scene (fig. 105), carved in relief, shows four farmhands engaged in the netting of a bevy of Common Quails in a grain field. It is the time of the harvest, and the crop is in the process of being gathered in.[413] The trapping takes place in a section of the field which the reapers have already mown, and all that remains is the long stubble of the stalks. Due to some unseen disturbance, or perhaps because of the approach of the men, the quails have been flushed from the cover of the field, where they have been feeding on the gleanings. The sculptor has caught the birds in the instant of their burst upward, some on the wing, others already entangled in the meshing of the mist-net. The quails have been well expressed, and most of the species' distinctive features are present. These comparatively tiny game birds, though, are shown disproportionately large in relation to their captors. The artist may have

been simply emphasizing the plumpness of their bodies from the cereal they have consumed. Scale is frequently ignored in Egyptian art. All four men wear short kilts which are open at the front, and have closely cropped hair. They are grouped in pairs on either side of the net, and are depicted briskly running through the field toward the right carrying the net. The two on the right side have their heads turned back viewing behind them. Each man grasps a rope which is attached to a corner of the net, and the two nearest the net hold on to the side of it with their other hand. Because of the often confusing conventions of Egyptian two-dimensional drawing and painting, it is extremely difficult to judge from the relief the exact form and workings of the net. However, the way in which Common Quails are trapped from the harvest fields in modern Egypt is of much help in our understanding of the mode of capture in this representation. The method is nicely described by the Swedish naturalist Frederick Hasselquist, who visited Egypt between May 1750 and March 1751, and noted this concerning Common Quails in the country: ''An amazing number of these birds come to Egypt at this time [March]; for in this month the wheat ripens. They conceal themselves amongst the corn, but the Egyptians know extremely well that there are thieves in their grounds; and when they imagine the field to be full of them, they spread a net over the corn, and surround the field, at the same time making a noise, by which the birds are frightened, and endeavouring to rise, are caught in the net in great numbers, and make a most delicate and agreeable dish.''[414] It is almost certainly this same technique, or some close variation of it, which is being used by the farmhands in the mastaba of Mereruka.

There is only one other instance of quail trapping in Egyptian art, which appears on a fragment of wall painting from a late Dynasty XIX tomb at Thebes (fig. 106a). The scene is no longer complete, but originally four men were portrayed (fig. 106b) standing amid the tall stubble of a recently cut grain field, holding a fine-meshed net over (horizontally) the field. Two other men have succeeded in flushing the quails from the field, and with their arms outstretched, are rushing toward the net to seize those birds which have flown up into it. This method of catching Common Quails has been

reported in Egypt from more recent times as well,[415] and although it is now illegal (but difficult to enforce), it probably continues to this day. It is not mentioned in Hasselquist's account, but this manner of quail capture usually takes place at night, when it is easier to flush the birds.

There is yet another way in which quails are netted in Egypt. This method uses long nets, some spanning more than 200 m, which are elevated on poles about 3.5 m high. These quail nets, however, are not used in fields, but are exclusively employed for catching the birds along the seashore (see below).

The hieroglyph  can be recognized during the Early Dynastic Period,[416] but it is not until the beginning of Dynasty IV that we can firmly establish the identity of the bird as being a young Common Quail.[417] Greatly aiding in this initial identification of it is a pristine example of the sign on a fragment of wall painting from the mastaba of Atet at Meidum (fig. 107). This ornamental hieroglyph is a superb likeness of a fledgling Common Quail, a bird approximately three weeks of age or less. The bird's downy

Fig. 108. (top) Relief showing Common Quails on the wing above a standing grain crop, from the tomb of Khaemhet (No. 57), Thebes. Dynasty XVIII.

Fig. 109. (bottom) Relief of an offering bearer holding a sheaf with Common Quails, from the tomb of Ramose (No. 55), Thebes. Dynasty XVIII.

plumage is colored golden yellow, with black streaks on its head and upper parts.[418] It also exhibits the typical undeveloped wings of a chick. While there are only two extant scenes showing the netting of Common Quails, other evidence suggests that it was a regular activity of the Egyptian harvest field. Several times quails are shown feeding in grain fields as the crop is being reaped.[419] A particularly interesting example occurs in the Dynasty XVIII tomb of Khaemhet (No. 57) at Thebes (fig. 108). Here the deceased is pictured inspecting two groups of men measuring a crop in order to assess the taxes due. As the team of surveyors work in the field with a measuring cord, they have disturbed a bevy of Common Quails feeding, and we see four of them flying low above the crop. In the Dynasty XVIII tomb of Nakht (No. 52) at Thebes, a scene shows Nakht seated and viewing farmers on his estates performing agricultural tasks related to the harvest.[420] Placed before him are offerings of produce from the fields, including sheaves which have quails tied to them. Quails are similarly depicted in a scene in the Dynasty XVIII tomb of Menna (No. 69) at Thebes.[421] Also, processions of offering bearers rendered on the walls of tombs sometimes bring to the owner sheaves with Common Quails (fig. 109), doubtless caught in the harvest fields, attached to them.[422] The remark made by Herodotus that in Egypt "quails and ducks and small birds are salted and eaten raw" may have had some truth.[423] There are numerous scenes, especially during the New Kingdom,[424] which illustrate

men plucking the feathers from a catch of waterfowl (usually ducks), then eviscerating them. After the carcasses have been allowed to hang and dry in the sun and breeze (fig. 110), they are then potted, possibly in salt.[425] This method of preserving may well have been used for quails and other small table birds too. Some indication of the species' frequency in the Egyptian diet may perhaps be told from Hipparchus' crack "and I liked not the life which the Egyptians lead, forever plucking quails and slimy magpies."[426]

The Common Quail is today,[427] as it apparently was in ancient Egypt,[428] highly esteemed as an article of food, most being obtained from along the Mediterranean Sea coast. This is because in the autumn great waves of migrating Common Quails arrive in Egypt, and being utterly exhausted after their long flight from Europe, are easily netted in large numbers as they alight.[429] It has been said that in Egypt during the autumn months practically the whole northern coast is lined with nets and snares of various sorts.[430] There is a strong market demand for these birds, and in the past a portion of the quail catch has been exported. To the best of our knowledge, there is no evidence for this kind of quail trapping in ancient Egypt, although one would assume that it probably took place in some form. The first time we hear of it is from Diodorus (mid-first century B.C.), who reports that quails were caught with long nets along the coast in northern Sinai.[431]

Fig. 110. A painting in the tomb of Nakht (No. 52), Thebes, showing ducks being plucked, drawn and hung up to dry before they are placed in the tall jars. Dynasty XVIII.

40. Red Junglefowl (*Gallus gallus*)

Fig. 111. An ostracon depicting a Red Junglefowl, from the Valley of the Kings. Probably Dynasty XIX.

Identification: The characteristic posture, the prominent comb, the hackle on the side of the neck, the lappet protruding from the base of the mandible, and the elongated tail-feathers which droop in sickle-shaped curves are diagnostic features of an adult male Red Junglefowl.

Distribution: The bird breeds and winters in parts of southern and southeast Asia. However, its domestic descendant, our common fowl (or chicken), has been introduced virtually world-wide.[432] In modern Egypt, the domestic fowl is found throughout the country in association with human habitation.

Comments: Representations of Red Junglefowl are extremely rare in Egyptian art. Potsherds and small, flat, white flakes of limestone were often used in ancient Egypt as a cheap alternative to costly papyrus for writing and drawing surfaces. The ostracon illustrated here (fig. 111) bears a charming sketch of a male Red Junglefowl facing toward the right. It was found by Howard Carter in the course of Lord Carnarvon's excavations in the Valley of the Kings during the winter of 1920-1. In dating the flake, Carter proposed that it was not earlier than the second half of Dynasty XVIII and not later than the time of the Dynasty XX tomb of Ramesses IX (No. 6) in the Valley.[433] More recently, some writers have offered a more specific date for the piece, suggesting that it is the work of an artist of Dynasty XIX,[434] and this may well be the case. The drawing is executed in black ink, and while it is only a simple statement, it has great vitality and successfully reproduces the essential features of the Red Junglefowl. The artist, with a few rapid strokes of his pen, has made a sketch which conveys a feeling for the strutting gait so characteristic of a living rooster. The picture seems very much the product of a moment, drawn while the artist was perhaps viewing this highly spirited and, what must certainly have been regarded at this age in Egypt, strange bird.

The Red Junglefowl arrived relatively late in Egypt. It may have been introduced by way of Mesopotamia,[435] where through trading links

79

with India, the bird, based upon textual evidence, was known by the time of the Third Dynasty of Ur (*c*.2113-2006).[436] However, the oldest clearly recognizable occurrence of the bird in art from there dates from the second half of the fourteenth century B.C., when four roosters and four hens (?) are depicted on an ivory vessel from Assur.[437] As with other exotic animals which were imported into Egypt, such as the Syrian Bear (*Ursus arctos syriacus*), the Red Junglefowl was probably brought to the country as something to be admired for its unusualness. The bird was not to become a regular feature of the Egyptian farmyard at least until the Ptolemaic Period. The earliest evidence for it in Egypt may perhaps come from the Middle Kingdom. A block from a now destroyed temple at Naga el-Madamud bears a rather crude graffito of what can only be a Red Junglefowl.[438] If we accept the dating of the delineation proposed by its excavator, it would be the first portrayal of the species in Egypt. However, we are very skeptical of a Middle Kingdom date for it, and believe that the graffito is likely to have come from a much later period. A short passage in the Dynasty XVIII "Annals" of Tuthmosis III at Karnak has been restored by Sethe to read that the king received from Syria "four birds which lay every day."[439] According to Sethe, these birds must be Red Junglefowl, and this has been uncritically accepted by Egyptologists.[440] Even if the restoration of the text is correct, it must remain an entirely open question, as Keimer has already pointed out,[441] whether the passage refers to Red Junglefowl or not.

The only other sure example of a Red Junglefowl from the New Kingdom known to us,[442] appears on a beautifully decorated silver bowl from late Dynasty XIX or early Dynasty XX (fig. 112), which was found at Tell Basta. In delicate repoussé work, the bird is shown in

Fig. 112. (top) Detail of a scene on an embossed silver bowl showing a Red Junglefowl with its young, and some Ostriches, from Tell Basta. Late Dynasty XIX - Dynasty XX.

Fig. 113. (center) Limestone relief with a fine Red Junglefowl sitting before the deceased. Dynasty XXX.

Fig. 114. (bottom) Bearer with an offering of a Red Junglefowl for Petosiris, from his tomb, Tuna el-Gebel. Time of Philip Arrhidaeus.

a scene which has been interpreted as taking place along the desert margin.[443] It is standing near a palm tree, and tagging along behind are two of its fledglings (only one appears in our photograph). Although small, the bird is superbly handled and well detailed. It is worth while to note here that by about the mid-seventh century B.C. the Red Junglefowl was also known in the Sudan, as the bird is represented on four ivory plaques from the tomb of Queen Yeturow at Nuri.[444] It is not until Dynasty XXX that the Red Junglefowl again appears in Egyptian art. A fragment of a lintel from the Dynasty XXX tomb of Hapiu is decorated with a scene showing an old harper playing his instrument in front of the deceased, who is seated for the performance (fig. 113). At Hapiu's feet sits a rooster, crisply carved in relief, and considering its tame appearance and close proximity to him, the bird was probably his pet. Whether the Red Junglefowl was consumed during the Dynastic Period is not known.[445] The first indication of its consumption comes from the tomb of Petosiris at Tuna el-Gebel, which dates to the reign of Philip Arrhidaeus (323-316 B.C.). Here in a mixture of Egyptian and Greek styles, processions of bearers are figured bringing offerings to the tomb owner, and included amongst the gifts are two Red Junglefowl (fig. 114). Perhaps also dating from about this time, or later, is a fine drawing of a cock on a papyrus sheet (fig. 115). The picture is especially noteworthy as it has been sketched within a squared grid, and was probably intended to serve as a standard reference for future representations of the bird.[446] With the coming of the Ptolemaic Period, and in the immediate centuries following, the Red Junglefowl was often portrayed in art.[447]

Sometime during the Late Dynastic and Ptolemaic Periods the Egyptian aviculturalists invented a method for artificially incubating fowls' eggs on a large scale. It is also possible that ibis and falcon eggs may have been incubated as well.[448] We learn of this from such classical authors as Diodorus, who remarks regarding the practice: "The men who have charge of poultry and geese, in addition to producing them in the natural way known to all mankind, raise them by their own hands, by virtue of a skill peculiar to them, in numbers beyond telling; for they do not use the birds for hatching the eggs, but in effecting this themselves artificially by their own wit and skill in

an astounding manner, they are not surpassed by the operations of nature."[449] What Diodorus was almost certainly referring to is the same method of hatching eggs that was extensively used in Egypt up to the last century. It involved placing the eggs of the domestic fowl inside large ovens to incubate for a period of time. Just a hundred and fifty years ago, there were 164 of these hatcheries in Egypt, which together hatched more than seventeen million eggs a year.[450] These establishments were great attractions to travelers of the day, and there are many accounts which relate this interesting process.[451] This method of artificial incubation is still in use, or was until recently at least, in some small villages of Upper Egypt.[452]

Fig. 115. Drawing of a rooster on a papyrus sheet. Ptolemaic Period.

41. Helmeted Guineafowl (*Numida meleagris*)

Fig. 116. Hieroglyph of a Helmeted Guineafowl, from the sed-*festival shrine of Sesostris I, Karnak. Dynasty XII.*

Identification: The heavy bill, the comparatively long legs, the horny helmet on the crown, the short, squared tail, the long pendant wattle, and the profusely spotted body plumage are features of the Helmeted Guineafowl.

Distribution: The bird breeds and winters in parts of the southwestern Arabian Peninsula, Morocco, and sub-Saharan Africa. The wild Helmeted Guineafowl has never been recorded in modern Egypt. However, its domestic descendant, our common guineafowl, is found in a few areas of the country,[453] and it is possible that some may revert back to a feral state.[454]

Comments: The Helmeted Guineafowl is common as an Egyptian hieroglyph;[455] it is extremely rare in art. This ornamental hieroglyph (fig. 116), from the Dynasty XII *sed*-festival shrine of Sesostris I at Karnak, is carved in relief and faces toward the left. Identification of it is certain, as the figure displays characteristics which are unmistakably those of the Helmeted Guineafowl. The artist

has, however, rendered several of its features incorrectly. The conspicuous horny helmet on the crown of the bird has been improperly fashioned. This rather large game bird only has a single knob on top of its head, not two. It should be noted that this spurious detail is often repeated on other examples of the sign. The wattle is shown too long and it is attached in the wrong location; it should connect at the base of the mandible, rather than the throat region. Also, the bill is excessively large. The species' heavily spotted body plumage, however, is well indicated on this representation by the use of rows of small incised marks in the relief. There is a great deal of variation in the form of this hieroglyphic sign.[456] It is occasionally portrayed with the horny helmet completely absent. Other times its outline suggests a raptorial species, to the extent that is has "boots". Sometimes the bird's wattle, instead of being attached at the base of the mandible or at least close to it, is placed much lower and gives the appearance of being a large breast-tuft. It is the exception when the Egyptian artist created an image of the species

82

which closely approaches the likeness of a living Helmeted Guineafowl. One of his better efforts, we believe, is this example from the *sed*-festival shrine of Sesostris I.

We first meet with this very distinctive looking bird during predynastic times. Helmeted Guineafowl can be recognized on the painted decoration of some ceramic vessels from the Gerzean Period (Naqada II). While the birds are vastly stylized and little detail is present on them, there is no mistaking the spotted plumage and ungainly appearance of the Helmeted Guineafowl.[457] On a fragment of the slate Battlefield Palette (fig. 117), which dates from the Late Predynastic Period, and on another fragment of the same palette which is now in a private collection in Lucerne,[458] there are representations of birds carved in relief that with only a slight element of doubt are Helmeted Guineafowl. On the piece we illustrate here, the bird is joined by a Gerenuk which is standing next to a palm, and is perhaps feeding. The identification of this odd looking bird has certainly run the gamut. Some have wished to see in it a Ground Hornbill (*Bucorvus abyssinicus*),[459] a chicken,[460] a duck,[461] a Crested Coot (*Fulica cristata*),[462] and others. But it was Keimer who aptly pointed to the bird's striking resemblance to the Helmeted Guineafowl,[463] and we are inclined to agree with him. Note that even at this early age, the bird is depicted with two protuberances on top of its head, instead of just one. These are the only examples of this species in art known to us. During the Dynastic Period the Helmeted Guineafowl appears only as a standard hieroglyphic sign.

The wild Helmeted Guineafowl has never been reported in modern Egypt. At one time the bird had a large distribution across North Africa.[464] As recently as two hundred years ago,[465] they were apparently still plentiful in some areas, but are nowadays extremely rare, and are confined to a small population in Morocco. The reasons for its disappearance from most of North Africa, including Egypt, have yet to be elucidated. Because of the lack of exact representations, the Helmeted Guineafowl may never have been common in ancient Egypt. Some support for this may perhaps be found in the fact that the species was sufficiently rare to be carried in cages **during Ptolemy II's great pageant.**[466]

Fig. 117. Fragment of the slate Battlefield Palette showing a Helmeted Guineafowl, from Abydos(?). Late Predynastic Period.

42. Common Crane (*Grus grus*)

Identification: The customary proportions, the long pointed bill, the very long neck and legs, and the diagnostic elongated bushy secondary feathers which droop over the tail are features of a Common Crane.

Distribution: The bird breeds in parts of Europe, Asia, and the Middle East. It winters in parts of southern Europe and Asia, the Middle East, and Africa north of the equator. In modern Egypt, the Common Crane is a winter visitor in the Nile Valley (along Lake Nasser) and northern Delta. However, migrating Common Cranes pass through the Nile Valley and Delta, the Faiyum, along the Red Sea coast, in the vicinity of the Suez Canal, and in the Dakhla, Kharga and Siwa Oases during the spring and fall.

Comments: The Common Crane is abundantly represented in Egyptian art. This picture (fig. 118) is part of a scene on a block of relief from

Fig. 118. *Relief of a man force-feeding a Common Crane, from Saqqara. Dynasty V.*

a Dynasty V mastaba at Saqqara which illustrates the activities of a poultry yard.[467] It shows an attendant of the yard inside an aviary, facing left and standing between two lotus bud columns, where he is in the process of cramming a Common Crane by hand. He is wearing a short kilt and a curled wig. Behind him to the left is a pair of Common Cranes roosting in a very lifelike manner on the ground, with their long legs folded beneath them. In the upper left hand corner there is part of a goose, which is resting on a perch. The man is depicted with his legs planted wide apart, and he is straddling the crane's back, so as to steady the struggling bird. He firmly grasps its long neck with his left hand, while with the right he has turned the bird's head around, and has managed to pry open its bill. In his thumb and index fingers he is holding a piece of food, which he has obtained from a bowl set on the ground in front of him, and is about to forcibly feed the bird by thrusting the food down its gullet. This task was not without its bodily risks, regardless of how tame the

Fig. 119. *A troop of six Common Cranes, from the mastaba of Kaemrehu (No. 79), Saqqara. Dynasty V.*

crane may have been, as this large bird could easily strike out with its strongly pointed bill and cause serious injury to the attendant if he was not careful. By force-feeding it, the Common Crane was certain to provide a plump and succulent dish for the table. This method of fattening is frequently represented, and was used on a variety of farm animals, including such birds as ducks, geese and doves. Cranes are occasionally figured in scenes being fed in this way (see below). The carving of this relief is of a high order, and it well conveys the elegant appearance of this long-legged bird. The artist has shown in a naturalistic fashion the greatly elongated and bushy secondary feathers which droop down and cover the tail. The general proportions of the species have also been correctly observed, that is all except for the bill, which is much too long, and looks more like the bill of a stork. This is true of a great many portrayals of cranes in Egyptian art, where the bills are rendered a good deal longer than that of the living bird (see fig. 122).

Cranes can first be recognized during Dynasty I. But it is not until Dynasty IV that the Common Crane can be specifically identified, and at this time they already appear in a domestic state. A charming example of the species occurs in a scene on a fragment from the Dynasty IV mastaba of Atet at Meidum, now in the Ny Carlsberg Glyptothek, Copenhagen, which shows one of Atet's sons playing with his pets, two monkeys and a Common Crane.[468] The species is frequently rendered in captivity in large troops,[469] which are sometimes tended by keepers that brandish long sticks. This is beautifully illustrated by a scene in the Dynasty V mastaba of Kaemrehu (No. 79) from Saqqara. Here a small flock of six individuals (fig. 119) is shown under the charge of two men who direct the group's movements by touching their legs with long sticks. The artist has pictured the troop in a most realistic fashion. However, the number of legs depicted is insufficient for the number of Common Cranes pictured. The birds seem remarkably well behaved, and there apparently was little concern of them taking to the wing. Perhaps their wings had been pinioned.

The Egyptians portrayed two species of crane in art,[470] the Common Crane and the Demoiselle Crane (*Anthropoides virgo*), see bird No. 43. Usually the flocks of cranes which appear are mixed (fig. 124), consisting of both species, but the Common Crane always far out-

Fig. 120. Offering of a Common Crane, from the mortuary temple of Queen Hatshepsut, Deir el-Bahari. Dynasty XVIII.

numbers the Demoiselle Crane in these troops. There are many scenes, particularly on walls of Old Kingdom tombs, featuring cranes in aviaries and poultry yards,[471] where they are feeding on grain distributed by attendants, and like in our fig. 118 are occasionally being force-fed. Common Cranes are often represented in bearers' arms in processions on tomb (fig. 123) and temple walls, bringing the birds as food offerings.[472] They are also depicted in the great piles of offerings after having been dispatched (fig. 120). Although Common Cranes have been known to breed successfully in captivity,[473] and the Egyptian aviculturalists may have experienced some breeding with them too,[474] it seems more likely to us that the cranes used to stock the aviaries were trapped in the wild while the birds were on their migrations.[475] An almost unique scene in the Dynasty VI mastaba of Mehu at Saqqara illustrates fowlers at work trapping a flock of cranes with a clap-net in the swamplands (fig. 121). Caught in the meshes of the net are two Common and two Demoiselle Cranes. The fowlers employed four decoy birds for the trapping, two *Ardea* herons (see bird No. 7), and two cranes, one Common and one Demoiselle. After being kept for a time, these wild birds would have become tame and manageable. It must be mentioned that there is one further example of crane trapping. A gaming disk from the Dynasty I tomb of Hemaka (S 3035) at Saqqara, now in the

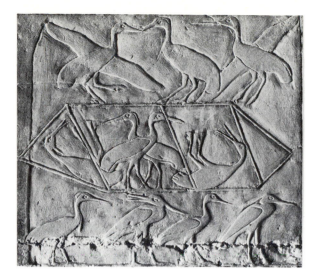

Fig. 121. Relief showing the trapping of cranes with a clap-net, from the mastaba of Mehu, Saqqara. Dynasty VI.

Egyptian Museum, Cairo, is decorated with a clap-net which has two long-legged birds in the middle of it.[476] There can be little doubt that these birds are meant to represent cranes.[477] These are the only instances known to us from Egyptian art where cranes are shown in anything but a domestic state. Crane was an extremely popular dish in ancient Egypt, and while it has a long history of being enjoyed in other cultures as well,[478] crane flesh today is generally regarded as unfit for human consumption.[479] However, it has been reported that if cranes are allowed to feed on grain for a while, they will lose their coarse flavor and then are quite delicious.[480] This is precisely what we see pictured in the Egyptian aviaries. The cranes were fed grain to fatten them, while at the same time it improved their taste. The long tradition of keeping cranes in Egypt has not survived into the modern era. It has been said, however, that Bedouins living in the Western Desert in the vicinity of Burg el-Arab sometimes eat crane (species not known). It is roasted and is supposedly highly regarded.[481]

43. Demoiselle Crane (*Anthropoides virgo*)

Fig. 122. Painted limestone relief of a Demoiselle Crane walking between two bearers, from the mortuary temple of Queen Hatshepsut, Deir el-Bahari. Dynasty XVIII.

Identification: The long neck and legs, the crest on the back of the head (ear-tuft), the elongated breast feathers, and the elongated secondary feathers which hang down and cover the tail are features of a Demoiselle Crane.

Distribution: The bird breeds in parts of eastern Europe, Asia, Turkey, and Morocco.[482] It winters in parts of southern Asia, and central Africa. In modern Egypt, the Demoiselle Crane is a migrant in the Nile Valley and Delta, and in the Dakhla and Kharga Oases.

Comments: Demoiselle Cranes are commonly figured in Egyptian art. From a scene in the Dynasty XVIII mortuary temple of Hatshepsut at Deir el-Bahari which depicts processions of bearers presenting offerings to the queen,[483] this picture (fig. 122) shows two of the offering bearers. Carved in relief and painted, the men are walking toward the right, and are wearing short kilts and curled wigs. The bearer on the left is carrying in his outstretched arms a tray which is heaped high with food offerings of vegetables and fruits, and includes a lettuce, figs, grapes, and squashes or gourds. The bearer on the right is carrying in his right hand what is probably a sealed beer jar with the stem of a lotus bud wrapped around it. Between the two men is a handsome Demoiselle Crane, which is walking in a very orderly fashion. Those familiar with this attractive species of crane will immediately notice that the bill on this representation is far too long in comparison with that of the living bird. We have

Fig. 123. Relief of an offering bringer with a White Oryx, and carrying a crane that has its bill securely tied to its neck, from the tomb of Paatenemhab, Saqqara. Dynasty XVIII.

Fig. 124. A flock of Demoiselle and Common Cranes, from the mastaba of Ti (No.60), Saqqara. Dynasty V.

87

Fig. 125. An offering of a Demoiselle Crane for the deceased, from the mastaba of Mereruka, Saqqara. Dynasty VI.

center of gravity in order to become airborne, and with the bill tied down in this way, the crane would not have been able to obtain the correct balance for take-off. The species' elongated breast feathers are well displayed on the bird, though the crest on the head should spring out from behind the eye, rather than from the occiput. The elongated secondary feathers which hang over the tail are too bushy, and seem more like those of the Common Crane.

The earliest representations known to us of the Demoiselle Crane are from Dynasty V. This species of crane is much less common in Egyptian art than the Common Crane. Like the Common Crane, the Demoiselle Crane was also domesticated. They can regularly be observed being kept along with them in aviaries, being trapped with them in a clap-net (fig. 121), and herded with them in large troops. We know of no better instance of a mixed flock of cranes than the magnificent relief example in the Dynasty V mastaba of Ti (No. 60) at Saqqara (fig. 124). A troop of fourteen cranes, only three of which are Demoiselle Cranes, are being tended by keepers wielding long sticks. These large overlapping birds, some facing toward the right, others to the left, and the three Demoiselle Cranes standing out from the rest, makes for both an attractive and busy scene. Note that the artist has omitted legs for some of the birds. The smaller number of the Demoiselle Cranes is typical of their minority status in relation to the Common Crane in these types of composition. Demoiselle Cranes are only occasionally depicted being carried by offering bearers (fig. 125) in processions on tomb and temple walls.[486] See under bird No. 42 for more on cranes.

already noted that Egyptian artists frequently rendered the bills of cranes unrealistically large (see under bird no. 42), but here, this abnormality has been taken to an extreme. A Demoiselle Crane has a fine and short bill. The bill on this portrayal is over twice the length it should be, and as a consequence looks very much like the bill of a stork. The bill is shown tied with a cord(?) to the lower portion of the bird's neck.[484] Cranes are sometimes depicted with their bills restrained in this manner (fig. 123), and the reasons for its being tied like this were probably twofold. First, it prevented the crane from lashing out with its pointed bill, which could cause injury. Secondly, it hindered the bird's ability to fly.[485] Cranes need to be able to throw out their necks to shift their

---

44. Purple Gallinule (*Porphyrio porphyrio*)

Identification: The characteristic stance, the long leg and toes, and the diagnostic massive bill are features of a Purple Gallinule.

Distribution: The bird breeds and winters in parts of southern Europe, the Middle East, and Africa. In modern Egypt, the Purple Gallinule is a permanent breeding resident in the Nile Delta.[487]

Comments: Purple Gallinules are frequently represented in Egyptian art. Executed in relief, this portrait of a Purple Gallinule (fig. 126) appears on a block from the Dynasty V mortuary temple of Userkaf at Saqqara, which illustrates a group of birds inhabiting a papyrus swamp.[488] A stock figure of swamp scenes, particularly during the Old Kingdom (see below), this Purple Gallinule is certainly one of the more lifelike examples of the species to have come down to us. Facing toward the left, and with its right leg placed forward, the bird is pictured ambling high on top of the delicate papyrus umbels. The bird is in an environment in which it would be very much at home, as the Purple Gallinule is a wetlands dweller and often haunts swamps. Sadly, the bird's left leg and hind region are missing from the block. The bird is depicted with its head angled upward and its large stout bill open, as if it were crying out with its loud hoarse trumpetlike call. Though damaged, and with no pigment preserved, this is a highly convincing image of a Purple Gallinule.

The first time we meet the Purple Gallinule in Egyptian art is during Dynasty IV. For example, a fragment from the Dynasty IV mastaba of Atet at Meidum, now in the Ashmolean Museum, Oxford, bears unmistakably the outline of a Purple Gallinule roosting on a stem in a papyrus swamp.[489] This species was one of the standard types that the Egyptian artists chose to include as part of the wildlife of the swamplands, and there are a number of fine representations of them. This is especially true in Old Kingdom times, when Purple Gallinules are repeatedly depicted in scenes perched amid the dense papyrus vegetation.[490] Typical is a swamp scene in the Dynasty IV tomb of Nebemakhet (LG 86) at Giza, where a pair of Purple Gallinules is walking on top of papyrus umbels,[491] just like the bird we exhibit here. In the Dynasty V mastaba of Niankhkhnum and Khnumhotep at Saqqara, there are two scenes showing Niankhkhnum fowling with throwsticks in the swamplands. In both instances he is followed by attendants who are holding his spare throwsticks and are bringing the birds that he has already felled.[492] In both scenes the bag includes Purple Gallinules, which are being carried by their wings, allowing their long legs to dangle down. Whether the birds were intended for the table cannot be said for certain, but it seems likely. Further evidence to suggest that the bird was consumed

Fig. 126. Purple Gallinule depicted on a block of relief, from the mortuary temple of Userkaf, Saqqara. Dynasty V.

Fig. 127. Purple Gallinule from the collection of birds in the tomb of Baket III (No. 15), Beni Hasan. Dynasty XI.

89

in ancient Egypt comes from the Dynasty VI tomb of Zauw at Deir el-Gebrawi. Here four fowlers are depicted trapping birds with a clapnet on a pond.[493] In the net there is a Purple Gallinule, while near the net are the birds which have already been taken, and one of them is unmistakably a Purple Gallinule. This species is nowadays thought to provide a rather poor meal, since its flesh has a strong fishy flavor to it, but it is not totally unpalatable.[494] Purple Gallinules are still consumed today in modern Egypt, and they can sometimes be found in the bird markets.[495] In the collection of birds painted in the Dynasty XI tomb of Baket III (No. 15) at Beni Hasan, see under bird No. 9, there is a representation of a Purple Gallinule (fig. 127). Although the figure is not an especially accomplished one, it does retain much of its coloring.[496] The back and wing are painted dark green, while the head, breast, underside and tail are in blue, and the bill, eye, legs and feet are red. This perfectly fits the coloring of the Egyptian race of the Purple Gallinule.[497]

45. European Coot (*Fulica atra*)

Identification: The somewhat rotund body, the entirely black body plumage, the short tail, the dark legs (only traces of the paint are extant), and the diagnostic short, light colored bill are features of a European Coot.

Fig. 128. European Coot from the collection of birds in the tomb of Baket III (No. 15), Beni Hasan. Dynasty XI.

Distribution: The bird breeds in parts of Europe, Asia, the Middle East, and North Africa. It winters in parts of Europe, Asia, the Middle East, and Africa north of the equator. In modern Egypt, the European Coot is a breeding resident in the Nile Valley and Delta, and the Dakhla Oasis. It commonly winters throughout the Nile Valley and Delta.

Comments: The European Coot is rarely represented in ancient Egyptian art. Shown at rest, and facing toward the right with its left leg in advance of the right, this picture of a European Coot (fig. 128) appears in the collection of birds painted in the Dynasty XI tomb of Baket III (No. 15) at Beni Hasan, see under bird No. 9. Although it is poorly preserved, the features of the coot are recognizable at once. There is no trace of pigment on the bird's bill, and it may never have been painted, but was left the color of the ground of the wall to suggest the species' white bill. Coot are the only completely black waterfowl with a conspicuous white bill occurring in the area, so there can be little real doubt as to the bird's identity. The shape of the body has been well enough observed, but note that the artist has given the coot a tiny spur on the back of each leg, a feature not present in the living bird. This same abnormality is repeatedly met with on other birds depicted in Baket III's tomb.

The earliest example of a European Coot known to us is from Dynasty XI.[498] Another instance of the species from this date comes from a model discovered in the tomb of Meketre (No. 280) at Thebes, now in the Metropolitan Museum of Art, New York.[499] A figure of a fowler on a wooden model of a boat is shown bringing to the seated Meketre what Winlock described as "a bunch of coots tied together by their legs."[500] There can be little doubt that he was correct. There are at least two scenes in Egyptian art which illustrate coots being trapped by fowlers using clap-nets in the swamplands. One example is in the Dynasty XVIII tomb of Nakht (No. 52) at

Fig. 129. Wall painting showing the trapping of European Coots and other waterfowl with a clap-net, from the tomb of Haremhab (No. 78), Thebes. Dynasty XVIII.

Thebes,[501] the other in the Dynasty XVIII tomb of Haremhab (No. 78) at Thebes. In the latter case (fig. 129) the scene is now damaged,[502] but originally a flock of seven European Coots was shown being netted along with various other waterfowl. Their plumage is painted wholly black, and the artist has even included the species' white frontal shield on them, a detail which is absent from the example in the tomb of Baket III, and clinches the identification of the flock. It is clear from these occurrences of the bird that it was regarded as a potential food item. As a table dish the European Coot is reported to be quite poor,[503] but its flesh is edible, and the bird is still eaten today in Egypt. They appear quite often in the bird markets.[504]

---

46. Painted Snipe (*Rostratula benghalensis*)

Identification: The long bill (only the slightest traces of it are now extant), the short tail, the completely white underside, the dark back and wing, and the distinctive white "shoulder stripe" are features of a Painted Snipe.

Distribution: The bird breeds and winters in parts of Asia and Africa. In modern Egypt, the Painted Snipe is a breeding resident in the Nile Delta, and the Faiyum.[505]

Comments: This is the only example of a Painted Snipe (fig. 130) that we have been able to identify from Egyptian art and hieroglyphs. So damaged that it contains only enough of the bird to make the identification certain, this representation of a Painted Snipe appears in the collection of birds painted in the Dynasty XI tomb of Baket III (No. 15) at Beni Hasan, see under bird No. 9. Pictured facing toward the right, the bird is shown standing at rest with its left leg placed forward. Almost all of the long slender bill and a good deal of the bird's head have been destroyed, but the species' striking plumage pattern is clearly recognizable, allowing for an easy and accurate identification.[506] When this figure is viewed in color,[507] the bird's back, wing, the lower two-thirds of the legs, and the feet are painted light green. The underside, and the "shoulder stripe" are white, while the head, neck, upper breast, and the upper portion of the legs are pinkish. This strongly suggests the brightly colored plumage of a living female Painted Snipe. Of interesting detail, attention should be drawn to the hind toes on the feet (the toe on the left foot is barely visible), which are rendered more or less as they are in nature.

Fig. 130. Painted Snipe from the collection of birds in the tomb of Baket III (No. 15), Beni Hasan. Dynasty XI.

47. Ringed Plover or Little Ringed Plover
(*Charadrius hiaticula* and *C. dubius*)

Identification: The short neck and bill, the completely white collar and underside, the dark crown, back and wing, and the diagnostic bold black facial mask and breast band are features of an adult ringed plover.

Distribution: The Ringed Plover breeds in parts of Europe and Asia. It winters in parts of southern Europe and Asia, the Middle East, and Africa. In modern Egypt, the Ringed Plover is a winter visitor in the Nile Valley and Delta, the Faiyum, and along the Red Sea coast. The Little Ringed Plover breeds in parts of Europe, Asia, the Middle East, and North Africa. It winters in parts of southern Europe, Asia, the Middle East, and Africa north of the equator. In modern Egypt, the Little Ringed Plover is a breeding resident in the Nile Delta, and the Faiyum. It winters in the Nile Valley and Delta, the Faiyum, along the Red Sea coast, and the Dakhla Oasis.

Comments: This is the only representation of a ringed plover (fig. 131) that we have been able to identify from Egyptian art and hieroglyphs. Executed facing toward the right, and shown in an attitude of repose, this portrayal of a ringed plover appears in the collection of birds in the Dynasty XI tomb of Baket III (No. 15) at Beni Hasan, see under bird No. 9. The picture has not fared particularly well with time, but there is no problem in our distinguishing it as a ringed plover, as the characteristic black facial mask and breast band are clearly visible. It is not possible to determine accurately whether it is one or the other species of ringed plover,[508] as the differences between the two are slight. In its own way this painting is both a careful and attractive rendering of this shore bird.

Fig. 131. Ringed Plover or Little Ringed Plover from the collection of birds in the tomb of Baket III (No. 15), Beni Hasan. Dynasty XI.

48. Lapwing (*Vanellus vanellus*)

Identification: The characteristic proportions, the short pointed bill, the rounded head, the squared tail, and the diagnostic long wispy crest on the head are features of an adult Lapwing.

Distribution: The bird breeds in parts of Europe, northern Asia, the Middle East, and Morocco. It winters in parts of Europe, southern Asia, the Middle East, and North Africa. In modern Egypt, the Lapwing is a winter visitor in the Nile Valley and Delta, the Faiyum, along the Mediterranean Sea coast west of Alexandria, in the vicinity of the Suez Canal, and the Dakhla and Siwa Oases.[509]

Comments: Lapwings are abundantly represented in both Egyptian art and hieroglyphs.[510] Carved in crisp relief, this charming picture (fig. 132) is from a scene in the Dynasty V tomb of Nefer at Saqqara which displays the

Fig. 132. Relief of young girl holding a Lapwing, from the tomb of Nefer, Saqqara. Dynasty V.

93

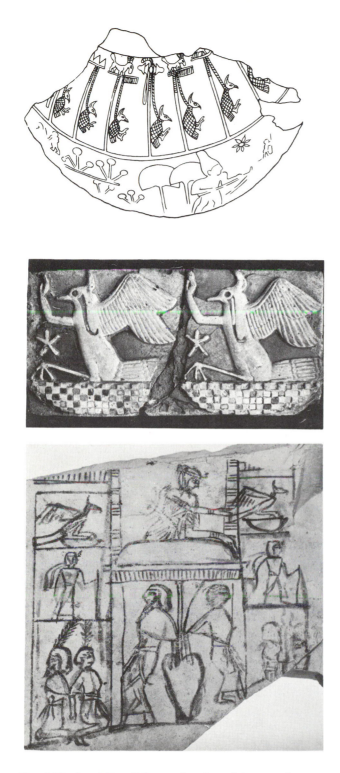

Fig. 133. (top) Detail from a drawing of the carved mace-head of King "Scorpion" showing the nomes capture of the Lapwings, from Hierakonpolis. Late Predynastic Period.

Fig. 134. (center) Inlaid faience tile with design of Lapwings, from the palace of Ramesses III, Medinet Habu. Dynasty XX.

Fig. 135. (bottom) Ostracon with a drawing of a king standing at the "window of appearance", which is decorated with a motif of Lapwings. Ramesside Period.

deceased tomb owner with his pet dog and young daughter, who is shown here, facing toward the right and viewing the activities of fishermen, herdsmen and fowlers on his estates.[511] The child has been reduced to a much smaller scale than her father, whose staff, kilt and left leg are partly visible in our illustration. The girl is naked. She is wearing a broad collar which is fringed with a row of drop-shaped beads, and a pendant which is suspended by straps. On her right wrist there is one or more bracelets. She wears her hair neatly braided into a long lock (a symbol of childhood), which falls past the shoulder. Her left arm is raised, holding a lotus blossom up to her nose, and she is sniffing its pleasant fragrance. The long stem of the flower is coiled around her hand. In her right hand, she clutches a Lapwing by its wings. The bird's form has been splendidly captured, and this is especially true of the long, thin erectile crest on its head, a diagnostic feature of the species. The manner in which she handles the bird, letting it dangle by the wings, is a method of carrying birds which is still routinely seen in villages in Egypt today. The plover was in all likelihood the girl's pet or plaything. Lapwings were apparently only rarely kept as pets in ancient Egypt.[512] However, there are numerous representations of children, similarly unclothed and close to their parents' side, also carrying their pet birds. The perky Hoopoe (*Upupa epops*) was seemingly by far the great favorite of the children, see under bird No. 62 and fig. 171. While there are many other Lapwing portraits with more detail and painted plumage features, this delightful picture of Nefer's daughter with her Lapwing ranks in this writer's eyes as one of the most memorable examples of the species in all of Egyptian art.

The Lapwing can first be identified during the Late Predynastic Period. An outstanding example from this era appears on a fragment of a slate palette, now in the Egyptian Museum, Cairo.[513] The bird is pictured above the deck of a ship, and there can be no mistaking what bird was intended here. This is similarly the case on the famous limestone ceremonial mace-head of King "Scorpion" from Hierakonpolis, which also dates from Late Predynastic times. A scene on it shows a row of standards with bows and Lapwings hanging from them by their necks (fig. 133). These have been interpreted as symbolizing the king's sovereignty over foreigners and part of the Egyptian people.[514] As a standard hieroglyphic sign the Lapwing signifies "common people" (*rekhyt*). During the New Kingdom human arms and hands upraised in an attitude of worship were added to the fronts of the birds. They frequently appear squatting on top of the hieroglyphic sign for "all" (*neb*) and with a five-pointed star "adore" (*dwa*) in front of it (fig. 134). Together they form a kind of monogram meaning "all the people in adoration" before the king.[515] It is in combination with the *neb*-sign and *dwa*-star that we most often meet with the Lapwing in Egyptian art. This device was an extremely popular motif. Friezes of them were used to decorate, among a great many things, the bases of statues and sphinxes,[516] the daises on which the king is pictured,[517] the king's footrest,[518] the base of columns, and very frequently on the jambs of doorways and windows.[519] From a doorway in the Dynasty XX palace of Ramesses III at Medinet Habu comes this fine polychrome inlaid faience tile (fig. 134) with two *rekhyt*-birds on it. Although the shape of the Lapwing has been vastly

conventionalized, their identification can be made with complete certainty. How this motif fits into the decorative program of the doorway is conveniently suggested by a drawing of the "window of appearance" on a Ramesside Period limestone ostracon (fig. 135). The Lapwings are depicted on the jambs flanking the window and occupying the uppermost register.

Fig. 136. (top) Lapwing from a swamp scene in the tomb of Montuemhet (No. 34), Thebes. Dynasty XXV-XXVI.
Fig. 137. (bottom) Painting of a Lapwing in flight above a papyrus thicket, from the tomb of Amenemhet (No. 82), Thebes. Dynasty XVIII.

Whenever Lapwings are figured in this motif they are invariably pictured with their wings twisted round one another. This had the effect of making them incapable of either walking or flying.[520] It also served to give the idea of utter helplessness before the king.

The Lapwing was also a stock item of scenes displaying a papyrus swamp. From Dynasty IV onward,[521] Lapwings appear roosting amid the stems and umbels (fig. 136) or more regularly winging above it (fig. 137) in scenes which illustrate the traditional hunting in the swamplands theme.

---

49. Spur-winged Plover (*Vanellus spinosus*)

Fig. 138. (top) Spur-winged Plover from the collection of birds in the tomb of Baket III (No. 15), Beni Hasan. Dynasty XI.

Fig. 139. (bottom) Relief of a Spur-winged Plover frequenting a papyrus swamp, from the mastaba of Ti (No. 60), Saqqara. Dynasty V.

Identification: The distinctive proportions, the black crown, crest, throat, breast, tail, bill, legs and feet, the dark back and wing, and the white cheek, side of the neck and underside are features of an adult Spur-winged Plover.

Distribution: The bird breeds and winters in parts of Greece, Crete, the Middle East, and Africa north of the equator. In modern Egypt, the Spur-winged Plover is a breeding resident in the Nile Valley and Delta, and the Faiyum.

Comments: The Spur-winged Plover is extremely rare in Egyptian art. This portrait (fig. 138) appears in the collection of birds painted in the Dynasty XI tomb of Baket III (No. 15) at Beni Hasan, see under bird No. 9. The bird is depicted at rest and facing toward the right, with its left leg placed in advance of its right. The painting is wonderfully true to nature. In both form and coloring, it is most lifelike. When viewed in color,[522] the back and wing are painted a pinkish-brown hue and the eye is red, which certainly adds to the figure's realism. The careful attention to details, such as the shape of the head and bill, and the faint indication of a short crest on the back of the head,[523] gives us a vivid picture of this plover. The cheek, side of the neck and underside of the figure seem to have been left unpainted so as to suggest by the color of the ground of the wall the species' white plumage parts. There is no trace of the spur on its wing to which the bird's name refers. As with a great many other birds pictured in this collection, the artist has given this Spur-winged Plover a tiny hind spur on each leg, a wholly fictitious feature.[524]

The first time we meet with the Spur-winged Plover in Egyptian art is during Dynasty V. In the mastaba of Ti (No. 60) at Saqqara, three Spur-winged Plovers are represented inhabiting a papyrus swamp.[525] Two of the birds are roosting on umbels (fig. 139), while the third is shown on its clutch of eggs. Although pigment is no longer extant on them, the species' outline and features are precisely captured in the relief. The Spur-winged Plover is one of the more common birds in Egypt,[526] and while we might have expected it to be figured more often in art, these are the only positive examples known to us. However, there are other renderings which appear to show the Spur-winged Plover,[527] but their details are insufficient for certain identification.

Some believe the Spur-winged Plover to be the bird which Herodotus said performed a service for Crocodiles (*Crocodilus niloticus*) in Egypt by entering their gaping mouths while they basked on shore eating the "leeches" from inside their jaws.[528] The identification of the Trochilus with the Spur-winged Plover cannot be made with certainty. Others have suggested that it may have been the Egyptian Plover (*Pluvianus aegyptius*).[529] Since there is evidence for both species of bird actually picking crocodiles' teeth, the Trochilus may cover them both.

---

50. Sandpiper (*Tringa* sp.)

Identification: The highly distinctive posture, the rather long, slender straight bill, the short tail, and the comparatively long neck and legs are features of a sandpiper belonging to the genus *Tringa*.

Distribution: There are seven species of *Tringa* sandpipers that have been reported in modern

Egypt. The Spotted Redshank (*T. erythropus*) is a winter visitor in the Nile Delta, the Faiyum, and the Dakhla Oasis. The Redshank (*T. totanus*) is a winter visitor in the Nile Valley and Delta, the Faiyum, along the Red Sea coast, in the vicinity of the Suez Canal, and the Dakhla Oasis. The Marsh Sandpiper (*T. stagnatilis*), the Green Sandpiper (*T. ochropus*),

Fig. 140. Sandpiper roosting on a papyrus umbel, from the mastaba of Ti (No. 60), Saqqara. Dynasty V.

Fig. 141. *Sandpiper from the "Botanical Garden" in the Festival Hall of Tuthmosis III, Karnak. Dynasty XVIII.*

and the Wood Sandpiper (*T. glareola*) are winter visitors in the Nile Valley and Delta, the Faiyum, in the vicinity of the Suez Canal, and the Dakhla Oasis. The Greenshank (*T. nebularia*) is a winter visitor in the Nile Valley and Delta, the Faiyum, in the vicinity of the Suez Canal, and the Dakhla Oasis. The Common Sandpiper (*T. hypoleucos*) is a winter visitor in the Nile Valley and Delta, the Faiyum and the Dakhla Oasis.

Comments: Sandpipers are quite rare in Egyptian art. Executed in relief, this elegant

sandpiper (fig. 140) appears amongst the great variety of bird life pictured in the magnificent swampland scene in the Dynasty V mastaba of Ti (No. 60) at Saqqara. It is shown just beneath the uppermost row of papyrus umbels, roosting on top of a blossom.[530] Facing toward the right, it is depicted with its tail partly open, revealing a notched terminal edge. The bird's features have been well carved, and they are decidedly those of a *Tringa* sandpiper. The sandpiper is joined elsewhere in the same composition by another of its kind,[531] and the pair have been placed into an environment in which some members of this genus are known to frequent. The absence of extant pigment and plumage pattern prevents us from identifying this example, or the other figure in the scene, to the species level.

It is during Dynasty V that sandpipers can first be recognized in Egyptian art. Another notable example of a sandpiper occurs in a scene from the Dynasty V mastaba of Hetep-herakhti (D 60) at Saqqara, now in the Rijksmuseum van Oudheden, Leiden. Here the bird is rendered high amid the stems and umbels of a dense papyrus thicket, where it has adopted the posture so typical of some *Tringa* sandpipers, and is ambling across the blossoms toward the right.[532] At the "Botanical Garden" in the Dynasty XVIII Festival Hall of Tuthmosis III at Karnak (see under bird No. 2), there is a bird which has the general profile and appearance of what can only be a *Tringa* sandpiper (fig. 141).

51. Avocet (*Recurvirostra avosetta*)

Identification: The distinctive proportions, the striking black and white plumage pattern, and the diagnostic long, thin upcurved bill are the unmistakable features of an Avocet.

Distribution: The bird breeds and winters in parts of Europe, Asia, the Middle East, and Africa. In modern Egypt, the Avocet is a breeding resident in the Nile Delta, and the Faiyum.[533] It winters in the Nile Delta, and in the vicinity of the Suez Canal.[534]

Fig. 142. *Avocet from the collection of birds in the tomb of Baket III (No. 15), Beni Hasan. Dynasty XI.*

Comments: Avocets are fairly rare in Egyptian art. This picture of an Avocet (fig. 142) appears in the collection of birds from the Dynasty XI tomb of Baket III (No. 15) at Beni Hasan, see under bird No. 9. Facing toward the right, the bird is shown in an attitude of repose, with its left leg placed forward. Sadly, the portrait has suffered, to the degree where even the species' characteristic upcurved bill is today rather difficult to make out. The artist has done a remarkable job of depicting the different areas of the Avocet's black and white plumage, and it looks very much as it does in nature. It is uncertain whether the crown of the bird, like the back of its neck, was ever painted black or not. The white portion of the bird's plumage was apparently not painted, but was allowed to remain the light color of the ground of the wall to suggest these areas. When the figure is viewed in color,[535] the legs and feet are painted green, which is an error, as on the living bird these bare parts are a bluish-grey. This painting is a simple yet skilled representation of an Avocet.

The first time we meet with this graceful wader in Egyptian art is in the Dynasty V mastaba of Ti (No. 60) at Saqqara (fig. 143). In a scene which illustrates a papyrus swamp teeming with wild life, two Avocets are rendered having alighted upon the tops of umbels.[536] The species' form, particularly the diagnostic upcurved bill, has been correctly indicated in the relief. They are pictured in a type of habitat in which they would be right at

Fig. 143. Relief of an Avocet in a swamp scene, from the mastaba of Ti (No. 60). Saqqara. Dynasty V.

home. The only other sure example of this species known to us appears in the Dynasty XII tomb of Djehutyhotep (No. 2) at El-Bersheh. Here there are two scenes which show Avocets as part of the catch of fowlers.[537] In one of these (fig. 144) a man is depicted inside a kiosk with crates holding waterfowl, and hanging from the roof-pole of the structure is a cluster of fourteen Avocets. The birds are still alive and they seem to be bobbing their heads as they dangle by their tied wings. This group of Avocets would probably have been eviscerated and prepared as a dish for the table of the

Fig. 144. Drawing of a painting showing a bunch of Avocets hanging in a fowler's hut, from the tomb of Djehutyhotep (No. 2), El-Bersheh. Dynasty XII.

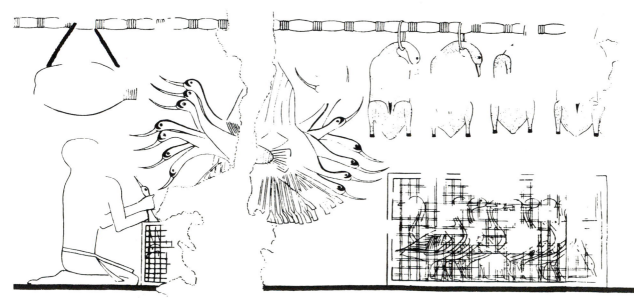

deceased tomb owner. Elsewhere in the same tomb comes a fine portrayal of an Avocet standing along the edge of a pond near a fowlers' clap-net.[538] In modern Egypt, Avocets are still regularly eaten,[539] even though their flesh is said to have a pungent fishy flavor.[540] We have seen them for sale in the bird markets of Cairo. They were plucked and thoroughly dressed, their long black upturned bills being the single clue for identification.

---

52. Pin-tailed Sandgrouse (*Pterocles alchata*)

Fig. 145. Pin-tailed Sandgrouse from the collection of birds in the tomb of Baket III (No. 15), Beni Hasan. Dynasty XI.

Identification: The rather thickset body, the short neck and legs, and the diagnostic broad dark breast band are features of a male Pin-tailed Sandgrouse.

Distribution: The bird breeds and winters in parts of southern Europe and Asia, the Middle East, and North Africa. In modern Egypt, the Pin-tailed Sandgrouse is thought to be an accidental visitor.[541]

Comments: This is the only representation of a Pin-tailed Sandgrouse (fig. 145) that we have been able to identify from Egyptian art and hieroglyphs. It appears amongst the collection of birds painted in the Dynasty XI tomb of Baket III (No. 15) at Beni Hasan, see under bird No. 9. The picture is poorly preserved, but enough of the bird is extant for us to recognize it as a Pin-tailed Sandgrouse.[542] The bird is uncolored except for the red breast band,[543] just like it is on the living male. This band, however, should not fully extend across the back as it does here. There is no trace of the long pinlike tail feathers to which the species' vernacular name refers. The bill is greatly damaged, but it seems too large in comparison with that of the living bird.

53. Rock Pigeon[544] (*Columba livia*)

Identification: The customary stance and proportions, the black bill, the swollen white cere, the rounded head and body, the distinctly marked upper breast and throat collar, and the black barring on the wing are features of a Rock Pigeon.

Distribution: The bird breeds and winters in parts of Europe, Asia, the Middle East, and Africa north of the equator. In modern Egypt, the Rock Pigeon is a permanent breeding resident in the Nile Valley and Delta, the Faiyum, along the Mediterranean Sea coast west of · Alexandria, and the Dakhla and Kharga Oases.

Fig. 146. Painting of a Rock Pigeon in a papyrus swamp, from the North Palace of Akhenaten, El-Amarna. Dynasty XVIII.

Comments: Rock Pigeons are not very commonly represented in Egyptian art. This wonderful portrait of a Rock Pigeon (fig. 146) appears on a fragment of a wall painting from one of the many small chambers, the so-called "green room", which opened on to a large garden court in the North Palace of King Akhenaten at El-Amarna. The walls of this little room were decorated with a scene showing a concourse of bird life inhabiting the lush greenery of a dense papyrus thicket.[545] Although the bird is damaged, its attractiveness is immediately apparent. The pigeon is pictured at repose facing left, with its wing tips turned upward, and long tail drooping. The bill is open, and its long tongue is visible. While we normally do not think of Rock Pigeons frequenting a waterside environment, since they prefer a more arid type of haunt, this example is just one of several fine renderings of them amid the swamp vegetation in this scene. Some of the other birds figured in the "green room" are depicted roosting on the papyrus stems which bend under their weight. This Rock Pigeon, however, is simply suspended in mid-air. The species' form has been carefully observed, and its plumage is executed in a very naturalistic style. When the bird is viewed in color,[546] the head, neck, breast, wing tips, and the tail are painted blue.

Fig. 147. (left) Bearer with an offering of pigeons for Nebseny, from his tomb (No. 108), Thebes. Dynasty XVIII.

Fig. 148. (right) Faience tile with pigeon in flight, from the palace of Ramesses III, Tell el-Yahudiya. Dynasty XX.

Fig. 149. (bottom) Detail of the painted ceiling in the tomb of Raya (No. 159), Thebes, showing a decorative design which includes pigeons. Dynasty XIX.

The underside, wing, and the cere are white. The tongue is red. The bill, and feather markings are black. The iris, and the legs and feet are brownish. The hatching on the neck and upper breast, used to denote the violet-green gloss located in this region on the living bird, is a most successful device. This Rock Pigeon is a masterpiece of Egyptian painting.

There are only a select number of representations in Egyptian art which can confidently be identified as a Rock Pigeon. In a great many instances it is impossible to determine with accuracy whether a figure should be thought of as a pigeon or a dove (see under bird No. 54), due to the absence of specific plumage features. The earliest example of a pigeonlike bird known to us is in the form of a vessel from the Gerzean Period (Naqada II). Fashioned from red breccia, the vase, now in the British Museum, London, is in the shape of a sitting pigeon,[547] and it well conveys the appearance of the bird. In the Dynasty XVIII tomb of Nebseny (No. 108) at Thebes, a scene shows an offering bearer carrying eight pigeons (fig. 147) and presenting them to the deceased. This instance of the species serves to indicate that the bird was regarded as a food item.[548]

Another outstanding depiction of a pigeon appears on a decorative faience tile from the Dynasty XX palace of Ramesses III at Tell el-Yahudiya (fig. 148). The bird is superbly rendered, and it makes for a convincing image of a pigeon on the wing. The blue color of the tile is also suggestive of the coloring of a pigeon. A pattern of pigeons, ducks, and flowers was used to decorate the ceiling of the Dynasty XIX tomb of Raya (No. 159) at Thebes (fig. 149).

The wild Rock Pigeon is the ancestor of our common domestic pigeon,[549] a bird virtually all of us are well acquainted with. Pigeons are still consumed today in modern Egypt, and can be considered as something of a national dish. They are kept in cotes of various sizes and designs which are a common sight of the countryside.[550] Their guano is much valued and is collected and used as a fertilizer in the cultivation of fruit trees and certain kinds of vegetables. Although an earlier date for their appearance has been suggested,[551] the first firm evidence for pigeon cotes in Egypt comes from the Greco-Roman Period.[552] For more on pigeons, see under bird No. 54.

---

54. Turtle Dove (*Streptopelia turtur*)

Identification: The short neck, the rounded head, the narrow black bill, the long tail, the mottled upper wing coverts, and the diagnostic patch of parallel lines on the side of the neck are features of an adult Turtle Dove.

Distribution: The bird breeds in parts of Europe, Asia, the Middle East, and North Africa. It winters in Africa north of the equator. In modern Egypt, the Turtle Dove is a breeding resident in the Nile Valley and Delta, the Faiyum, and the Dakhla, Kharga and Siwa Oases. However, large numbers of migratory Turtle Doves pass through the Nile Valley and Delta, the Faiyum, along the Mediterranean Sea coast west of Alexandria, the general vicinity of the Suez Canal, along the Red Sea coast, and the Dakhla, Kharga and Siwa Oases.

Comments: Turtle Doves are abundantly pictured in Egyptian art. Executed on an inner face of the Dynasty XII cedarwood coffin of Djehutynekht from El-Bersheh, this exquisite portrayal of a Turtle Dove (fig. 150) appears in a scene amid the various offerings of vegetables, waterfowl, cuts of meat, cakes, fruits, flowers, and drink laid before the deceased owner.[553] Facing toward the left, the dove is painted with its wings outstretched, as if it were momentarily about to take to the air. The species' form and salient plumage features are deftly captured in this representation. Care has been taken to put into this figure such naturalistic details as the orbital skin and the mottling on the upper wing coverts, which further enhances its realism. The dove can best be appreciated when it is viewed in color.[554] Both its plumage and bare parts are strikingly like those of the living bird. It must be noted, however, that while the Turtle Dove is depicted with its wings extended upward, the painter has simultaneously shown it with a second left wing which is folded at the side.[555] As a result of this, the upraised wings lack conviction and look

Fig. 150. *Detail of a Turtle Dove amid the offerings painted on the wooden coffin of Djehutynekht, from El-Bersheh. Dynasty XII.*

very much out of place. In spite of this fault, this is a beautiful and accomplished rendering of a Turtle Dove.

The first time that Turtle Doves can positively be identified is during Dynasty V. This species is most often met with in Old Kingdom art. They often appear along with other domestic birds in processions on tomb and temple walls, sometimes labeled with captions giving their respective names or numbers, where they were intended to serve as provisions in the beyond.[556] Typical of this standard scene is an example in the Dynasty V mastaba of Ti (No. 60) at Saqqara (fig. 101), which shows thirteen birds, mainly ducks and geese, in neat rows and under the charge of an attendant. A pair of Turtle Doves appears among them, and although they are without pigment, their conspicuous neck patch makes for instant recognition. Also from the mastaba of Ti comes a very fine group of Turtle Doves (fig. 151). One cannot help but admire the attractive arrangement of these captive doves. In the Dynasty VI mastaba of Mereruka at Saqqara, a scene illustrates Turtle Doves housed in an aviary.[557] A man is pictured cramming one of the doves by hand in order to fatten it for the table. Turtle Doves are easily domesticated and are energetic breeders in captivity,[558] and the Egyptian aviculturalists probably had great success with them. These Turtle Doves are accompanied in the aviary by a number of birds with a very similar appearance, but which quite noticeably lack the characteristic neck stripes. Some writers have

wished to see these birds, and others like them (see below), as pigeons (see bird No. 53), and have stated that the ancient Egyptians kept large numbers of pigeons as they did doves.[559] The identification of these birds as pigeons is, in our view, rather doubtful. They were probably meant to represent another species of dove, one that does not exhibit prominent neck markings, perhaps the Laughing Dove (*S. senegalensis*). Two examples can be cited to support our viewpoint. In the Dynasty VI mastaba of Kaemankh (G 4561) at Giza, two birds which are unmistakably doves are painted in a procession with other poultry.[560] Neither of these handsome birds possesses neck markings. In the mastaba of Mereruka at Saqqara, one of these "pigeons" is displayed nesting in a swamp scene.[561] Although it does not bear a neck patch, clearly indicated in the relief is a distinction on the tail of the prominent white edging belonging to that of a dove. It is our contention then that the Egyptians were familiar with and domesticated two species of dove, the Turtle Dove and another variety without any neck markings, maybe the Laughing Dove, and commonly used one name (*mnwt*) for both. This other kind is frequently shown in the same types of scenes which feature Turtle Doves.[562] How the Egyptians captured doves to stock their aviaries is illustrated by what is almost a unique scene in the Dynasty V mastaba of Neferherptah at Saqqara. Here a huge flock of doves (or pigeons?) is depicted being trapped in a clap-net,[563] and then being placed into cages for

Fig. 151. Relief showing an offering of Turtle Doves for Ti, from his mastaba (No. 60), Saqqara. Dynasty V.

transport. The Turtle Dove can frequently be observed being carried by offering bearers (fig. 152) on tomb and temple walls.[565] The species can also sometimes be seen frequenting papyrus swamps, roosting amid the vegetation or flying above it (fig. 153). Second only to the dove on Djehutynekht's coffin is a superb portrait of a Turtle Dove painted in the Dynasty XII tomb of Khnumhotep III (No. 3) at Beni Hasan (fig. 154), where it is pictured having come to rest on a branch of an acacia tree. Elsewhere in the same tomb, there is a scene showing eleven Turtle Doves being herded along with flocks of ducks and geese.[565] On at least one occasion the Turtle Dove was kept for pleasure. In the mastaba of Ti (No. 60) at Saqqara, Ti's young son is depicted clutching a Turtle Dove by its wings,[566] probably the boy's pet or plaything. Remains of four Turtle Doves were found in the queens' burial chambers in the Dynasty XII pyramid of King Amenemhat III at Dahshur,[567] where they had been placed as food offerings. Turtle Doves are excellent birds for the table,[568] and are said by some to excel pigeon in flavor. They are still consumed today in Egypt, and can sometimes be found in the bird markets.[569]

Fig. 152. Drawing of a relief of a woman bringing gifts for the deceased, including a Turtle Dove, from the mastaba of Ti (No. 60), Saqqara. Dynasty V.

Fig. 153. (bottom) Turtle Dove winging above a papyrus thicket, from the mastaba of Kaemnofret (No. 57), Saqqara. Dynasty V.

Fig. 154. Turtle Dove roosting on a branch of an acacia tree, from the tomb of Khnumhotep III (No. 3), Beni Hasan. Dynasty XII.

55. Great Spotted Cuckoo (*Clamator glandarius*)

Identification: The slender proportions, the short legs, and the diagnostic exceptionally long tail and fully erect crest are features of an adult Great Spotted Cuckoo.

Distribution: The bird breeds in parts of southern Europe, the Middle East, and Africa. It winters in parts of the Middle East, and Africa. In modern Egypt, the Great Spotted Cuckoo is a permanent breeding resident in the Nile Valley.[570]

Comments: This is the only example of a Great Spotted Cuckoo (fig. 155) that we have been able to identify from Egyptian art and hieroglyphs. Carved in relief, this representation appears amid the collection of fauna and flora depicted in the so-called "Botanical Garden" in the Dynasty XVIII Festival Hall of Tuthmosis III at Karnak, see under bird No. 2. Its presence here indicates that the bird was to be thought of as an exotic and not a native species. The cuckoo is shown facing toward the right in an attitude of repose, with one leg placed in advance of the other. The species' long tail and erectile crest are pictured here considerably more pronounced in length than they are in nature, and yet there is no mistaking this for any other bird but the Great Spotted Cuckoo.[571] Based upon present-day distribution, the ancient naturalists would not necessarily have had to journey to Western Asia to obtain or view a Great Spotted Cuckoo, since the bird is today a breeding resident in Egypt. The Great Spotted Cuckoo is parasitic in its breeding habits, in that it lays its eggs in the nests of other kinds of birds. In this way the cuckoo solely relies on the host to incubate its eggs and to raise their brood of young once they have hatched. Throughout the Middle East the principal host species is the Magpie (*Pica pica*),[572] while in Egypt it is the

107

Fig. 155. Great Spotted Cuckoo from the "Botanical Garden" in the Festival Hall of Tuthmosis III, Karnak. Dynasty XVIII.

Hooded Crow (*Corvus corone*).[573] Directly in front of this portrayal of the Great Spotted Cuckoo there is a nest containing two eggs. This is the only instance of a nest pictured in the "Botanical Garden". Could it be that the artist was aware of the Great Spotted Cuckoo's parasitic habits and associated the nest with the bird to express this idea? While nothing can be said with certainty, it seems to us that this is how the nest should be interpreted. Other ancient cultures knew the parasitic ways of the cuckoo,[574] so why not the Egyptians? It may have been a bit of knowledge gathered during Tuthmosis III's Syrian travels. However, it must be remembered that the Egyptians probably need not have looked any further than their own countryside for the Great Spotted Cuckoo and its nesting habits.

56. Barn Owl (*Tyto alba*)

Identification: The upright stance, the large head, the darkish back, wing and crown, the wholly white breast and underside, and the diagnostic heart-shaped facial discs are features of a Barn Owl.

Distribution: The bird breeds and winters in parts of Europe, southern Asia, the Middle East, and Africa. In modern Egypt, the Barn Owl is a permanent breeding resident in the Nile Valley and Delta, the Faiyum, along the Mediterranean Sea coast west of Alexandria, the general vicinity of the Suez Canal, and Dakhla and Kharga Oases.

Fig. 156. Painted relief hieroglyph of a Barn Owl, from the temple of Tuthmosis III, Deir el-Bahari. Dynasty XVIII. (see the frontispiece for this in color).

Comments: The Barn Owl is extremely common as an Egyptian hieroglyph;[575] it is only rarely represented in art. Well cut and faithfully painted, this ornamental hieroglyph of a Barn Owl (fig. 156) is carved on a block from the Dynasty XVIII temple of Tuthmosis III at Deir el-Bahari. The sign survives in a particularly good state of preservation and is a superlative example of a Barn Owl. In Egyptian drawing and painting the human and animal head is as a rule shown in a profile view only. One of the few exceptions to this is the owl. As our illustration shows, the owl's body, right wing and feet are seen from the side, but the head is turned toward us, and is viewed full face, which distinguishes it from all other birds. Its large eyes are wide open and stare ahead with a humanlike appearance, and help to create the owls' legendary concentrated facial expression. It should come as no surprise that the Egyptians chose to picture the owl frontally. When a living owl is alerted to some object or movement, it cannot move its eyes to observe it, since they are fixed in their sockets. As a result, the entire head must move for the bird to shift its gaze, and owls are capable of turning their heads 270°. The Egyptian artists simply captured the owl as they most often viewed it in nature, with the head turned full face and the eyes looking forward. Modern illustrators usually depict owls *en face* as well and nearly all other birds in profile, as this is how they most frequently appear in the field.[576] The Barn Owl has been typified in this relief portrait. The species' distinctive flattened face, with its heart-shaped facial discs,[577] is most admirably defined. The plumage pattern on the wing and back is indicated by the use of cross-hatching, and with neat rows of short black strokes on the light brown plumage to suggest barring. Also, note that a feature of the owl sign is that it does not have a hind toe.[578] On the bird's brow there is a pair of large erect black feather tufts, which we call "ears" (they have absolutely nothing to do with hearing). Although these tufts may seem a genuine morphological feature of a Barn Owl, those familiar with this bird of prey will immediately recognize them to be a spurious detail.[579] Barn Owls do not possess "ears"; they are a feature of the "eared" owl group, see under bird No. 57. When carefully executed, the owl hieroglyph is almost always figured with "ears" (until the Late Dynastic Period, see below), regardless of whether the species of owl

Fig. 157. Detail from a fragment of wall painting showing a Barn Owl nesting in a papyrus swamp, from the tomb of Neferhotep (A. 5), Thebes. Dynasty XVIII.

Fig. 158. Limestone sculptor's model of a head of a Barn Owl. Late Dynastic-Ptolemaic Period.

109

that was being rendered actually had them or not. That is why our Barn Owl has "ears". But unlike a true "eared" owl, the feather tufts on this sign do not protrude above the head of the bird as they do on an "eared" species (fig. 159). While this error certainly detracts from its overall fidelity, this is still a most accomplished illustration of a Barn Owl.

There is evidence for the owl sign showing influence from the Barn Owl as early as Dynasty I,[580] but it is not until the beginning of Dynasty IV that this species can be positively identified.[581] We know of just three extant examples of the Barn Owl appearing in Dynastic Egyptian art. They are all from the New Kingdom, and in two cases they are depicted in papyrus swamps.[582] Of these two, the far more interesting is displayed on a fragment of a wall painting from the Dynasty XVIII tomb of Neferhotep (A.5) at Thebes,[583] where amid a dense papyrus thicket with variegated bird life, a Barn Owl is shown on a nest which is filled with eggs (fig. 157). The bird is pictured sheltering the clutch beneath its outstretched wings in an attempt to protect them from an Egyptian Mongoose (*Herpestes ichneumon*), which is approaching the nest with plans of making a meal of the eggs, one of their favorite foods.[584] What makes this representation so remarkable is that the Barn Owl's head is shown in a profile view[585] rather than frontally, and we believe it to be without parallel. It is looking toward the right, in the direction of the oncoming invader. Being able to see the head from the side we are better able to observe the species' flattened face and short hooked bill, which are well conveyed here. It also appears that the owl is portrayed without "ears". Barn Owls, however, do not nest in waterside habitats as this painting would have us believe. They prefer the nooks and crannies of buildings and ruins, and in the hollows of trees and rocks, etc. The third occurrence of a Barn Owl is figured in a humorous scene on an ostracon dating from the Ramesside Period, see under bird No. 70 with fig. 191.

There are a considerable number of sculptors' models dating from the Late Dynastic and Ptolemaic Periods which feature depictions of Barn Owls.[586] These are usually in the form of plaques with the birds carved in relief on them, and were used in the training of apprentice sculptors. Many of these pieces are the work of students, but others are without doubt the product of master sculptors (fig. 158) and are among the most attractive portraits of the species from ancient Egypt. Most of these owl models do not have any trace of "ears". The owl hieroglyph during this era is also quite often pictured without "ears",[587] a feature which had been standard on the sign for centuries. From the late Greco-Roman Period come a few more examples of the owl in art. During this time the owl apparently had religious associations.[588] For more on owls, see under bird No. 57.

---

57. "Eared" Owl (*Bubo bubo* and/or *Asio otus*)

Identification: The erect carriage, the rather stocky build, the large eyes, and the diagnostic erect feather tufts on the head are features of an "eared" owl.

Distribution: There are two species of owl occurring in modern Egypt that exhibit prominent feather tufts ("ears"). The Eagle Owl (*Bubo bubo*) breeds and winters in parts of Europe, Asia, the Middle East, and North Africa. In modern Egypt, the Eagle Owl is a breeding resident in the Nile Valley and Delta, the Faiyum, along the Red Sea coast, and the Kharga Oasis. The Long-eared Owl (*Asio otus*) breeds and winters in parts of Europe, Asia, the Middle East, and Africa north of the equator. In modern Egypt, the Long-eared Owl is a winter visitor in the Nile Delta.

Comments: An "eared" owl frequently appears as an Egyptian hieroglyph. This detail of relief (fig. 159) is from a fragment of a Dynasty I schist palette known as the Libya Palette. The palette records the victories of a king over fortified settlements in the Nile Delta and in Libya, and the taking of plants and animals as booty.[589] Our picture shows a crenellated town represented in plan. Within the walls is a group of eight buildings, and an owl hieroglyph which identifies the city's name. The fortress is being symbolically attacked by a falcon, which is hacking down a wall with a mattock. The owl, which even at this very early date is already conventionally portrayed with its head turned full face, has been carved with care. Conspicuous are the large eyes and the erect "ears". Note that on this sign the "ears" are positioned on the head as one would actually see them on an "eared" owl in nature, and are not like those depicted on the Barn Owl (fig. 156). In attempting to identify this figure, several writers have thought that it is probably the Eagle Owl.[590] However, we do not believe that it is possible to establish firmly which species of "eared" owl served as the model for the sign, though it has to be either the Eagle Owl or the Long-eared Owl, if indeed it is to be regarded as specific, since each of these birds possesses very prominent feather tufts.

As shown by our example from the Libya Palette, the owl hieroglyph is met with at the beginning of Dynasty I. At this time the owl is represented with "ears" correctly placed on top of its head, but later in Dynasty I the owl was also rendered with the "ears" shown on its brow.[591] This latter type is suggestive of the Barn Owl, which as we have already seen was depicted in the same manner (see under bird No. 56). The owl sign with true "ears" on it was quite frequently pictured up until Dynasty V,[592] then the Barn Owl with "ears" on its brow became more or less the standard way of illustrating it. That is all except for in linear or "semicursive" hieroglyphic writing,[593] when the owl is generally always drawn with the "ears" on top of its head (fig. 77). Thus it can be confidently said that the owl hieroglyph was

Fig. 159. Detail of the Libya Palette showing an "eared" owl hieroglyph within the walls of a city, from Abydos(?). Dynasty I.

originally fashioned after some species of "eared" owl, surely either the Eagle Owl or the Long-eared Owl, or both. The "ears" which were spuriously added to the Barn Owl were a carrying over of this earlier tradition. Sometimes one also sees painted examples of the owl sign which display plumage features more reminiscent of an Eagle Owl or a Long-eared Owl than a Barn Owl.[594]

---

58. Roller (*Coracias garrulus*)

Identification: The wholly light colored body plumage, long squared tail and wing coverts, the dark "shoulders", and the black flight feathers are features of a Roller.

Distribution: The bird breeds in parts of Europe, Western Asia, the Middle East, Morocco, Algeria, and Tunisia. It winters in parts of the Middle East, and Africa. In

modern Egypt, the Roller is a migrant in the Nile Valley and Delta, the Faiyum, the general vicinity of the Suez Canal, along the Red Sea coast, and the Dakhla, Kharga and Siwa Oases.[595]

Comments: Representations of Rollers are extremely rare in Egyptian art. This picture of a Roller (fig. 160) is from the Dynasty XI tomb

Fig. 160. *Painting of a Roller on the wing, from the tomb of Baket III (No. 15), Beni Hasan. Dynasty XI.*

of Baket III (No. 15) at Beni Hasan. It is shown in a scene flying alongside of a Golden Oriole (*Oriolus oriolus*), see bird No. 69, and the pair is about to alight upon a branch of a fruit tree, possibly a Sycamore fig (*Ficus sycomorus*).[596] Beneath the tree, to the right, a man is kneeling on the ground with a small spring-trap positioned in front of him. While the Roller is primarily insectivorous, they do occasionally consume fruit (e.g., figs, grapes, etc.), and although they are far less troublesome than the

Golden Oriole, flocks of Rollers can sometimes cause considerable damage to fruit crops.[597] It seems likely that this Roller is fluttering down to the tree to pilfer its ripened fruit. The trapper under the tree is attempting to capture these marauding birds. This scene is reminiscent of a kind of bird netting scene which was sometimes depicted during the Old Kingdom, showing flocks of Golden Orioles being trapped in orchards as they feed on figs in sycamore trees (see under bird No. 69). The

Fig. 161. *Roller from the collection of birds in the tomb of Baket III (No. 15), Beni Hasan. Dynasty XI.*

112

Roller cannot be recognized with the oriole in any of these earlier trapping scenes, but its flying with the bird near a fruit tree in the tomb of Baket III, and also in the Dynasty XI tomb of Khety (No. 17) at the same site (see below), indicates that both these migrants were regarded by the Egyptians as crop pests. Whether any of the captured Rollers were bound for the table is not clear, but it is said that their flesh is quite palatable.[598] In this portrayal the painter has done a fine job of suggesting the species' brightly colored and conspicuously patterned plumage. The body plumage, tail and wing coverts are shown light green, the "shoulders" bluish-green, the flight feathers are black, and the legs and feet are orange.[599] There can be no question that this is the correct identification of the bird. It appears as if we are viewing the Roller from below, as we can see the junction of the legs to the underside. However, the underside of its wings are depicted with the characteristic bluish-green "shoulders" of the upper wing surface, making it seem that we are viewing the wings from above.

The only other occurrence of a Roller in flight known to us is represented in the Dynasty XI tomb of Khety at Beni Hasan.[600] It is pictured in a scene which is a direct parallel to the one just described in the tomb of Baket III, and here the wings are executed as they are on this figure. This was probably a device to let us see what the Egyptians perceived as one of the Roller's most arresting plumage features so there could be no chance for ambiguity as to what bird was meant. The tomb of Baket III provides us with another example of a Roller (fig. 161). It is painted amid the famous collection of birds (see under bird No. 9). The Roller is shown at rest facing toward the right. Here again the coloring suggests the living bird, and the artist has even correctly painted its back reddish to indicate the species' chestnut back.[601]

Based upon textual evidence, we know that it is the Roller which is sometimes depicted in scenes (other times it is the Pintail, see bird No. 37) being ritually set free to the four cardinal points at festivals.[602] They served as messengers to announce festivals of enthronement and victory.

---

59. Kingfisher (*Alcedo atthis*)

Fig. 162. Kingfisher depicted on a block of relief, from the mortuary temple of Userkaf, Saqqara. Dynasty V.

113

Identification: The characteristic upright posture, the relatively large head, the short neck and legs, the long daggerlike bill, and the diagnostic malar stripe and fine barring on the crown are features of a Kingfisher.

Distribution: The bird breeds in parts of Europe, Asia, the Middle East, Morocco, Algeria, and Tunisia. It winters in parts of Europe, southern Asia, the Middle East, and North Africa. In modern Egypt, the Kingfisher is a winter visitor in the Nile Valley and Delta, along the Mediterranean Sea coast west of Alexandria, the general vicinity of the Suez Canal, along the Red Sea coast, and the Siwa Oasis.[603]

Comments: The Kingfisher is very frequently represented in Egyptian art. Executed in relief, this handsome example (fig. 162) of the species appears on a block from the now destroyed Dynasty V mortuary temple of Userkaf at Saqqara, which shows part of a swamp scene with a variety of birds roosting amid and flying above a papyrus thicket.[604]

Facing toward the right, the Kingfisher is pictured in an attitude of repose perched on top of an umbel. The bird may perhaps be scanning the surface of the water in search of a meal, and once it had zeroed in on its prey, a sudden steep headlong plunge into the water would have followed to secure it. The outline of the bird is crisply cut, and the delicate detailing of its features is extraordinary. This is especially evident in the fine hatching on the crown and the malar stripe. Its upright posture is free and natural, doubtless the product of careful observation. There is, unfortunately, no trace of the species' brightly colored plumage, and its tail is lost.

The first time we meet with this pert little bird is during Dynasty IV, when for example, a Kingfisher can be recognized in the tomb of Nebemakhet (LG 86) at Giza, figured on top of an umbel in a papyrus swamp.[605] Almost always associated with scenes of fowling or hunting in the swamps, the bird is a stock figure of the wild life depicted therein,[606] particularly in the Old Kingdom.

60. Pied Kingfisher (*Ceryle rudis*)

Identification: The highly distinctive diving posture, the large head, the long pointed black bill, the short shaggy crest on the back of the head, and the diagnostic boldly patterned black and white plumage are features of a Pied Kingfisher.

Distribution: The bird breeds in parts of Asia, the Middle East, and Africa. It winters in parts of southern Europe, Asia, the Middle East, and Africa. In modern Egypt, the Pied Kingfisher is a breeding resident in the Nile Valley (south of Sohag) and Delta, the Faiyum,[607] and the general vicinity of the Suez Canal.

Comments: Pied Kingfishers are abundantly represented in Egyptian art. The Pied Kingfisher's spectacular hunting method in which it hovers virtually motionless, except for the rapid beating of its wings, over shallow water until it has sighted a fish, at which time it hurls itself headfirst, like and arrow, into the water to seize it, was very well known to the ancient

Egyptians. Sometimes the descent is so great that the bird momentarily vanishes beneath the surface of the water. If the attempt was successful, the bird would then fly to a nearby perch, dispatch the catch, and then consume it. This splendid portrait of a Pied Kingfisher (fig. 163), which dates from Dynasty XVIII, appears on a fragment of a wall painting from one of the small chambers, the so-called "green room",[608] which opened on to a large garden court in the North Palace of King Akhenaten at El-Amarna. The bird is shown amid the stems and umbels of a dense papyrus thicket and is pictured in the instant of its bold vertical plummet to the water. The action has been frozen as if a single frame had been removed from a motion picture. Deftly painted, the artist has captured the swiftness and beauty of a Pied Kingfisher in flight in a very convincing manner. Care has been taken to depict the species' major morphological features and its pied plumage markings, and except for the slightest point of error, it is completely faithful to the living bird. To prevent us from making a

Fig. 163. Painting of a Pied Kingfisher swooping down, from the North Palace of Akhenaten, El-Amarna. Dynasty XVIII.

mistake in recognizing which bird was intended, the painter, while having executed its body and wings as if we are viewing them from above, has rendered the head in profile, so that we would not miss its character. In nature, however, a Pied Kingfisher would not adopt a posture like this while in a swoop, and this aspect of the illustration is purely conventionalized. There are many outstanding examples of Pied Kingfishers in art, but this figure, even though it is damaged, is one of the most lovely.

This distinctive waterside bird can first be identified during Dynasty V. Other representations show them in different stages of their remarkable hover-and-dive hunting technique. For instance, on a block of relief from the Dynasty V mortuary temple of Userkaf (fig. 164) at Saqqara, a Pied Kingfisher is beautifully depicted poised on outstretched wings above a dense papyrus thicket only seconds before its dart down to the water. One is perplexed by the

Egyptians' accurate observation of the species' method of fishing, in contrast to their complete misunderstanding of its nesting habits. As a stock element of swamp scenes, the Pied Kingfisher frequently appears, particularly during the Old Kingdom, nesting out in the open amongst the lush papyrus vegetation.[609] Typical of this standard detail is our example of it from the Dynasty V mastaba of Hetepherakhti (D 60) at Saqqara (fig. 165). Here we see the fluttering parent Pied Kingfishers defending their nest from a Common Genet (*Genetta genetta*) which has come to prey upon their young. Note that the nest is imaginatively placed resting on a bending papyrus stem. While on a fragment of relief from the "Chamber of the Seasons" in the Dynasty V sun temple of Niuserre at Abu Gurob, a Pied Kingfisher is portrayed sitting on a nest in a tree.[610] These natural history observations are entirely fanciful, because the Pied Kingfisher's

115

mode of nesting is nothing like this at all,[611] as it drills a deep horizontal hole into steep banks of rivers and canals, and places its eggs in an expanded chamber at the rear of the tunnel.[612] The reason for this abnormality in Egyptian art is not clear, but perhaps an explanation can be found in the practical difficulties of attempting to render the bird nesting in a burrow. Another hole nester, the Hoopoe (see bird No. 62), was also depicted nesting incorrectly (fig. 170), and perhaps the Egyptian artists simply chose the most convenient manner of expressing the idea of nesting.

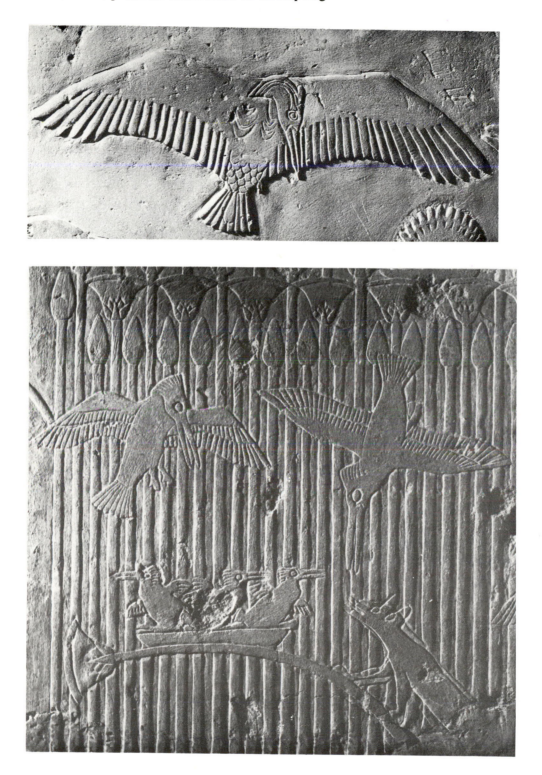

Fig. 164. (top) Pied Kingfisher depicted on a block of relief, from the mortuary temple of Userkaf, Saqqara. Dynasty V. Fig. 165. (bottom) Relief of Pied Kingfishers nesting in a papyrus swamp, from the mastaba of Hetepherakhti (D 60), Saqqara. Dynasty V.

116

61. Bee-eater (*Merops* sp.)

Identification: The long, slender and slightly downcurved bill, the short neck, the rather long pointed wing, and the diagnostic long squared tail with the two narrow projecting feathers are features of an adult bee-eater.

Distribution: There are three species of *Merops* bee-eaters that have been reported in modern Egypt. The Little Green Bee-eater (*M. orientalis*) is a common breeding resident in the Nile Valley and Delta, and the Faiyum. It winters throughout the Nile Valley and Delta, the Faiyum, and the general vicinity of the Suez Canal. The Bee-eater (*M. apiaster*) is a common migrant in the Nile Valley and Delta, the Faiyum, along the Red Sea coast, and the Dakhla, Kharga and Siwa Oases.[613] The Blue-cheeked Bee-eater (*M. superciliosus*) is a breeding resident in the Nile Valley north of Beni Suef, and the Delta. However, migratory Blue-cheeked Bee-eaters pass through the Nile Valley and Delta, the Faiyum, along the Mediterranean Sea coast west of Alexandria, along the Red Sea coast, and the Dakhla, Kharga and Siwa Oases.

Comments: This is the only representation of a bee-eater (fig. 166) that we have been able to identify positively in Egyptian art and hieroglyphs.[614] The walls of the southern half of the middle colonnade of the mortuary temple of Queen Hatshepsut at Deir el-Bahari are decorated with scenes which record the events of her great sea-borne trading expedition to the far-off land of Punt.[615] The location of Punt has yet to be firmly established, but it is generally thought to lie along the coast of what is now modern Eritrea or Somalia.[616] Punt was a tropical land, and the queen's artists took great care in capturing the region's exotic character, including the local fauna and flora. Pictured in the reliefs is the Puntite village which the expedition visited, situated amid a grove of tall trees. Wandering about the trees and dwellings is a host of handsomely depicted animals: monkeys, bovines, dogs, a Giraffe, a

Fig. 166. Relief of a bee-eater in flight, from the mortuary temple of Queen Hatshepsut, Deir el-Bahari. Dynasty XVIII

rhinoceros, birds, etc. This is the setting of the scene illustrated here (fig. 166), a detail of the Puntite village. We view through the trees a dome-shaped mat hut built on piles and reached by a ladder. Between the trees and flying toward the left is a bee-eater, which has been carved in a most accomplished manner. Although it is severely damaged (the crevice between the two adjoining blocks has in a restorative effort been filled with mortar), and no trace of its colorful plumage is extant, identification of the bird as a bee-eater can be made with complete confidence.[617] On a living *Merops* bee-eater, however, the pair of elongated tail feathers protrude directly out from the middle of the tail, but on our figure they have been slightly moved to one side,

probably so they would not become confused with the branches of the tree. Because the bird is associated with the land of Punt, it is clear that it was to be regarded as an exotic species. However, the artist who portrayed the bird would not necessarily have had to travel to Punt to observe a bee-eater, since these striking birds must surely have existed in Egypt during ancient times as they do nowadays. There is, of course, the possibility that the bird may represent a bee-eater other than one belonging to the genus *Merops*, as other varieties of bee-eater do occur in East Africa which are not found in Egypt.[618] It is something of a surprise that these brightly colored birds do not appear more often in Egyptian art, but apparently they were not part of the artistic tradition.

62. Hoopoe (*Upupa epops*)

Identification: The upright stance, the long slender and slightly downcurved black bill, the boldly patterned black and white wing, and the diagnostic black-tipped erect crest are features of a Hoopoe.

Fig. 167. Painting of a Hoopoe roosting on a branch of an acacia tree, from the tomb of Khnumhotep III (No. 3), Beni Hasan. Dynasty XII.

Distribution: The bird breeds in parts of Europe, Asia, the Middle East, and Africa. It winters in parts of Asia, the Middle East, and Africa. In modern Egypt, the Hoopoe is a common breeding resident in the Nile Valley and Delta, the Faiyum, the general vicinity of the Suez Canal, and the Dakhla and Kharga Oases.

Comments: Hoopoes are frequently pictured in both Egyptian art and hieroglyphs.[619] Of all the representations of birds that have survived from ancient Egypt, perhaps the most famous and most often reproduced, after the "Geese of Meidum" (see bird No. 29), is a group which appears in a scene in the Dynasty XII tomb of Khnumhotep III (No. 3) at Beni Hasan, of which this splendid Hoopoe (fig. 167) is a part. Nine birds have been executed perching on the branches of two flowering acacia trees, which flank a pond on which the tomb owner is shown trapping waterfowl with a clap-net (fig. 94). When compared with much of the painted decoration in the tombs at Beni Hasan, the scene has fared exceptionally well with the passage of time, owing to its great distance from the ground, away from human hands, and for the most part having escaped the thick coating of grey film. Although they have been described as resembling stuffed museum specimens,[620] because they look rather stiff and lack any of the vitality of living birds, W. S. Smith has said of them that they are "one of the most charming pieces of observation on the part of an ancient painter and a fine instance of the naturalistic impulse that remains constantly near the surface in all Egyptian work."[621] Five species can clearly be distinguished and each is accurately expressed, with details well tended to. The Hoopoe has been marvelously captured in this portrait. Facing toward the left, it is shown in an attitude of repose with its right leg placed forward, roosting on a lower branch of one of the acacias, a favorite haunt of Hoopoes in Egypt. The artist has depicted the bird with its erectile crest fully raised, like a fan, a characteristic feature of this species and one that allows us to identify it as a Hoopoe at a glance. The Hoopoe's strongly barred black and white wing, the cinnamom body plumage,[622] and the long downcurved black bill are especially well indicated. The single deviation is that a Hoopoe possesses a rounded tail, and not a slightly forked one as it is rendered here.

Fig. 168. (top) Hoopoe flying above a papyrus thicket, from the mastaba of Kaemnofret (No. 57), Saqqara. Dynasty V.

Fig. 169. (center) Relief of a Hoopoe having come to rest on an umbel in a papyrus swamp, from the mortuary temple of Userkaf, Saqqara. Dynasty V.

Fig. 170. (bottom) Hoopoe nesting in a swamp scene, from the mastaba of Mereruka, Saqqara. Dynasty VI.

119

Fig. 171. Relief of young boy holding a Hoopoe, from the mastaba of Ptahhotep II (D 64), Saqqara. Dynasty V.

The first time the Hoopoe can positively be identified is during Dynasty IV, when for example, two can be recognized perched on top of papyrus umbels in a swamp scene in the tomb of Nebemakhet (LG 86) at Giza.[623] Hoopoes, however, are not true waterside dwellers, but prefer grassy and wooded areas, farmlands, orchards and the like. In spite of this though, they repeatedly occur in Egyptian art inhabiting a papyrus swamp environment (figs. 168-9).[624] While in the Dynasty VI mastaba of Mereruka at Saqqara, a Hoopoe is shown nesting in the swamps (fig. 170). This scene is entirely imaginary as the Hoopoe is a hole nester and lays its clutch of eggs in cavities of trees, walls, etc., and would not build its nest in the middle of a papyrus swamp. We have already noted a similar anomaly with the nesting habits of the Pied Kingfisher, see under

bird No. 60. Hoopoes also appear in a number of scenes during the Old Kingdom which illustrate the netting of flocks of Golden Orioles in orchards (fig. 183). The orioles were trapped because they were regarded as a crop pest, since they pilfered the fruit of the sycamore fig tree (see under bird No. 69). The few Hoopoes shown in these scenes would not have done any damage to the crop because they are not fruit eaters. Whether their being trapped along with the Golden Orioles was simply unavoidable because of their presence in the orchards or was purposely planned is not clear. The inscriptions which accompany these scenes only speak of the trapping of orioles. When Golden Orioles are trapped today in Egypt using a very similar method of netting, there is no effort made to catch Hoopoes along with them. The Hoopoes might have been captured for the table. Although the palatability of their flesh is reported to be quite poor,[625] Hoopoes are known to be eaten in modern Egypt and they can sometimes be found in the bird markets.[626] Another possibility is that they were obtained to serve as pets or playthings for children. The species is routinely pictured in Old Kingdom art being clutched in the hands of children (fig. 171), who typically are shown standing at their parents' side holding the bird by its wings, just as Nefer's daughter does with her Lapwing (fig. 132). It has been said that the Hoopoe will become very tame in captivity,[627] and apparently this gaily colored bird was a favorite pet of the Egyptian young during the Pyramid Age.[628] That this may have been at least part of the reason for their capture is suggested by a scene preserved in the mastaba of Mereruka at Saqqara.[629] It depicts children engaged in various games. In one register several boys are shown leaving an orchard in which figs are being harvested and birds are being caught with small spring-traps. They are carrying the birds that have just been removed from the traps, possibly to play with (or maybe bringing them as offerings?), and one of them is a Hoopoe. According to Keimer, the Hoopoe is still a plaything for children in Egypt today.[630]

Although not a sacred bird, the Hoopoe apparently did possess some religious associations.[631] It is pictured in vignettes on several funerary papyri[632] and on coffins[633] perching on top of a sycamore fig tree, and in one instance on a papyrus umbel.

63. Crag Martin or Pale Crag Martin (*Hirundo rupestris* and *H. obsoleta*)

Fig. 172. Crag Martin or Pale Crag Martin depicted in a vignette on the papyrus "Book of the Dead" belonging to Mahirper, from his tomb (No. 36), Valley of the Kings. Dynasty XVIII.

Identification: The long pointed wings, the comparatively small bill, the short unfeathered legs and feet, the slightly forked tail, the light underside, and the dark back and wing are features of a crag martin.

Distribution: The Crag Martin breeds in parts of southern Europe, Asia, the Middle East, Morocco, and Algeria. It winters in parts of southern Europe, Asia, the Middle East, and Africa north of the equator. In modern Egypt, the Crag Martin is a winter visitor in the Nile Valley, and along the Mediterranean coast west of Alexandria. The Pale Crag Martin breeds and winters in portions of Asia, the Middle East, and Africa north of the equator. In modern Egypt, the Pale Crag Martin is a permanent breeding resident in the Nile Valley, the Faiyum, along the Red Sea coast, and the Dakhla and Kharga Oases.

Comments: This is the only representation of crag martin (fig. 172) that we have been able to identify from Egyptian art and hieroglyphs.[634] The bird is pictured in a vignette on a papyrus copy of the "Book of the Dead" which was prepared for Mahirper, and was found in his Dynasty XVIII tomb (No. 36) in the Valley of the Kings.[635] The vignette accompanies a spell (Chapter 86) of that work which allows the deceased owner to become transformed into a swallow.[636] The crag martin is shown at rest, facing toward the right and perched on a low platform. The features of a crag martin have been well observed here. This is very much apparent in the detailing of its plumage, which when it is viewed in color,[637] is wholly brown with paler underparts. However, neither the Crag Martin nor the Pale Crag Martin possesses elongated central tail feathers. Because of this abnormality, and given the close resemblance between the two crag martins in nature, it is not possible to determine which species is portrayed here. For more on swallows, see under bird Nos. 64-5.

121

64. Swallow (*Hirundo rustica*)

Identification: The characteristic build, the short neck, the long pointed wings, the black crown, neck, rump and back, the lighter colored facial mask, and the long streamerlike outer tail feathers which give the tail a forked appearance are features of an adult Swallow.

wearing a broad collar, a kilt, a short beard, a shoulder length wig, a fillet with streamers, and on top of his head a cone of perfumed fat. On board the vessel there is an empty throne, with the symbol of the god Nefertum placed in front of it.[639] Above, the rays of the sun disk stream

Fig. 173. *Scene from the funerary papyrus of the scribe Panebenkemtnakht showing a pair of fine Swallows, from Deir el-Bahari. Dynasty XXI.*

Distribution: The bird breeds in parts of Europe, Asia, the Middle East, and North Africa. It winters in parts of southern Asia, the Middle East, and Africa. In modern Egypt, the Swallow is a common breeding resident in the Nile Valley and Delta, the Faiyum, and the general vicinity of the Suez Canal. However, migrating Swallows pass through the Nile Valley and Delta, the Faiyum, along the Mediterranean Sea coast west of Alexandria, along the Red Sea coast, and the Dakhla, Kharga and Siwa Oases.

Comments: Representations of the Swallow are extremely rare in Egyptian art. This scene (fig. 173) executed in black and red ink, is from the Dynasty XXI funerary papyrus of the scribe Panebenkemtnakht.[638] It shows the deceased owner seated in a papyrus raft, which has a bow and stern that terminate in large stylized papyrus umbels, and he is paddling it across the waters of the underworld. The water is conventionally depicted as an area of zigzags. Panebenkemtnakht is pictured facing left, and

down upon the throne. In front of the raft are two black mounds with doors,[640] perhaps tomb buildings, and perched on top of each is a large Swallow. This detail evidently refers to a spell (Chapter 86) of the "Book of the Dead" which enables the deceased owner to become transformed into a swallow. Facing toward the right, the birds are portrayed at rest, each with one leg placed forward. To prevent us from making an error in identifying the type of bird that was intended here, the artist has labeled each of them with the appropriate hieroglyphic name. The species' morphological features have been nicely described in these drawings. Of signal value is the rendering of their characteristic deeply forked tail. Also, when they are viewed in color,[641] their facial masks are colored red, which further adds to their realism and clinches the identification of them as Swallows. There is, however, no trace of the species' white underpart (or which can be chestnut red, depending upon the subspecies) on the figures. These are by any standard top quality drawings of Swallows.

Although swallows are frequently represented in Egyptian art, it is the exception when one can be identified to the species level. This is because they are usually illustrated with little in the way of specific plumage features and are sometimes given imaginative coloring. We know of just one other example of a swallow that can confidently be called the

sun greeting bird and would proclaim the approach of the dawn.[644] The bird would soon fly from its perch on the bark and announce the first light of the new day. The swallow played a similar role in a love poem from the New Kingdom:

Swallow. It appears in a vignette on a funerary papyrus,[642] and is a fine picture of the species. In mythological scenes on the walls of New Kingdom tombs and particularly on funerary papyri,[643] swallows very commonly appear standing on the prow of the bark of the sun god. This detail is exceptionally well shown in a scene on the Dynasty XXI papyrus of Hirweben (fig. 174), which depicts the sun god Re-Harakhty's journey through the night. The god's bark is being towed by four jackals and four uraei, while the god Seth is standing in the bow repelling the Apopis snake with a spear. Small, but distinct, is a bird on the prow, which from comparison with other similar scenes where more detail is present, can be recognized as a swallow. Here the swallow served as a

Fig. 174. (top) Scene from the funerary papyrus of Hirweben showing a swallow on the prow of the sun bark, from Deir el-Bahari. Dynasty XXI.

Fig. 175. (center) A swallow represented on a mound in a vignette on the papyrus "Book of the Dead" prepared for the scribe Ani. Dynasty XIX.

Fig. 176. (bottom) Drawing of the top half of a limestone stela showing a swallow receiving adoration, from Deir el-Medina. Dynasty XIX.

The voice of the swallow says:
'It's light already. Mustn't you go now?'
Don't, little bird. You bring dispute.
I have found my brother [= lover] in his bed.
My heart overflows with happiness.
We say: I will not go away
As long as my hand is in your hand.
I still go for walks
While I am with you
To all the beautiful spots.
He made me the first of the maidens
And he does not pain my heart. [645]

In the poem the swallow has awakened the lovers with its song in the early morning and signals the break of dawn. Further evidence for the swallow as a sun bird is suggested by an amuletic bracelet found in the Dynasty XVIII tomb of Tutankhamun (No. 62) in the Valley of the Kings.[646] It shows a swallow with the sun's disk resting upon its rump. This piece may allude to the bird's function as a

messenger of day and light. Swallows are also frequently depicted in tombs and on papyri standing on top of small hills (fig. 175) or mounds,[647] and it is thought that these may be symbolic of the first piece of earth that rose up out of the primeval waters.[648] While the vast majority of these swallows cannot be specifically identified, one gets the impression from many of them that the Swallow served as the principal model.

The swallow represented a minor deity who was closely connected with the region of the Theban necropolis.[649] The upper part of a Dynasty XIX stela (fig. 176) from the artisans' village at Deir el-Medina shows the swallow being worshipped.[650] The bird is perched on top of a shrine and there is a table with offerings in front, with the text: "The beautiful swallow who remains and remains in eternity."[651] The swallow also had associations with the goddess Isis.[652]

65. House Martin (*Delichon urbica*)

Fig. 177. Painted relief hieroglyph of a House Martin, from the tomb of Meketre (No. 280), Thebes. Dynasty XI.

Identification: The small black bill, the short neck, the comparatively short and slightly forked tail, the prominent pure white underside, and the diagnostic blue head, back,

wing and tail (see Comments) are features of an adult House Martin.

Distribution: The bird breeds in parts of

124

Europe, Asia, the Middle East, Morocco, Algeria, and Tunisia. It winters in southern Asia, and sub-Saharan Africa. In modern Egypt, the House Martin is a migrant in the Nile Valley and Delta, the Faiyum, along the Mediterranean Sea coast west of Alexandria, along the Red Sea coast, and the Dakhla, Kharga and Siwa Oases.

Comments: The House Martin routinely appears as a standard Egyptian hieroglyph. This handsome ornamental hieroglyph (fig. 177) occurs on a fragment of painted relief from the Dynasty XI tomb of Meketre (No. 280) at Thebes. In this small portrait the species' principal morphological features and diagnostic plumage coloring have been authoritatively reproduced.[653] The underside is painted completely white, while the head, back, wing and tail are dark blue, exactly as on the living bird. Executed facing right, the House Martin is shown at rest with its left leg placed forward. Because it is depicted with its wings folded at the side, we are prevented from seeing the species' characteristic white rump, and this holds true for every example of the sign. But this in no way hinders our identification of the bird as a House Martin.

Positive identification of the House Martin cannot be made first until Dynasty IV,[654] owing to the absence of preserved pigment on earlier examples of the sign. When carefully executed, the form of the hieroglyph remains more or less the same throughout all periods, but there is a good deal of variation in its coloring and markings. Sometimes the bird is shown with greyish upper parts and with a dark spot on its breast,[655] and other times the upper parts are painted all green and with the underside entirely white.[656] On at least one occasion, the bird has a green back and the underside is tinted an orange color.[657] It seems quite likely therefore that from time to time other species of swallow may have influenced the appearance of the sign. Because of this it is usually said that it is impossible to define precisely the species of bird the sign represents.[658] In our view, however, there are a sufficient number of examples of the hierolgyph with dark blue upper parts, only slightly forked tail, and pure white underside for us to establish that the sign was chiefly fashioned after the House Martin.[659]

66. White/Pied Wagtail[660]

(*Motacilla alba*)

Fig. 178. Painting of a White/Pied Wagtail in a papyrus swamp, from the unlocated tomb of Nebamun, Thebes. Dynasty XVIII.

125

Identification: The distinguishing proportions, the short neck, the slender body, the black bill and legs, the conspicuous black and white plumage combination, and the long black tail are features of an adult White/Pied Wagtail.

Distribution: The bird breeds in parts of Europe, Asia, the Middle East, and Africa. It winters in parts of southern Europe and Asia, the Middle East, and Africa. In modern Egypt, the Pied Wagtail is a breeding resident in the Nile Valley south of Aswan.[661] However, large numbers of migratory White Wagtails winter in the Nile Valley and Delta, the Faiyum, along the Red Sea coast, and the Dakhla, Kharga and Siwa Oases.

Comments: White/Pied Wagtails are extremely rare in Egyptian art. This example of a White/Pied Wagtail (fig. 178) is depicted on a scene on a fragment of a wall painting from the Dynasty XVIII tomb of Nebamun at Thebes, which shows the tomb owner, accompanied by his wife and small daughter, engaged in fowling from a papyrus raft in the swamplands (fig. 85). The wagtail is clutched in the hind paws of Nebamun's cat, who is busily retrieving the birds that his master's throwstick has brought down. The species' features have been, on the whole, accurately observed and well rendered here, but there has been some deviation from the living bird. In nature the bird possesses a black throat and facial markings, and these are subject to a great deal of variation in their size and prominence, depending upon the subspecies, age and the time of year. Neither of these details are indicated on the painting. Their absence is probably due to the artist's oversight rather than lack of knowledge. That it is a White/Pied Wagtail can be asserted with near certainty,[662] as its form and other plumage features so closely resemble this species. Its presence in an aquatic environment is in keeping with the habits of the bird, since the species often frequents the waterside.

The only other sure occurrence of a White/Pied Wagtail known to us appears in the Dynasty V mastaba of Ti (No. 60) at Saqqara.[663] It is perched on a papyrus umbel in a swamp scene, and although paint is no longer extant on the bird, the species' characteristics have been precisely carved in the relief. The artist has pictured the wagtail with the throat collar which is absent on the example from the tomb of Nebamun.

---

67. Red-backed Shrike (*Lanius collurio*)

Identification: The characteristic proportions, the black legs, feet, slightly hooked bill and mask, the bluish-grey crown and nape, the chestnut back and wing (see Comments), the white underparts, and the long black tail which has white outermost feathers are features of an adult male Red-backed Shrike.

Distribution: The bird breeds in parts of Europe, Asia, and the Middle East. It winters in parts of southern Asia, the Middle East, and sub-Saharan Africa. In modern Egypt, the Red-backed Shrike is a migrant in the Nile Valley and Delta, the Faiyum, along the Mediterranean Sea coast west of Alexandria, along the Red Sea coast, and the Dakhla, Kharga and Siwa Oases.[664]

Comments: This is the only example of a Red-backed Shrike (fig. 179) that we have been able to identify in Egyptian art and hieroglyphs.[665] From the Dynasty XII tomb of Khnumhotep III (No. 3) at Beni Hasan, this delightful picture of a Red-backed Shrike appears in the famous scene showing a number of birds roosting on the branches of two acacia trees (fig. 94). Facing toward the right, the bird is at rest, standing with its left leg in advance of the right. The artist seems to have worked directly from life. He has depicted it frequenting a habitat in which the living bird would be very much at home. Red-backed Shrikes can regularly be viewed in the wild conspicuously perched on small trees and shrubs, which in Egypt is often the acacia tree, where they are on the lookout for their prey. The species' features, both in regards to form and plumage coloring, have been painted with extraordinary fidelity. The naturalism of this portrait led the ornithologist R. E. Moreau to remark that "it is probably the most excellent and faithful of all the coloured bird-pictures of Ancient

Fig. 179. Painting of a Red-backed Shrike on a branch of an acacia tree, from the tomb of Khnumhotep III (No. 3), Beni Hasan. Dynasty XII.

Egypt."[666] The coloring in particular is extremely lifelike,[667] the tints of the bluish-grey crown and nape and the chestnut back and wing are nearly exact. Also, note for example, the authentic rendering of the slightly hooked bill, the eye stripe, and the long black tail which has its sides fringed with white, which are the result of keen observation of the Red-backed Shrike.

68. Masked Shrike (*Lanius nubicus*)

Identification: The typical build, the dark bill, crown, mask, nape and back, and the white forehead, throat, underside, wing patch and outer edges of the long dark tail are features of an adult Masked Shrike.

Distribution: The bird breeds in parts of southeastern Europe, and the Middle East. It winters in parts of the Middle East, and Africa north of the equator. In modern Egypt, the Masked Shrike is an uncommon winter visitor to the Upper Nile Valley.[668] However, migrating Masked Shrikes pass through the Nile Valley and Delta, the Faiyum, along the Red Sea coast, and the Dakhla and Kharga Oases during the spring and fall.

Comments: Masked Shrikes are very rare in Egyptian art. This striking representation of a Masked Shrike (fig. 180) is from the Dynasty XII tomb of Khnumhotep III (No. 3) at Beni Hasan, where it is figured in the celebrated scene showing a group of birds roosting on the branches of two acacia trees (fig. 94). Depicted in an attitude of repose, the bird is facing right with its left leg forward. Here, the artist has once again created a picture both of great beauty and of surpassing accuracy. The

Fig. 180. (top) Painting of a Masked Shrike roosting on a branch of an acacia tree, from the tomb of Khnumhotep III (No. 3), Beni Hasan. Dynasty XII.

Fig. 181. (bottom) Masked Shrike from the collection of birds in the tomb of Baket III (No. 15), Beni Hasan. Dynasty XI.

placement of it in a tree is in full accordance with the nature of the Masked Shrike, though the living bird is somewhat retiring and often conceals itself in the foliage, and is therefore less likely to be exposed to view than the Red-backed Shrike (fig. 179). The species' distinctive plumage pattern, by using a combination of black, white and brown, has been admirably expressed. Further adding to its realism, the artist has painted the flank area of the plumage a dull reddish color.[669] Note too, that the shrike is portrayed standing "flat-footed" on the branch, and that no attempt has been made to show the toes wrapped around the branch gripping it, as the actual bird would do in life. This is not the only

Masked Shrike in the scene; a total of four appear, a pair located in each of the acacias. Two are completely at rest, while the other two have their wings outstretched. Like the one illustrated in fig. 180, the others too have been conveyed in a masterly fashion.

We are aware of only one other extant depiction of this species in Egyptian art. It appears in the collection of birds in the Dynasty XI tomb of Baket III (No. 15) at Beni Hasan (see under bird No. 9). Although it has suffered considerably and is not as detailed a picture as those in the tomb of Khnumhotep III, there is no difficulty in distinguishing it as a Masked Shrike (fig. 181).

69. Golden Oriole (*Oriolus oriolus*)

Identification: The moderately long and slightly downcurved dark bill, the light colored head, neck underside, under wing coverts and terminal tail band, and the black flight feathers and tail are features of an adult male Golden Oriole.

Distribution: The bird breeds in parts of Europe, Asia, the Middle East, Morocco, Algeria, and Tunisia. It winters in parts of southern Asia, and sub-Saharan Africa. In modern Egypt, the Golden Oriole is a migrant in the Nile Valley and Delta, the Faiyum, and the Dakhla, Kharga and Siwa Oases.

Fig. 182. (top) Painting of a Golden Oriole on the wing, from the tomb of Baket III (No. 15), Beni Hasan. Dynasty XI.

Fig. 183. (bottom) A scene from the mastaba of Akhethotep, Saqqara, showing the trapping of Golden Orioles, with a few Hoopoes, in a sycamore fig tree. Dynasty V.

129

Fig. 184. (left) Fragment of relief with two Golden Orioles in a sycamore fig tree engaged in playful conflict, from a trapping scene in the mortuary temple of Userkaf, Saqqara. Dynasty V. Fig. 185. (right) Detail of painted relief showing a Golden Oriole stuck in the meshing of a net covering a sycamore fig tree, from the mastaba of Niankhkhnum and Khnumhotep, Saqqara. Dynasty V.

Comments: Golden Orioles are frequently pictured in Egyptian art. The Golden Oriole is primarily an arboreal bird, only occasionally descending to the ground, preferring to perch high in the canopy of trees. True to its nature, this unmistakable representation of a male Golden Oriole (fig. 182), from the Dynasty XI tomb of Baket III (No. 15) at Beni Hasan, is shown in a scene flying just to the left of a fruit tree, possibly a sycamore fig, and is about to alight upon one of its branches.[670] It is flying next to a Roller (see bird No. 58), which is also headed toward the tree, where many of each of their respective kinds(?) have already gathered to feed. Beneath the tree, to the right, a man is kneeling on the ground with a small spring-trap positioned in front of him. The Golden Oriole is partly frugivorous, and flocks of these birds can sometimes consume large portions of economically important fruit crops. Because of this they continue to be persecuted in some areas of the world to this day. It seems quite clear that this oriole is about to land in the tree to pilfer the ripe fruit (figs?). The trapper under the tree is attempting to capture these marauding birds.

There are other scenes which illustrate this species being similarly caught with small spring-traps while they feed in orchards. In the Dynasty XI tomb of Khety (No. 17) at Beni Hasan, there is a scene which is a direct parallel to the one in the tomb of Baket III,[671] and from the time of the Old Kingdom there are at least two instances of it.[672] But the clever Egyptian farmer had a more effective method of trapping and protecting their fruit crops from this pesky bird (see below). In this portrayal we view the bird from below. The species' features, both in form and color, have been very accurately painted, from its yellow plumage to the red coloring of the bill.[673]

This attractive and brightly colored bird can first be identified during Dynasty V. It is in the Old Kingdom that this species is most frequently met with in Egyptian art. Flocks of Golden Orioles are shown in scenes which decorate tomb and temple walls, being trapped in orchards as they feed on figs in sycamore trees. Rather than using small spring-traps which can only catch a few birds at a time, extremely large fine-meshed nets were employed, allowing great numbers to be caught at once. This trapping technique is uniquely confined to its appearance during the Old Kingdom,[674] and the number of extant scenes picturing it is comparatively small.[675] An outstanding example of it is preserved on a wall from the Dynasty V mastaba of Akhethotep at Saqqara (fig. 183). Here a large triangular mist-net has been placed over the side of a sycamore fig tree which is heavy with fruit. One corner of the net is attached at the crown of the tree, and the net reaches all the way down to the ground, where presumably it has been fastened as well.

130

A flock of Golden Orioles has invaded the tree to pilfer the ripe figs. It is now that two men, one a dwarf, swiftly approach the tree from the left, the opposite side that the net has been set. As they advance they are shouting and making noise, and each of them is waving in his hand a small strip of cloth. All of this has the effect of greatly startling the feedings birds, which in their panic take wing, most of them in the direction of the outstretched net, only to hit it and instantly become entangled in its meshes (figs. 184-5). Other men would then rush to the net and remove those birds that have been caught. We then view them on the right being placed into crates for transport. As is usually the case in these scenes, the flock of Golden Orioles is mixed with a sprinkling of Hoopoes (see bird No. 62). Their presence here is not entirely clear, since this species is not frugivorous. The main reason for the trapping of the Golden Orioles was most assuredly to protect the fig crop from their ravenous pilfering,[676] but they were probably also caught for the table. This is suggested by the fact that the captured birds are shown being put into crates, and in an example of this type of netting scene in the Dynasty V mastaba of Niankh-khnum and Khnumhotep at Saqqara,[677] one of the trappers is depicted plucking the feathers from the carcass of one of the orioles. The flesh of this bird is said to be fairly good,[678] and its taste would have been improved after feeding on sweet fruit. Golden Orioles are also occasionally eaten in modern Egypt.[679] The species continues to do considerable damage to Egyptian fruit crops. They do not just feed on figs, but also enjoy dates (*Phoenix dactylifera*)[680] and especially mulberries (*Morus* sp.).[681] It is because of their harmfulness to these economically important crops that Golden Orioles are persecuted by farmers in Egypt today.[682] They are trapped nowadays in Egypt using a method that is essentially the same as we have already described from the mastaba of Akhethotep. In the spring of 1984 a short distance from the city of Port Said, we witnessed a large flock of orioles being so netted in a small mulberry grove while the birds were feeding in the trees.

From inscriptions which accompany scenes that illustrate the tomb owner fowling with throwsticks in the swamplands, we know that the Golden Oriole was sometimes one of the birds the deceased would try to bag.[683]

---

70. Crow (*Corvus* sp.)

Identification: The moderately long black bill and legs, the short thick neck, and the diagnostic wholly dark plumage are features of a crow belonging to the genus *Corvus*.

Distribution: There are six species of *Corvus* crows that have been reported in modern Egypt. The House Crow (*C. splendens*) is a breeding resident at Suez and Ras Gharib.[684] The Rook (*C. frugilegus*) is a reputed winter visitor to the Nile Delta.[685] The Hooded Crow (*C. corone*) is a breeding resident in the Nile Valley (north of Aswan) and Delta, the Faiyum, and in the vicinity of the Suez Canal. The Brown-necked Raven (*C. ruficollis*) is a breeding resident throughout the semiarid parts of the country. The Raven (*C. corax*) is a breeding resident along the Mediterranean Sea coast west of Alexandria.[686] The Fan-tailed Raven (*C. rhipidurus*) is a breeding resident in the extreme southeastern part of the country (near Gebel Elba).

Fig. 186. *An ostracon depicting a pair of crows, from Thebes. Ramesside Period.*

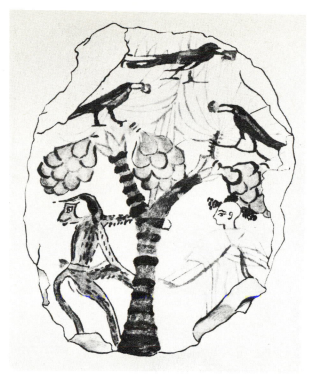

Fig. 187. Drawing of an ostracon showing a monkey climbing a palm and three crows feeding on fruit above, from Deir el-Medina. Ramesside Period.

Comments: Crows are fairly common in Egyptian art. The work of a Ramesside Period artist, this limestone ostracon (fig. 186), chipped at the lower right hand corner, bears two sketches which at first appear to be separate and not connected with one another.[687] However, upon investigation, it is very possible that these motifs are in fact related. The main drawing consists of a naked boy who is depicted in the act of driving an animal, which is on all fours, toward the right. Although most of the figure is now lost (only the extreme rear of its body, long tail, and right hind leg remain), on the basis of numerous parallels to this scene on figured ostraca,[688] it is probably a Hamadryas Baboon (*Papio hamadryas*). The boy is brandishing in his right hand a short crook, used to prod the animal along, and with his left he holds onto a leash, the other end of which is tied around the monkey's waist. This activity is believed to have been part of the training process in domesticating wild baboons for pets and as workers.[689] The other sketch is of two large black crows which are facing each other, with an egg(?) placed between them. They are engaged in what looks to be a very lively discussion, one that perhaps centers on the action below. The pair have been expeditiously

drawn, but there can be no mistaking what kind of bird the artist intended, as he has successfully captured the unique form of a *Corvus* crow. In ancient Egypt baboons were trained to help harvest fruit from trees.[690] Many ostraca have been found which illustrate scenes showing monkeys scampering up the trunks of the Dom Palm (*Hyphaene thebaica*) to gather the fruit for their masters.[691] Most of these flakes come from the artisans' village at Deir el-Medina, and date to the Ramesside Period. On several of these ostraca as the baboons are pictured climbing up the trees, one or more crows are perched on its branches (figs. 187-8), pilfering the ripe dom nuts before the monkeys could pick them.[692] The crows were apparently in competition with the baboons for the fruit, an interesting race between these two highly intelligent species. The appearance of crows feeding in fruit trees is realistic, as some species of *Corvus* crow are known to be great fruit eaters.[693] It seems highly likely to us therefore, that the juxtaposing of these two motifs on the ostracon was not accidental. It is not very difficult for us to imagine the birds to be making light of the child's attempt to manage the not yet tamed monkey, all the while knowing that in spite of this training, they will be able to pilfer their share of fruit crop that the monkey may in future try to harvest. Whatever the real reason may have been for including the pair of chattering crows here, the humorous nature of this detail is immediately evident.

The earliest extant representation of a *Corvus* crow is preserved on a fragment of the Battlefield Palette, now in the British Museum, London, which dates from the Late Predynastic Period.[694] In a scene which pictures the gruesome aftermath of a battle, a flock of birds, consisting of large vultures and a few superbly carved crows, is shown preying upon the bodies of the fallen men. Crows are omnivorous in their feeding habits, and not only do they sometimes consume fruit, but if given the opportunity will feed on flesh. It is interesting to note that bodies of Egyptian soldiers slain in battle have actually been found with marks indicating that they had been attacked by birds of prey as they lay on the battlefield.[695]

It is however in comical situations that we most often meet with the crow in Egyptian art. On the extraordinary so-called "Erotic and

Fig. 188. (left) Ostracon with a drawing of a monkey climbing a Dom Palm and a crow perched above, from Deir el-Medina. Ramesside Period.

Fig. 189. (right) An episode from the "Erotic and Satirical Papyrus" showing a crow climbing a ladder to reach a fruit tree. Dynasty XX.

Satirical Papyrus" from Dynasty XX, there is a small scene (fig. 189) which depicts a crow, and not a swallow as it is so often called,[696] attempting to pilfer figs from a sycamore fig tree in a most laughable manner. Instead of flying up to the branches of the tree to reach the fruit, the ingenious crow has opted to ascend the tree by means of a ladder, and we view the bird slowly making its way up the rungs. Already perched up in the tree is a Hippopotamus that is either guarding the fruit crop from the hungry bird or is himself gathering the ripe figs into a basket.[697] The humor in this detail is of course self-explanatory. On another satirical papyrus dating from the same general period, the crow is again figured in association with a fruit tree (fig. 190). Unfortunately, there is a break in the papyrus and the scene in which the bird appears is no longer complete, making the interpretation of it rather uncertain. It may originally have been similar to the episode illustrated on the other papyrus (fig. 189), but part of the humor here may lie in the fact that the crow, which is on the ground beneath the tree, is standing next to a basket of brightly colored fruit and is simply ignoring the sweet morsels as if this tasty meal did not appeal to

him. The crow and the Hippopotamus appear together again in an interesting and not very well known limestone ostracon from the Ramesside Period (fig. 191). It is an outstanding example of the topsy-turvy brand of humor that commonly occurs on figured ostraca. The drawing on the flake shows what is seemingly a parody of the traditional scene of weighing the deceased's heart against a feather on a scale pictured in the "Book of the Dead."[698] The hippo and the crow are depicted standing on either end of the scale, while below, an owl (see bird No. 56) and a cat(?) serve as the judge and jury and check the balance to determine the outcome. It is possible that some of these scenes that the crow appears in are illustrations of Egyptian folktales or fables, now lost, in which this crafty black bird had a role.[699] In other scenes in art, crows are also portrayed feeding on figs[700] and dates[701] in trees.

Probably the best and most accurate example of the crow in Egyptian art appears on a Dynasty XII cloisonné work pectoral from a tomb at El-Riqqa (fig. 192). The two crows are pictured on the jewel in a place that we would normally expect to see falcons,[702] symbol of the god Horus. Their presence here seems to

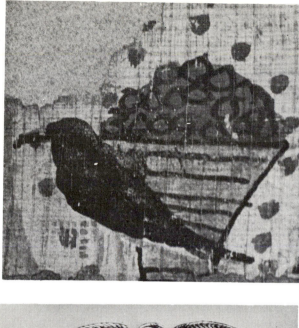

Fig. 190. (top left) Detail from a comic papyrus showing a crow with a basket of fruit. Ramesside Period.

Fig. 191. (top right) Drawing of an ostracon with a scene showing a crow and a Hippopotamus on a scale, from Thebes. Ramesside Period.

Fig. 192. (bottom) Back view of a shrine-shaped pectoral depicting two crows, from El-Riqqa. Dynasty XII.

suggest that the crow had some minor religious associations. We view the pectoral from its reverse side, which allows us to see more clearly the details of the birds. The features of a Corvus crow have been well observed in these renderings. However, they cannot be identified to the species level.

71. Redstart (*Phoenicurus phoenicurus*)

Identification: The upright stance and diminutive proportions, the black bill, cheek and throat, the white facial marking bordering the black cheek, the darkish crown, nape, back and wing, the light colored underside, and the greyish tail are features of an adult male Redstart.

Distribution: The bird breeds in parts of Europe, Western Asia, the Middle East, Morocco, Algeria, and Tunisia. It winters in parts of the southern Arabian Peninsula, and sub-Saharan Africa. In modern Egypt, the Redstart is a migrant in the Nile Valley and Delta, the Faiyum, and in the Dakhla, Kharga and Siwa Oases.

Fig. 193. Painting of a Redstart on a branch of an acacia tree, from the tomb of Khnumhotep III (No. 3), Beni Hasan. Dynasty XII.

Comments: Redstarts are extremely rare in Egyptian art. This painted representation of a Redstart (fig. 193), one of only two examples of the species known to us, is from the Dynasty XII tomb of Khnumhotep III (No. 3) at Beni Hasan, where it is figured in the famous scene showing a group of birds roosting on the branches of two acacia trees (fig. 94). In repose, the bird is shown facing toward the right, with its left leg forward. Evincing a great familiarity with the species, the artist has beautifully reproduced the features of a male Redstart in this portrayal. A rather common passage migrant in modern Egypt, as they pause on their long flights,[703] they can be routinely observed perching in acacia trees, and it is one such occasion that our picture captures. The bird's coloring closely approaches that of a living male Redstart,[704] making the identification of it quite straight-forward. The crown, nape and back are painted bluish-grey, and the wing is mainly brownish, with some bluish-grey. The breast and underparts are white, tinged with yellowish brown, while the legs, bill, eye, cheek, throat and edges of the feathers on the wing are black, and the tail is entirely reddish. Of noticeable error, however, the white which borders the black cheek extends too far, and should be confined to the forehead. Sadly, the painting has suffered, and a small portion of the face and bill, and the terminal of the tail is now lost. Although the bird is surely meant to be thought of as roosting in the tree, the artist has not rendered it on a branch, and it looks as if it were standing on the back of a Pintail which is swimming in the pool on which the tomb owner has laid his clap-net. The other occurrence of a Redstart appears in the second acacia tree in the same scene,[705] and it is the better preserved of the two. Like the Redstart pictured here, it too is an outstanding depiction of this handsome and unmistakable bird.

135

72. House Sparrow (*Passer domesticus*)

Fig. 194. House Sparrows feeding in a sycamore fig tree, from the tomb of Userhet (No. 51), Thebes. Dynasty XIX.

Identification: The grey back and upper wing coverts with black markings, the black face and crown, the white cheek and underside, and the diagnostic black upper breast patch which is fringed with white are features of an adult male House Sparrow.

Distribution: The bird breeds and winters in parts of Europe, Asia, the Middle East, and Africa.[706] In modern Egypt, the House Sparrow is an abundant permanent breeding resident in the Nile Valley and Delta, the Faiyum, along the Mediterranean Sea coast west of Alexandria, the general vicinity of the Suez Canal, and in the Dakhla and Kharga Oases.

Comments: The House Sparrow is a commonly represented Egyptian hieroglyph;[707] it is extremely rare in art. This painting of two House Sparrows (fig. 194) is from a scene in the Dynasty XIX tomb of Userhet (No. 51) at Thebes, which shows the deceased tomb owner, with his wife and mother, seated beside a T-shaped pool and a great sycamore fig,

about to drink the cool refreshment that the goddess of the tree has poured for them.[708] Amid the thick green foliage of the tree, three House Sparrows are flitting about and nibbling at the ripened pink figs. This is the only sure instance of the species in Egyptian art known to us. The pair which we illustrate here, surrounded by broad leaves and neatly arranged clusters of figs, makes for an exquisite and charming picture. These pesky little birds have invaded the tree to pilfer the fruit. They have been painted in a most stylized fashion. Their bills really do not look much like the short, thick bill of the living species, and the head markings were hastily executed, sacrificing some of the birds' realism. Nature has not been totally forsaken with regard to detail, however, as the hatching on the back and upper wing coverts (though incorrectly oriented), and the subtle stippling fringing the black breast patch is entirely authentic. There can be but little doubt regarding their identification as House Sparrows.[709] Note that the lower bird is perching in a manner which suggests that its toes have hold of the branch,

136

something which was all too often overlooked by the Egyptian artist. The House Sparrow is an omnivorous feeder, and it is not surprising to see them enjoying figs, although they are best known in Egypt for their damage to grain crops (see below).

The sparrow hieroglyph 𓅓 can be clearly identified from Dynasty III onward;[710] it is often difficult to distinguish it from the swallow sign 𓏲 , except for the shape of the tail, and this is not always clearly shown.[711] The ubiquitous House Sparrow is a species that most of us are very familiar with. Often inhabiting human settlements, these highly gregarious birds frequently feed in cultivated areas and can sometimes cause great damage to crops, particularly to grain. In modern Egypt, House Sparrows consume vast quantities of ripe grain, a considerable problem.[712] The battle between man and the House Sparrow over valuable crops is by no means a recent development, but is probably as old as agriculture itself. A short didactic text of Ramesside date, which relates the miseries of the farmer's lot, while extolling that of the professional scribe, mentions that part of the farmer's hardship is due to sparrows, which "bring want upon the cultivator."[713]

---

73. Bat (Order Chiroptera)

Identification: The characteristic proportions, the foxlike head, the long pointed snout, the pricked ears, the small hind limbs, the comparatively long tail, and the broad membraneous wings are the unmistakable features of a bat.

Distribution: Bats are found throughout Europe, Asia, the Middle East, and Africa. In modern Egypt, sixteen species of bat are known to occur.[714]

Fig. 195. Drawing of a bat on a limestone ostracon, from Deir el-Medina. Ramesside Period.

Comments: Bats are extremely rare in Egyptian art. Today we know that bats are *not* birds, but mammals, and as such really do not have any claim to appear in this work. Man, however, has not always been quite so clear-cut in distinguishing between bat and bird scientifically, and it is clear that the Egyptians regarded the two as related. We therefore include this mammal here at the end of our catalogue.

This limestone ostracon (fig. 195) from Deir el-Medina, about the size of a man's hand, bears a fine, though somewhat faded drawing of a bat in black ink. While it is only a quick sketch, it is obviously the work of a skilled

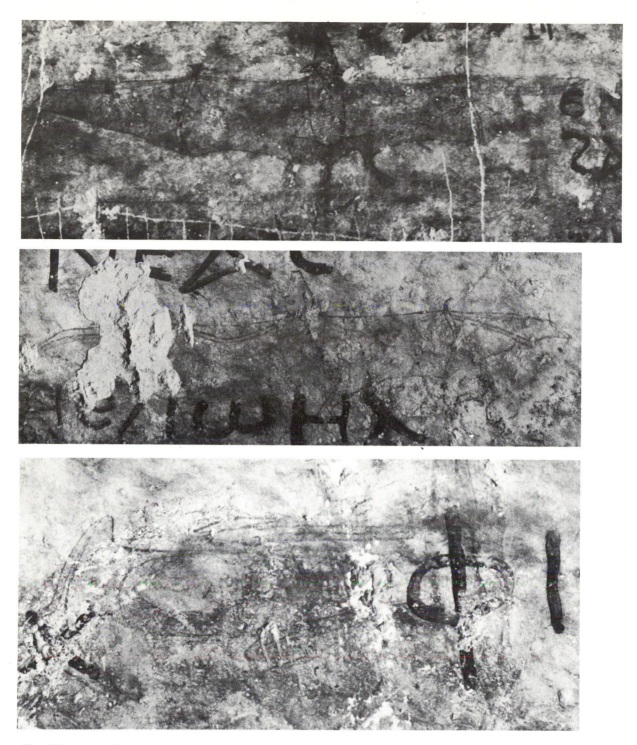

Fig. 196. (top) Larger bat from the collection of birds in the tomb of Baket III (No. 15), Beni Hasan. Dynasty XI.
Fig. 197. (center) Smaller bat from the collection of birds in the tomb of Baket III.
Fig. 198. (bottom) Bat depicted at rest from the collection of birds in the tomb of Baket III.

hand—as indeed might be expected from an artisans' village—and the animal has been vividly portrayed. It is pictured with its large wings outstretched as if it were in flight. The head is turned toward the right and the mouth is gaping open. Although the head is shown in profile, the ears are conventionally shown in a frontal view. Details such as the tragi (external ear flaps), the bones of the forearms, the tail, and the foxlike head seem to indicate that the artist had more than just a passing familiarity with the beast. It is worth noting that the bat is represented with a comparatively long tail, which extends beyond the interfemoral membrane, a characteristic feature of the rat-tailed bat (*Rhinopoma* sp.).[715] Given the rarity of the subject, this figure may have been executed for the artist's own enjoyment, perhaps drawn in an idle moment, rather than it being a trial study for the placement of its form elsewhere.

The only other extant and indisputable example of a bat from Dynastic times known to us,[716] is preserved in the Dynasty XI tomb of Baket III (No. 15) at Beni Hasan, where three bats are painted in the well known collection of birds, see under bird No. 9. The bats, of two varieties, large (fig. 196), and small (fig. 197), have been drawn with deft certainty.[717] They are displayed with considerable realistic detail. The two types are further distinguished by differing hieroglyphic names. Two of the bats are shown upright, with their wings outstretched and their heads turned and facing upward. The third is between them (fig. 198), but instead of being upright it is depicted horizontally on the wall, in an attitude of repose with its wings retracted and folded at the side. Some have regarded the three distinct enough to identify them as old world fruit bats (family Pteropodidae),[718] while others have been more precise still, seeing them as a pair of Rousette Fruit Bats (*Rousettus aegyptiacus*) and a Tomb Bat (*Taphozous perforatus*).[719] Owing to the rather poor condition of the representations today and because of the similarity between the many species of bat in present-day Egypt, we prefer simply an ordinal recognition of them.

Their inclusion in the scene amid the collection of birds indicates that the Egyptians considered bats and birds as a collective group of animals.[720] To the modern scientist the only similarity shared by these animals, other than being vertebrates, is their capability for sustained flight. Bats have fur, give live birth and nourish their young with milk, while birds have feathers, lay eggs and do not suckle their young. Thus, the phylogenetic relationship between bats and birds is distant. To regard the bat as a type of bird, like the Egyptians, is not uncommon in the history of man. For instance, in the Old Testament the bat was among the birds that the Hebrews were supposed to abstain from eating;[721] and a score of early Western zoologists also looked upon the bat as a kind of bird.[722] A parallel to the Egyptians' classification of the bat can be found in the fact that they thought of the turtle as a type of fish.[723] From the Ptolemaic Period comes a bronze statuette in the shape of a bat (fig. 199). It is quite stylized, but there can be no mis-taking it for anything else.[724] During this era the bat evidently had some religious associations.[725]

It is surprising how very few pictures of bats have come down to us. Bats are extremely abundant in Egypt today, often roosting in large numbers inside of pyramids, temples and particularly in rock cut tombs.[726] The modern visitor to these ancient monuments often quickly, and sometimes most unexpectedly, becomes aware of their presence. Their scarcity in art must surely not reflect their numbers in antiquity, but probably some inhibition on the part of the artists in portraying them. It is quite likely that the Egyptians, just like people the world over today, regarded the bat with some degree of fear, on account perhaps of its strange squeaks, its nocturnal habits and its mysterious dark haunts.

Fig. 199. Bronze statuette of a bat shown with its wings wrapped around its body, from Benha. Ptolemaic Period.

APPENDIX I
The Mummified Birds

The following is a list of those species of birds that have been identified from mummified remains.[1] The mummies themselves range in date from the New Kingdom through the Greco-Roman Period, with the vast majority coming from the Late Dynastic and Greco-Roman Periods.

Abdim's Stork	*Sphenorhynchus abdimii*
Glossy Ibis	*Plegadis falcinellus*
Sacred Ibis	*Threskiornis aethiopicus*
Osprey	*Pandion haliaetus*
Honey Buzzard	*Pernis apivorus*
Black-shouldered Kite	*Elanus caeruleus*
Red Kite	*Milvus milvus*
Black Kite	*Milvus migrans*
White-tailed Eagle	*Haliaeetus albicilla*
Egyptian Vulture	*Neophron percnopterus*
Griffon Vulture	*Gyps fulvus*
Lappet-faced Vulture	*Aegypius tracheliotus*
Short-toed Eagle	*Circaetus gallicus*
Hen Harrier	*Circus cyaneus*
Pallid Harrier	*Circus macrourus*
Montagu's Harrier	*Circus pygargus*
Marsh Harrier	*Circus aeruginosus*
Levant Sparrowhawk	*Accipiter brevipes*
Sparrowhawk	*Accipiter nisus*
Gabar Goshawk	*Melierax gabar*
Buzzard	*Buteo buteo*
Long-legged Buzzard	*Buteo rufinus*
Greater Spotted Eagle	*Aquila clanga*
Imperial Eagle	*Aquila heliaca*
Booted Eagle	*Hieraaetus pennatus*
Lesser Kestrel	*Falco naumanni*
Kestrel	*Falco tinnunculus*
Red-footed Falcon	*Falco vespertinus*
Merlin	*Falco columbarius*

Hobby	*Falco subbuteo*
Lanner Falcon	*Falco biarmicus*
Saker Falcon	*Falco cherrug*
Peregrine Falcon	*Falco peregrinus*
Egyptian Goose	*Alopochen aegyptiaca*
Stone Curlew	*Burhinus oedicnemus*
Spotted Sandgrouse	*Pterocles senegallus*
Cuckoo	*Cuculus canorus*
Barn Owl	*Tyto alba*
Eagle Owl	*Bubo bubo*
Long-eared Owl	*Asio otus*
Short-eared Owl	*Asio flammeus*
Scops Owl	*Otus scops*
Roller	*Coracias garrulus*
Swallow	*Hirundo rustica*

The following is a list of those species of birds that have been identified from bone remains found in tombs and from King Tutankhamun's funerary meal which were intended or known to have served as articles of food in ancient Egypt.[2] It also includes those birds which were mummified for the sole purpose of serving as food in the beyond. All of the material dates from the Middle and New Kingdoms.

Greylag Goose	*Anser anser*
White-fronted Goose	*Anser albifrons*
Bean Goose	*Anser fabalis*
Brent Goose	*Branta bernicla*
Green-winged Teal	*Anas crecca*
Gadwall	*Anas strepera*
Pintail	*Anas acuta*
Garganey	*Anas querquedula*
Shoveler	*Anas clypeata*
Turtle Dove	*Streptopelia turtur*

---

1. This list is based upon the identifications in Lortet and Gaillard 1903; Lortet and Gaillard 1905; Lortet and Gaillard 1908; Gaillard and Daressy 1905; Nicoll 1919; Hanzák 1977.

2. This list is based upon the identifications in Lortet and Gaillard 1905; Lortet and Gaillard 1907; Lortet and Gaillard 1908; Gaillard and Daressy 1905; Winlock 1941; Boessneck and von den Driesch 1982.

APPENDIX II
A Preliminary Checklist to the Birds of Egypt
(Excluding the Sinai)

by Steven M. Goodman

Introduction

Scope of the work

There are two intended purposes of this checklist. Firstly, I have attempted to provide an accurate, updated and concise list to the birds of the country for both the scholar and bird enthusiast. A considerable amount of new information has been collected on Egyptian birds since 1930, when Meinertzhagen published the last major review of the topic. Secondly, a complete list of transliterated colloquial Egyptian Arabic bird names has never been available, and through the careful work of Dr. Joseph J. Hobbs, an effort has been made to fill this need.

The geographic area covered herein includes all of present-day Egypt, excluding the Sinai. For the sake of clarity, Egypt is defined as the area south of the Mediterranean Sea, east of the Libyan border, west of the Suez Canal and Red Sea, and north of the Sudan border (including the Sudan Government Administration Area). The omission of Sinai from the checklist has no political motive. This preliminary checklist includes a total of 408 species, 11 of which are hypothetical.

Brief history of modern Egyptian ornithology

Three major works can be recognized as landmarks in modern Egyptian ornithology: G. E. Shelley (1872), *A Handbook to the Birds of Egypt*; M. J. Nicoll (1919), *Handlist of the Birds of Egypt*; and R. Meinertzhagen (1930, two vols.), *Nicoll's Birds of Egypt*. Meinertzhagen's work remains to this day the *magnum opus* of modern Egyptian ornithology and forms to some extent the foundation of this checklist.

The literature and work on Egyptian ornithology from the eighteenth to the early twentieth century has been summarized by Meinertzhagen.[1] Alexander Koenig traveled extensively in the country obtaining collections and distributional information, and between 1907 and 1932 published many substantial papers on modern Egyptian birds in the *Journal für Ornithologie*. While Egypt was a United Kingdom Protectorate (1914-22) and under military occupation (until 1936) a tremendous amount of information was published on the birds of the country. One individual at the forefront was R. E. Moreau who lived in Egypt from 1920 to 1928, and whose publishing record on works dealing exclusively with Egyptian ornithology spans the years from 1926 to 1970.

Abdallah El Negumi made important collections in the late 1940s and early 1950s, particularly in the Eastern Desert. These collections are housed in the Giza Zoological Gardens. El Negumi also co-authored a book in Arabic on Egyptian birds.[2] Another important contributor was A. H. Al Hussaini who wrote a series of papers on the birds of the Western Desert and Red Sea coast,[3] and a book in Arabic on the birds of the country.[4] In 1959, Dr. Lajos Horváth published a report on ornithological observations and materials obtained by the Natural History Museum, Budapest, on a 1957 expedition to Egypt.[5] Dr. Horváth named the most recently described endemic form from the country, a Desert Lark (*Ammomanes deserti borosi*), from some material collected during this trip.

Much of the new specimen material presented in this checklist comes from two recent bird collections. One of these was assembled by Dr. Harry Hoogstraal and the staff of the United States Naval Medical Research Unit No. 3 (NAMRU-3), Cairo, and is for the most part housed in the Field Museum of Natural History, Chicago. Since the early 1950s researchers from NAMRU-3 have been studying aspects of arboviruses, ticks and their vertebrate hosts. This work has added in countless ways to our knowledge of Egyptian zoology. The second major collection was obtained by the Palearctic Migratory Bird Survey (PMS), under the direction of Dr. G. E. Watson. The purpose of the PMS project was to study serology and ectoparasites of migratory birds in northeast Africa. During this survey, large collections of voucher specimens were made and all were deposited in the National Museum of Natural History, Washington, D.C.

The recent work of two Dutch ornithologists, Peter L. Meininger and W. C. Mullié, on the distribution of Egyptian birds and the importance of Egyptian wetlands for waterbirds have been important in establishing the need for habitat and bird conservation in the country. Since the late 1970s a renewed interest has arisen in the avifauna of Egypt resulting in a considerable amount of new information. Excluding our own work and notes, only material published before December 1983 has been included in this work.

Explanatory Notes for the Annotated Checklist

Systematic sequence and English vernacular names
The systematic order we have adopted is somewhat eclectic. The orders Struthioniformes through Falconiformes except for some minor deviations follow Mayr and Cottrell,[6] and the Anseriformes are after Delacour.[7] The remaining orders, including Passeriformes, generally follow Vaurie[8] for Palearctic species and numerous other sources for the few Afrotropical (= Ethiopian) species. Most English vernacular, colloquial, common or trivial names, as they are variously called, are generally after Voous.[9] However, when other English vernacular names are in wide use for any species, these have been listed in the "Comments" section.

Brief description of nomenclature and the use of this checklist
Following the classical scheme of taxonomy, in which animals are grouped and ranked in a hierarchical arrangement, the class Aves (all birds) is divided into orders, orders into families, families into genera, and genera into species. Species showing distinct geographical variation are divided into subspecies.

This system of classification has several advantages; perhaps foremost is that it has been almost universally adopted by taxonomists, which affords great stability to the scheme. The roots employed in scientific names are often of Latin and Greek origin. Regardless of the native tongue of researchers using this taxonomic system, the use of scientific names should eliminate any ambiguity as to which animal they are referring. As one can imagine, such stability would be impossible on an international scale solely with vernacular names. We must emphasize that it is precisely for this reason that archaeologists, art historians, philologists, etc., should use scientific names when they want to refer to a specific organism. It is our hope that this checklist will facilitate easier access to current scientific names, as well as English and Arabic vernacular names, for both the scholar and bird enthusiast alike, to the birds of the country.

Such a classical hierarchical system has been used in our arrangement. The birds are grouped by orders, and then subdivided within each order into families, genera, species and where appropriate into subspecies. The following example is presented to clarify, for those unfamiliar with this type of arrangement, how to interpret the entries used in this checklist.

1. **Black Kite** *Milvus migrans* (Boddaert)
2. *Milvus migrans migrans* (Boddaert)
3.   *Falco migrans* Boddaert, 1783, *Table Planches Enlum.*, p. 28, France.
4. *Milvus migrans aegyptius* (Gmelin)
5.   *Falco aegyptius* Gmelin, 1788, *Syst. Nat.*, 1, pt. 1, p. 261, Egypt.

Entry 1: Here the currently recognized genus (*Milvus*) and species (*migrans*) of the Black Kite are listed. Boddaert is the name of the author who published the first recognizable description of the species according to the rules set by the International Commission on Zoological Nomenclature. In cases such as this, when the author originally placed the species in a genus to which it is no longer assigned (see entry 3), the author's name is put in parentheses (cf. *Struthio camelus*, p. 144). An asterisk (*) before the scientific name denotes species whose known Egyptian occurrence is restricted to ancient times.

Entry 2: Here the genus, species and subspecies (the second *migrans*) are given along with the name of the author who described this subspecies. In this case the subspecies has the same name as the species and is termed the "nominate subspecies". For those animals which show no distinct intraspecific variation, a parallel to this entry would not be included (cf. *Sula bassana*, p. 145).

Entry 3: The genus and species are listed as given in Boddaert's original type description of the bird. This is followed by the citation where it was originally published, and type locality ("France").

Entry 4: For several species more than one subspecies has been recorded in the country. Other than the nominate subspecies *migrans*, a second subspecies, called *aegyptius* and named by Gmelin, also occurs in Egypt.

Entry 5: Here the name originally used by Gmelin for his description of *aegyptius*, the type citation and type locality are given. Note that although Gmelin described *aegyptius* as a distinct species and in the genus *Falco*, subsequent work showed that it was a subspecies of *migrans* and generically distinct from the genus *Falco* (the "true falcons").

In modern usage the first letter of the genus is capitalized whereas that of the species is always uncapitalized. All of the species (abbreviated sp. singular, spp. plural) and subspecies (subsp. singular, subspp. plural) and currently recognized genera used in this checklist are listed in the scientific index at the end of the book.

Egyptian Arabic Vernacular Names
Included in the checklist under the heading "Arabic name(s)" are the bird names most likely to be met with during field work in Egypt. Vernacular names are most problematic, for a single species may have different names in Upper and Lower Egypt, and between the Bedouin tribes of the Eastern and

Western Deserts. Also, in the region of the Siwa Oasis the names are generally of Berber origin.

Often the Egyptian Arabic bird name is "generic" in that it is used to designate several species. Many animals lumped under a generic name are closely related, in the modern taxonomic sense, while others show only gross similarities in external morphology or some aspect of natural history and are not closely related (e.g. swifts and swallows). Other names are strictly onomatopoetic (e.g., Hoopoe, *Hudhud*). The generic names provided in this list should be consulted first; where specific names are given for those also with generic names, these are separated by "and". Not surprisingly, birds which are conspicuous by virtue of size, number, coloring, habits, habitat or economic importance tend to have specific names.

Further collection of vernacular names and the study of their distribution and etymology is needed. The field student is encouraged to collect all, even conflicting, renditions, with the use of a field guide to the birds of North Africa or with the bird in hand, being careful to note the location where the name was given and to identify some socioeconomic characteristics of the informant. The Egyptian vernacular names have been adapted and/or transliterated from several works.[10]

Pronunciation, Spelling and Transliteration Guide

The hamza or glottal stop is represented by a single closing quote mark ('). It is here omitted when in an initial position or following a definite article ("al"). The glottal stop is produced by momentary closure of the glottis, "stopping" the outgoing breath.

Consonant sequences sh, gh, kh, dh, and th represent the single Arabic letters shiin, ghayn, khaa', dhaal, and thaa' respectively.

The slash (e.g., Mus/har) distinguishes two independent letters from the consonant sequences noted above.

The emphatic consonants are indicated by a dot beneath the letter, thus distinguishing the separate Arabic letters ṣaad, ḍaad, ṭaa', ẓaa', and ḥaa' from their softer counterparts siin, daal, taa', zaay, and haa' (s, d, t, z, h).

The opening quote represents the consonant 'ayn, which resembles a deep "a" emanating from the throat cavity.

Alif maqṣuura and alif maddah are written as "aa". Adjectival endings are "ii" for masculine and "iyya" for feminine.

Regional Variation in Pronunciation

The linguistic pattern of Egypt is very complex. Generalizations about regional pronunciation are offered with reservations. In particular, pronunciation of the literary Arabic qaaf (q) and jiim (j) varies considerably. Qaaf is probably not pronounced as "q" anywhere in Egypt; in Cairo and in some other places it becomes a glottal stop, indis-

tinguishable in speech from the hamza, while in rural areas and among the Bedouin it is often pronounced as gimm (a hard "g"). Thus ṣaqr (generic for falcons) may be heard as ṣa'r or as ṣagr, but probably not as ṣaqr. The jiim (j) in Cairo and many other localities becomes hard "g". In general, it may be said that where the qaaf is pronounced as "g" the jiim will be retained as a soft "j". The letter dhaal (dh) is pronounced often as a true "d", but in literal pronunciation resembles the "th" of "this". Thaa' (th) is pronounced in literary Arabic as in "thing", but often becomes "s" in spoken usage.

Comments Section

The annotations in this section are meant to serve several functions. In recent years a considerable amount of ornithological field work has been conducted in Egypt, resulting in new distributional information and species for the country. Although the annotations are succinct, we have attempted to include both literature and specimen references that augment the information presented by Meinertzhagen.[11] We have relied more heavily on museum specimens than published field observations for documentary purposes. The complete names of the museums abbreviated in the annotations can be found in the "Acknowledgements" section below. English vernacular names other than those we have adopted in this checklist that are in wide use are also included here.

Differences of opinion exist among systematists as to the higher level, generic and specific relationships and limits of some birds. In this section we have attempted to include the major divergences, particularly at the genus and species levels from other works.

Acknowledgements

While preparing this checklist assistance was received from many people. The fine section on Arabic bird names was compiled and transliterated by Dr. Joseph J. Hobbs, to whom I am indebted. The help and encouragement of Mr. Patrick F. Houlihan was important in the production of this work. I am also grateful to the following people for loaning or allowing access to specimen material under their care: Dr. Lester L. Short and Mrs. Mary K. LeCroy, American Museum of Natural History (AMNH), New York; Messrs. I. C. J. Galbraith and Michael P. Walters, British Museum (Natural History) (BMNH), Tring; Dr. David M. Niles, Delaware Museum of Natural History, Greenville; the late Dr. Abdel Hakim M. Kamel, Entomological Society of Egypt, Cairo; Dr. John W. Fitzpatrick and Dr. David E. Willard, Field Museum of Natural History (FMNH), Chicago; Dr. Mervat

Marcos, Dr. Mohamed Amir, and Dr. Mohamed Abdel Rahim, Giza Zoological Museum (GZM), Cairo; Dr. Pierre Devillers, Institut Royal des Sciences Naturelles Belgique, Brussels; Dr. Charles G. Sibley and Mrs. Eleanor H. Stickney, Peabody Museum of Natural History, New Haven; Dr. G. F. Mees, Rijksmuseum van Natuurlijke Historie, Leiden; Dr. Robert B. Payne and Dr. Robert W. Storer, The University of Michigan Museum of Zoology (UMMZ), Ann Arbor; Dr. George E. Watson, National Museum of Natural History, formerly United States National Museum (USNM), Washington, D.C.; and Dr. Karl-L. Schuchmann, Zoologisches Forschunginstitut und Museum Koenig (ZFMK), Bonn. For answering inquiries, and help in other ways, I would like to thank: Dr. Peter L. Ames, Dr. R. D. Etchécopar, Dr. Lajos Horváth, Dr. Thomas E. Lovejoy, Mr. Peter L. Meininger, Mr. Wim C. Mullié, Dr. Goetz Rheinwald, and Dr. Uriel Safriel. The University of Michigan Museum of Zoology generously provided workspace and materials during the writing of this checklist. Dr. Harry Hoogstraal, and Messrs. Ibrahim Helmy and Sherif Tewfik of the U.S. Naval Medical Research Unit No. 3, Cairo, provided assistance in countless ways while in Egypt. Some of the museum work was financed by grants from (in chronological order) from the Frank M. Chapman Fund, The University of Michigan Museum of Zoology and School of Graduate Studies, and the National Geographic Society. Mr. Patrick F. Houlihan, Dr. Robert B. Payne, and Dr. Robert W. Storer read an earlier version of this checklist and offered most useful comments.

ANNOTATED CHECKLIST

Order STRUTHIONIFORMES

Family STRUTHIONIDAE

Ostrich   *Struthio camelus* Linnaeus
Struthio camelus camelus Linnaeus
  Struthio Camelus Linnaeus, 1758, *Syst. Nat.*, ed. 10, p. 155, "Syria, Arabia, Lybia, Africa."
Arabic name: Na'aam.
Comments: This species has recently been "rediscovered" in Egypt, see Distribution of bird No. 1.[12]

Order PROCELLARIIFORMES

Family PROCELLARIIDAE

Cory's Shearwater   *Calonectris diomedea* (Scopoli)
Calonectris diomedea diomedea (Scopoli)
  Procellaria diomedea Scopoli, 1769, *Annus 1 Hist.-Nat.*, p. 74, no locality, but designated as Adriatic Sea, Brit. Ornith. Union, List Committee's Report, 1946, Ibis, p. 534.
Comments: Sometimes placed in the genus *Puffinus* as *P. diomedea*. Four specimens in the AMNH (527354-7) collected on 2 March 1885 at Abu Qir Bay. Another specimen from Abu Qir Bay in the GZM (A2040) collected on 12 September 1916. Several recent records from the country.[13] Called Mediterranean Shearwater in some other works.

Manx Shearwater   *Puffinus puffinus* (Brünnich)
Puffinus puffinus yelkouan (Acerbi)
  Procellaria Yelkouan Acerbi, 1827, *Biblioteca Italiana*, 47, p. 297, Hellespont, Bosphorus, and Black Sea [reference not verified].

Comments: Three specimens in the BMNH (91.6.18.101, 1941:5:30:3058 and 1941:5:30:3059) collected in 1879 at Damietta and on 9 September 1917 and 4 September 1918 at Ras el Bar (respectively). Another six specimens in the GZM (5884, 5989-90, 6938, 7896-7) obtained on 16 August 1916 at Burullus Beach, 8 September 1916 at Ras el Bar, 12 September 1916 at Abu Qir Bay, and 5 September 1917 and 4 September 1918 (two) at Ras el Bar (respectively). Called Levantine Shearwater or Common Shearwater in some other works.

[Order GAVIIFORMES

Family GAVIIDAE

Red-throated Diver   *Gavia stellata* (Pontoppidan)
Gavia stellata stellata (Pontoppidan)
  Colymbus Stellatus Pontoppidan, 1763, *Danske Atlas*, 1, p. 621, no locality, but presumed to be Denmark.
Comments: We are not aware of any specimens of this species from Egypt. Until documentation is available it should be considered hypothetical in this country. See under bird No. 2 for further comments. Called Red-throated Loon in some works.

Black-throated Diver   *Gavia arctica* (Linnaeus)
Gavia arctica arctica (Linnaeus)
  Colymbus arcticus Linnaeus, 1758, *Syst. Nat.*, ed. 10, p. 135, Europe and America.
Arabic name: Ghawwaaṣ (generic for loons and grebes).
Comments: We are not aware of any specimens of this species from Egypt. Until documentation is

available it should be considered hypothetical in the country. See under bird No. 2 for further comments. Called Black-throated Loon, Arctic Diver, or Arctic Loon in some other works.]

Order PODICIPEDIFORMES

Family PODICIPEDIDAE

Little Grebe *Tachybaptus ruficollis* (Pallas)
Tachybaptus ruficollis ruficollis (Pallas)
  Colymbus ruficollis Pallas, 1764, in Vroeg, *Cat. Adumbratiunculae*, p. 6, Holland, *fide* Sherborn, 1905, Smiths. Misc. Collect., 47.
Arabic name: Zahuut.
Comments: Sometimes placed in the genus *Podiceps* as *P. ruficollis*. A specimen in the USNM (550933) collcted on 8 January 1971 at Lake Manzala is referable to this subspecies.[14] Called Dabchick in some other works.

  Tachybaptus ruficollis capensis (Salvadori)
  Podiceps capensis Salvadori, 1884, Ann. Mus. Civ. Genova, 21, p. 252, Rugghiè and Lake Cialalakà, Shoa, Ethiopia.

[**Red-necked Grebe** *Podiceps grisegena* (Boddaert)
Podiceps grisegena grisegena (Boddaert)
  Colymbus grisegena Boddaert, 1783, *Table Planches Enlum.*, p. 28, France.
Comments: Inclusion of this species is based on several sight records.[15] We are not aware of any specimens from Egypt, and until further documentation is available this species should be considered hypothetical in the country. The subspecies *grisegena* is the one more likely to occur.]

Great Crested Grebe *Podiceps cristatus* (Linnaeus)
Podiceps cristatus cristatus (Linnaeus)
  Colymbus cristatus Linnaeus, 1758, *Syst. Nat.*, ed. 10, p. 135, Europe.

Black-necked Grebe *Podiceps nigricollis* Brehm
Podiceps nigricollis nigricollis Brehm
  Podiceps nigricollis C. L. Brehm, 1831, *Handb. Naturgesch. Vögel Deutschl.*, p. 963, Germany.
Comments: Called Eared Grebe in some other works. Also called *P. caspicus* in some earlier works.

Order PELECANIFORMES

Family PHAETHONTIDAE

Red-billed Tropicbird *Phaethon aethereus* Linnaeus
Phaethon aethereus indicus Hume
  Phaeton [sic] *indicus* Hume, 1876, Stray Feathers, 4, p. 481, Indian Ocean and Gulf of Oman.
Arabic name: Ra'iis Al-bahr.
Comments: Sometimes this subspecies is considered a distinct species and is called the Lesser Red-billed Tropicbird. A chick was reported to have been collected in April 1942 on an island off Hurghada.[16] There are numerous other records of this species in Egypt.[17]

Family PHALACROCORACIDAE

Great Cormorant *Phalacrocorax carbo* (Linnaeus)
Phalacrocorax carbo sinensis (Blumenbach)
  Pelecanus Sinensis Blumenbach, 1789, *Abbildungen Naturhist., Gegenstände*, no. 25, plate and text, China.
Arabic names: Abuu Ghaṭaas, and 'Aqaq, Ghuraab Al-bahr (generic for cormorant).
Comments: Called Greater Cormorant or White-breasted Cormorant in some other works.

Shag *Phalacrocorax aristotelis* (Linnaeus)
Phalacrocorax aristotelis desmarestii (Payraudeau)
  Carbo Desmarestii Payraudeau, 1826, Ann. Sci. Nat., 8, p. 464, Sardinia and Corsica.
Arabic name: Qaaq Al-maaya.

Long-tailed Cormorant *Phalacrocorax africanus* (Gmelin)
Phalacrocorax africanus africanus (Gmelin)
  Pelecanus africanus J. F. Gmelin, 1789, *Syst. Nat.*, 1, pt. 2, p. 577, "Africa."
Comments: Sometimes placed in the genus *Halietor* as *H. africanus*. This species has not been recorded in Egypt since 1875 when a specimen was collected on 2 June in the Faiyum.[18] Called Long-tailed Shag, Reed Cormorant, Reed Duiker, or African Pygmy Cormorant in some other works.

*****Darter** *Anhinga rufa* (Daudin)
Anhinga rufa (subsp.?) (Daudin)
  Plotus rufus Daudin, 1802, in Buffon, *Hist. Nat.*, ed. Didot, Quadr., 14, p. 319, Senegal.
Comments: Sometimes placed in the Family ANHINGIDAE and also regarded as conspecific with *A. melanogaster*. This species does *not* occur in modern Egypt, see bird No. 4 for further comments.

Family SULIDAE

Gannet *Sula bassana* (Linnaeus)
  Pelecanus Bassanus Linnaeus, 1758, *Syst. Nat.*, ed. 10, p. 133, "Scotia, America", restricted to Bass Rock, Scotland, *fide* Hartert, 1920, *Vögel Pal. Fauna*, 2, p. 1406.
Arabic name: Atiish (generic for *Sula* spp.)
Comments: Sometimes placed in the genus *Morus* as *M. bassanus*. Specimen in ZFMK (4175) taken at Port Said on 20 September 1905.[19] One observed relatively recently off the coast of Alexandria.[20]

Brown Booby *Sula leucogaster* (Boddaert)
Sula leucogaster plotus (Forster)
  Pelecanus Plotus Forster, 1844, *Descriptiones Animalium*, p. 278, near New Caledonia.

Family PELECANIDAE

White Pelican   *Pelecanus onocrotalus* Linnaeus
Pelecanus Onocrotalus Linnaeus, 1758, *Syst. Nat.*,
   ed. 10, p. 132, "Africa, Asia."
Arabic names: Baja', Jamal Al-baḥr (both generic
for pelicans).
Comments: Called Rosy Pelican in some other
works.

Pink-backed Pelican   *Pelecanus rufescens* Gmelin
Pelecanus rufescens J. F. Gmelin, 1789, *Syst. Nat.*,
   1, pt. 2, p. 571, West Africa.
Comments: There are a few records of this species
in Egypt.[21] Called Rose-backed Pelican in some
other works.

Dalmatian Pelican   *Pelecanus crispus* Bruch
Pelecanus crispus Bruch, 1832, Isis von Oken, col.
   1109, Dalmatia.
Comments: Sometimes regarded as conspecific with
P. philippensis.

Order CICONIIFORMES

Family ARDEIDAE

Grey Heron   *Ardea cinerea* Linnaeus
Ardea cinerea cinerea Linnaeus
   Ardea cinerea Linnaeus, 1758, *Syst. Nat.*, ed. 10,
   p. 143, Europe.
Arabic names: Naghaaj, and Balashuun, Waaq
(generic for herons and egrets).

Goliath Heron   *Ardea goliath* Cretzschmar
Ardea goliath Cretzschmar, 1827, *Atlas Reise
   Rüppell, Vögel*, p. 39, pl. 26, "Baḥr el Abiad."
Arabic name: Mirra.
Comments: Records of this species in Egypt,
including breeding, have been recently reviewed.[22]

Purple Heron   *Ardea purpurea* Linnaeus
Ardea purpurea purpurea Linnaeus
   Ardea purpurea purpurea Linnaeus, 1766, *Syst.
   Nat.*, ed. 12, p. 236, "Oriente."
Arabic names: Jaḥfa, Maalik Al-ḥaziin.

Great Egret   *Egretta alba* (Linnaeus)
Egretta alba alba (Linnaeus)
   Ardea alba Linnaeus, 1758, *Syst. Nat.*, ed. 10,
   p. 144, Europe.
Arabic names: Balashuun Abyaḍ, Ghayṭii, Waaq
Abyaḍ.
Comments: Sometimes placed in the genus *Cas-
merodias* as *C. albus*. Called Great White Egret,
Large Egret, or Common Egret in some other
works.

Cattle Egret   *Egretta ibis* (Linnaeus)
Egretta ibis ibis (Linnaeus)
   Ardea Ibis Linnaeus, 1758, *Syst. Nat.*, ed. 10,
   p. 144, Egypt.
Arabic name: Abuu Qurdaan.
Comments: Called Buff-backed Egret or Buff-
backed Heron in some other works.

Little Egret   *Egretta garzetta* (Linnaeus)
Egretta garzetta garzetta (Linnaeus)
   Ardea Garzetta Linnaeus, 1766, *Syst. Nat.*, ed. 12,
   p. 237, "Oriente."
Arabic names: Abuu Baliiqa, Bayaaḍii.

Western Reef Heron   *Egretta gularis* (Bosc)
Egretta gularis schistacea (Hemprich & Ehrenberg)
   Ardea Lepterodas schistacea Hemprich and
   Ehrenberg, 1828, *Symbolae Physicae, Aves*,
   pt. 1, pl. 6, and text, sig. i (1833), Red Sea.
Arabic names: Balashuun Baḥrii, Abuu Ṣarraaḥ.
Comments: Sometimes this subspecies is placed
under *E. garzetta* or considered a distinct species.
Called African Reef Heron in some other works.

Squacco Heron   *Ardeola ralloides* (Scopoli)
   Ardea ralloides Scopoli, 1769, *Annus 1 Hist.-
   Nat.*, p. 88, "In Carniolica."
Arabic names: Sabiisa, Waaq Abyaḍ Ṣughayyar.

Striated Heron   *Ardeola striata* (Linnaeus)
Ardeola striata brevipes (Hemprich & Ehrenberg)
   Ardea, Nycticorax, brevipes Hemprich and Ehrenberg, 1833, *Symbolae Physicae, Aves*, pt. 1, sig.
   m, note 2, "Habitat ad ripas Nili et ad Maris
   rubri littus."
Comments: Sometimes placed in the genus *Butori-
des* as *B. striatus brevipes*. This subspecies has been
considered a distinct species in some other works.
Records of this species in Egypt have been recently
summarized.[23] Called Green-backed Heron, Little
Mangrove Heron or Little Green Heron in some
other works.

Night Heron   *Nycticorax nycticorax* (Linnaeus)
Nycticorax nycticorax nycticorax (Linnaeus)
   Ardea Nycticorax Linnaeus, 1758, *Syst. Nat.*, ed.
   10, p. 142, Europe.
Arabic names: Ghuraab Al-layl, Waaq Ash-shajar.
Comments: Called Black-crowned Night Heron in
some other works.

Little Bittern   *Ixobrychus minutus* (Linnaeus)
Ixobrychus minutus minutus (Linnaeus)
   Ardea minuta Linnaeus, 1766, *Syst. Nat.*, ed. 12,
   p. 240, "Helvetia, Aleppo", restricted to Switzer-
   land, *fide* Vaurie, 1965, *Birds Pal. Fauna. Non-
   Pass.*, p. 57.
Arabic name: Maliiḥa.

Bittern   *Botaurus stellaris* (Linnaeus)
Botaurus stellaris stellaris (Linnaeus)
   Ardea stellaris Linnaeus, 1758, *Syst. Nat.*, ed. 10,
   p. 144, Europe.
Arabic name: Buubuu.

Family CICONIIDAE

Wood Ibis   *Mycteria ibis* (Linnaeus)
Tantalus Ibis Linnaeus, 1766, *Syst. Nat.*, ed. 12,
   p. 241, Egypt.
Comments: Sometimes placed in the genus *Ibis* as
I. ibis. On 29 November 1982 a skull was collected

from a bird found dead on an island off Hurghada.[24] On 21 October 1957, twelve birds were observed on the Nile bank opposite El Bayana and four birds on 22 October 1957 below Luxor.[25] There is also an earlier sight record.[26] Also note that the type locality is Egypt. Called Yellow-billed Stork in some other works.

White Stork   *Ciconia ciconia* (Linnaeus)
Ciconia ciconia ciconia (Linnaeus)
  Ardea Ciconia Linnaeus, 1758, *Syst. Nat.*, ed. 10, p. 142, Europe, Asia, Africa.
Arabic names: 'Anaz, Balaaraj, Laqlaq.

Black Stork   *Ciconia nigra* (Linnaeus)
  Ardea nigra Linnaeus, 1758, *Syst. Nat.*, ed. 10, p. 142, northern Europe.
Arabic names: 'Anaz Aswad, Laqlaq Aswad.

*Saddlebill Stork   *Ephippiorhynchus senegalensis* (Shaw)
  Mycteria Senegalensis Shaw, 1800, Trans. Linn. Soc. London, 5, p. 35, pl. 3, Senegal.
Comments: This species does *not* occur in modern Egypt, see under bird No. 12 for further comments. Called Jabiru in some other works.

[Family BALAENICIPITIDAE

*Whale-headed Stork   *Balaeniceps rex* Gould
Balaeniceps rex Gould, 1850, Athenaeum, no. 1207, p. 1315, upper White Nile.
Comments: This species does *not* occur in modern Egypt and the evidence for it in ancient Egypt may be inconclusive. See under bird No. 13 for further comments. Called Shoe-billed Stork or Whale-billed Stork in some other works.]

Family THRESKIORNITHIDAE

Glossy Ibis   *Plegadis falcinellus* (Linnaeus)
  Tantalus Falcinellus Linnaeus, 1766, *Syst. Nat.*, ed. 12, p. 241, "Austria, Italia."
Arabic names: Abuu Minjal Aswad, and Abuu' Minjal (generic for ibis).

Sacred Ibis   *Threskiornis aethiopicus* (Latham)
Threskiornis aethiopicus aethiopicus (Latham)
  Tantalus aethiopicus Latham, 1790, *Index Ornith.*, 2, p. 706, "Aethiopia."
Arabic name: Abuu Ḥannash.
Comments: Specimen in the BMNH (93.8.4.6) collected in November 1877 at Damietta.[27] Also in the BMNH is a clutch of four eggs (1914.10.1. 3522-5) from the Radcliffe-Saunders collection, obtained in May 1896 at Damietta. The data for specimens in the Radcliffe-Saunders collection is notorious for its uncertainty[28] and this record cannot be accepted. Thus the last reliable record of this species in Egypt is November 1877.

Hermit Ibis   *Geronticus eremita* (Linnaeus)
  Upupa Eremita Linnaeus, 1758, *Syst. Nat.*, ed. 10, p. 118, Switzerland.

Comments: This species has been documented only once in modern Egypt. See under bird No. 14 for further comments. Called Waldrapp or Bald Ibis in some other works.

European Spoonbill   *Platalea leucorodia* Linnaeus
Platalea leucorodia leucorodia Linnaeus
  Platalea Leucorodia Linnaeus, 1758, *Syst. Nat.*, ed. 10, p. 139, Europe.
Arabic name: Abuu Mil'aqa.
Comments: Called Common Spoonbill in some other works.

  Platalea leucorodia archeri Neumann
  Platalea leucorodia archeri Neumann, 1928, J. f. Ornith., 7, p. 283, Dahlak Islands, Ethiopia.
Comments: This subspecies has been found breeding in Egypt.[29]

Order PHOENICOPTERIFORMES

Family PHOENICOPTERIDAE

Greater Flamingo   *Phoenicopterus ruber* Linnaeus
Phoenicopterus ruber roseus Pallas
  Phoenicopterus roseus Pallas, 1811, *Zoographia Rosso-Asiatica*, 2, p. 207, "ad ostia Volgae et Rhymni."
Arabic names: Bashaaruush, Nuḥaam.
Comments: Called Rosy Flamingo in some other works.

Order FALCONIFORMES[30]

Family ACCIPITRIDAE

Osprey   *Pandion haliaetus* (Linnaeus)
Pandion haliaetus haliaetus (Linnaeus)
  Falco Haliaetus Linnaeus, 1758, *Syst. Nat.*, ed. 10, p. 91, Europe.
Arabic names: Mansuurii, Naasuurii.
Comments: Sometimes this genus is placed in the Family PANDIONIDAE.

Honey Buzzard   *Pernis apivorus* (Linnaeus)
  Falco apivorus Linnaeus, 1758, *Syst. Nat.*, ed. 10, p. 91, Europe.
Arabic name: Ḥuwwaam An-naḥl.

Black-shouldered Kite   *Elanus caeruleus* (Desfontaines)
Elanus caeruleus caeruleus (Desfontaines)
  Falco caeruleus Desfontaines, 1789, Hist. Acad. Roy. Sci., Paris (for 1787), p. 503, pl. 15, Algeria.
Arabic names: Kuuhiya, Zurraq, and Ḥidaaya, Ḥid'a (generic for kite).
Comments: Called Black-winged Kite in some other works.

Red Kite   *Milvus milvus* (Linnaeus)
Milvus milvus milvus (Linnaeus)
  Falco Milvus Linnaeus, 1758, *Syst. Nat.*, ed. 10,

147

p. 89, "Europa, Asia, Africa."
Comments: Specimen in the GZM (B452) collected at Abu Rawash and which later died in the Giza Zoo on 14 September 1942.[31] There are a few other records of this species in Egypt.[32]

Black Kite   *Milvus migrans* (Boddaert)
Milvus migrans migrans (Boddaert)
Falco migrans Boddaert, 1783, *Table Planches Enlum.*, p. 28, France.
Arabic name: Hidaaya Maṣriyya.
Comments: Called Black-billed Kite in some other works.

Milvus migrans aegyptius (Gmelin)
Falco aegyptius J. F. Gmelin, 1788, *Syst. Nat.*, 1, pt. 1, p. 261, Egypt.

African Fish Eagle   *Haliaeetus vocifer* (Daudin)
Falco vocifer Daudin, 1800, *Traité Ornith.*, 2, p. 65; based on Levaillant, 1796, *Hist. Nat. Oiseaux Afrique*, 1, p. 11, pl. 14, Cape Province.
Comments: An adult specimen (in GZM) was collected south of Aswan in the first half of November 1947.[33]

White-tailed Eagle   *Haliaeetus albicilla* (Linnaeus)
Falco Albicilla Linnaeus, 1758, *Syst. Nat.*, ed. 10, p. 89, Europe, America.
Arabic names: Shumiiṭa, 'Uqaab Al-baḥr.
Comments: Called Grey Sea Eagle or White-tailed Sea Eagle in some other works.

Lammergeyer   *Gypaetus barbatus* (Linnaeus)
Gypaetus barbatus meridionalis Keyserling and
                                                    Blasius
Gypaetus meidionalis [sic] Keyserling and Blasius, 1840, *Wirbelthiere Europa's*, p. XXVIII, South Africa.
Arabic names: Abuu Dhiqan, Kaasir Al-'iẓaam, and Nasr, Nisr, Rakhama (generic for vulture).
Comments: Specimen in the FMNH (312438) collected on 27 February 1964 at Wadi Akwamtra, Gebel Elba.[34] A few recent sight records from the Red Sea Mountains.[35] Called Bearded Vulture or Lammergeier in some other works.

Egyptian Vulture   *Neophron percnopterus*
                                                    (Linnaeus)
Neophron percnopterus percnopterus (Linnaeus)
Vultur Perenopterus [sic] Linnaeus, 1758, *Syst. Nat.*, ed. 10, p. 87, Egypt.
Arabic name: Anuuq.

Rüppell's Vulture   *Gyps rueppellii* (Brehm)
Gyps rueppellii rueppellii (Brehm)
Vultur Rueppellii A. E. Brehm, 1852, Naumannia, 2, p. 44, Khartoum, Sudan.

Griffon Vulture   *Gyps fulvus* (Hablizl)
Gyps fulvus fulvus (Hablizl)
Vultur fulvus Hablizl, 1783, *Neue Nordische Beyträge*, 4, p. 58, Samamisian Alps, Gilan, northern Iran.

Black Vulture   *Aegypius monachus* (Linnaeus)
Vultur Monachus Linnaeus, 1766, *Syst. Nat.*, ed. 12, p. 122, Arabia.
Comments: Specimen in the GZM (4983) collected on 4 March 1911 at El Mansuriya. This specimen has been previously reported.[36] Called Cinereous Vulture in some other works.

Lappet-faced Vulture   *Aegypius tracheliotus*
                                                    (Forster)
Vultur tracheliotus Forster, 1791, in Levaillant, *Reise Afrikas*, 3, p. 363, pl. 12, Great Namaland.
Arabic name: Abuu Wudaan.
Comments: Specimens in the FMNH (299495) and GZM (A2468) collected on 14 February 1967 at Wadi Yoider, Gebel Elba and on 30 December 1938 at Wadi Shallal, Gebel Elba (respectively).[37] Called Nubian Vulture in some other works.

Short-toed Eagle   *Circaetus gallicus* (Gmelin)
Circaetus gallicus gallicus (Gmelin)
Falco gallicus J. F. Gmelin, 1788, *Syst. Nat.*, 1, pt. 1, p. 259, France.
Arabic names: Ṣaraara, 'Uqaab Abyaḍ.
Comments: Called Snake Eagle, Short-toed Snake Eagle or Short-toed Harrier Eagle in some other works.

Hen Harrier   *Circus cyaneus* (Linnaeus)
Circus cyaneus cyaneus (Linnaeus)
Falco cyaneus Linnaeus, 1766, *Syst. Nat.*, ed. 12, p. 126, Europe, Africa.
Arabic names: Abuu Ḥuṣn, Murza Ad-dajaaj, 'Uqaab Ad-dajaaj, and Murza (generic for harrier).
Comments: Called Northern Harrier or Marsh Hawk in some other works.

Pallid Harrier   *Circus macrourus* (Gmelin)
Falco macrourus S. G. Gmelin, 1770, *Reise Russland*, 1, p. 48, Voronezh, Russia.
Arabic name: Murza Baghthaa'.
Comments: Called Pale Harrier in some other works.

Montagu's Harrier   *Circus pygargus* (Linnaeus)
Falco Pygargus Linnaeus, 1758, *Syst. Nat.*, ed. 10, p. 89, Europe.
Arabic name: Abuu Sharada.

Marsh Harrier   *Circus aeruginosus* (Linnaeus)
Circus aeruginosus aeruginosus (Linnaeus)
Falco aeruginosus Linnaeus, 1758, *Syst. Nat.*, ed. 10, p. 91, Europe.
Arabic names: Darraa'a, Durii'a.

Levant Sparrowhawk   *Accipiter brevipes* (Severtzov)
Astur brevipes Severtzov, 1850, Bull. Soc. Imp. Nat. Moscou, 23, no. 3, p. 234 (first), pls. 1-3, southern Russia.
Arabic names: Baydaq, and Baashiq, Baaz, Baazii (generic for *Accipiter* spp.).
Comments: Sometimes considered conspecific with

A. badius. Specimen in the USNM .(569005) collected on 5 May 1971 at Bahig.

Sparrowhawk   *Accipiter nisus* (Linnaeus)
Accipiter nisus nisus (Linnaeus)
 Falco Nisus Linnaeus, 1758, *Syst. Nat.*, ed. 10, p. 92, Europe.

Accipiter nisus nisosimilis (Tickell)
 Falco Nisosimilis Tickell, 1833, *J. Asiat. Soc. Bengal*, 2, p. 571, "Marcha, in Borabhúm", India.
Comments: There are several published records of this subspecies in Egypt.[38]

Goshawk   *Accipiter gentilis* (Linnaeus)
Accipiter gentilis gentilis (Linnaeus)
 Falco gentilis Linnaeus, 1758, *Syst. Nat.*, ed. 10, p. 89, Alps, Sweden.
Comments: Called Northern Goshawk in some other works.

Buzzard   *Buteo buteo* (Linnaeus)
Buteo buteo buteo (Linnaeus)
 Falco Buteo Linnaeus, 1758, *Syst. Nat.*, ed. 10, p. 90, Europe.
Arabic names: Ṣaqr Ḥuwwam, and Ḥamiimaq, Ṣaqr Jarraaḥ (generic for buzzard).

Buteo buteo vulpinus (Gloger)
 ?*Falco vulpinus* Gloger, 1833, *Abändern der Vögel Einfluss Klima's*, p. 141 [south] Africa.
Comments: Called Steppe Buzzard in some other works.

Long-legged Buzzard   *Buteo rufinus* (Cretzschmar)
Buteo rufinus rufinus (Cretzschmar)
 Falco rufinus Cretzschmar, 1827, *Atlas Reise Rüppell, Vögel*, p. 40, pl. 27, upper Nubia, Shendi, Sennar, and Ethiopia.
Arabic name: Siqaawa.

Buteo rufinus cirtensis (Levaillant)
 Falco cirtensis Levaillant, 1850, *Expl. Sci. Algérie, Hist. Nat. Ois., Atlas*, pl. 3, no locality, but presumed to be northeastern Algeria, *fide* Loche, 1867, *Expl. Sci. Algérie, Hist. Nat. Ois.*, 1, p. 44.

Lesser Spotted Eagle   *Aquila pomarina* Brehm
Aquila pomarina pomarina Brehm
 Aquila Pomarina C. L. Brehm, 1831, *Handb. Naturgesch. Vögel Deutschl.*, p. 27, Pomerania, northern Germany.
Arabic name: 'Uqaab (generic for large falconiforms).

Greater Spotted Eagle   *Aquila clanga* Pallas
 Aquila Clanga Pallas, 1811, *Zoographia Rosso-Asiatica*, 1, p. 351, Russia and Siberia.
Comments: Called Spotted Eagle in some other works.

Steppe Eagle   *Aquila rapax* (Temminck)
Aquila rapax orientalis Cabanis
 Aq[uila] orientalis Cabanis, 1854, *J. f. Ornith.*, 2, p. 369, footnote, Sarepta, southeastern Russia.

Aquila rapax belisarius (Levaillant)
 Falco Belisarius Levaillant, 1850, *Expl. Sci. Algérie, Hist. Nat. Ois., Atlas*, pl. z, no locality, but presumed to be northeastern Algeria, *fide* Loche, 1867, *Expl. Sci. Algérie, Hist. Nat. Ois.*, 1, p. 24.
Comments: Specimen in GZM (7975) taken on 20 January 1924 at Giza.[39] Called Tawny Eagle in some other works.

Imperial Eagle   *Aquila heliaca* Savigny
Aquila heliaca heliaca Savigny
 Aquila heliaca Savigny, 1809, *Descr. de l'Égypte, Hist. Nat.*, 1, *Syst. Ois.*, p. 82, pl. 12, Thebes, upper Egypt.
Arabic name: Khaaṭiya.

Golden Eagle   *Aquila chrysaetos* (Linnaeus)
Aquila chrysaetos homeyeri Severtzov
 Aq[uila] Fulva Homeyeri Severtzov, 1888, *Nouv. Mém. Soc. Imp. Nat. Moscou*, 15, p. 184, livr. 5, Balearic Islands and Algeria.

[Verreaux's Eagle   *Aquila verreauxii* Lesson
 Aquila Verreauxii Lesson, 1830, *Centurie Zool.*, p. 105, pl. 38, Cape of Good Hope.
Comments: Previously it was reported that a specimen was captured near the Suez Canal on 1 November 1916.[40] However, this record has been questioned,[41] and it is best to consider this species hypothetical in Egypt until further documentation is available. Called Black Vulture in some other works.]

Bonelli's Eagle   *Hieraaetus fasciatus* (Vieillot)
Hieraaetus fasciatus fasciatus (Vieillot)
 Aquila fasciata Vieillot, 1822, *Mém. Soc. Linn. Paris*, 2, pt. 2, p. 152, "Fontaineblau and Sardinia."
Arabic name: 'Uqaab Masiira.

Booted Eagle   *Hieraaetus pennatus* (Gmelin)
Hieraaetus pennatus pennatus (Gmelin)
 Falco pennatus J. F. Gmelin, 1788, *Syst. Nat.*, 1, pt. 1, p. 272, no locality; France suggested by Swann, 1922, *Synopsis Accipitres*, ed. 2, p. 113.
Arabic name: 'Uqaab Masiira Ṣaghirra.

Family FALCONIDAE

Lesser Kestrel   *Falco naumanni* Fleischer
 Falco Naumanni Fleischer, 1818, in Fischer, *Sylvan Jahrb.* for 1817-8, p. 174, southern Germany and Switzerland.
Arabic names: 'Awiisuq, Burgayz, Ṣaqr Al-jaraad, and Ṣaqr (generic for *Falco* spp.).

Kestrel   *Falco tinnunculus* Linnaeus
Falco tinnunculus tinnunculus Linnaeus
 Falco Tinnunculus Linnaeus, 1758, *Syst. Nat.*, ed. 10, p. 90, Europe.
Arabic names: 'Aasuuq, Ṣaqr Baladii.

Falco tinnunculus rupicolaeformis (Brehm)

Cerchneis rupicolaeformis C. L. Brehm, 1855, *Der Vollständige Vogelfang*, p. 29, Egypt.

Red-footed Falcon   *Falco vespertinus* Linnaeus
Falco vespertinus Linnaeus, 1766, *Syst. Nat.*, ed. 12, p. 129, "Ingria", designated as Province of St. Petersburg, *fide* Hartert, 1913, *Vögel Pal. Fauna*, 2, p. 1078.
Arabic name: Luziiq.

Eleonora's Falcon   *Falco eleonorae* Gené
Falco Eleonorae Gené, 1839, Rev. Zool., p. 105, Sardinia.
Comments: Specimen in the BMNH (94.6.16.368) collected in 1878 at Damietta.[42]

Sooty Falcon   *Falco concolor* Temminck
Falco concolor Temminck, 1825, in Temminck and Laugier, *Planches Col.*, livr. 56, pl. 330 and text, "Sénégal, sur les côtes de Barbarie, en Égypte et en Arabie", restricted to Barqan Island, Gulf of Aqaba, *fide* Vaurie, 1965, *Birds Pal. Fauna. Non-Pass.*, p. 227.
Arabic name: Ṣaqr Al-ghuruub.
Comments: Three specimens in the FMNH (296929-296931) collected on 14 June 1974 and 17 June 1974 (two) in the Bahariya Oasis. A specimen in the BMNH (1955.6.N.20-1721) collected on 10 September 1861 in the Nubian Desert at "Rowan-kab". There are numerous sight records of this species in Egypt.[43]

Merlin   *Falco columbarius* Linnaeus
Falco columbarius aesalon Tunstall
Falco Aesalon Tunstall, 1771, *Ornith. Brit.*, p. 1, France.
Arabic names: Abuu Riyaaḥ, Yu'yu'.
Comments: Called Pigeon Hawk in some other works.

Falco columbarius insignis (Clark)
Aesalon regulus insignis Clark, 1907, Proc. U.S. Natl. Mus., 32, p. 470, Fusan, Korea.

Hobby   *Falco subbuteo* Linnaeus
Falco subbuteo subbuteo Linnaeus
Falco Subbuteo Linnaeus, 1758, *Syst. Nat.*, ed. 10, p. 89, Europe.
Arabic name: Kuunig.

Lanner Falcon   *Falco biarmicus* Temminck
Falco biarmicus tanypterus Schlegel
Falco tanypterus Schlegel, 1843, *Abh. Gebiete Zool. Vergleich. Anat.*, 3, p. 8, pls. 12-13, Nubia and Ethiopia.
Arabic names: (Ṣaqr) Ḥurr, Shaahiin.

Saker Falcon   *Falco cherrug* Gray
Falco cherrug cherrug Gray
Falco cherrug J. E. Gray, 1834, in Hardwicke, *Illustr. Indian Zool.* 2, pts. 15-16, pl. 25, India.
Arabic name: Ṣaqr Al-ghazaal.
Comments: Specimen in the FMNH (284696) taken on 21 December 1967, 15 miles southeast of Bahig.

Peregrine Falcon   *Falco peregrinus* Tunstall
Falco peregrinus peregrinus Tunstall
Falco Peregrinus Tunstall, 1771, *Ornith. Brit.*, pl. 1, Great Britain.

Falco peregrinus calidus Latham
Falco calidus Latham, 1790, *Index Ornith.*, 1, p. 41, India.
Comments: Specimen in the USNM (152776) collected on 12 March 1895 at Helwan, and another in the FMNH (222415) taken on 22 April 1954 near Sidi Barrani.

Falco peregrinus pelegrinoides Temminck
Falco pelegrinoides Temminck, 1829, in Temminck and Laugier, *Planches Col.*, livr. 81, pl. 479, Nubia.
Comments: Sometimes this subspecies is regarded as a distinct species. Called Barbary Falcon or Shaheen in some other works.

Order ANSERIFORMES

Family ANATIDAE

Mute Swan   *Cygnus olor* (Gmelin)
Anas Olor J. F. Gmelin, 1789, *Syst. Nat.*, 1, pt. 2, p. 502, "Russia, Sibiria, Persico etiam littore maris Caspii."
Arabic names: Timm, Wizz 'Iraaqi (generic for swan).
Comments: Specimen in the GZM (12289) collected on 7 December 1931 at Lake Maryiut. There are several other records of this species in Egypt.[44]

Whooper Swan   *Cygnus cygnus* (Linnaeus)
Anas Cygnus Linnaeus, 1758, *Syst. Nat.*, ed. 10, p. 122, Europe, America.
Comments: There are several records of this species in Egypt.[45]

[*Bewick's Swan   *Cygnus bewickii* Yarrell
Cygnus Bewickii Yarrell, 1830, Trans. Linn. Soc. London, 16, p. 453, pl. 24, England.
Comments: This species does *not* occur in modern Egypt, but either it and/or *C. cygnus* occurred in ancient Egypt, see bird No. 27 for further comments. *C. bewickii* is sometimes regarded as conspecific with *C. columbianus*.]

Greylag Goose   *Anser anser* (Linnaeus)
Anser anser [*anser*] (Linnaeus)
Anas Anser Linnaeus, 1758, *Syst. Nat.*, ed. 10, p. 123, Europe, America.
Arabic names: Iwazz, Wizz (generic for geese).
Comments: One individual was collected out of a flock of six in January 1942 at Lake Maryiut.[46] The specimen cannot be traced. The subspecies that is most likely to occur is *anser*, but this needs specimen confirmation.

White-fronted Goose   *Anser albifrons* (Scopoli)
Anser albifrons albifrons (Scopoli)

Branta albifrons Scopoli, 1769, *Annus 1 Hist.-Nat.*, p. 69, no locality, thought to be Italy, *fide* Vaurie, 1965, *Birds Pal. Fauna. Non-Pass.*, p. 96.
Comments: Called Greater White-fronted Goose in some other works.

Lesser White-fronted Goose   *Anser erythropus* (Linnaeus)
Anas erythropus Linnaeus, 1758, *Syst. Nat.*, ed. 10, p. 123, Europe.

Bean Goose   *Anser fabalis* (Latham)
Anser fabalis fabalis (Latham)
Anas Fabalis Latham, 1787, *Gen. Synopsis Birds, Suppl.* 1, p. 297, Great Britain.
Comments: Two wings in the GZM (2038) collected in December 1922 at "Hod el Raml."[47]

Barnacle Goose   *Branta leucopsis* (Bechstein)
A.[nas] *leucopsis* Bechstein, 1803, *Ornith. Taschenb.*, p. 424, Germany.
Comments: A female was collected on 16 April 1931 near Helwan.[48] We have examined this specimen in the Entomological Society collection, Cairo.

Red-breasted Goose   *Branta ruficollis* (Pallas)
Anser ruficollis Pallas, 1769, *Spicilegia Zool.*, fasc. 6, p. 21, pl. 4, lower Ob River, Siberia [reference not verified].
Comments: This species has not been documented in Egypt since the late nineteenth century.[49] See under bird No. 31 for further comments.

Brent Goose   *Branta bernicla* (Linnaeus)
Branta bernicla bernicla (Linnaeus)
Anas Bernicla Linnaeus, 1758, *Syst. Nat.*, ed. 10, p. 124, "Europa boreali; migrat supra Sveciam."
Comments: Called Brant in some other works.

Egyptian Goose   *Alopochen aegyptiaca* (Linnaeus)
Anas aegyptiaca Linnaeus, 1766, *Syst. Nat.*, ed. 12, p. 197, Egypt.
Arabic name: Shayyiqa.

Ruddy Shelduck   *Tadorna ferruginea* (Pallas)
Anas ferruginea Pallas, 1764, in Vroeg, *Cat. Adumbratiunculae*, p. 5, "Tartary", *fide* Sherborn, 1905, *Smiths. Misc. Collect.*, 47.
Arabic name: Abuu Farwa.

Common Shelduck   *Tadorna tadorna* (Linnaeus)
Anas Tadorna Linnaeus, 1758, *Syst. Nat.*, ed. 10, p. 122, Europe.
Arabic name: Shaharamaan.

Mallard   *Anas platyrhynchos* Linnaeus
Anas platyrhynchos platyrhynchos Linnaeus
Anas platyrhynchos Linnaeus, 1758, *Syst. Nat.*, ed. 10, p. 125, Europe.
Arabic names: Burkaawaa, Khuḍaarii, and Baṭṭ (generic for duck).

Green-winged Teal   *Anas crecca* Linnaeus
Anas crecca crecca Linnaeus
Anas Crecca Linnaeus, 1758, *Syst. Nat.*, ed. 10, p. 126, Europe.

Arabic name: Sharshiir Shatawii.
Comments: Called Common Teal in some other works.

Gadwall   *Anas strepera* Linnaeus
Anas strepera strepera Linnaeus
Anas strepera Linnaeus, 1758, *Syst. Nat.*, ed. 10, p. 125, Europe.
Arabic name: Samaarii.

European Wigeon   *Anas penelope* Linnaeus
Anas Penelope Linnaeus, 1758, *Syst. Nat.*, ed. 10, p. 126, Europe.
Arabic name: Ṣiwwaay.

Pintail   *Anas acuta* Linnaeus
Anas acuta acuta Linnaeus
Anas acuta Linnaeus, 1758, *Syst. Nat.*, ed. 10, p. 126, Europe.
Arabic name: Balbuul.
Comments: Called Northern Pintail in some other works.

Marbled Duck   *Anas angustirostris* Ménétries
Anas angustirostris Ménétries, 1832, *Cat. Raisonné Obj. Zool. Caucase*, p. 58, Lenkoran, Talych.
Arabic name: Minya.
Comments: Sometimes placed in the genus *Marmaronetta* as *M. angustirostris*.

Garganey   *Anas querquedula* Linnaeus
Anas Querquedula Linnaeus, 1758, *Syst. Nat.*, ed. 10, p. 126, Europe.
Arabic names: Karkaj, Sharshiir Ṣayfii.

Shoveler   *Anas clypeata* Linnaeus
Anas clypeata Linnaeus, 1758, *Syst. Nat.*, ed. 10, p. 124, Europe.
Arabic name: Kiish.
Comments: Called Northern Shoveler in some other works.

Red-crested Pochard   *Netta rufina* (Pallas)
Anas rufina Pallas, 1773, *Reise Versch. Prov. Russ. Reichs*, 2, p. 713, Caspian Sea and lakes of Tartarian Desert.
Arabic name: Wanas.

Common Pochard   *Aythya ferina* (Linnaeus)
Anas ferina Linnaeus, 1758, *Syst. Nat.*, ed. 10, p. 126, Europe.
Arabic names: Baṭṭ Aḥmar, Ḥumraay.
Comments: Called European Pochard in some other works.

White-eyed Pochard   *Aythya nyroca* (Güldenstädt)
Anas nyroca Güldenstädt, 1770, Novi Comm. Acad. Sci. Imp. Petropol., 14 (for 1769), pt. 1, p. 403, southern Russia.
Arabic names: Zariiqal, Zurqaay Aḥmar.
Comments: Called Ferruginous Duck in some other works.

Tufted Duck   *Aythya fuligula* (Linnaeus)
Anas Fuligula Linnaeus, 1758, *Syst. Nat.*, ed. 10, p. 128, Europe.

Arabic name: Zurqaay.

Spur-winged Goose   *Plectropterus gambensis*
(Linnaeus)
Plectropterus gambensis gambensis (Linnaeus)
  Anas gambensis Linnaeus, 1766, *Syst. Nat.*, ed.
  12, p. 195, Gambia.
Comments: Solitary birds were observed on four occasions in March 1962 at Abu Simbel.[50] It is impossible to determine whether these animals were wild or feral domestics.

Velvet Scoter   *Melanitta fusca* (Linnaeus)
Melanitta fusca fusca (Linnaeus)
  Anas fusca Linnaeus, 1758, *Syst. Nat.*, ed. 10,
  p. 123, coasts of Sweden.
Comments: Two sight records from Egypt. One was noted off the Red Sea coast, near Halaib, on 14 January 1896[51] and one female was observed in Suez Bay by several observers on four days between 24 February and 12 March 1982.[52] Called White-winged Scoter in some other works.

Smew   *Mergus albellus* Linnaeus
  Mergus Albellus Linnaeus, 1758, *Syst. Nat.*, ed.
  10, p. 129, Europe.
Arabic name: Balqasha (generic for merganser).

Red-breasted Merganser   *Mergus serrator* Linnaeus
Mergus serrator serrator Linnaeus
  Mergus Serrator Linnaeus, 1758, *Syst. Nat.*, ed.
  10, p. 129, Europe.
Comments: Specimen in the GZM (8617) collected on 15 June 1926 at Suez.[53] There are a few other specimen records from Egypt.[54]

White-headed Duck   *Oxyura leucocephala* (Scopoli)
  Anas leucocephala Scopoli, 1769, *Annus 1 Hist.-
  Nat.*, p. 65, no locality, thought to be northern
  Italy, *fide* Vaurie, 1965, *Birds Pal. Fauna. Non-
  Pass.*, p. 142.
Arabic name: Abuu Mirwaha.

Order GALLIFORMES

Family PHASIANIDAE

Barbary Partridge   *Alectoris barbara* (Bonaterre)
Alectoris barbara barbata (Reichenow)
  C.[accabis] barbata Reichenow, 1896, Ornith.
  Monatsber., 4, p. 76, bird in Cologne Zoo.
Arabic names: Shinaar, and Ḥajal (generic for partridge).
Comments: Two specimens (one of which is a nestling) in the BMNH (1965 M.1905 and 1965 M.1906) were collected on 30 January 1928 at Mersa Matruh.

Sand Partridge   *Ammoperdix heyi* (Temminck)
Ammoperdix heyi nicolli Hartert
  Ammoperdix heyi nicolli Hartert, 1919, Bull. Brit.
  Ornith. Club, 40, p. 4, Wadi Hof, near Cairo.
Comments: Spelled *hayi* in some other works.[55]

Ammoperdix heyi cholmleyi Ogilvie-Grant
  Ammoperdix cholmleyi Ogilvie-Grant, 1897,
  Handb. Game Birds, 2, p. 293, "Egypt and
  Nubia", restricted to Jebel Erba, Suakin, Sudan,
  fide Vaurie, 1965, *Birds Pal. Fauna. Non-Pass.*,
  p. 280.

Common Quail   *Coturnix coturnix* (Linnaeus)
Coturnix coturnix coturnix (Linnaeus)
  Tetrao Coturnix Linnaeus, 1758, *Syst. Nat.*, ed.
  10, p. 161, Europe, Asia, Africa.
Arabic names: Salwaa, Summaan.
Comments: Called African Quail in some other works.

Red Junglefowl or **Domestic Fowl**   *Gallus gallus*
(Linnaeus)
Gallus gallus subsp.
  Phasianus Gallus Linnaeus, 1758, *Syst. Nat.*, ed.
  10, p. 158, "India Orientali: Pouli candor."
Arabic names: Dajaaj, Firaakh.
Comments: This species has been introduced to Egypt, see under bird No. 40 for further comments.

Family NUMIDIDAE

***Helmeted Guineafowl**   *Numida meleagris*
(Linnaeus)
Numida meleagris subsp. (Linnaeus)
  Phasianus Meleagris Linnaeus, 1758, *Syst. Nat.*,
  ed. 10, p. 158, Africa.
Comments: This species does not exist in a wild state in modern Egypt, see under bird No. 41 for further comments. Called Tufted Guineafowl or Crowned Guineafowl in some other works.

Order GRUIFORMES

Family GRUIDAE

Common Crane   *Grus grus* (Linnaeus)
Grus grus grus (Linnaeus)
  Ardea Grus Linnaeus, 1758, *Syst. Nat.*, ed. 10,
  p. 141, Europe, Africa.
Arabic names: Ghurnuuq, Kurkii, Rahuu (generic for cranes).
Comments: Called European Crane or Grey Crane in some other works.

Demoiselle Crane   *Anthropoides virgo* (Linnaeus)
  Ardea Virgo Linnaeus, 1758, *Syst. Nat.*, ed. 10,
  p. 141, "Oriente."

Family OTIDIDAE

Little Bustard   *Otis tetrax* Linnaeus
  Otis Tetrax Linnaeus, 1758, *Syst. Nat.*, ed. 10,
  p. 154, Europe.
Arabic name: Ḥubaarii (generic for bustard).
Comments: Sometimes placed in the genus *Tetrax* as *T. tetrax*. Specimen in the GZM (9306) collected on 8 December 1922 at Gattah.[56]

Houbara Bustard *Chlamydotis undulata* (Jacquin)
Chlamydotis undulata undulata (Jacquin)
  Psophia (*undulata*) Jacquin, 1784, *Beyträge Gesch. Vögel*, p. 24, pl. 9, "Afrika."
Comments: Four relatively recent specimens in the FMNH (219670, 18930 CC, 18931 CC, 18932 CC) collected on 23 October 1953, twenty miles southeast of Salum, on 20 April 1954, two miles south of Sidi Barrani, and on 23 April 1954, ten miles east of Sidi Barrani (two) (respectively).

Chlamydotis undulata macqueenii (Gray)
  Otis Macqueenii J. E. Gray, 1832, in Hardwicke, *Illustr. Indian Zool.*, 2, pt. 12, pl. 47, "Himalaya Mountains."

Family RALLIDAE

Water Rail *Rallus aquaticus* Linnaeus
Rallus aquaticus aquaticus Linnaeus
  Rallus aquaticus Linnaeus, 1758, *Syst. Nat.*, ed. 10, p. 153, Europe.
Arabic names: Kalb Al-baḥr, 'Uṣfuur Kalb Al-maaya, and Mur'a (generic for rail and crake).

Spotted Crake *Porzana porzana* (Linnaeus)
  Rallus Porzana Linnaeus, 1766, *Syst. Nat.*, ed. 12, p. 262, Europe.

Little Crake *Porzana parva* (Scopoli)
  Rallus parva Scopoli, 1769, *Annus 1 Hist.-Nat.*, p. 108, Carniola.

Baillon's Crake *Porzana pusilla* (Pallas)
Porzana pusilla pusilla (Pallas)
  Rallus pusillus Pallas, 1776, *Reise Versch. Prov. Russ. Reichs*, 3, p. 700, Dauria, Transbaicalia.
Comments: Called Lesser Spotted Crake in some other works.

Porzana pusilla intermedia (Hermann)
  Rallus intermedius Hermann, 1804, *Observ. Zool.*, p. 198, Strassburg, Germany.

Corncrake *Crex crex* (Linnaeus)
  Rallus Crex Linnaeus, 1758, *Syst. Nat.*, ed. 10, p. 153, Europe.
Arabic names: Mur'a Al-ghalla, Ṣifrad.
Comments: Called Landrail in some other works.

Moorhen *Gallinula chloropus* (Linnaeus)
Gallinula chloropus chloropus (Linnaeus)
  Fulica Chloropus Linnaeus, 1758, *Syst. Nat.*, ed. 10, p. 152, Europe.
Arabic name: Dajaaja Al-maaya.
Comments: Called Common Gallinule or Common Moorhen in some other works.

Purple Gallinule *Porphyrio porphyrio* (Linnaeus)
Porphyrio porphyrio aegyptiacus Heuglin
  Porphyrio aegyptiacus Heuglin, 1856, Sitzungber. Akad. Wiss. Wien, Math.-Naturwiss. Klasse, 19, p. 317, Egypt.
Arabic names: Dajaaja Sulṭaaniyya, Farkha Sulṭaaniyya.

Comments: Sometimes the Egyptian population is regarded as a race of the Green-backed Gallinule and is designated *P. m. madagascariensis*, or is synonymized with *P. p. madagascariensis*. Called King Reed-hen, Purple Waterhen, Blue Gallinule, Purple Coot or Purple Swamphen in some other works.

Allen's Gallinule *Porphyrio alleni* Thomson
  Porphyrio Alleni Thomson, 1842, Mag. Nat. Hist., 10, p. 204, Idda, Niger River.
Arabic name: Furfuur.
Comments: Sometimes placed in the genus *Porphyrula* as *P. alleni*. Called Allen's Reed-hen or Lesser Gallinule in some other works.

European Coot *Fulica atra* Linnaeus
Fulica atra atra Linnaeus
  Fulica atra Linnaeus, 1758, *Syst. Nat.*, ed. 10, p. 152, Europe.
Arabic names: Ghurr, Ghurra.
Comments: Called Common Coot or Black Coot in some other works.

Order CHARADRIIFORMES

Family ROSTRATULIDAE

Painted Snipe *Rostratula benghalensis* (Linnaeus)
Rostratula benghalensis benghalensis (Linnaeus)
  Rallus benghalensis Linnaeus, 1758, *Syst. Nat.*, ed. 10, p. 153, Asia.
Arabic names: Bakaashiina, Shunqub.

Family HAEMATOPODIDAE

European Oystercatcher *Haematopus ostralegus* Linnaeus
Haematopus ostralegus ostralegus Linnaeus
  Haematopus Ostralegus Linnaeus, 1758, *Syst. Nat.*, ed. 10, p. 152, Europe, America.
Arabic name: Aakil Al-maḥaar.
Comments: Called Pied Oystercatcher in some other works.

Family CHARADRIIDAE

Ringed Plover *Charadrius hiaticula* Linnaeus
Charadrius hiaticula tundrae (Lowe)
  Aegialitis hiaticola [sic] *tundrae* Lowe, 1915, Bull. Brit. Ornith. Club, 36, p. 7, Yenisei Valley, Siberia.
Arabic names: Abuu Ar-ru'uus, Qaṭqaaṭ, Zaqzaaq (all generic for plover).
Comments: Called Great Ringed Plover in some other works.

Little Ringed Plover *Charadrius dubius* Scopoli
Charadrius dubius curonicus Gmelin
  Charadrius curonicus J. F. Gmelin, 1789, *Syst. Nat.*, 1, pt. 2, p. 692, "Curonia."

153

Kittlitz's Plover *Charadrius pecuarius* Temminck
Charadrius pecuarius Temminck, 1823, in Temminck and Laugier, *Planches Col.*, livr. 31, p. 183, Cape of Good Hope.

Kentish Plover *Charadrius alexandrinus* Linnaeus
Charadrius alexandrinus alexandrinus Linnaeus
Charadrius alexandrinus Linnaeus, 1758, *Syst. Nat.*, ed. 10, p. 150, Egypt.
Comments: Called Snowy Plover in some other works.

Geoffrey's Plover *Charadrius leschenaultii* Lesson
Charadrius Leschenaultii Lesson, 1826, *Dict. Sci. Nat.*, ed. Levrault, 42, p. 36, India.
Comments: Called Greater Sand Plover in some other works.

Caspian Plover *Charadrius asiaticus* Pallas
Charadrius asiaticus Pallas, 1773, *Reise Versch. Prov. Russ. Reichs*, 2, p. 715, "Lacus salsos deserti australioris."
Comments: Sometimes placed in the genus *Eupoda* as *E. asiatica*. Specimen in the FMNH (23734 CC) collected on 14 October 1962 at Bahig.[57] There are a few recent sight records from Egypt.[58]

Dotterel *Eudromias morinellus* (Linnaeus)
Charadrius Morinellus Linnaeus, 1758, *Syst. Nat.*, ed. 10, p. 150, Europe.
Comments: Sometimes placed in the genus *Charadrius* as *C. morinellus*.

Grey Plover *Pluvialis squatarola* (Linnaeus)
Tringa Squatarola Linnaeus, 1758, *Syst. Nat.*, ed. 10, p. 149, Europe.
Comments: Called Black-bellied Plover or Silver Plover in some other works.

Golden Plover *Pluvialis apricaria* (Linnaeus)
Pluvialis apricaria altifrons (Brehm)
Charadrius altifrons C. L. Brehm, 1831, *Handb. Naturgesch. Vögel Deutschl.*, p. 542, Faroes.
Comments: Called Eurasian Golden Plover or Greater Golden Plover in some other works.

White-tailed Plover *Vanellus leucurus* (Lichtenstein)
Charadrius leucurus Lichtenstein, 1823, in Eversmann, *Reise von Orenburg nach Buchara*, p. 137, "Kuman und Jan-Darja."
Arabic name: Ṭaqṭiiqa Shumiiṭa.
Comments: Sometimes placed in the genus *Chettusia* as *C. leucura*.

Sociable Plover *Vanellus gregarius* (Pallas)
Charadrius gregarius Pallas, 1771, *Reise Versch. Prov. Russ. Reichs*, 1, p. 456, Volga, Jaiku, and Samara.
Comments: Sometimes placed in the genus *Chettusia* as *C. gregaria*.

Lapwing *Vanellus vanellus* (Linnaeus)
Tringa Vanellus Linnaeus, 1758, *Syst. Nat.*, ed. 10, p. 148, Europe, Africa.
Arabic name: Zaqzaaq Shaamii.

Comments: Called Northern Lapwing in some other works.

Spur-winged Plover *Vanellus spinosus* (Linnaeus)
Charadrius spinosus Linnaeus, 1758, *Syst. Nat.*, ed. 10, p. 151, Egypt.
Arabic name: Abuu Ẓufur.

Family SCOLOPACIDAE

Turnstone *Arenaria interpres* (Linnaeus)
Arenaria interpres interpres (Linnaeus)
Tringa Interpres Linnaeus, 1758, *Syst. Nat.*, ed. 10, p. 148, Europe, America.
Arabic name: Qunbura Al-maaya.
Comments: Called Ruddy Turnstone in some other works.

Little Stint *Calidris minuta* (Leisler)
Tringa minuta Leisler, 1812, *Nachträge zu Bechsteins Naturgesch. Deutschl.*, p. 74, Germany.
Arabic names: Durrayga, Fuṭayra, Karawaan Al-maaya (all generic for *Calidris* spp.)

Temminck's Stint *Calidris temminckii* (Leisler)
Tringa Temminckii Leisler, 1812, *Nachträge zu Bechsteins Naturgesch. Deutschl.*, p. 63, Germany.

Dunlin *Calidris alpina* (Linnaeus)
Calidris alpina alpina (Linnaeus)
Tringa alpina Linnaeus, 1758, *Syst. Nat.*, ed. 10, p. 149, Lapland.

Calidris alpina schinzii (Brehm)
Tringa Schinzii C. L. Brehm, 1822, *Beiträge zur Vögelkunde*, 3, p. 355, Baltic coast and Germany.
Comments: Two specimens in the FMNH (22317 CC and 22482 CC) collected on 3 February 1959 along the shore of Lake Qarun, Faiyum, and on 11 December 1959, five miles north of Qantara (respectively).

Curlew Sandpiper *Calidris ferruginea* (Pontoppidan)
Tringa Ferrugineus Pontoppidan, 1763, *Danske Atlas*, 1, p. 624, no locality, but presumed to be Denmark.

Knot *Calidris canutus* (Linnaeus)
Calidris canutus canutus (Linnaeus)
Tringa Canutus Linnaeus, 1758, *Syst. Nat.*, ed. 10, p. 149, Europe.
Comments: One individual was collected out of a small flock on 5 March 1903 at Suez.[59] The specimen cannot be traced. Recent records include two on 30 March 1982 and one on 23 April 1982 at Suez.[60]

Sanderling *Calidris alba* (Pallas)
Trynga alba Pallas, 1764, in Vroeg, *Cat. Adumbratiunculae*, p. 7, coast of the North Sea, *fide* Sherborn, 1905, Smiths. Misc. Collect., 47.
Arabic name: Midrawaan.

Buff-breasted Sandpiper   *Tryngites subruficollis*
                                                                    (Vieillot)
Tringa subruficollis Vieillot, 1819, *Nouv. Dict.*
d'Hist. Nat., nouv. éd., 34, p. 465, Paraguay.
Comments: A female specimen (BMNH 1965.
M.3659) was collected at Quseir on 21 February
1928.[61]

Ruff   *Philomachus pugnax* (Linnaeus)
Tringa Pugnax Linnaeus, 1758, *Syst. Nat.*, ed. 10,
    p. 148, Europe.
Arabic names: Ḥajwaala, Shaqiiy.

Broad-billed Sandpiper   *Limicola falcinellus*
                                                                 (Pontoppidan)
Limicola falcinellus falcinellus (Pontoppidan)
Scolopax Falcinellus Pontoppidan, 1763, *Danske
    Atlas*, 1, p. 623, no locality, but presumed to be
    Denmark.

Spotted Redshank   *Tringa erythropus* (Pallas)
Scolopax erythropus Pallas, 1764, in Vroeg, *Cat.
    Adumbratiunculae*, p. 6, Holland, *fide* Sherborn,
    1905, Smiths. Misc. Collect., 47.
Arabic names: Ṭawṭaw, Tiyṭawaa (both generic for
Tringa spp.).

Redshank   *Tringa totanus* (Linnaeus)
Tringa totanus totanus (Linnaeus)
Scolopax Totanus Linnaeus, 1758, *Syst. Nat.*, ed.
    10, p. 145, Europe.

Marsh Sandpiper   *Tringa stagnatilis* (Bechstein)
T. [*otanus*] *stagnatilis* Bechstein, 1803, *Ornith.
    Taschenb.*, p. 292, pl. 29, Heerden, Germany.

Greenshank   *Tringa nebularia* (Gunnerus)
Scolopax nebularia Gunnerus, 1767, in Leem,
    Beskrivelse over Finmarkens Lapper, p. 251,
    Norway [reference not verified].

Green Sandpiper   *Tringa ochropus* Linnaeus
Tringa Ocrophus [sic] Linnaeus, 1758, *Syst. Nat.*,
    ed. 10, p. 149, Europe.

Wood Sandpiper   *Tringa glareola* Linnaeus
Tringa Glareola Linnaeus, 1758, *Syst. Nat.*, ed.
    10, p. 149, Europe.

Common Sandpiper   *Tringa hypoleucos* Linnaeus
Tringa Hypoleucos Linnaeus, 1758, *Syst. Nat.*,
    ed. 10, p. 149, Europe.
Comments: Sometimes placed in the genus *Actitis*
as *A. hypoleucos*.

Terek Sandpiper   *Xenus cinereus* (Güldenstädt)
Scolopax cinerea Güldenstädt, 1775, Novi Comm.
    Acad. Sci. Imp. Petropol., 19 (for 1774), p. 473,
    pl. 19, shores of Caspian Sea near mouth of
    Terek River.
Comments: Sometimes placed in the genus *Tringa*
as *T. cinerea* or in the genus *Terekia* as *T. cinerea*.
There are several recent sight records of this species
in Egypt.[62]

Black-tailed Godwit   *Limosa limosa* (Linnaeus)
Limosa limosa limosa (Linnaeus)
Scolopax Limosa Linnaeus, 1758, *Syst. Nat.*, ed.
    10, p. 147, Europe.
Arabic name: Biqwayqa Sulṭaaniyya.

Bar-tailed Godwit   *Limosa lapponica* (Linnaeus)
Limosa lapponica [*lapponica*] (Linnaeus)
Scolopax lapponica Linnaeus, 1758, *Syst. Nat.*,
    ed. 10, p. 147, Lapland.
Comments: An individual was collected on 26
February 1941 at the Bitter Lakes.[63] The specimen
cannot be traced. There are several sight records of
this species in Egypt.[64] The subspecies *lapponica* is
the one most likely to occur, but this needs specimen confirmation.

Common Curlew   *Numenius arquata* (Linnaeus)
Numenius arquata arquata (Linnaeus)
Scolopax Arquata Linnaeus, 1758, *Syst. Nat.*, ed.
    10, p. 145, Europe.
Arabic names: Karawaan Ghayṭii, and Karawaan
(generic for *Numenius* spp.).

Numenius arquata orientalis Brehm
Numenius orientalis C. L. Brehm, 1831, *Handb.
    Naturgesch. Vögel Deutschl.*, p. 610, East Indies.
Comments: Specimen in the BMNH (91.8.1.129)
collected on 20 February 1821 in the Faiyum. There
are a few recent records of this subspecies in
Egypt.[65]

Slender-billed Curlew   *Numenius tenuirostris*
                                                                      Vieillot
Numenius tenuirostris Vieillot, 1817, *Nouv. Dict.
    d'Hist. Nat.*, nouv. éd., p. 302, Egypt.
Comments: An old specimen housed in the BMNH
(92.8.3.451) is labeled "Egypt" and another in
ZFMK was taken in October 1903 near Abu Qir.

Whimbrel   *Numenius phaeopus* (Linnaeus)
Numenius phaeopus phaeopus (Linnaeus)
Scolopax Phaeopus Linnaeus, 1758, *Syst. Nat.*,
    ed. 10, p. 146, Europe.
Arabic name: Karawaan Ghayṭii Ṣughayyar.

Eurasian Woodcock   *Scolopax rusticola* Linnaeus
Scolopax Rusticola Linnaeus, 1758, *Syst. Nat.*,
    ed. 10, p. 146, Europe.
Arabic names: Dajaaja Al-arḍ, Ḥimaar Al-ḥajal.

Common Snipe   *Gallinago gallinago* (Linnaeus)
Gallinago gallinago gallinago (Linnaeus)
Scolopax Gallinago Linnaeus, 1758, *Syst. Nat.*,
    ed. 10, p. 147, Europe.
Arabic names: Bakashiin, Shunqub (both generic
for snipe).
Comments: Sometimes placed in the genus *Capella*
as *C. gallinago*.

Great Snipe   *Gallinago media* (Latham)
Scolopax Media Latham, 1787, *Gen. Synopsis
    Birds*, Suppl. 1, p. 292, England.
Comments: Sometimes placed in the genus *Capella*
as *C. media*.

155

Jack Snipe   *Lymnocryptes minimus* (Brünnich)
Scolopax Minima Brünnich, 1764, *Ornith. Borealis*, p 49, Denmark [reference not verified].

Family RECURVIROSTRIDAE

Black-winged Stilt   *Himantopus himantopus* (Linnaeus)
Himantopus himantopus himantopus (Linnaeus)
Charadrius Himantopus Linnaeus, 1758, *Syst. Nat.*, ed. 10, p. 151, Europe.
Arabic names: Abuu Maghaazil, Abuu Qaṣaba.

Avocet   *Recurvirostra avosetta* Linnaeus
Recurvirostra Avosetta Linnaeus, 1758, *Syst. Nat.*, ed. 10, p. 151, Europe.
Arabic names: Ḥaliibii, Nakkaat.
Comments: Called Pied Avocet in some other works.

Family PHALAROPODIDAE

Red-necked Phalarope   *Phalaropus lobatus* (Linnaeus)
Tringa tobata [sic] Linnaeus, 1758, *Syst. Nat.*, ed. 10, p. 148, Europe, America.
Comments: Admitted on sight record. One was observed between 1 and 7 May 1982 near Suez.[66] Called Northern Phalarope in some other works.

Family DROMADIDAE

Crab Plover   *Dromas ardeola* Paykull
Dromas Ardeola Paykull, 1805, Nya Handl. Kongl. Vet. Akad., 26, p. 182, 188, pl. 8, "Ost-indien."
Arabic name: Ḥunkuur.
Comments: An individual was reported to have been shot from a flock in October 1946 along the Red Sea coast.[67] The specimen cannot be traced. There are numerous sight records of this species in Egypt.[68]

Family BURHINIDAE

Common Thick-knee   *Burhinus oedicnemus* (Linnaeus)
Burhinus oedicnemus oedicnemus (Linnaeus)
Charadrius Oedicnemus Linnaeus, 1758, *Syst. Nat.*, ed. 10, p. 151, England.
Arabic names: Karawaan, Karawaan Jabalii (both generic for *Burhinus* spp.).
Comments: Called Stone Curlew in some other works.

Burhinus oedicnemus saharae (Reichenow)
Oedicnemus oedicnemus saharae Reichenow, 1894, J. f. Ornith., 42, p. 102, Tunis.

Senegal Thick-knee   *Burhinus senegalensis* (Swainson)
Burhinus senegalensis inornatus (Salvadori)
Oedicnemus inornatus Salvadori, 1865, Atti Soc.
Italiana Sci. Nat., Milano, 8, p. 381, "Abissinia."
Comments: Called Senegal Stone Curlew in some other works.

Family GLAREOLIDAE

Egyptian Plover   *Pluvianus aegyptius* (Linnaeus)
Charadrius aegyptius Linnaeus, 1758, *Syst. Nat.*, ed. 10, p. 150, Egypt.
Arabic name: Ṭayr At-timsaaḥ.
Comments: Called Crocodile Bird in some other works.

Cream-colored Courser   *Cursorius cursor* (Latham)
Cursorius cursor cursor (Latham)
Charadrius Cursor Latham, 1787, *Gen. Synopsis Birds*, Suppl. 1, p. 293, Kent, England.
Arabic names: Galiil, Karawaan Jabalii.

Collared Pratincole   *Glareola pratincola* (Linnaeus)
Glareola pratincola pratincola (Linnaeus)
Hirundo Pratincola Linnaeus, 1766, *Syst. Nat.*, ed. 12, p. 345, "Europae australioris; in Austriae pratis apricis."
Arabic name: Abuu Yusr (generic for pratincole).
Comments: Called Common Pratincole or Red-winged Pratincole in some other works.

Black-winged Pratincole   *Glareola nordmanni* Fischer
Glareola Nordmanni Fischer, 1842, Bull. Soc. Imp. Nat. Moscou, 15, p. 314, pl. 2, fig. 2, a-c, Russia.
Comments: Sometimes regarded as conspecific with *G. pratincola*.

Family STERCORARIIDAE

Great Skua   *Stercorarius skua* (Brünnich)
Stercorarius skua [*skua*] (Brünnich)
Catharacta Skua Brünnich, 1764, *Ornith. Borealis*, p. 33, Faroes and Iceland [reference not verified].
Comments: There are several recent observations from Egyptian waters.[69] These may have at least in part been of *Stercorarius* (*skua*) *maccormicki*. We are unaware of specimens of this species from Egypt.

Pomarine Skua   *Stercorarius pomarinus* (Temminck)
Lestris pomarinus Temminck, 1815, *Manuel d'Ornith.*, ed. 1, p. 514, "Les régions du cercle arctique; de passage accidentel sur les côtes maritimes de Hollande et de France."
Comments: One preserved wing in the BMNH uncataloged) collected on 11 May 1921 at Ashrafi Island and numerous sight records from the country.[70] Called Pomarine Jaeger or Pomatarhine Skua in some other works.

Arctic Skua *Stercorarius parasiticus* (Linnaeus)
Larus parasiticus Linnaeus, 1758, *Syst. Nat.*, ed.
10, p. 136, within the Tropic of Cancer, Europe,
America, Asia.
Comments: One was shot in September 1941 along
the Red Sea coast and preserved in the collection of
Mr. Hassan Galal El Din.[71] The specimen cannot be
traced. Numerous sight records of this species in
Egypt.[72] Called Parasitic Jaeger or Richardson's
Skua in some other works.

Long-tailed Skua *Stercorarius longicaudus* Vieillot
Stercorarius longicaudus Vieillot, 1819, Nouv.
Dict. d'Hist. Nat., nouv. éd., 32, p. 157, the
north of Europe, Asia, and America, restricted to
northern Europe.
Comments: Numerous observations from the
country.[73] Called Long-tailed Jaeger in some other
works.

Family LARIDAE

Hemprich's Gull *Larus hemprichii* (Bruch)
Adelarus Hemprichii Bruch, 1853, J. f. Ornith., 1,
p. 106, pl. 3, Red Sea.
Arabic names: Nawras, Nuuras (both generic for
gull).
Comments: Called Sooty Gull or Aden Gull in some
other works.

White-eyed Gull *Larus leucophthalmus* Temminck
Larus leucophthalmus Temminck, 1825, in Temminck and Laugier, *Planches Col.*, livr. 62,
pl. 366, coasts of Red Sea.
Arabic name: 'Ajama.

Great Black-headed Gull *Larus ichthyaetus* Pallas
Larus Ichthyaetus Pallas, 1773, *Reise Versch.
Prov. Russ. Reichs*, 2, p. 713, Caspian Sea.

Mediterranean Black-headed Gull
Larus melanocephalus Temminck
Larus melanocephalus Temminck, 1820, *Manuel
d'Ornith.*, ed. 2, 2, p. 777, coast of the Adriatic
Sea.

Little Gull *Larus minutus* Pallas
Larus minutus Pallas, 1776, *Reise Versch. Prov.
Russ. Reichs*, 3, p. 702, rivers of Siberia and in
Russia.

Black-headed Gull *Larus ridibundus* Linnaeus
Larus ridibundus Linnaeus, 1766, *Syst. Nat.*, ed.
12, p. 225, "Mari Europaeo", restricted to
England, *fide* Vaurie, 1965, *Birds Pal. Fauna.
Non-Pass.*, p. 463.
Comments: Called Common Black-headed Gull in
some other works.

Slender-billed Gull *Larus genei* Brême
Larus genei Brême, 1840, Rev. Zool., 321,
Sardinia.

Lesser Black-backed Gull *Larus fuscus* Linnaeus
Larus fuscus fuscus Linnaeus

Larus fuscus Linnaeus, 1758, *Syst. Nat.*, ed. 10,
p. 136, Europe.
Arabic name: Juukaa.

Herring Gull *Larus argentatus* Pontoppidan
Larus argentatus cachinnans Pallas
Larus cachinnans Pallas, 1811, *Zoographia
Rosso-Asiatica*, 2, p. 318, Caspian Sea.
Comments: Sometimes this subspecies is regarded
as a distinct species and is called the Yellow-legged
Herring Gull.

[Glaucous Gull *Larus hyperboreus* Gunnerus
Larus hyperboreus hyperboreus Gunnerus
Larus hyperboreus Gunnerus, 1767, in Leem,
Beskrivelse over Finmarkens Lapper, p. 226,
Norway [reference not verified].
Comments: Hypothetical in Egypt until its occur-
rence can be better documented.]

Common Gull *Larus canus* Linnaeus
Larus canus canus Linnaeus
Larus canus Linnaeus, 1758, *Syst. Nat.*, ed. 10,
p. 136, Europe.
Arabic name: Zummaj Al-maaya.
Comments: Called Mew Gull or Short-billed Gull in
some other works.

Audouin's Gull *Larus audouinii* Payraudeau
Larus Audouinii Payraudeau, 1826, Ann. Sci.
Nat., 8, p. 462, Sardinia and Corsica.

Black-legged Kittiwake *Rissa tridactyla* (Linnaeus)
Larus tridactyla Linnaeus, 1758, *Syst. Nat.*, ed.
10, p. 136, Europe, restricted to Great Britain.
Comments: One individual was found dead near
Baltim on 10 May 1983 (skull in UMMZ).

Family STERNIDAE

Black Tern *Chlidonias niger* (Linnaeus)
Chlidonias niger niger (Linnaeus)
Sterna nigra Linnaeus, 1758, *Syst. Nat.*, ed. 10,
p. 137, Europe.
Arabic names: Shakiitii, Shaniifa, Khuttaaf Al-
baḥr, and Kharshana, Khuṭṭaaf, Marshak (generic
for tern).
Comments: Called Black Marsh Tern in some other
works.

White-winged Black Tern *Chlidonias leucopterus*
(Temminck)
Sterna leucoptera Temminck, 1815, *Manuel
d'Ornith.*, ed. 1, p. 483, coasts of the Mediter-
ranean Sea.
Arabic name: Abuu Daqqa.
Comments: Called White-winged Marsh Tern in
some other works.

Whiskered Tern *Chlidonias hybridus* (Pallas)
Chlidonias hybridus hybridus (Pallas)
Sterna hybrida Pallas, 1811, *Zoographia Rosso-
Asiatica*, 2, p. 338, southern Volga.
Comments: Called Whiskered Marsh Tern in some
other works.

Gull-billed Tern   *Gelochelidon nilotica* (Gmelin)
Gelochelidon nilotica nilotica (Gmelin)
  Sterna nilotica J. F. Gmelin, 1789, *Syst. Nat.*, 1,
    pt. 2, p. 606, Egypt.
Arabic name: Uwayq.

Caspian Tern   *Hydroprogne caspia* (Pallas)
  Sterna caspia Pallas, 1770, Novi Comm. Acad.
    Sci. Imp. Petropol., 14 (for 1769), pt. 1, p. 582,
    pl. 22, fig. 2, Caspian Sea.
Arabic names: Abuu Balḥa, Abuu Jirra.
Comments: In some other works the name *Hydro-progne tschegrava* (Lepechin) is used for this species.[74]

Swift Tern   *Sterna bergii* Lichtenstein
Sterna bergii velox Cretzschmar
  Sterna Velox Cretzschmar, 1827, *Atlas Reise
    Rüppell, Vögel*, p. 21, pl. 13, coasts of the Red
    Sea.
Comments: Called Great Crested Tern in some other works.

Lesser Crested Tern   *Sterna bengalensis* Lesson
  Sterna bengalensis Lesson, 1831, *Traité d'Ornith.*,
    p. 621, livr. 8, coasts of India.

Sandwich Tern   *Sterna sandvicensis* Latham
Sterna sandvicensis sandvicensis Latham
  Sterna Sandvicensis Latham, 1787, *Gen. Synopsis
    Birds*, Suppl. 1, p. 296, England.

Common Tern   *Sterna hirundo* Linnaeus
Sterna hirundo hirundo Linnaeus
  Sterna Hirundo Linnaeus, 1758, *Syst. Nat.*, ed.
    10, p. 137, Europe.
Arabic name: Khuṭṭaaf Al-baḥr.

Roseate Tern   *Sterna dougallii* Montagu
Sterna dougallii dougallii Montagu
  Sterna Dougallii Montagu, 1813, *Ornith. Dict.
    Suppl.*, text and plate to "Tern-Roseate",
    Scotland.
Comments: Admitted on sight record of Sherif
Baha el Din.[75] He observed it in May 1980 at Suez.
There is no evidence that this species breeds in
Egyptian waters.[76]

White-cheeked Tern   *Sterna repressa* Hartert
  Sterna repressa Hartert, 1916, Novitates Zool.,
    23, p. 288, Persian Gulf.
Arabic name: Abuu Baṭn.

Bridled Tern   *Sterna anaethetus* Scopoli
Sterna anaethetus anaethetus Scopoli
  Sterna Anaethetus Scopoli, 1786, *Deliciae Florae
    Faunae Insubr.*, fasc. 2, p. 92, "In Guinea", in
    error; type from Philippines, *fide* Vaurie, 1965,
    Birds Pal. Fauna. Non-Pass., p. 500.

Little Tern   *Sterna albifrons* Pallas
Sterna albifrons albifrons Pallas
  Sterna albifrons Pallas, 1764, in Vroeg, *Cat.
    Adumbratiunculae*, p. 6, Netherlands, *fide* Sher-
    born, 1905, Smiths. Misc. Collect., 47.
Arabic name: Dughbaz.

Saunder's Little Tern   *Sterna saundersi* Hume
  Sterna Saundersi Hume, 1877, Stray Feathers, 5,
    p. 324, Karachi.
Comments: Sometimes regarded as conspecific with
S. albifrons. A carcass (USNM 557822) found on 21
May 1982 on an island off Hurghada is referable to
S. saundersi.[77]

Family RYNCHOPIDAE

African Skimmer   *Rynchops flavirostris* Vieillot
  Rhynchops [sic] *flavirostris* Vieillot, 1816, *Nouv.
    Dict. d'Hist. Nat.*, nouv. éd., 3, p. 388, "Austra-
    lasie", in error; type from Senegal River, *fide*
    Vieillot, 1819, *ibid.*, 29, p. 283.
Arabic names: Abuu Miqaṣṣ, 'Ujhuum.
Comments: Specimen in the BMNH (91.6.18.89)
collected in 1878 at Damietta appears to be the last
known taken in Egypt. Recent observations include
a flock of forty birds on 17 October 1979 near Kom
Ombo[78] and one individual on 15 May 1982 at
Hurghada.[79] Called Scissor-billed Tern in some
other works.

[Family ALCIDAE

Razorbill   *Alca torda* Linnaeus
Alca torda islandica Brehm
  Alca Islandica C. L. Brehm, 1831, *Handb. Natur-
    gesch. Vögel Deutschl.*, p. 1005, pl. 46, fig. 2,
    Iceland.
Comments: A Razorbill was found dead on the
beach near Ramleh in the winter of 1908-9.[80] It is
impossible to know if the bird reached Egyptian
waters alive. Until further documentation is
available this species should be considered hypothetical in Egypt.]

Order PTEROCLIDIFORMES[81]

Family PTEROCLIDIDAE

Lichtenstein's Sandgrouse   *Pterocles lichtensteinii*
                                          Temminck
Pterocles lichtensteinii lichtensteinii Temminck
  Pterocles lichtensteinii Temminck, 1825, in Tem-
    minck and Laugier, *Planches Col.*, livr. 60,
    pls. 335, 361, Nubia.
Arabic name: Qaṭaa (generic for sandgrouse).
Comments: Several recent specimen records from
the Gebel Elba region.[82]

Black-bellied Sandgrouse   *Pterocles orientalis*
                                          (Linnaeus)
Pterocles orientalis orientalis (Linnaeus)
  Tetrao orientalis Linnaeus, 1758, *Syst. Nat.*, ed.
    10, p. 161, "Oriente."
Comments: One bird recently collected in Wadi
Araba, west of Zafarana.[83] Called Imperial Sand-
grouse in some other works.

[**Pin-tailed Sandgrouse** *Pterocles alchata* (Linnaeus)]

Pterocles alchata caudacutus (Gmelin)
Tetrao caudacutus S. G. Gmelin, 1774, *Reise Russland*, 3, p. 93, pl. 18, Iran.
Comments: Hypothetical in Egypt until its occurrence can be better documented,[84] but see under bird No. 52.]

Spotted Sandgrouse *Pterocles senegallus* (Linnaeus)
Tetrao senegallus Linnaeus, 1771, *Mantissa*, p. 526, "Senegallia", in error; type from Algeria, *fide* Hartert, 1924, Novitates Zool., 31, p. 7.

Coronetted Sandgrouse *Pterocles coronatus* Lichtenstein
Pterocles coronatus coronatus Lichtenstein
Pt.[erocles] coronatus Lichtenstein, 1823, *Verz. Doubl. Zool. Mus. Berlin*, p. 65, Nubia.
Comments: This species has recently been collected in the Eastern Desert.[85] Called Crowned Sandgrouse in some other works.

Chestnut-bellied Sandgrouse *Pterocles exustus* Temminck
Pterocles exustus floweri Nicoll
Pterocles senegalensis floweri Nicoll, 1921, Bull. Brit. Ornith. Club, 41, p. 128, Faiyum, Egypt.
Arabic name: Ghaṭaaṭ.

Order COLUMBIFORMES

Family COLUMBIDAE

Stock Pigeon *Columba oenas* Linnaeus
Columba oenas oenas Linnaeus
Columba Oenas Linnaeus, 1758, *Syst. Nat.*, ed. 10, p. 162, Europe.
Arabic names: Al-waraqaa', Ḥamaam Barrii, and Ḥamaam, Qimrii, Yamaam (generic for pigeon and dove).

Rock Pigeon *Columba livia* Gmelin
Columba livia schimperi Bonaparte
Columba schimperi Bonaparte, 1854, Compt. Rend. Acad. Sci. Paris, 39, p. 1107, "Abyssinie", in error; type from Egypt, *fide* Hartert, 1920, *Vögel Pal. Fauna*, 2, p. 1468.
Arabic names: Ḥamaam Azraq. Ḥamaam Jabalii.
Comments: Called Rock Dove in some other works.

Columba livia dakhlae Meinertzhagen
Columba livia dakhlae Meinertzhagen, 1928, Bull. Brit. Ornith. Club, 48, p. 116, Dakhla Oasis, Egypt.

Pink-headed Turtle Dove *Streptopelia roseogrisea* (Sundevall)
Streptopelia roseogrisea arabica (Neumann)
Turtur roseogriseus arabicus Neumann, 1904, Ornith. Monatsber., 12, p. 31, Arabia.
Arabic name: Yamaam Wardii Ar-ra's.

Comments: Sometimes regarded as conspecific with *S. decaocto*. Numerous specimens have been taken in the extreme southeastern part of the country.[86] A specimen was obtained at Hurghada in 1933.[87] However, the circumstances of its collection are ambiguous and it is impossible to say if it "reached the area by natural means." Called African Collared Dove or Rose-grey Dove in some other works.

Collared Turtle Dove *Streptopelia decaocto* (Frivaldszky)
Streptopelia decaocto subsp. (Frivaldszky)
Columba decaocto Frivaldszky, 1838, A Magyar Tudos Társasàg Evkönyvei, 3 (1834-6), pt. 3, p. 183, pl. 8, Balkans.
Comments: Specimen in UMMZ (201,255) collected on 9 February 1979 at Cairo.[88] There are several recent observations of this species in Egypt.[89] The subspecific identity of these birds still needs to be worked out.

Turtle Dove *Streptopelia turtur* (Linnaeus)
Streptopelia turtur turtur (Linnaeus)
Columba Turtur Linnaeus, 1758, *Syst. Nat.*, ed. 10, p. 164, "India", in error; type from England, *fide* Vaurie, 1965, *Birds Pal. Fauna. Non-Pass.*, p. 553.
Arabic names: Ṣalṣal, Turghul.

Streptopelia turtur arenicola (Hartert)
Turtur turtur arenicola Hartert, 1894, Novitates Zool., 1, p. 42, Iraq.
Comments: Specimen in the FMNH (22332 CC) collected on 27 April 1959, nine miles southeast of Mersa Matruh.

Streptopelia turtur isabellina (Bonaparte)
T.[urtur] isabellinus Bonaparte, 1856, Compt. Rend. Acad. Sci. Paris, 43, p. 942, upper Egypt.

Streptopelia turtur rufescens (Brehm)
Peristera (Turtur) rufescens C. L. Brehm, 1845, Isis von Oken, col. 348, "Griechenland", in error; type from Dongola, Sudan, *fide* Vaurie, 1965, *Birds Pal. Fauna. Non-Pass.*, p. 555.

Laughing Dove *Streptopelia senegalensis* (Linnaeus)
Streptopelia senegalensis senegalensis (Linnaeus)
Columba senegalensis Linnaeus, 1766, *Syst. Nat.*, ed. 12, p. 283, Senegal.
Arabic name: Yamaam Baladii.
Comments: Called Palm Dove in some other works.

Streptopelia senegalensis aegyptiaca (Latham)
Columba aegyptiaca Latham, 1790, *Index Ornith.*, 2, p. 607, Egypt.

Namaqua Dove *Oena capensis* (Linnaeus)
Oena capensis capensis (Linnaeus)
Columba capensis Linnaeus, 1766, *Syst. Nat.*, ed. 12, p. 286, Cape of Good Hope, Cape Province, *fide* Clancey, 1966, Bull. Brit. Ornith. Club, 86, p. 114.
Arabic names: Baaluum, Yamaam Al-kaab.

Comments: Two specimens in the USNM (551110-1) collected on 27 December 1971 at Kom Ombo. Another specimen in the FMNH (25104 CC) was taken on 16 February 1967 at Wadi Akwamtra, Gebel Elba.[90] Called Long-tailed Dove or Masked Dove in some other works.

Order PSITTACIFORMES

Family PSITTACIDAE

Rose-ringed Parakeet   *Psittacula krameri* (Scopoli)
Psittacula krameri manillensis (Bechstein)
  Psittacus Manillensis Bechstein, 1800, *Stuben-vögel*, 2nd Gotha ed., p. 612, Philippines, in error; type from Ceylon, *fide* Ali and Ripley, 1969, *Handb. Birds India and Pakistan*, 3, p. 171.
Arabic name: Duuduu.
Comments: This subspecies was introduced into Egypt.[91] The form *borealis* (Neumann) may also have been introduced, but referable specimens are lacking. Called Long-tailed Parakeet or Senegal Parakeet in some other works.

Order CUCULIFORMES

Family CUCULIDAE

Cuckoo   *Cuculus canorus* Linnaeus
Cuculus canorus canorus Linnaeus
  Cuculus canorus Linnaeus, 1758, *Syst. Nat.*, ed. 10, p. 110, Europe.
Arabic names: Huuhuu, Shakhfuut, and Waqwaaq (generic for cuckoo).
Comments: Called Common Cuckoo in some other works.

Great Spotted Cuckoo   *Clamator glandarius* (Linnaeus)
  Cuculus glandarius Linnaeus, 1758, *Syst. Nat.*, ed. 10, p. 111, "Africa septentrionali & Europa australi."
Arabic name: Qamiiḥa.

Senegal Coucal   *Centropus senegalensis* (Linnaeus)
Centropus senegalensis aegyptius (Gmelin)
  Cuculus aegyptius J. F. Gmelin, 1788, *Syst. Nat.*, 1, pt. 1, p. 420, Egypt.
Arabic names: Mukk, Kuukuu.

Order STRIGIFORMES

Family TYTONIDAE

Barn Owl   *Tyto alba* (Scopoli)
Tyto alba alba (Scopoli)
  Strix alba Scopoli, 1769, *Annus 1 Hist.-Nat.*, p. 21, "Ex Foro Juli", thought to be northern Italy, *fide* Hartert, 1913, *Vögel Pal. Fauna*, 2, p. 1031.

Arabic names: Haama, Maṣṣaaṣa, Umm Aṣ-ṣakhr, and Buuma (generic for owl).

Tyto alba affinis (Blyth)
  Strix affinis Blyth, 1862, Ibis, p. 388, Cape, South Africa.
Comments: The inclusion of this subspecies is based on the specimen reported by Meinertzhagen.[92] Several specimens examined from Egypt approach *affinis* from sub-Saharan Africa in plumage color, but cannot be confidently referred to this form (e.g., BMNH 94.8.15.104).

Family STRIGIDAE

Eagle Owl   *Bubo bubo* (Linnaeus)
Bubo bubo ascalaphus Savigny
  Bubo Ascalaphus Savigny, 1809, *Descr. de l'Égypte, Hist. Nat.*, 1, *Syst. Ois.*, p. 110, pl. 3, fig. 2, "la haute Égypte."
Arabic name: Ba'afa.
Comments: Sometimes this subspecies is regarded as a distinct species. We consider the form *desertorum* a synonym of *ascalaphus*. Called Pharaoh Owl or Desert Eagle Owl in some other works.

Long-eared Owl   *Asio otus* (Linnaeus)
Asio otus otus (Linnaeus)
  Strix Otus Linnaeus, 1758, *Syst. Nat.*, ed. 10, p. 92, Europe.

Short-eared Owl   *Asio flammeus* (Pontoppidan)
Asio flammeus flammeus (Pontoppidan)
  Strix Flammea Pontoppidan, 1763, *Danske Atlas*, 1, p. 617, pl. 25, no locality, but presumed to be Denmark.
Arabic name: Haama.

Scops Owl   *Otus scops* (Linnaeus)
Otus scops scops (Linnaeus)
  Strix Scops Linnaeus, 1758, *Syst. Nat.*, ed. 10, p. 92, Europe.
Arabic names: Buuh, Sabaj, Thabaj.

Little Owl   *Athene noctua* (Scopoli)
Athene noctua glaux (Savigny)
  Noctua Glaux Savigny, 1809, *Descr. de l'Égypte, Hist. Nat.*, 1, *Syst. Ois.*, p. 105, no locality, but presumed to be Egypt.
Arabic names: Umm As-sahar, Umm Quwayq.

Athene noctua saharae (Kleinschmidt)
  Strix saharae Kleinschmidt, 1909, Falco, 5, p. 19, southern Algeria.

Hume's Tawny Owl   *Strix butleri* (Hume)
  Asio butleri Hume, 1878, Stray Feathers, 7, p. 316, Omara, Makran coast, Baluchistan.
Comments: Sometimes regarded as conspecific with *S. aluco*. A specimen was taken on 16 February 1982 in Wadi Nugrus, central Red Sea mountains.[93]

Order CAPRIMULGIFORMES

Family CAPRIMULGIDAE

European Nightjar   *Caprimulgus europaeus*
                                                        Linnaeus
Caprimulgus europaeus europaeus Linnaeus
    Caprimulgus europaeus Linnaeus, 1758, *Syst. Nat.*, ed. 10, p. 193, Europe.
Arabic names: Abuu An-nawm, Qirra, Subad (all generic for nightjar).

Caprimulgus europaeus meridionalis Hartert
    Caprimulgus europaeus meridionalis Hartert, 1896, Ibis, p. 370, southern Europe and north-western Africa.

Egyptian Nightjar   *Caprimulgus aegyptius*
                                                        Lichtenstein
Caprimulgus aegyptius aegyptius Lichtenstein
    C.[aprimulgus] aegyptius Lichtenstein, 1823, *Verz. Doubl. Zool. Mus. Berlin*, p. 59, upper Egypt.
Arabic name: Al-bakhaakh.

Caprimulgus aegyptius saharae Erlanger
    Caprimulgus aegyptius saharae Erlanger, 1899, J. f. Ornith., 47, p. 525, pl. 12, Tunisia.

Order APODIFORMES

Family APODIDAE

House Swift   *Apus affinis* (Gray)
Apus affinis [affinis] (Gray)
    Cypselus affinis J. E. Gray, 1830, in Gray and Hardwicke, *Illustr. Indian Zool.*, 1, pt. 2, pl. 35, fig. 2, no locality, but accepted as Ganges.
Arabic names: Khuṭṭaaf, Samaama, Samiima (all generic for swift).
Comments: Admitted on sight record.[94] One bird was observed on 5 September 1957 at Alexandria.[95] The subspecies *galilejensis* (Antinori) is the one that has been previously recorded in North Africa, and perhaps this observation was of this subspecies rather than *affinis* as identified by Horváth, but further documentation is necessary. Called Little Swift in some other works.

Pallid Swift   *Apus pallidus* (Shelley)
Apus pallidus brehmorum Hartert
    Apus apus Brehmorum Hartert, 1901, in Naumann, *Naturgesch. Vögel Mitteleuropas*, 4, p. 233, Madeira, Spain.
Comments: A specimen in the FMNH (256970) collected on 4 December 1959 in the Faiyum and two in the USNM (551165-6) taken in the Kharga Oasis on 16 January 1972 and in the Dakhla Oasis on 12 January 1972 are referable to this subspecies.[96] Called Mouse-colored Swift in some other works.

Apus pallidus illyricus Tschusi

Apus murinus illyricus Tschusi, 1907, Ornith. Jahrb., 18, p. 29, Dalmatia.
Comments: A series of twenty-eight specimens (FMNH and USNM) taken near Bahig are referable to this subspecies.[97]

Apus pallidus pallidus (Shelley)
    Cypselus pallidus Shelley, 1870, Ibis, p. 445, Egypt.

Swift   *Apus apus* (Linnaeus)
Apus apus apus (Linnaeus)
    Hirundo Apus Linnaeus, 1758, *Syst. Nat.*, ed. 10, p. 192, Sweden.
Comments: Specimen (UMMZ 207, 151) collected on 27 May 1984 in Wadi Natroun. There are numerous sight records from the country.[98] Some of these sightings could be of *A. a. pekinensis* (Swinhoe). Called Common Swift in some other works.

Alpine Swift   *Apus melba* (Linnaeus)
Apus melba melba (Linnaeus)
    Hirundo melba Linnaeus, 1758, *Syst. Nat.*, ed. 10, p. 192, "Herculeum", designated as Gibraltar, *fide* Hartert, 1912, *Vögel Pal. Fauna*, 2, p. 834.
Comments: Specimen in the GZM (uncataloged) collected on 31 October 1957 at Dokki, by Cairo.[99] There are numerous sight records of this species from Egypt.[100] Some of these could be of *A. m. tuneti* Tschusi. Sometimes placed in the genus *Tachymarptis* as *T. melba*.

Order CORACIIFORMES

Family CORACIIDAE

Roller   *Coracias garrulus* Linnaeus
Coracias garrulus garrulus Linnaeus
    Coracias garrulus garrulus Linnaeus, 1758, *Syst. Nat.*, ed. 10, p. 107, Europe.
Arabic names: Ghurrab Zaytuunii, Shiqirraaq.

Abyssinian Roller   *Coracias abyssinicus* Hermann
    Coracias abyssinica Hermann, 1783, *Tabula Affinitatum Animalium*, p. 197, Ethiopia [reference not verified].
Comments: Specimens in the BMNH (1965 M.6011) and the FMNH (40783) collected on 14 February 1928 at Abu Simbel and in 1874 in "Egypt" (respectively). A wing and tail of this species were found at Abd el Malek, Gebel Uweinat on 22 November 1968.[101]

Family ALCEDINIDAE

Kingfisher   *Alcedo atthis* (Linnaeus)
Alcedo atthis atthis (Linnaeus)
    Gracula Atthis Linnaeus, 1758, *Syst. Nat.*, ed. 10, p. 109, Egypt.
Arabic names: Abuu Mumbalad, Rafraaf, and Ṣayyaad As-samak (generic for kingfishers).

Comments: Called Little Blue Kingfisher or Common Kingfisher in some other works.

Pied Kingfisher   *Ceryle rudis* (Linnaeus)
Ceryle rudis rudis (Linnaeus)
  Alcedo rudis Linnaeus, 1758, *Syst. Nat.*, ed. 10, p. 116, "Persia, Aegypto."
Arabic name: Qirillaa.
Comments: Called Lesser Pied Kingfisher in some other works.

White-breasted Kingfisher   *Halcyon smyrnensis* (Linnaeus)
Halcyon smyrnensis smyrnensis (Linnaeus)
  Alcedo smyrnensis Linnaeus, 1758, *Syst. Nat.*, ed. 10, p. 116, "Africa & Asia."
Arabic name: Qaawanad.
Comments: One observed on 23 and 24 February 1982 near Suez.[102]

Family MEROPIDAE

Little Green Bee-eater   *Merops orientalis* Latham
Merops orientalis cleopatra Nicoll
  Merops viridis cleopatra Nicoll, 1910, Bull. Brit. Ornith. Club, 27, p. 11, Cairo, Egypt.
Arabic names: 'Uṣfuur Al-janna, and Khuḍḍiir, Warwaar (generic for bee-eater).

Bee-eater   *Merops apiaster* Linnaeus
Merops Apiaster Linnaeus, 1758, *Syst. Nat.*, ed. 10, p. 117, "Europa australi, Oriente."
Arabic name: 'Uṣfuur Al-janna.

Blue-cheeked Bee-eater   *Merops superciliosus* Linnaeus
Merops superciliosus persicus Pallas
  Merops persica Pallas, 1773, *Reise Versch. Prov. Russ. Reichs*, 2, p. 708, Caspian Sea.
Comments: Sometimes this subspecies is regarded as a distinct species.

Family UPUPIDAE

Hoopoe   *Upupa epops* Linnaeus
Upupa epops epops Linnaeus
  Upupa Epops Linnaeus, 1758, *Syst. Nat.*, ed. 10, p. 117, Europe.
Arabic name: Hudhud.

Upupa epops major Brehm
  Upupa major C. L. Brehm, 1855, *Der Vollständige Vogelfang*, p. 78, "Er besucht im Winter Aegypten."

Order PICIFORMES

Family PICIDAE

Wryneck   *Jynx torquilla* Linnaeus
Jynx torquilla torquilla Linnaeus
  Jynx Torquilla Linnaeus, 1758, *Syst. Nat.*, ed. 10, p.112, Europe.
Arabic names: Lawwaa', Umm Al-waa.

Jynx torquilla tschusii Kleinschmidt
  Jynx torquilla tschusii Kleinschmidt, 1907, Falco, 3, p. 103, Sardinia.
Comments: Two specimens in the USNM (552625 and 569056) collected on 10 March 1971 and 18 April 1971 (respectively) at Bahig.[103]

Order PASSERIFORMES

Family HIRUNDINIDAE

Sand Martin   *Riparia riparia* (Linnaeus)
Riparia riparia riparia (Linnaeus)
  Hirundo riparia Linnaeus, 1758, *Syst. Nat.*, ed. 10, p. 192, Europe.
Arabic names: Khuṭṭaaf, Sunuunuu, 'Uṣfuur Al-janna (all generic for swallows and martins).
Comments: Called Bank Swallow or European Sand Martin in some other works.

Riparia riparia shelleyi (Sharpe)
  Cotile shelleyi Sharpe, 1885, *Cat. Birds Brit. Mus.*, 10, p. 96 (in key), p. 100, Egypt.

Riparia riparia diluta (Sharpe and Wyatt)
  Cotile diluta Sharpe and Wyatt, 1893, *Monogr. Hirundinidae*, 1, p. 41 (in key), p. 63, Russian Turkestan.

Crag Martin   *Hirundo rupestris* Scopoli
  Hirundo rupestris Scopoli, 1769, *Annus I Hist.-Nat.*, p. 167, Tirol.
Comments: Specimen in the USNM (537997) collected on 24 March 1967 at Bahig. Sometimes placed in the genus *Ptyonoprogne* as *P. rupestris*.

Pale Crag Martin   *Hirundo obsoleta* (Cabanis)
Hirundo obsoleta obsoleta (Cabanis)
  C.[*otyle*] *obsoleta* Cabanis, 1850, *Mus. Heineanum*, 1, p. 50, northeast Africa, restricted to "lower Egypt on the right bank of the Nile in the region of Cairo and neighboring Moqattam Hills", *fide* Vaurie, 1951, Amer. Mus. Novitates, no. 1529, p. 16.
Comments: Sometimes placed in the genus *Ptyonoprogne* as *P. obsoleta*. Also regarded by some as conspecific with *H. rupestris* and *H. fuligula*.

Hirundo obsoleta arabica (Reichenow)
  Riparia arabica Reichenow, 1905, *Vögel Afrikas*, 3, pt. 2, p. 828, Lahej, Aden.
Comments: Specimen in the BMNH (1965 M.8315) collected on 20 March 1928 at Gebel Elba. This is most likely the same specimen reported by Meinertzhagen.[104]

Swallow   *Hirundo rustica* Linnaeus
Hirundo rustica rustica Linnaeus
  Hirundo rustica Linnaeus, 1758, *Syst. Nat.*, ed. 10, p. 191, Europe.
Comments: Called Barn Swallow in some other works.

Hirundo rustica transitiva (Hartert)

Chelidon rustica transitiva Hartert, 1910, *Vögel Pal. Fauna*, 1, p. 802, Palestine.

Comments: Three specimens in the USNM (550109, 551297, 551300) obtained on 24 March 1967 at Bahig, 30 April 1970 at Burg el Arab, and 1 May 1970 at Abu Rawash (respectively).

Hirundo rustica savignii Stephens
   Hirundo Savignii Stephens, 1817, in Shaw, *Gen. Zool.*, 10, pt. 1, p. 90, Egypt.

Red-rumped Swallow   *Hirundo daurica* Linnaeus
Hirundo daurica rufula Temminck
   Hirundo rufula Temminck, 1835, *Manuel d'Ornith.*, ed. 1, 3, p. 298, Africa, Egypt, Sicily, Japan.

House Martin   *Delichon urbica* (Linnaeus)
Delichon urbica urbica (Linnaeus)
   Hirundo urbica Linnaeus, 1758, *Syst. Nat.*, ed. 10, p. 192, Europe.

Family ALAUDIDAE

Black-crowned Finch Lark   *Eremopterix nigriceps* (Gould)
Eremopterix nigriceps melanauchen (Cabanis)
   C.[oraphites] melanauchen Cabanis, 1851, *Mus. Heineanum*, 1, p. 124, Africa, in error; type from Jidda, Arabia, *fide* Vaurie, 1959, *Birds Pal. Fauna. Pass.*, p. 19.

Arabic names: Qubbara, Qunburra (both generic for lark).

Comments: Specimens in the GZM (A2429, A2456, and A2455) collected on 23 December 1938 and 27 December 1938 in the Eastern Desert and 27 December 1938 at Wadi Sid Abgouab (respectively). Two more specimens in the GZM (A2080 and A2081) collected on 27 December 1938 at Gebel Elba.[105] There is also a record of this form from between the Dakhla Oasis and Gebel Uweinat.[106] Called White-fronted Sparrow Lark in some other works.

Desert Lark   *Ammomanes deserti* (Lichtenstein)
Ammomanes deserti deserti (Lichtenstein)
   A.[lauda] deserti Lichtenstein, 1823, *Verz. Doubl. Zool. Mus. Berlin*, p. 28, upper Egypt.

Arabic name: Qunburra Al-baadiya.

Comments: Called Sand Lark in some other works.

Ammomanes deserti isabellinus (Temminck)
   Alauda isabellina Temminck, 1823, in Temminck and Laugier, *Planches Col.*, livr. 41, pl. 244, fig. 2, Jordan.

Ammomanes deserti borosi Horváth
   Ammomanes deserti borosi Horváth, 1958, *Bull. Brit. Ornith. Club*, 78, p. 124, Bir Abbad, Egypt.
Comments: We have not been able to examine specimens of this subspecies and its validity cannot be evaluated.

Bar-tailed Desert Lark   *Ammomanes cincturus* (Gould)
Ammomanes cincturus arenicolor (Sundevall)
   Alauda arenicolor Sundevall, 1850, *Öfver. Kongl. Sv. Vet. Akad. Förh.*, Stockholm, 7, p. 128, lower Egypt.
Comments: Called Black-tailed Desert Lark in some other works.

Hoopoe Lark   *Alaemon alaudipes* (Desfontaines)
Alaemon alaudipes desertorum (Stanley)
   Alauda Desertorum Stanley, 1814, in Salt, *Voyage Abyssinia*, app., p. LX, no locality, but designated as Amphila Island, Red Sea, *fide* Latham, *op. cit.*, app., p. XLIX.
Comments: Called Bifasciated Lark in some other works.

Alaemon alaudipes alaudipes (Desfontaines)
   Upupa alaudipes Desfontaines, 1789, *Mém. Acad. Sci. Paris* (for 1787), p. 504, pl. 16, Tunisia.

Dupont's Lark   *Chersophilus duponti* (Vieillot)
Chersophilus duponti margaritae (Koenig)
   Alaemon Margaritae Koenig, 1888, *J. f. Ornith.*, 36, p. 228, pl. 2, Tunisia.
Comments: Specimens in the FMNH (297023) and USNM (568934) collected on 23 May 1975 at El Hammam and on 2 September 1971 at Bahig (respectively). The El Hammam specimen is a nestling.

Short-toed Lark   *Calandrella cinerea* (Gmelin)
Calandrella cinerea brachydactyla (Leisler)
   Alauda brachydactila [sic] Leisler, 1814, *Ann. Wetterauischen Gesell.*, 3, p. 357, pl. 19, southern France and Italy [reference not verified].
Comments: Sometimes this subspecies is considered a distinct species and is called the Greater Short-toed Lark. Also called Red-capped Lark in some other works.

Calandrella cinerea hermonensis Tristram
   Calandrella hermonensis Tristram, 1864, *Proc. Zool. Soc. London*, p. 434, "slopes of Hermon and Lebanon."
Comments: Specimens in the BMNH (1965 M.7159, 1965 M.7155, and 1965 M.7154) taken on 5 March 1905 at Port Said, 15 April 1923 at Wadi Natroun, and on 24 March 1928 between the Kharga and Dakhla Oases (respectively).[107] Other specimens include two in the GZM (A2082 and A2083) collected on 23 February 1938 at Wadi Shaab.[108]

Calandrella cinerea longipennis (Eversmann)
   Alauda longipennis Eversmann, 1848, *Bull. Soc. Imp. Nat. Moscou*, 21, pt. 1, p. 219, Dzungaria, Turkestan.

Lesser Short-toed Lark   *Calandrella rufescens* (Vieillot)
Calandrella rufescens minor (Cabanis)
   C.[alandritis] minor Cabanis, 1851, *Mus. Heineanum*, 1, p. 123, "N.O. Africa", restricted to Bir

Hamman, southwest of Alexandria, Egypt, *fide* Vaurie, 1959, *Birds Pal. Fauna, Pass.*, p. 31.
Comments: Called Rufous Short-toed Lark in some other works.

Calandrella rufescens nicolli Hartert
Calandrella minor nicolli Hartert, 1909, Bull. Brit. Ornith. Club, 25, p. 9, Damietta, Egypt.

Calandrella rufescens heinei (Homeyer)
Calandritis Heinei Homeyer, 1873, J. f. Ornith., 21, p. 197, Volga region.
Comments: Specimen in the BMNH (1934.1.1.7796) taken on 21 October 1906 at Port Said.[109]

Calandra Lark   *Melanocorypha calandra* (Linnaeus)
Melanocorypha calandra calandra (Linnaeus)
Alauda Calandra Linnaeus, 1766, *Syst. Nat.*, ed. 12, p. 288, Pyrenees.

Eastern Calandra Lark   *Melanocorypha bimaculata* (Ménétries)
Melanocorypha bimaculata rufescens Brehm
Melanocorypha rufescens C. L. Brehm, 1855, *Der Vollständige Vogelfang*, p. 120, Sudan.
Comments: Specimen in the BMNH (1965 M.7075) collected on 20 February 1928 at Luxor. This is most likely the same specimen mentioned by Meinertzhagen.[110] Called Bimaculated Lark in some other works.

Thick-billed Lark   *Rhamphocorys clotbey* (Bonaparte)
Melanocorypha clot-bey Bonaparte, 1850, *Conspectus Generum Avium*, 1, p. 242, Egyptian desert.
Comments: Sometimes the genus is spelled *Ramphocoris*. Specimen in the GZM (B472) obtained on 16 September 1941 at Mersa Matruh.[111] There are several earlier specimen records.[112] Also note that the type locality is Egypt. Called Clot-bey Lark in some other works.

Temminck's Horned Lark   *Eremophila bilopha* (Temminck)
Alauda bilopha Temminck, 1823, in Temminck and Laugier, *Planches Col.*, livr. 41, pl. 244, fig. 1, Jordan.
Arabic name: Qunburra Aṣ-ṣaḥraa'.

Crested Lark   *Galerida cristata* (Linnaeus)
Galerida cristata nigricans (Brehm)
Galerita nigricans C. L. Brehm, 1855, *Der Vollständige Vogelfang*, p. 123, Egypt.
Arabic name: Qunburra Bashuusha.

Galerida cristata maculata (Brehm)
Galerita cristata maculata C. L. Brehm, 1858, Naumannia, 8, p. 208, Aswan, Egypt.

Galerida cristata altirostris (Brehm)
Galerita altirostris C. L. Brehm, 1855, *Der Vollständige Vogelfang*, p. 124, upper Egypt.

Thekla Lark   *Galerida theklae* Brehm
Galerida theklae superflua Hartert
G. [alerida] cristata superflua Hartert, 1897, Novitates Zool., 4, p. 144, Tunis.

Wood Lark   *Lullula arborea* (Linnaeus)
Lullula arborea arborea (Linnaeus)
Alauda arborea Linnaeus, 1758, *Syst. Nat.*, ed. 10, p. 166, Europe.

Lullula arborea pallida Zarudny
Lullula arborea pallida Zarudny, 1902, Ornith. Monatsber., 10, p. 54, Transcaspia.

Skylark   *Alauda arvensis* Linnaeus
Alauda arvensis cantarella Bonaparte
Alauda cantarella Bonaparte, 1850, *Conspectus Generum Avium*, 1, p. 245, central Italy.

Family MOTACILLIDAE

Richard's Pipit   *Anthus novaeseelandiae* (Gmelin)
Anthus novaeseelandiae richardi Vieillot
Anthus Richardi Vieillot, 1818, *Nouv. Dict. d'Hist. Nat.*, nouv. éd., 26, p. 491, France.
Arabic name: Abuu Fuṣṣiya (generic for pipit).
Comments: Sometimes this subspecies is regarded as a distinct species.

Tawny Pipit   *Anthus campestris* (Linnaeus)
Anthus campestris campestris (Linnaeus)
Alauda campestris Linnaeus, 1758, *Syst. Nat.*, ed. 10, p. 166, Europe.

Anthus campestris griseus Nicoll
Anthus campestris griseus Nicoll, 1920, Bull. Brit. Ornith. Club, 41, p. 25, Russian Turkestan.

Tree Pipit   *Anthus trivialis* (Linnaeus)
Anthus trivialis trivialis (Linnaeus)
Alauda trivialis Linnaeus, 1758, *Syst. Nat.*, ed. 10, p. 166, Sweden.

Meadow Pipit   *Anthus pratensis* (Linnaeus)
Anthus pratensis pratensis Linnaeus, 1758, *Syst. Nat.*, ed. 10, p. 166, Europe.

Red-throated Pipit   *Anthus cervinus* (Pallas)
Motacilla Cervina Pallas, 1811, *Zoographia Rosso-Asiatica*, 1, p. 511, Siberia.

Water Pipit   *Anthus spinoletta* (Linnaeus)
Anthus spinoletta coutellii Audouin
Anthus Coutellii Audouin, 1828, in Savigny, *Descr. de l'Égypte*, 23, p. 360, pl. 5, fig. 5, Egypt.
Comments: Some other subspecies are called Rock Pipit.

(Wagtails: see under subspp.)   *Motacilla flava* Linnaeus
Motacilla flava flavissima (Blyth)   **Yellow Wagtail**
Budytes flava, or better, perhaps, *flavissima* Blyth, 1834, Mag. Nat. Hist., 7, p. 342, England.
Arabic name: Abuu Fiṣaada (generic for wagtail).

Motacilla flava flava Linnaeus   **Blue-headed Wagtail**
Motacilla flava Linnaeus, 1758, *Syst. Nat.*, ed. 10, p. 185, Europe.

Comments: Several examples of *M. f. "dombrow-skii"* have been obtained in Egypt, which are best considered *M. f.* subspp. hybrids. One such specimen is in the USNM (551826) collected on 16 April 1970 at Bahig.

Motacilla flava cinereocapilla Savi   **Ashy-headed Wagtail**
Motacilla cinereocapilla Savi, 1831, Nuovo Giornale de' Letterati, no. 57, p. 190, Italy [reference not verified].

Motacilla flava pygmaea (Brehm)   **Egyptian Wagtail**
B. [*udytes*] *pygmaeus* A. E. Brehm, 1854, J. f. Ornith., 2, p. 74, footnote, "Northeast Africa."

Motacilla flava thunbergi Billberg   **Grey-headed Wagtail**
Motacilla Thunbergi Billberg, 1828, *Synopsis Fauna Scand.*, 1, pt 2, Aves, p. 50, "Lapponia ad Enontekis et Enara" [reference not verified].

Motacilla flava feldegg Michahelles   **Black-headed Wagtail**
Motacilla Feldegg Michahelles, 1830, Isis von Oken, col. 812, southern Dalmatia.

Grey Wagtail   *Motacilla cinerea* Tunstall
Motacilla cinerea cinerea Tunstall
Motacilla Cinerea Tunstall, 1771, *Ornith. Brit.*, p. 2, no locality, but presumed to be England, *fide* Clancey, 1946, Bull. Brit. Ornith. Club, 66, p. 28.

(Wagtails: see under subspp.)   *Motacilla alba* Linnaeus

Motacilla alba alba Linnaeus   **White Wagtail**
Motacilla alba Linnaeus, 1758, *Syst. Nat.*, ed. 10, p. 185, Europe.

Motacilla alba vidua Sundevall   **Pied Wagtail**
Motacilla vidua Sundevall, 1850, Öfver. Kongl. Sv. Vet. Akad. Förh., Stockholm, 7, p. 128, "Syene, Aegypti."
Comments: Sometimes the African breeding populations are considered a distinct species, *M. aquimp*, in which case this subspecies becomes *M. aquimp vidua*. Called African Pied Wagtail in some other works.

Family LANIIDAE

Red-backed Shrike   *Lanius collurio* Linnaeus
Lanius collurio collurio Linnaeus
Lanius Collurio Linnaeus, 1758, *Syst. Nat.*, ed. 10, p. 94, Europe.
Arabic names: Daqnaash, Nuhas, Ṣurad (all generic for shrike).

Lanius collurio isabellinus Hemprich and Ehrenberg
Lanius isabellinus Hemprich and Ehrenberg, 1833, *Symbolae Physicae, Aves*, pt. 1, sig. e, footnote 2, Arabia.
Comments: This subspecies is regarded in some

works as a distinct species and is called the Isabelline Shrike or Red-tailed Shrike. Specimens in the BMNH (1965 M.9865 and 1965 M.9856) collected on 28 March 1928 at Gebel Elba and on 21 February at Quseir (respectively).[113] There are a few other records of this form in Egypt.[114]

Masked Shrike   *Lanius nubicus* Lichtenstein
L. [*anius*] *nubicus* Lichtenstein, 1823, *Verz. Doubl. Zool. Mus. Berlin*, p. 47, Nubia.
Comments: Called Nubian Shrike in some other works.

Woodchat Shrike   *Lanius senator* Linnaeus
Lanius senator senator Linnaeus
Lanius Senator Linnaeus, 1758, *Syst. Nat.*, ed. 10, p. 94, "Indiis", in error; type from the Rhine, *fide* Hartert, 1907, *Vögel Pal. Fauna*, 1, p. 434.
Arabic name: Daqnaash Niilii.

Lanius senator niloticus (Bonaparte)
E. [*nneoctonus*] *niloticus* Bonaparte, 1853, Rev. Zool., p. 439, White Nile.

Lesser Grey Shrike   *Lanius minor* Gmelin
Lanius minor minor Gmelin
Lanius minor J. F. Gmelin, 1788, *Syst. Nat.*, 1, pt. 1, p. 308, Italy.
Arabic name: Daqnaash Ṣurdii.

Great Grey Shrike   *Lanius excubitor* Linnaeus
Lanius excubitor elegans Swainson
Lanius elegans Swainson, 1831, *Fauna Boreali-Americana*, 2, p. 122, "Hudson Bay", in error; type from Algeria or Tunisia, *fide* Hartert, 1907, *Vögel Pal. Fauna*, 1, p. 427.
Comments: This subspecies is regarded in some other works as a distinct species and is called the Grey Shrike. Called Northern Shrike in some other works.

Lanius excubitor aucheri Bonaparte
Lanius aucheri Bonaparte, 1853, *Rev. Zool.*, p. 294, Persia.
Comments: There are several recent records of this subspecies in Egypt.[115]

Lanius excubitor pallidirostris Cassin
Lanius pallidirostris Cassin, 1852, Proc. Acad. Nat. Sci., Philadelphia, 5, p. 244, East Africa.
Comments: Specimen in the BMNH (1965 M.10092) collected on 20 February 1928 at Quseir.[116]

Rosy-patched Shrike   *Tchagra cruenta* (Hemprich and Ehrenberg)
Tchagra cruenta cruenta (Hemprich and Ehrenberg)
Lanius cruentus Hemprich and Ehrenberg, 1828, *Symbolae Physicae, Aves*, pt. 1, pl. 3, and text, sig. c, Arkiko, near Massawa, Ethiopia.
Comments: Sometimes placed in the genus *Rhodo-phoneus* as *R. cruentus*. Specimens examined include one in the FMNH (222436) collected on 7 March 1954, eleven in the BMNH (1929.1.3.13-23) in March-April 1928, and two in the GZM (A2098

and A2751) on 4 March 1938 and 26 December 1938 (respectively), all in the general vicinity of Gebel Elba.[117]

Family ORIOLIDAE

Golden Oriole   *Oriolus oriolus* (Linnaeus)
Oriolus oriolus oriolus (Linnaeus)
  Coracias Oriolus Linnaeus, 1758, *Syst. Nat.*, ed. 10, p. 107, Europe, Asia.
Arabic names: Ṣufaariya, Ṣuffayr, 'Uṣfuur At-tuut.

Family STURNIDAE

Rose-colored Starling   *Sturnus roseus* (Linnaeus)
Turdus roseus Linnaeus, 1758, *Syst. Nat.*, ed. 10, p. 170, Lapland, Switzerland.
Comments: Sometimes placed in the genus *Pastor* as *P. roseus*. Called Rosy Pastor in some other works. The inclusion of this species is based on the specimens mentioned in Meinertzhagen[118] and a recent sight record near Suez.[119]

Starling   *Sturnus vulgaris* Linnaeus
Sturnus vulgaris vulgaris Linnaeus
  Sturnus vulgaris Linnaeus, 1758, *Syst. Nat.*, ed. 10, p. 167, Europe, Africa.
Arabic name: Zurzuur.

Sturnus vulgaris tauricus Buturlin
  Sturnus tauricus Buturlin, 1904, *Ornith. Jahrb.*, 15, p. 209, Crimea, Russia.

Sturnus vulgaris purpurascens Gould
  Sturnus purpurascens Gould, 1868, *Proc. Zool. Soc. London*, p. 219, Erzurum, Armenia.

Family CORVIDAE

[Chough   *Pyrrhocorax pyrrhocorax* (Linnaeus)
Pyrrhocorax pyrrhocorax docilis (Gmelin)
  Corvus docilis S. G. Gmelin, 1774, *Reise Russland*, 3, p. 365, pl. 39, northern Iran.
Arabic name: Ghuraab 'Aṣam.
Comments: Two birds were observed on 13 September 1957 at Gebel Mokattam, near Cairo and assigned to this subspecies.[120] Hypothetical in the country until further evidence is available.]

House Crow   *Corvus splendens* Vieillot
Corvus splendens [*splendens*] Vieillot
  Corvus splendens Vieillot, 1817, *Nouv. Dict. d'Hist. Nat.*, nouv. éd., 8, p. 44, India.
Arabic name: Ghuraab (generic for *Corvus* spp.).
Comments: This species has recently established itself in the country.[121] The subspecies that occurs in Egypt is unknown and is tentatively assigned to the nominate form until Egyptian material is available. Called Indian House Crow in some other works.

Rook   *Corvus frugilegus* Linnaeus
Corvus frugilegus frugilegus Linnaeus
  Corvus frugilegus Linnaeus, 1758, *Syst. Nat.*, ed. 10, p. 105, Europe.
Arabic name: Ghudaaf.
Comments: Inclusion of this species is based on the records reported by Meinertzhagen.[122]

Hooded Crow   *Corvus corone* Linnaeus
Corvus corone cornix Linnaeus
  Corvus Cornix Linnaeus, 1758, *Syst. Nat.*, ed. 10, p. 105, Europe.
Arabic names: Ghuraab Baladii, Zaagh.
Comments: Some other forms of this species are called the Carrion Crow.

Corvus corone sardonius Kleinschmidt
  Corvus sardonius Kleinschmidt, 1903, *Ornith. Monatsber.*, 11, p. 92, Sardinia.

Brown-necked Raven   *Corvus ruficollis* Lesson
Corvus ruficollis ruficollis Lesson
  Corvus ruficollis Lesson, end of 1830 or early 1831, *Traité d'Ornith.*, p. 329, no locality, accepted as Cape Verde Archipelago, *fide* Hartert, 1921, *Vögel Pal. Fauna*, 3, p. 2020.
Arabic name: Ghuraab Nuuḥii.
Comments: Sometimes this species is considered conspecific with *C. corax*. Called Desert Raven in some other works.

Raven   *Corvus corax* Linnaeus
Corvus corax tingitanus Irby
  Corvus tingitanus Irby, 1874, *Ibis*, p. 264, Tangier, Morocco.
Arabic name: Ghuraab Nuuḥii.

Fan-tailed Raven   *Corvus rhipidurus* Hartert
  Corvus rhipidurus Hartert, 1918, *Bull. Brit. Ornith. Club*, 39, p. 21, Ethiopia.

Family BOMBYCILLIDAE

Grey Hypocolius   *Hypocolius ampelinus* Bonaparte
  Hypocolius ampelinus Bonaparte, 1850, *Conspectus Generum Avium*, 1, p. 336, "California", in error; type from Ethiopia, *fide* Heuglin, 1868, *Ibis*, p. 182.
Comments: Sometimes placed in its own family, the HYPOCOLIDAE. Specimen in the GZM (A2424) obtained on 22 December 1938 at Gebel Elba.[123]

Family PYCNONOTIDAE

Common Bulbul   *Pycnonotus barbatus*
                                      (Desfontaines)
Pycnonotus barbatus arsinoe (Lichtenstein)
  T.[*urdus*] *Arsinoe* Lichtenstein, 1823, *Verz. Doubl. Zool. Mus. Berlin*, p. 39, Faiyum, Egypt.
Arabic name: Bulbul.
Comments: Called Black-eyed Bulbul or White-vented Bulbul in some other works.

Pycnonotus barbatus xanthopygos (Hemprich and Ehrenberg)

Ixus xanthopygos Hemprich and Ehrenberg, 1833, *Symbolae Physicae, Aves*, pt. 1, sig. bb, footnote 7, Arabia.

Comments: A male of this form in the GZM (8329) was collected on 11 April 1920 at the Delta Barrage. The bird was "apparently paired with *P. arsinoe*." Yellow-vented bulbuls have recently been observed near Suez.[124] This subspecies is considered specifically distinct in some other works and is called the Yellow-vented Bulbul.

Family PRUNELLIDAE

Dunnock   *Prunella modularis* (Linnaeus)
Prunella modularis modularis (Linnaeus)
Motacilla modularis Linnaeus, 1758, *Syst. Nat.*, ed. 10, p. 184, Europe.
Arabic name: 'Uṣfuur Ash-shawk.
Comments: Called Hedge Sparrow in some other works.

Prunella modularis obscura (Hablizl)
Motacilla obscura Hablizl, 1783, *Neue Nordische Beyträge*, 4, p. 56, mountains of Gilan, northern Iran.
Comments: Specimens in the USNM (533469, 550596, and 550594) collected on 23 November 1966, 4 November 1969, and 12 November 1969 (respectively) at Bahig.[125] The 1966 specimen was previously identified as *P. m. modularis*,[126] but is referable to *P. m. obscura*.

Family SYLVIIDAE[127]

Cetti's Warbler   *Cettia cetti* (Temminck)
Cettia cetti [*orientalis*] Tristram
Cettia (*Potamodus*) *orientalis* Tristram, 1867, Ibis, p. 79, Palestine.
Comments: One bird observed and heard vocalizing on 30 March 1982 south of Suez.[128] The subspecies that occurs in Egypt is unknown and is tentatively assigned to *orientalis* until Egyptian material is available.

Savi's Warbler   *Locustella luscinioides* (Savi)
Locustella luscinioides luscinioides (Savi)
Sylvia luscinioides Savi, 1824, Nuovo Giornale de' Letterati, 7, no. 14, p. 341, Pisa, Italy [reference not verified].
Arabic names: Bulbul Al-ghaab, and Haazija, Khansha' (generic for *Locustella*, *Lusciniola*, *Acrocephalus*, and *Hippolais* spp.).

Locustella luscinioides fusca (Severtzov)
Cettia fusca Severtzov, 1872, *Vertikal Turkestan. Zhivotn*, p. 131, south Kazakstan [reference not verified].
Comments: Inclusion of this subspecies is based on a previously reported specimen.[129]

River Warbler   *Locustella fluviatilis* (Wolf)
Sylvia fluviatilis Wolf, 1810, in Meyer and Wolf, *Taschenb. Deutsch. Vögelkunde*, 1, p. 229, Austria.

Comments: The USNM has a series of eight recent specimens from Egypt.[130]

Grasshopper Warbler   *Locustella naevia* (Boddaert)
Locustella naevia naevia (Boddaert)
Motacilla naevia Boddaert, 1783, *Table Planches Enlum.*, p. 35, Italy.

Moustached Warbler   *Lusciniola melanopogon* (Temminck)
Lusciniola melanopogon melanopogon (Temminck)
Sylvia melanopogon Temminck, 1823, in Temminck and Laugier, *Planches Col.*, livr. 41, pl. 245, fig. 2, Rome, Italy.
Comments: Sometimes placed in the genus *Acrocephalus* as *A. melanopogon*.

Sedge Warbler   *Acrocephalus schoenobaenus* (Linnaeus)
Motacilla Schoenobaenus Linnaeus, 1758, *Syst. Nat.*, ed. 10, p. 184, Europe.
Arabic name: Wish Ad-diiba.

Marsh Warbler   *Acrocephalus palustris* (Bechstein)
Motacilla s. Sylvia palustris Bechstein, 1798, in Latham, *Allg. Uebersicht der Vögel*, 3, p. 545, Germany.

Reed Warbler   *Acrocephalus scirpaceus* (Hermann)
Acrocephalus scirpaceus fuscus (Hemprich and Ehrenberg)
C. [*urruca*] *fusca* Hemprich and Ehrenberg, 1833, *Symbolae Physicae, Aves*, pt. 1, sig. cc, footnote 4, northern Arabia.
Arabic name: Abuu Dukhna.

Clamorous Reed Warbler   *Acrocephalus stentoreus* (Hemprich and Ehrenberg)
Acrocephalus stentoreus stentoreus (Hemprich and Ehrenberg)
Curruca stentorea Hemprich and Ehrenberg, 1833, *Symbolae Physicae, Aves*, pt. 1, sig. bb, footnote 2, Damietta, Egypt.
Comments: Called Southern Great Reed Warbler in some other works.

Great Reed Warbler   *Acrocephalus arundinaceus* (Linnaeus)
Acrocephalus arundinaceus arundinaceus (Linnaeus)
Turdus arundinaceus Linnaeus, 1758, *Syst. Nat.*, ed. 10, p. 170, Europe.

Acrocephalus arundinaceus zarudnyi Hartert
Acrocephalus arundinaceus zarudnyi Hartert, 1907, Bull. Brit. Ornith. Club, 21, p. 26, Djarkent, Turkestan.

Icterine Warbler   *Hippolais icterina* (Vieillot)
Sylvia icterina Vieillot, 1817, *Nouv. Dict. d'Hist. Nat.*, nouv. éd., 11, p. 194, France.

Olivaceous Warbler   *Hippolais pallida* (Hemprich and Ehrenberg)
Hippolais pallida pallida (Hemprich and Ehrenberg)

C.[*urruca*] *pallida* Hemprich and Ehrenberg, 1833, *Symbolae Physicae, Aves*, pt. 1, sig. bb, footnote 3, "Nilum Aegypti et Nubiae."
Arabic name: Zaqq.

Hippolais pallida elaeica (Lindermayer)
Salicaria elaeica Lindermayer, 1843, *Isis von Oken*, col. 343, Greece.

Olive-tree Warbler   *Hippolais olivetorum* (Strickland)
Salicaria Olivetorum Strickland, 1837, in Gould, *Birds of Europe*, 2, pl. 107, and text, Ionian Islands, Greece.

Barred Warbler   *Sylvia nisoria* (Bechstein)
Sylvia nisoria nisoria (Bechstein)
  Motacilla nisoria Bechstein, 1795, *Gemein. Naturgesch. Deutschl.*, 4, p. 580, pl. 17, Germany.
Arabic names: Dukhkhala, Zurayqa (both generic for *Sylvia* spp.).
Comments: Specimen in the FMNH (268674) collected on 13 October 1962 at Bahig. The USNM also has a series of seventeen specimens from Egypt.[131]

Orphean Warbler   *Sylvia hortensis* (Gmelin)
Sylvia hortensis crassirostris Cretzschmar
  Sylvia crassirostris Cretzschmar, 1830, *Atlas Reise Rüppell, Vögel*, p. 49, pl. 33, fig. a, Nubia.
Arabic name: Zurayqa Mughanniyya.
Comments: Six recent specimens from Egypt in the USNM.[132]

Garden Warbler   *Sylvia borin* (Boddaert)
Sylvia borin borin (Boddaert)
  Motacilla Borin Boddaert, 1783, *Table Planches Enlum.*, p. 35, France.
Arabic names: Dukhkhala Kuḥlaa', Qarqafanna.

Sylvia borin woodwardi (Sharpe)
  Bradyornis woodwardi Sharpe, 1877, *Cat. Birds Brit. Mus.*, 3, p. 311, Natal.

Blackcap   *Sylvia atricapilla* (Linnaeus)
Sylvia atricapilla atricapilla (Linnaeus)
  Motacilla Atricapilla Linnaeus, 1758, *Syst. Nat.*, ed. 10, p. 187, Europe.
Arabic name: Abuu Qalansuwa.

Whitethroat   *Sylvia communis* Latham
Sylvia communis communis Latham
  Sylvia Communis Latham, 1787, *Gen. Synopsis Birds*, Suppl. 1, p. 287, England.
Arabic name: Zurayqa Fiiraanii.

Sylvia communis icterops Ménétries
  Sylvia icterops Ménétries, 1832, *Cat. Raisonné Obj. Zool. Caucase*, p. 34, eastern Transcaucasia.

Lesser Whitethroat   *Sylvia curruca* (Linnaeus)
Sylvia curruca curruca (Linnaeus)
  Motacilla Curruca Linnaeus, 1758, *Syst. Nat.*, ed. 10, p. 184, Europe.

Sylvia curruca blythi Ticehurst and Whistler

Sylvia curruca blythi Ticehurst and Whistler, 1933, Ibis, p. 556, Siberia.

Desert Warbler   *Sylvia nana* (Hemprich and Ehrenberg)
Sylvia nana nana (Hemprich and Ehrenberg)
  C.[*urruca*] *nana* Hemprich and Ehrenberg, 1833, *Symbolae Physicae, Aves*, pt. 1, sig. cc, footnote 5, El Tor, Sinai.
Comments: Specimen in GZM (A2404) collected on 21 February 1938 at Halaib abd another in UMMZ (207,186) taken on 13 February 1984 near Hamra Dom.

Sylvia nana deserti (Loche)
  Stoparola Deserti Loche, 1858, Rev. Zool., p. 394, pl. 11, fig. 1, Algerian Sahara.
Comments: Specimen in the BMNH (1965 M.13939) collected on 28 January 1920, at the Libyan frontier, ten miles west of Salum.[133]

Rüppell's Warbler   *Sylvia rueppelli* Temminck
Sylvia ruppeli [sic] Temminck, 1823, in Temminck and Laugier, *Planches Col.*, livr. 41, pl. 245, fig. 1, Crete.
Arabic name: Zurayqa Quṣṣaabii.

Sardinian Warbler   *Sylvia melanocephala* (Gmelin)
Sylvia melanocephala melanocephala (Gmelin)
  Motacilla melanocephala J. F. Gmelin, 1789, *Syst. Nat.*, 1, pt. 2, p. 970, Sardinia.
Arabic name: Dukhkhala Ra'saa'.

Sylvia melanocephala momus (Hemprich and Ehrenberg)
  C.[*urruca*] *Momus* Hemprich and Ehrenberg, 1833, *Symbolae Physicae, Aves*, pt. 1, sig. bb, footnote 7, Egypt.

Sylvia melanocephala norrisae Nicoll
  Sylvia norrisae Nicoll, 1917, Bull. Brit. Ornith. Club, 37, p. 28, Faiyum, Egypt.

Sylvia melanocephala melanothorax Tristram
  Sylvia melanothorax Tristram, 1872, Ibis, p. 296, Jordan Valley.
Comments: Several specimens have been taken in Egypt.[134] Some authors consider this subspecies a distinct species, and call it the Cyprus Warbler.

Ménétries' Warbler   *Sylvia mystacea* Ménétries
Sylvia mystacea Ménétries, 1832, *Cat. Raisonné Obj. Zool. Caucase*, p. 34, eastern Transcaucasia.
Comments: Sometimes regarded as conspecific with *S. melanocephala* or *S. cantillans*.

Subalpine Warbler   *Sylvia cantillans* (Pallas)
Sylvia cantillans albistriata (Brehm)
  Curruca albistriata C. L. Brehm, 1855, *Der Vollständige Vogelfang*, p. 229, "Aegypten, wahrscheinlich auch in Südosteuropa."

Spectacled Warbler   *Sylvia conspicillata* Temminck
Sylvia conspicillata conspicillata Temminck
  Sylvia conspicillata Temminck, 1820, *Manuel d'Ornith.*, ed. 2, 1, p. 210, Sardinia.

168

Marmora's Warbler   *Sylvia sarda* Temminck
Sylvia sarda sarda Temminck
  Sylvia sarda Temminck, 1820, *Manuel d'Ornith.*, ed. 2, 1, p. 204, Sardinia.

Willow Warbler   *Phylloscopus trochilus* (Linnaeus)
Phylloscopus trochilus trochilus (Linnaeus)
  Motacilla Trochilus Linnaeus, 1758, *Syst. Nat.*, ed. 10, p. 188, Europe.
Arabic names: Haazija, Niqshaara (both generic for *Phylloscopus* spp.).

Phylloscopus trochilus acredula (Linnaeus)
  Motacilla Acredula Linnaeus, 1758, *Syst. Nat.*, ed. 10, p. 189, Europe.

Chiffchaff   *Phylloscopus collybita* (Vieillot)
Phylloscopus collybita collybita (Vieillot)
  Sylvia collybita Vieillot, 1817, *Nouv. Dict. d'Hist. Nat.*, nouv. éd., 11, p. 235, France.
Arabic names: Al-mughannaa Al-akhḍar, Suksuka.

Phylloscopus collybita abietinus (Nilsson)
  Sylvia abietina Nilsson, 1819, Nya Handl. Kongl. Vet. Akad., p. 115, pl. 5, Sweden.

Bonelli's Warbler   *Phylloscopus bonelli* (Vieillot)
Phylloscopus bonelli bonelli (Vieillot)
  Sylvia Bonelli Vieillot, 1819, *Nouv. Dict. d'Hist. Nat.*, nouv. éd., 28, p. 91, "Piémont."

Phylloscopus bonelli orientalis (Brehm)
  Phyllopneuste orientalis C. L. Brehm, 1855, *Der Vollständige Vogelfang*, p. 232, Wadi Halfa, Sudan.

Wood Warbler   *Phylloscopus sibilatrix* (Bechstein)
  Motacilla Sibilatrix Bechstein, 1793, Der Naturforscher, Halle, 27, p. 47, mountains of Thuringia, Germany [reference not verified].
Arabic names: Al-mughannaa Al-aṣfar, Ṭarghaluus Shimaaliyya.
Comments: Called Wood Wren in some other works.

Yellow-browed Warbler   *Phylloscopus inornatus* (Blyth)
Phylloscopus inornatus inornatus (Blyth)
  Regulus inornatus Blyth, 1842, J. Asiat. Soc. Bengal, 11, p. 191, no locality, thought to be near Calcutta, *fide* Vaurie, 1959, *Birds Pal. Fauna. Pass.*, p. 284.
Comments: Two specimens in the USNM (533475 and 551636) collected on 17 October 1966 and 22 October 1969 (respectively) at Bahig.[135] Called Inornate Leaf Warbler in some other works.

Goldcrest   *Regulus regulus* (Linnaeus)
Regulus regulus regulus (Linnaeus)
  Motacilla Regulus Linnaeus, 1758, *Syst. Nat.*, ed. 10, p. 188, Europe.
Comments: Specimen in the USNM (550804) collected on 30 October 1968 at Bahig.

Firecrest   *Regulus ignicapillus* (Temminck)
Regulus ignicapillus ignicapillus (Temminck)
  Sylvia ignicapilla Temminck, 1820, *Manuel d'Ornith.*, ed. 2, 1, p. 231, France and Germany.
Comments: Specimen in the NAMRU-3 collection, Cairo, collected on 5 March 1973 at Bahig.[136]

Graceful Prinia   *Prinia gracilis* (Lichtenstein)
Prinia gracilis carlo Zedlitz
  Prinia gracilis carlo Zedlitz, 1911, J. f. Ornith., 59, p. 610, Somaliland.
Arabic name: Fuṣṣiya.
Comments: Called Graceful Warbler, Streaked Wren Warbler, and Striped-backed Prinia in some other works. Two specimens in the BMNH (1965 M.14655-6) collected on 18 April 1928 at Gebel Elba. These are presumably the same specimens reported by Meinertzhagen,[137] but the date differs.

Prinia gracilis deltae Reichenow
  Prinia gracilis deltae Reichenow, 1904, J. f. Ornith., 52, p. 307, Alexandria, Nile Delta, Egypt.

Prinia gracilis gracilis (Lichtenstein)
  S.[ylvia] gracilis Lichtenstein, 1823, *Verz. Doubl. Zool. Mus. Berlin*, p. 34, Nubia.

Prinia gracilis natronensis Nicoll
  Prinia gracilis natronensis Nicoll, 1917, Bull. Brit. Ornith. Club, 37, p. 29, Wadi Natroun, Egypt.
Comments: The validity and relationships of this subspecies have recently been reviewed.[138]

Streaked Scrub Warbler   *Scotocerca inquieta* (Cretzschmar)
Scotocerca inquieta inquieta (Cretzschmar)
  Malurus inquietus Cretzschmar, 1830, *Atlas Reise Rüppell, Vögel*, p. 55, pl. 36, fig. b, Arabia Petraea.
Arabic names: Dukhkhala Ad-daghal, Nimnima Ash-shajar, Shuwaala.

Fan-tailed Warbler   *Cisticola juncidis* (Rafinesque)
Cisticola juncidis juncidis (Rafinesque)
  Sylvia Juncidis Rafinesque, 1810, *Caratteri Animali Sicilia*, p. 6, Sicily.
Arabic name: Umm Al-fuṣṣii.
Comments: Called Zitting Cisticola, Fantail Cisticola or Streaked Fan-tailed Warbler in some other works.

Family MUSCICAPIDAE

Pied Flycatcher   *Ficedula hypoleuca* (Pallas)
Ficedula hypoleuca hypoleuca (Pallas)
  Motacilla hypoleuca Pallas, 1764, in Vroeg, *Cat. Adumbratiunculae*, p. 3, Holland, *fide* Sherborn, 1905, Smiths. Misc. Collect., 47.
Arabic names: Khaaṭif Adh-dhubaab, Shuurib (both generic for flycatchers).

Collared Flycatcher   *Ficedula albicollis* (Temminck)
Ficedula albicollis albicollis (Temminck)
  Muscicapa albicollis Temminck, 1815, *Manuel d'Ornith.*, ed. 1, p. 100, Germany.
Arabic name: Abuu Shayquuna.

Ficedula albicollis semitorquata (Homeyer)
  Muscicapa semitorquata Homeyer, 1885, Zeitschr. Gesamm. Ornith., 2, p. 185, pl. 10, Caucasus.
Comments: Sometimes this subspecies is regarded as a distinct species and is called the Eastern Collared Flycatcher, White-collared Flycatcher or Semi-collared Flycatcher.

Red-breasted Flycatcher *Ficedula parva* (Bechstein)
Ficedula parva parva (Bechstein)
  Muscicapa parva Bechstein, 1794, in Latham, *Allg. Uebersicht der Vögel*, 2, p. 356, fig. on title page of vol. 3 (1796), Thüringer Wald, Germany.

Spotted Flycatcher *Muscicapa striata* (Pallas)
Muscicapa striata striata (Pallas)
  Motacilla striata Pallas, 1764, in Vroeg, *Cat. Adumbratiunculae*, p. 3, Holland, *fide* Sherborn, 1905, Smiths. Misc. Collect., 47.

Muscicapa striata neumanni Poche
  Muscicapa grisola neumanni Poche, 1904, Ornith. Monatsber., 12, p. 26, northern Tanganyika Territory.

Family TURDIDAE

Whinchat *Saxicola rubetra* (Linnaeus)
  Motacilla Rubetra Linnaeus, 1758, *Syst. Nat.*, ed. 10, p. 186, Europe.
Arabic name: Qulayʻii (generic for *Saxicola* spp.).

Stonechat *Saxicola torquata* (Linnaeus)
Saxicola torquata armenica Stegmann
  Saxicola torquata armenica Stegmann, 1935, Doklady Akad. Nauk. S.S.S.R., new ser., 3, p. 47, Kurdistan.

Saxicola torquata rubicola (Linnaeus)
  Motacilla Rubicola Linnaeus, 1766, *Syst. Nat.*, ed. 12, p. 332, Europe.

Saxicola torquata variegata (Gmelin)
  Parus Varietagus [sic] S. G. Gmelin, 1774, *Reise Russland*, 3, p. 105, pl. 20, fig. 3, eastern Transcaucasia.

Wheatear *Oenanthe oenanthe* (Linnaeus)
Oenanthe oenanthe oenanthe (Linnaeus)
  Motacilla Oenanthe Linnaeus, 1758, *Syst. Nat.*, ed. 10, p. 186, Europe.
Arabic names: Abuu Bulayq, and Ablaq, Abuu Ghamiira, Slaygaw (generic for wheatear).
Comments: Called Northern Wheatear in some other works.

Pied Wheatear [139] *Oenanthe pleschanka* (Lepechin)
Oenanthe pleschanka pleschanka (Lepechin)
  Motacilla pleschanka Lepechin, 1770, Novi Comm. Acad. Sci. Imp. Petropol., 14 (for 1769), pt. 1, p. 503, pl. 14, fig. 2, lower Volga.
Arabic name: Ablaq Muraqqaṭ.
Comments: Called Pleschanka's Wheatear in some other works.

Oenanthe pleschanka cypriaca (Homeyer)
  Saxicola cypriaca Homeyer, 1884, Zeitschr. Gesamm. Ornith., 1, p. 397, Cyprus.
Comments: Specimen in the BMNH (1941:5:30-5465) obtained on 30 October 1918 at Abu Zabal. Previously reported by Meinertzhagen.[140] Recently evidence has been presented that *cypriaca* should be considered specifically distinct from nominate *pleschanka*.[141]

Black-eared Wheatear *Oenanthe hispanica* (Linnaeus)
Oenanthe hispanica melanoleuca (Güldenstädt)
  Muscicapa melanoleuca Güldenstädt, 1775, Novi Comm. Acad. Sci. Imp. Petropol., 19 (for 1774), p. 468, pl. 15, Transcaucasia.
Comments: Called Spanish Wheatear or Black-throated Wheatear in some other works.

Mourning Wheatear *Oenanthe lugens* (Lichtenstein)
Oenanthe lugens halophila (Tristram)
  Saxicola halophila Tristram, 1859, Ibis, p. 59, Algerian Sahara.
Comments: Specimen in the USNM (551440) collected on 17 December 1971 at Dandara.

Oenanthe lugens lugens (Lichtenstein)
  S.[axicola] lugens Lichtenstein, 1823, *Verz. Doubl. Zool. Mus. Berlin*, p. 33, Nubia.

Oenanthe lugens persica (Seebohm)
  Saxicola persica Seebohm, 1881, *Cat. Birds Brit. Mus.*, 5, p. 372, Iran.

Desert Wheatear *Oenanthe deserti* (Temminck)
Oenanthe deserti homochroa (Tristram)
  Saxicola homochroa Tristram, 1859, Ibis, p. 59, "Sahara Tunitana", determined to be near the border of Algeria and Tunisia, *fide* Vaurie, 1959, *Birds Pal. Fauna. Pass.*, p. 347.

Oenanthe deserti deserti (Temminck)
  Saxicola deserti Temminck, 1825, in Temminck and Laugier, *Planches Col.*, livr. 60, pl. 359, fig. 2, Egypt.

Oenanthe deserti [atrogularis] (Blyth)
  S.[axicola] atrogularis Blyth, 1847, J. Asiat. Soc. Bengal, 16, p. 131, Upper Provinces, Sind.
Comments: Two males and a female collected on 27 March 1928 in the Dakhla Oasis were assigned to this form.[142] These specimens have been examined (BMNH 1965 M.11935-7) and are referable to nominate *deserti*. Until further documentation is available *atrogularis* should be considered hypothetical in the country.

Finsch's Wheatear *Oenanthe finschii* (Heuglin)
Oenanthe finschii finschii (Heuglin)
  Saxicola Finschii Heuglin, 1869, *Ornith. Nordost-Afrika's*, 1, p. 350, "Siberia", in error; type from Syria, *fide* Meinertzhagen, 1930, *Nicoll's Birds Egypt*, 1, p. 273.

Arabic name: Ablaq 'Arabii.
Comments: Specimen in the FMNH (297038) taken on 11 May 1975 at El Maghra.[143] Called Arabian Wheatear in some other works.

Red-rumped Wheatear — *Oenanthe moesta* (Lichtenstein)
Oenanthe moesta moesta (Lichtenstein)
  S.[axicola] *moesta* Lichtenstein, 1823, *Verz. Doubl. Zool. Mus. Berlin*, p. 33, Egypt.

Red-tailed Wheatear — *Oenanthe xanthoprymna* (Hemprich and Ehrenberg)
Oenanthe xanthoprymna xanthoprymna (Hemprich and Ehrenberg)
  S.[axicola] *xanthoprymna* Hemprich and Ehrenberg, 1833, *Symbolae Physicae, Aves*, pt. 1, sig. dd, footnote 2, Nubia.
Comments: Specimens in the BMNH (1905.6.28. 502), FMNH (126566) and USNM (552691) taken on 17 February 1896 at Giza, 2 November 1891 at Thebes, and 30 December 1970 at Abu Rawash (respectively). There are several additional records from the country.[144] Called Rufous-tailed Wheatear in some other works.

Isabelline Wheatear — *Oenanthe isabellina* (Temminck)
  Saxicola isabellina Temminck, 1829, in Temminck and Laugier, *Planches Col.*, livr. 79, pl. 472, fig. 1, Nubia.
Arabic name: Ablaq Ash/hab.

Hooded Wheatear — *Oenanthe monacha* (Temminck)
  Saxicola monacha Temminck, 1825, in Temminck and Laugier, *Planches Col.*, livr. 60, pl. 359, fig. 1, Nubia, determined to be Luxor, Egypt, *fide* Stresemann, 1954, Abh. Deutsch. Akad. Wiss., Math.-Naturwiss. Klasse, 1, p. 174.
Arabic name: Ablaq Mutaqallas.

Black Wheatear — *Oenanthe leucura* (Gmelin)
Oenanthe leucura syenitica (Heuglin)
  Saxicola syenitica Heuglin, 1869, J. f. Ornith., 17, p. 155, El Kab, Egypt.
Comments: Two specimens in the BMNH (1965 M.12257-8) collected at the Libyan frontier, twelve miles west of Salum, on 28 January 1928. Other than the type specimen, these are the only documented records from the country.

White-crowned Black Wheatear — *Oenanthe leucopyga* (Brehm)
Oenanthe leucopyga peucopyga (Brehm)
  Vitiflora leucopyga C. L. Brehm, 1855, *Der Vollständige Vogelfang*, p. 225, upper Egypt.
Arabic names: Abuu Futfuut, Abuu Slimaan, Ṭaa'irat Ash-shaykh.
Comments: Called White-crowned Wheatear or White-tailed Wheatear in some other works.

Oenanthe leucopyga [*ernesti*] Meinertzhagen
  Oenanthe leucopyga ernesti Meinertzhagen, 1930, *Nicoll's Birds Egypt*, 1, p. 280, Wadi Feiran, Sinai.

Comments: Two specimens (BMNH 1965 M.12250 and 1965 M.12251) were collected on 17 March 1928 and 8 April 1928 at Gebel Elba were reported to be referable to this form.[145] However, these specimens have been examined and they appear closer in coloring to the nominate form.[146] Until further documentation is available *ernesti* should be considered hypothetical in Egypt (excluding the Sinai).

Blackstart — *Cercomela melanura* (Temminck)
Cercomela melanura lypura (Hemprich and Ehrenberg)
  Sylvia lypura Hemprich and Ehrenberg, 1833, *Symbolae Physicae, Aves*, pt. 1, sig. ee, footnote 1, Ethiopia.
Arabic name: Qulay'ii Aswad Adh-dhanab.
Comments: Three specimens in the BMNH (1965 M.11351-3) were collected on 20 March 1928 (two) and 4 April 1928 at Gebel Elba (respectively). There are recent records from the Gebel Uweinat region.[147] Called Black-tailed Rock Chat in some other works.

Rufous Bush Robin — *Cercotrichas galactotes* (Temminck)
Cercotrichas galactotes galactotes (Temminck)
  Sylvia galactotes Temminck, 1820, *Manuel d'Ornith.*, ed. 2, 1, p. 182, southern Spain.
Comments: Sometimes placed in the genus *Erythropygia* as *E. galactotes*. Called Rufous Scrub Robin, Rufous Warbler, Rufous-tailed Chat or Rufous Bush Chat in some other works.

Rock Thrush — *Monticola saxatilis* (Linnaeus)
  Turdus saxatilis Linnaeus, 1766, *Syst. Nat.*, ed. 12, p. 294, "Helvetiae, Austriae, Borussiae montibus."
Arabic name: Sakala.
Comments: Called Rufous-tailed Rock Thrush in some other works.

Blue Rock Thrush — *Monticola solitarius* (Linnaeus)
Monticola solitarius solitarius (Linnaeus)
  Turdus solitarius Linnaeus, 1758, *Syst. Nat.*, ed. 10, p. 170, "Oriente", in error; type from Italy, *fide* Hartert, 1910, *Vögel Pal. Fauna*, 1, p. 674.
Arabic name: Ḥamaama Zarqaa'.

Monticola solitarius longirostris (Blyth)
  P.[etrocincla] *longirostris* Blyth, 1847, J. Asiat. Soc. Bengal, 16, p. 150, between Sind and Ferozepore, India.

Black Redstart — *Phoenicurus ochruros* (Gmelin)
Phoenicurus ochruros gibraltariensis (Gmelin)
  Motacilla gibraltariensis J. F. Gmelin, 1789, *Syst. Nat.*, 1, pt. 2, p. 987, Gibraltar.
Arabic names: Abuu Ḥumra, Ḥumayraa' (both generic for *Phoenicurus* spp.).

Phoenicurus ochruros semirufus (Hemprich and Ehrenberg)
  S.[ylvia] *semirufa* Hemprich and Ehrenberg,

1833, *Symbolae Physicae, Aves*, pt. 1, sig. bb, footnote 1, "Egypt", in error; type from Syria, *fide* Stresemann, 1954, Abh. Deutsch. Akad. Wiss., Math.-Naturwiss. Klasse, 1, p. 175.

Phoenicurus ochruros phoenicuroides (Horsfield and Moore)
Ruticilla phoenicuroides Horsfield and Moore, 1854, *Cat. Birds Mus. East India Co.*, 1, p. 301, Shikarpur, Sind.

Redstart   *Phoenicurus phoenicurus* (Linnaeus)
Phoenicurus phoenicurus phoenicurus (Linnaeus)
Motacilla Phoenicurus Linnaeus, 1758, *Syst. Nat.*, ed. 10, p. 187, Europe.

Phoenicurus phoenicurus samamisicus (Hablizl)
Motacilla samamisica Hablizl, 1783, *Neue Nordische Beyträge*, 4, p. 60, northern Iran.
Comments: Two specimens in the USNM (551497 and 548292) collected on 17 March 1970 at Mersa Matruh and 8 September 1966 at Bahig are referable to this subspecies.

European Robin   *Erithacus rubecula* (Linnaeus)
Erithacus rubecula rubecula (Linnaeus)
Motacilla Rubecula Linnaeus, 1758, *Syst. Nat.*, ed. 10, p. 188, Europe.
Arabic names: Abuu Al-ḥinnaa', Abuu Ṣadr, Al-ḥusn.

Nightingale   *Luscinia megarhynchos* Brehm
Luscinia megarhynchos megarhynchos Brehm
Luscinia megarhynchos C. L. Brehm, 1831, *Handb. Naturgesch. Vögel Deutschl.*, p. 356, Germany.
Arabic names: Al-mughannaa Al-asmar, Atbaz, Hazaar.
Comments: Sometimes placed in the genus *Erithacus* as *E. megarhynchos*.

Thrush Nightingale   *Luscinia luscinia* (Linnaeus)
Motacilla Luscinia Linnaeus, 1758, *Syst. Nat.*, ed. 10, p. 184, Europe.
Arabic name: 'Andaliib.
Comments: Sometimes placed in the genus *Erithacus* as *E. luscinia*. Called Sprosser in some other works.

Bluethroat   *Luscinia svecica* (Linnaeus)
Luscinia svecica cyanecula (Meisner)
Sylvia Cyanecula Meisner, 1804, *Syst. Verz. Vögel Schweiz*, p. 30, northern France.
Arabic name: Ḥusaynii.
Comments: Sometimes placed in the genus *Erithacus* as *E. svecica*.

Luscinia svecica svecica (Linnaeus)
Motacilla svecica Linnaeus, 1758, *Syst. Nat.*, ed. 10, p. 187, Europe.

Luscinia svecica volgae (Kleinschmidt)
Erithacus volgae Kleinschmidt, 1907, *Falco*, 3, p. 47, lower Volga.

Fieldfare [148]   *Turdus pilaris* Linnaeus
Turdus pilaris Linnaeus, 1758, *Syst. Nat.*, ed. 10, p. 168, Europe.
Arabic names: Dujj, Sumna (both generic for *Turdus* spp.).

Ring Ouzel   *Turdus torquatus* Linnaeus
Turdus torquatus alpestris (Brehm)
Merula alpestris C. L. Brehm, 1831, *Handb. Naturgesch. Vögel, Deutschl.*, p. 377, pl. 21, fig. 6, Tirol.
Comments: Specimens in the USNM (551350-1 and 568985) collected on 15 November 1969, 16 November 1969, and 25 October 1972 at Bahig (respectively).

Blackbird   *Turdus merula* Linnaeus
Turdus merula merula Linnaeus
Turdus Merula Linnaeus, 1758, *Syst. Nat.*, ed. 10, p. 170, Europe.
Arabic name: Shuḥuur.
Comments: Specimen in the FMNH (296938) obtained on 10 February 1974 at El Maghra. [149]

Turdus merula syriacus Hemprich and Ehrenberg
T.[urdus] Merula var. *syriaca* Hemprich and Ehrenberg, 1833, *Symbolae Physicae, Aves*, pt. 1, sig. bb, footnote 2, Syria.

Redwing   *Turdus iliacus* Linnaeus
Turdus iliacus iliacus Linnaeus
Turdus iliacus Linnaeus, 1766, *Syst. Nat.*, ed. 12, p. 292, Europe.
Comments: Called *T. musicus* in some earlier works.

Song Thrush   *Turdus philomelos* Brehm
Turdus philomelos philomelos Brehm
Turdus philomelos C. L. Brehm, 1831, *Handb. Naturgesch. Vögel Deutschl.*, p. 382, Germany.

Mistle Thrush   *Turdus viscivorus* Linnaeus
Turdus viscivorus viscivorus Linnaeus
Turdus viscivorus Linnaeus, 1758, *Syst. Nat.*, ed. 10, p. 168, Europe.
Arabic name: Sumna Ad-dibaq.

Family TIMALIIDAE

Fulvous Babbler   *Turdoides fulvus* (Desfontaines)
Turdoides fulvus acaciae (Lichtenstein)
S.[phenura] Acaciae Lichtenstein, 1823, *Verz. Doubl. Zool. Mus. Berlin*, p. 40, Nubia.
Arabic name: Tharthaara.
Comments: Called Egyptian Bush Babbler or Fulvous Chatterer in some other works. Numerous specimens have been taken in the Gebel Elba area. [150]

Family REMIZIDAE

Penduline Tit   *Remiz pendulinus* (Linnaeus)
Remiz pendulinus [menzbieri] (Zarudny)
Remiza pendulina menzbieri Zarudny, 1913,

172

Messager Ornith., p. 50, Karun River, southwestern Iran.

Comments: Up to twenty individuals were noted at Suez between 24 February and 31 March 1982.[151] The subspecies that occurs in Egypt is unknown and is tentatively assigned to *menzbieri* until material is available.

Family NECTARINIIDAE

Pygmy Sunbird   *Anthreptes platurus* (Vieillot)
Anthreptes platurus metallicus (Lichtenstein)
> *N.*[*ectarinia*] *metallica* Lichtenstein, 1823, *Verz. Doubl. Zool. Mus. Berlin*, p. 15, Dongola, Sudan.

Arabic names: Abuu Riish, Tumayr (both generic for sunbird).

Comments: Sometimes this subspecies is considered a distinct species. Called Nile Valley Sunbird in some other works.

Shining Sunbird   *Nectarinia habessinica* Hemprich and Ehrenberg
Nectarinia habessinica habessinica Hemprich and Ehrenberg
> *Nectarinia* (*Cinnyris*) *habessinica* Hemprich and Ehrenberg, 1828, *Symbolae Physicae, Aves*, pt. 1, pl. 4, and text, sig. a, "ex ora Habessiniae ad Eilet."

Comments: Sometimes placed in the genus *Cinnyris* as *C. habessinicus*. The identification of *N. h. hellmayri* (Neumann) as occurring at Gebel Elba is incorrect,[152] and *N. h. habessinica* is the form that occurs there.[153] Examined specimens include three in the FMNH (222865, 222466, and 107786) collected on 3 March 1954, 7 March 1954, and 16 February 1964 (respectively), two in the BMNH (1929.1.3.11-12) taken on 17 March 1928, and three in the GZM (A2092, A2089, and A2444) obtained on 26 February 1938, 28 February 1938, and 25 December 1938 (respectively), all from Gebel Elba. Called Abyssinian Sunbird in some other works.

Family ESTRILDIDAE

Avadavat   *Amandava amandava* (Linnaeus)
Amandava amandava amandava (Linnaeus)
> *Fringilla Amandava* Linnaeus, 1758, *Syst. Nat.*, ed. 10, p. 180, "india orientali."

Comments: Specimen in the USNM (569000) collected on 30 August 1971 at Abu Rawash. There are several recent records of this introduced species in Egypt.[154] Called Red Munia, Red Avadavat, Strawberry Finch or Amadavat in some other works.

African Silverbill   *Lonchura malabarica* (Linnaeus)
Lonchura malabarica [*cantans*] (Gmelin)
> *Loxia cantans* J. F. Gmelin, 1789, *Syst. Nat.*, 1, pt. 2, p. 859, Senegal.

Comments: Sometimes placed in the genus *Euodice*

as *E. malabarica cantans*. This subspecies is also regarded as a distinct species in some other works. Six specimens in the GZM (A2074-5 and A2474-7) taken on 6 March 1938 at Gebel Elba and on 1 January 1939 at Gebel Shallal (respectively). The subspecies still needs to be verified.[155] Called Warbling Silverbill or White-throated Munia in some other works.

Family PLOCEIDAE

Golden Sparrow   *Passer luteus* (Lichtenstein)
> *F.*[*ringilla*] *lutea* Lichtenstein, 1823, *Verz. Doubl. Zool. Mus. Berlin*, p. 24, Dongola, Sudan.

Arabic names: Ḥuzwii, 'Uṣfuur (both generic for *Passer* spp.).

Comments: Sometimes placed in the genus *Auripasser* as *A. luteus*. Also considered conspecific with *P. euchlorus* in some other works. Two specimens in the FMNH (107784-5) collected on 16 January 1964 at Wadi Akwamtra, Gebel Elba.[156] Called Sudan Golden Sparrow in some other works.

House Sparrow   *Passer domesticus* (Linnaeus)
Passer domesticus niloticus Nicoll and Bonhote
> *Passer domesticus niloticus* Nicoll and Bonhote, 1909, *Bull. Brit. Ornith. Club*, 23, p. 101, Faiyum, Egypt.

Spanish Sparrow   *Passer hispaniolensis* (Temminck)
Passer hispaniolensis hispaniolensis (Temminck)
> *Fringilla hispaniolensis* Temminck, 1820, *Manuel d'Ornith.*, ed. 2, 1, p. 353, southern Spain.

Passer hispaniolensis transcaspicus Tschusi
> *Passer hispaniolensis transcaspicus* Tschusi, 1902, *Ornith. Monatsber.*, 10, p. 96, Transcaspia.

[**Tree Sparrow**   *Passer montanus* (Linnaeus)
Passer montanus montanus (Linnaeus)
> *Fringilla montanus* Linnaeus, 1758, *Syst. Nat.*, ed. 10, p. 183, Europe, restricted to Bagnacavallo, Ravenna, Italy, *fide* Clancey, 1948, *Bull. Brit. Ornith. Club*, 68, p. 135.

Comments: One was recently observed at Suez on 29 April 1982.[157] We are unaware of specimens of this species from Egypt. Until further documentation is available it should be considered hypothetical in the country. The subspecies *montanus* is the one likely to occur.]

Desert Sparrow   *Passer simplex* (Lichtenstein)
Passer simplex [*simplex*] (Lichtenstein)
> *F.*[*ringilla*] *simplex* Lichtenstein, 1823, *Verz. Doubl. Zool. Mus. Berlin*, p. 24, Ambukol, Sudan.

Comments: Admitted on sight records from the Gebel Uweinat region.[158] Five were observed on 21 October 1968 at Ain Zuweina, and twenty-two between 27 and 28 December 1968 at Karkur Talh. The subspecies *simplex* is the one most likely to occur, but this needs specimen documentation.

Streaked Weaver   *Ploceus manyar* (Horsfield)
Ploceus manyar [*peguensis*] Baker
Ploceus manyar peguensis Baker, 1925, Bull. Brit.
Ornith. Club, 45, p. 58, Pegu, Burma.
Comments: This species has recently been found nesting in the Nile Delta.[159] The subspecies *peguensis* is the one suspected of occurring in Egypt. Specimen material is lacking.

Family FRINGILLIDAE

Chaffinch   *Fringilla coelebs* Linnaeus
Fringilla coelebs coelebs Linnaeus
Fringilla coelebs Linnaeus, 1758, *Syst. Nat.*, ed. 10, p. 179, Europe.
Arabic name: Ẓaalim.

Brambling   *Fringilla montifringilla* Linnaeus
Fringilla Montifringilla Linnaeus, 1758, *Syst. Nat.*, ed. 10, p. 179, Europe.
Arabic names: Shurshuur Jabalii, Zaghaarii.

Gold-fronted Serin   *Serinus pusillus* (Pallas)
Passer pusillus Pallas, 1811, *Zoographia Rosso-Asiatica*, 2, p. 28, pl. 43, fig. 1, "Circa Caucasum et mare caspium."
Comments: Specimen in the USNM (533477) collected on 18 March 1967 at Bahig.[160] Called Red-fronted Serin or Gold-fronted Finch in some other works.

Serin   *Serinus serinus* (Linnaeus)
Fringilla Serinus Linnaeus, 1766, *Syst. Nat.*, ed. 12, p. 320, Europe.
Arabic names: Ṣayyaah, 'Uṣfuur Na''aar.
Comments: Sometimes regarded as conspecific with *S. canaria*.

Syrian Serin   *Serinus syriacus* Bonaparte
Serinus syriacus Bonaparte, 1850, *Conspectus Generum Avium*, 1, p. 523, "ex As. occ. Bischerra."
Comments: Specimen in the USNM (551963) collected on 25 November 1969 at Bahig. Called Tristram's Serin in some other works.

Greenfinch   *Carduelis chloris* (Linnaeus)
Carduelis chloris chloris (Linnaeus)
Loxia Chloris Linnaeus, 1758, *Syst. Nat.*, ed. 10, p. 174, Europe.
Arabic name: Khuḍayrii.

Carduelis chloris aurantiiventris (Cabanis)
L.[*igurinus*] *aurantiiventris* Cabanis, 1851, *Mus. Heineanum*, 1, p. 158, southern France.
Comments: Two specimens in the USNM (551928 and 548644) collected on 15 March 1970 at Bahig and 12 November 1966 at Port Said (respectively).[161]

Carduelis chloris chlorotica (Bonaparte)
Chlorospiza chlorotica Bonaparte, 1850, *Conspectus Generum Avium*, 1, p. 514, western Asia,

restricted to Syria, *fide* Hartert, 1903, *Vögel Pal. Fauna*, 1, p. 63.

Siskin   *Carduelis spinus* (Linnaeus)
Fringilla Spinus Linnaeus, 1758, *Syst. Nat.*, ed. 10, p. 181, Europe.
Arabic name: Sumaylii.

Goldfinch   *Carduelis carduelis* (Linnaeus)
Carduelis carduelis [*carduelis*] (Linnaeus)
Fringilla Carduelis Linnaeus, 1758, *Syst. Nat.*, ed. 10, p. 180, Europe.
Arabic names: Abuu Zaqaaya, Ḥassuun.
Comments: A specimen in the USNM (549073) collected on 18 December 1966 at Port Said may be referable to this subspecies.

Carduelis carduelis niediecki Reichenow
Carduelis carduelis niediecki Reichenow, 1907, J. f. Ornith., 55, p. 623, Asia Minor.

Linnet   *Acanthis cannabina* (Linnaeus)
Acanthis cannabina cannabina (Linnaeus)
Fringilla cannabina Linnaeus, 1758, *Syst. Nat.*, ed. 10, p. 182, Europe.
Arabic name: Tuffaaḥii.
Comments: Sometimes placed in the genus *Carduelis* as *C. cannabina*.

Acanthis cannabina bella (Brehm)
Fringilla bella C. L. Brehm, 1845, Isis von Oken, col. 348, "Egypt or Nubia", in error; type from Lebanon, *fide* Vaurie, 1959, *Birds Pal. Fauna. Pass.*, p. 616.

Trumpeter Finch   *Rhodopechys githaginea*
(Lichtenstein)
Rhodopechys githaginea zedlitzi (Neumann)
Erythrospiza githaginea zedlitzi Neumann, 1907, Ornith. Monatsber., 15, p. 145, Biskra, Algeria.
Comments: Sometimes placed in the genus *Bucanetes* as *B. githagineus*. Called Trumpeter Bullfinch in some other works,

Rhodopechys githaginea githaginea (Lichtenstein)
F.[*ringilla*] *githaginea* Lichtenstein, 1823, *Verz. Doubl. Zool. Mus. Berlin*, p. 24, upper Egypt.

Common Rose Finch   *Carpodacus erythrinus*
(Pallas)
Carpodacus erythrinus [*kubanensis*] Laubmann
Carpodacus erythrinus kubanensis Laubmann, 1915, Verhandl. Ornith. Gesell. Bayern, 12, p. 93, Karaul Kisha, northwestern Caucasus.
Comments: Three specimens in the USNM (533478, 550324, and 551960) collected on 22 May 1967, 7 October 1968, and 21 October 1969 (respectively) at Bahig.[162] All three specimens are in first basic plumage and it is difficult to assign them to any subspecies. However, they are similar to a series of *kubanensis* in the same plumage, to which they are tentatively assigned. Called Scarlet Rosefinch or Scarlet Grosbeak in some other works.

Hawfinch   *Coccothraustes coccothraustes*
                                    (Linnaeus)
Coccothraustes   coccothraustes   coccothraustes
(Linnaeus)
Loxia Coccothraustes Linnaeus, 1758, *Syst. Nat.,*
ed. 10, p. 171, Europe.
Arabic name: Bulbul Zaytuunii.

Family EMBERIZIDAE

Corn Bunting   *Emberiza calandra* Linnaeus
Emberiza calandra calandra Linnaeus
Emberiza Calandra Linnaeus, 1758, *Syst. Nat.,*
ed. 10, p. 176, Europe.
Arabic names: Darrusa, and Bulbul Ash-sha'iir
(generic for bunting).
Comments: Sometimes placed in the genus *Milaria*
as *M. calandra*.

Ashy-headed Bunting   *Emberiza cineracea* Brehm
Emberiza cineracea semenowi Zarudny
Emberiza (Hypocentor) semenowi Zarudny, 1904,
Ornith. Jahrb., 15, p. 217, Jebel Tnüe, Arabi-
stan.
Comments: Specimen in the BMNH (1965 M.16237)
obtained on 12 April 1928 at Gebel Elba.[163] Called
Cinereous Bunting in some other works.

Ortolan Bunting   *Emberiza hortulana* Linnaeus
Emberiza Hortulana Linnaeus, 1758, *Syst. Nat.,*
ed. 10, p. 177, Europe.

Cretzschmar's Bunting   *Emberiza caesia*
                                    Cretzschmar
Emberiza caesia Cretzschmar, 1830, *Atlas Reise
Rüppell, Vögel,* p. 17, pl. 10, fig. b, Sudan.

Cirl Bunting   *Emberiza cirlus* Linnaeus
Emberiza cirlus cirlus Linnaeus
Emberiza Cirlus Linnaeus, 1766, *Syst. Nat.,* ed.
12, p. 311, Europe.
Comments: The inclusion of this species is based on
an old published specimen record.[164]

Striped Bunting   *Emberiza striolata* (Lichtenstein)
Emberiza striolata sahari Levaillant
Emberiza Sahari Levaillant, 1850, *Expl. Sci.*

Algérie, Hist. Nat. Ois., Atlas, pl. 9 *bis,* fig. 2, no
locality, but presumed to be southern Algeria, *fide*
Loche, 1867, *ibid.,* p. 182.
Comments: Specimen in the BMNH (1965 M.16315)
collected on 28 January 1928.[165] Called House
Bunting or Striolated Bunting in some other works.

Emberiza striolata striolata (Lichtenstein)
F.[ringilla] striolata Lichtenstein, 1823, *Verz.
Doubl. Zool. Mus. Berlin,* p. 24, Ambukol,
Nubia.
Comments: Specimens in the GZM (A2073 and
A2473) taken on 22 February 1938 at Gebel Elba
and on 1 January 1939 at Gebel Shallal (res-
pectively).[166] There are also recent records from the
Gebel Uweinat region.[167]

Rustic Bunting   *Emberiza rustica* Pallas
Emberiza rustica rustica Pallas
Emberiza rustica Pallas, 1776, *Reise Versch.
Prōv. Russ. Reichs,* 3, p. 698, Dauria, Trans-
baicalia.
Comments: Specimen in the USNM (568990)
collected on 22 October 1971 at Bahig.[168]

Black-headed Bunting   *Emberiza melanocephala*
                                    Scopoli
Emberiza melanocephala Scopoli, 1769, *Annus* 1
Hist.-Nat., p. 142, Carniola.
Comments: No Egyptian specimens (excluding the
Sinai) of this species have been examined. One
recent observation of a male at Suez on 3 May
1982.[169]

Reed Bunting   *Emberiza schoeniclus* (Linnaeus)
Emberiza schoeniclus schoeniclus (Linnaeus)
Fringilla Schoeniclus Linnaeus, 1758, *Syst. Nat.,*
ed. 10, p. 182, Europe.

Emberiza schoeniclus [intermedia] Degland
Emb.[eriza] intermedia Degland, 1849, *Ornith.
Europ.,* 1, p. 264 [misprinted as p. 164], Dalmatia.
Comments: Specimen in the BMNH (1965 M.16564)
collected on 28 January 1928 at Salum may be
referable to this subspecies.[170]

NOTES TO THE CATALOGUE

1. It appears that the Ostrich has been all but totally exterminated by man throughout the Middle East, see Cramp and Simmons 1977, p. 38.
2. Meinertzhagen 1930, p. 650; Vaurie 1965, p. 1.
3. Cramp and Simmons 1977, p. 38.
4. Al-Hussaini 1959, p. 3.
5. For a summary of the distribution of the Ostrich in modern Egypt, and a description of the specimens collected at Gebel Elba in 1967, see Goodman *et al.* 1984, pp. 39-44.
6. For references, see Gardiner 1957, p. 470, Sign-list G34.
7. For a more detailed discussion of this piece, see Edwards 1976a, pp. 126-7 and his references.
8. *Ibid.*, p. 126.
9. For another example of Tutankhamun hunting juvenile Ostriches, see Davies and Gardiner 1962, pl. III.
10. For the reverse side of the fan, see Carter 1927, pl. LXII(b); Edwards 1976a, pl. 11.
11. Cramp and Simmons 1977, p. 37.
12. This irregularity is commented upon by Edwards 1979, pp. 205-6. Also see Houlihan and Goodman 1979, pp. 219-25.
13. Butzer 1959, pp. 81-2; Hayes 1965, pp. 73, 89-90.
14. See Petrie 1953, pl. A, fig. 3; Spencer 1980, pl. 63, cat. no. 575.
15. Other than the several Ostriches pictured at the sun temple of Niuserre, we are aware of only one other example of an Ostrich from the Old Kingdom. See Keimer 1957a, p. 100, fig 4 and n. 1.
16. See Edel 1963, fig. 12; Smith 1965b, fig. 178 (a).
17. See Newberry 1893b, pl. IV. But also a fragment from Dynasty XI, see Davies 1913, pl. XLI.
18. E.g., Newberry 1895, pl. VII; Wreszinski 1923, pl. 353; Davies 1922, pl. VII; Davies 1943, pl. XLIII.
19. E.g., Wreszinski 1923, pl. 53 (a); Keimer 1940, pl. III.
20. E.g., Moreau 1930, p. 71.
21. E.g., Davies and Davies 1933, pl. IX; Ricke *et al.* 1967, pls. 7 and 9.
22. Keimer 1956a, p. 7; Simpson 1959, p. 38.
23. E.g., Caminos 1954, pp. 437-8.
24. Rice 1983, pp. 19 and 90.
25. Laufer 1926, pp. 41-2; Simon 1952, p. 577.
26. Bagnold 1935, pp. 297-8.
27. Caminos 1975, p. 1186 with n. 16.
28. Lucas 1962, p. 38. Ostrich eggs have also been found in predynastic burials, see Capart 1905, pp. 39-40; Kantor 1948, pp. 46-51.
29. See Davies 1905, pl. XL.
30. See Naville 1898, pl. LXXX; Davies 1943, pl. XVII.
31. See Brack and Brack 1980, pl. 49 (a).
32. E.g., Davies 1936, pl. XVI; Davies and Davies 1940, pl. XXIV; Davies 1942, pl. V; Ricke *et al.* 1967, pls. 7 and 9.
33. Kuentz 1924, pp. 85-8.
34. Johnson and West 1949, p. 211.
35. Martin 1891, p. 101; Taylor 1891, p. 474; Sclater 1895, pp. 400-1.
36. Sonnini 1800, p. 336.
37. Darby *et al.* 1977, p. 318.
38. Etchécopar and Hüe 1967, p. 4.
39. *Ibid.*, p. 4.
40. Breasted 1906, p. 193, nos. 451-2.
41. For the complete publication of the "Botanical Garden", see Wreszinski 1935, pls. 26-33.
42. Schweinfurth 1919, p. 464.
43. Keimer 1925, p. 154. Also see the remarks of Davies 1930b, pp. 34-5; Prideaux 1978, pp. 22-5.
44. Cramp and Simmons 1977, p. 52.
45. *Ibid.*, pp. 50-2.
46. Meinertzhagen 1930, p. 487.
47. For cormorant hieroglyphs, see Smith 1946, pl. B; Bissing 1956, pl. I.

48. For the entire scene, see Duell 1938, pl. 19.
49. See Hassan 1943, p. 135, fig. 77 and pl. XXXVII.
50. E.g., Blackman 1914, pl. II; Keimer 1936, pl. I; Wreszinski 1936, pl. 41; Wild 1953, pl. CXIX; Moussa and Altenmüller 1977, pl. 4 and fig. 5.
51. For the bird in color, see Newberry 1900, pl. XI.
52. Störk 1980, pp. 741-2.
53. E.g., Davies 1958, pl. IV, no. 6; Thausing and Goedicke 1971, pl. 82; Gaillard 1933, pl. I, figs. 1-2.
54. It appears that the Darter may no longer breed in Turkey, see Cramp and Simmons 1977, pp. 223-224.
55. Heinzel *et al.* 1977, p. 32. The authors state that the Darter occurs in modern Egypt. However, in a personal communication dated 19 October 1979, Mr. Heinzel states that the record for the Darter in Egypt is an error.
56. Kumerloeve 1967, p. 255.
57. Arnold 1962, p. 103.
58. Moreau 1966, p. 76.
59. Ballmann 1980, p. 310.
60. Boessneck and von den Driesch 1982, p. 96.
61. Nicoll 1919, p. 61; Flower 1933, p. 42; Horváth 1959, p. 453.
62. These inscriptions have been studied by Edel 1961, pp. 209-55 and Edel 1963, pp. 89-217.
63. For the entire fragment on which the birds appear, see Wreszinski 1936, pl. 84; Bissing 1956, pl. XII; Edel 1963, fig. 11.
64. Edel 1961, p. 239.
65. Vandier 1969, p. 428; Störk 1982, pp. 923-4.
66. Kaiser 1967, p. 16, cat. no. 147.
67. Moussa and Altenmüller 1977, pl. 31.
68. See Bissing 1956, pl. XVIII; Edel 1963, p. 193, fig. 16.
69. For the entire scene, see Wreszinski 1923, pl. 249; Brack and Brack 1980, pls. 76 (a), 73 (b) and 89.
70. These pelicans have often been incorrectly referred to as domesticated birds. E.g., Zeuner 1963, pp. 471-2; Aldred 1972, p. 60.
71. Davies 1936, p. 83.
72. Wilkinson 1878, Vol. III, p. 328; Macpherson 1897, pp. 203-4.
73. Cott 1954, pp. 354-5.
74. Horapollo I, 54.
75. Belzoni 1820, p. 387; Wilkinson 1878, Vol. III, p. 328.
76. Jourdain and Lynes 1936, p. 45; Bulman 1944, pp. 486-7.
77. Smith 1960, p. 41; Simpson 1978, p. 3. Herons are similarly shown in a scene in the Dynasty V mastaba of Rashepses (LS 16) at Saqqara. See Boreux 1925, p. 213, fig. 58.
78. Among the many examples, see Petrie 1892, pl. XXVIII; Murray 1905, pl. XI; Naville 1908, pl. CLXIII; Wreszinski 1923, pl. 146; Wreszinski 1936, pl. 73 (a); Vigneau 1935, pl. 24; Hayes 1953, p. 97, fig. 55.
79. Macpherson 1897, pp. 213-4.
80. Markham 1621, p. 15.
81. Chapman 1930, pp. 72-3.
82. E.g., Newberry 1900, pl. VIII; Davies 1936, pl. XIX; Moussa and Altenmüller 1971, pl. 5.
83. E.g., Davies 1922, pls. IX-X; Wild 1953, pl. CXIX; Berlandini 1982, p. 87, fig. 1 and pl. VII.
84. On the subject of the phoenix, see van den Broek 1972; Kákosy 1982, pp. 1030-9.
85. E.g., Davis 1908b, pl. VII; Piankoff 1957, pls. 3 and 10; Faulkner 1972; Vandersleyen 1975, pl. 341.
86. E.g., Vandier 1954, pls. IV and XXXI; Bruyère 1959, pl. XXV; Thausing and Goedicke 1971, pls. 22 and 133.
87. For the birds in color, see Forman and Kischkewitz 1972, pl. 28.
88. Boussac 1905b, pp. 41-4; Carter 1927, p. 121; Posener 1959, p. 217.
89. Gardiner 1957, p. 470, Sign-list G33. Here a hieroglyph is identified as a Cattle Egret(?). This sign is indeed very egretlike, and we would lean toward such an identification.

176

But, Gardiner is correct in questioning it, as positive identification does not seem possible.

90. For the entire scene, see Davies and Gardiner 1915, frontispiece; Davies 1936, pl. XIX.
91. E.g., Gauthier 1908, pl. XI; Duell 1938, pls. 10-11; Werbrouck 1938, p. 139, fig. 12 and p. 141, fig. 14; Moussa and Altenmüller 1977, pls. 4-5 and figs. 5-6.
92. Wild 1953, pl. CXIX.
93. E.g., Wreszinski 1923, pls. 24, 121 (a) and 214.
94. See Wreszinski 1923, pl. 184; Vandier 1969, pl. XXII, fig. 169, 3.
95. Davis 1968, pp. 91-3.
96. Macpherson 1897, p. 214.
97. Chapman 1930, pp. 72-3.
98. A good example of this indifference is the large Cattle Egret heronry located in the trees adjacent to the Giza Zoological Gardens and a busy street (Shari el-Giza) in Giza.
99. Kadry 1942, pp. 20-6. For a nice illustration of Cattle Egrets feeding in this manner, see Kees 1961, pl. 5 (a).
100. E.g., Hasselquist 1766, p. 198. Also see the remarks of Keimer 1955, p. 17.
101. We have already noted a somewhat similar irregularity as this on the Ostrich, see under bird No. 1.
102. There is some evidence to suggest that originally there may have been more than twenty-nine birds.
103. For the individual members of the collection, see Rosellini 1834, pls. IX-X and XIV (includes most); Wilkinson 1878, Vol. II, pp. 112-13, nos. 368-9 (includes most); Davies 1949, pls. II-III.
104. To see the scene in its context on the wall, see Newberry 1893b, pl. IV.
105. Aldred 1980, p. 122; Wilson-Yang and Burns 1982, pp. 115-17.
106. See Wreszinski 1923, pl. 67 (a); Wreszinski 1936, pl. 83 (b).
107. See Bissing 1905, pl. IX.
108. For the entire block, see Firth 1929, pl. II; Smith 1965a, pl. 47.
109. E.g., Bissing 1905, pl. IX; Wreszinski 1936, pl. 73 (a).
110. Wild 1953, pl. CXXII.
111. E.g., Macramallah 1935, frontispiece and pl. VII; Junker 1940, fig. 8; Blackman and Apted 1953b, pls. XIII and XXVII no. 1; Wild 1953, pls. LXXXII (a) and CXIX.
112. E.g., Duell 1938, pls. 10 and 11; Wild 1953, pl. CXIX.
113. See Blackman and Apted 1953b, pl. XIII.
114. Bitterns have been reported as pets elsewhere, see Macpherson 1897, p. 214.
115. For the bird in color, see Rosellini 1834, pl. X, fig, 12; Newberry 1900, pl. XIII, fig. 2 (the coloring of the figure is less accurate here than in Rosellini).
116. Davies 1949, p. 16, no. 7 states that Black Storks are rarely found in Egyptian paintings. This could be taken to infer that there is more than one extant example. If so, we are completely unaware of their location.
117. For a Black Stork shown in this posture, see Etchécopar and Hüe 1967, p. 61; Cramp and Simmons 1977, p. 327, fig. (b).
118. Davies 1949, p. 16, no. 7. The early copyists apparently also viewed the bird with the same unpainted area on the shoulder.
119. Throughout much of the Egyptological literature, the Saddlebill Stork is referred to by an archaic vernacular name "Jabiru". However, due to an attempt to standardize English vernacular bird names, the name Jabiru is now generally attributed to a South American stork, *Jabiru mycteria*. The Jabiru identified and referred to by so many past authors is actually the Saddlebill Stork.
120. Lucas 1962, pp. 32-3.
121. For the reverse side of the knife handle, see Bénédite 1918, pls. I and II; Vandier 1952, p. 541, fig. 362.
122. Keimer 1947, pp. 26-31.
123. Bénédite 1918, p. 1.
124. Bannerman 1930, p. 105; Jackson 1938, p. 76.
125. Vandier 1952, pp. 542-4; Edwards 1955, p. 1061.
126. Lortet and Gaillard 1909, pp. 254-258; Bothmer and Keith 1974, pp. 18-19.
127. Firth 1927, p. 205, fig. 8 and pl. XVIII.
128. See Quibell and Green 1902, pl. LIX, no. 4; Burgess and Arkell 1958, pl. IX, no. 4.
129. E.g., Murray 1905, pl. XXXVII, no. 21; Borchardt 1928, pl. I(a); Lacau and Chevrier 1969, pl. IX.
130. For the birds in color, see Smith 1946, pl. A.
131. E.g., Griffith 1896, pl. II, figs. 3 and 10; Murray 1937, pl. VI, nos. 34 and 35.
132. Some very stylized examples of the sign have recently been mistaken for the Wattled Ibis (*Bostrychia carunculata*), see Kumerloeve 1983, pp. 218-21.
133. E.g., Terrace 1967, pl. XXXII.
134. Keimer 1930a, pp. 17-18; Keimer 1954b, p. 134.
135. Bannerman 1930, p. 105; Jackson 1938, p. 76.
136. Butzer 1959, pp. 67-74; Butzer 1976, pp. 26-7; Butzer 1980, pp. 455-7.
137. *Ibid.*
138. Snow 1978, p. 28.
139. Rosen 1961, pp. 174-8. Here the author publishes a fragment of a marsh scene, now in the Museo Gregoriano Egizio, Vatican, which he believes is of Dynasty V date. He states that a bird depicted on the piece is a Whale-headed Stork. However, this fragment is not from the Old Kingdom, but from the Dynasty XXV-XXVI tomb of Montuemhet (No. 34) at Thebes. Through the courtesy of the Vatican Museum, a detailed photograph of the bird in question was made available to us. It revealed that the bird is not a Whale-headed Stork, but a cormorant. The fragment can also be viewed in Wreszinski 1936, p. 82, fig. 41, 5; Botti and Romanelli 1951, pl. LIII, cat. no. 111.
140. For the entire scene, see Wild 1953, pl. CXIX.
141. Those who have identified the bird as a Whale-headed Stork, or at least have accepted the identification are many. See, e.g., Boussac 1910b, pp. 309 and 312; Boussac 1912, pp. 163-5; Koenig 1926, pp. 323-5; Keimer 1927, p. 227, n. 1; Moreau 1930, pp. 65-6; Wreszinski 1936, p. 234; Moreau 1966, p. 69; Schüz 1966, p. 264; Bodenheimer 1972, p. 3; Rich 1974, p. 184; Störk 1977a, p. 131.
142. Etchécopar and Hüe 1967, p. 67; Heinzel *et al.* 1977, p. 40. It is stated in both works that the Glossy Ibis breeds in the Nile Delta. However, this cannot be supported by any published records or museum specimens that we are aware of. Thus, the bird should be considered a migrant in Egypt until such time that breeding can be substantiated.
143. For the stela, see Firth and Gunn 1926, pl. 5 (d).
144. Firth and Gunn 1926, p. 109, n. 4; Keimer 1930a, pp. 20-3.
145. *Ibid.*
146. Keimer 1930a, p. 23 and n. 4. Keimer identifies a Glossy Ibis depicted on a fragment from the Dynasty V sun temple of Niuserre. The bird may in fact have been intended to represent a Glossy Ibis, based on its hieroglyphic caption, but there is absolutely nothing about its form and color that could lead to a more precise identification of it other than "ibis".
147. See Junker 1940, pl. XI.
148. E.g., Capart 1907, pl. XXXVIII; Wreszinski 1923, pl. 146.
149. See Firth and Gunn 1926, pls. 23, 25 and 26; Mogensen 1930, pl. LXV (A 514).
150. Caminos 1954, p. 127.
151. Herodotus II, 76.
152. Keimer 1930a, p. 23, n. 6; Zivie 1980, p. 116. Some still maintain that it was the Hermit Ibis (*Geronticus eremita*), see Lloyd 1976, p. 328-9.
153. Meinertzhagen 1930, p. 438. Meinertzhagen's records for the Sacred Ibis in Egypt at the very beginning of the nineteenth century are based upon Savigny 1805.
154. Gurney 1876, p. 298 (see Sacred Ibis in the Checklist).
155. For Sacred Ibis hieroglyphs, see Griffith 1898, pl. IX, fig. 168; Mekhitarian 1954, p. 21; Davies 1958, pl. III, no. 4.
156. For the entire scene, see Newberry 1893a, pl. XXXIV.
157. See Newberry 1900, pl. IX.
158. For example in the Dynasty IV mastaba of Meresankh III (G 7530-7540) at Giza.
159. Cramp and Simmons 1977, p. 348.
160. E.g., Davies 1930a, pl. LI(a); Junker 1940, pl. XI; Smith 1965a, pl. 47.
161. E.g., Blackman 1914, pl. II; Davies 1920, pl. IV; Duell 1938, pl. 19.
162. Boylan 1922; Bleeker 1973.
163. E.g., Vandier 1950, pl. IV; Clark 1955, p. 182; Roemer-und Pelizaeus-Museum 1979, cat. no. 185.

164. See Roeder 1956, pls. 57-8.
165. E.g., Petrie 1914, pl. XLII, fig. 247; Mogensen 1930, pl. LV (A 412); David 1980, p. 31, no. 46.
166. Herodotus II, 65.
167. Smith 1974, p. 25; Zivie 1980, p. 118; Martin 1981, p. 8.
168. For references, see Zivie 1980, p. 118.
169. The major works dealing with ibis mummies and their identification are Lortet and Gaillard 1903, pp. 117-23 and pp. 171-7; Gaillard and Daressy 1905.
170. Preliminary reports on the Society's excavations at Saqqara are published annually in *JEA*, beginning with 1965. Also see Smith 1974, pp. 21-63 and Martin 1981.
171. Smith 1974, p. 27.
172. Sclater 1878, pp. 449-51; Risdon 1971, p. 131.
173. See under bird No. 40 with note 448.
174. See Wreszinski 1923, pl. 395; Klebs 1934, p. 70, fig. 51; Vandier 1969, pp. 437-8.
175. Etchécopar and Hüe 1967, p. 65.
176. For a review of the breeding and wintering ranges as well as the migratory routes of this bird, see Smith 1970, pp. 18-24.
177. Moreau 1930, p. 67.
178. For Hermit Ibis hieroglyphs, see Griffith 1896, pl. II, fig. 4; Petrie 1927, pl. XIII, nos. 307-12; Smith 1946, pl. B; Davies 1958, pl. IV, no. 10.
179. Schäfer 1974, pp. 255-8.
180. For the bird in color, see Holwerda *et al.* 1908, pl. XV.
181. Petrie 1953, pl. B, figs. 6-7; Asselberghs 1961, pl. LI, figs. 84-5.
182. Cramp and Simmons 1977, pp. 343-4.
183. See Wreszinski 1936, pl. 41; Keimer 1954a, p. 240, fig. 34.
184. Dunham 1946, pp. 23-9; Abu-Bakr 1953, p. 84, fig. 69; Kerrn 1959, pp. 168-71.
185. Kumerloeve 1977, pp. 319-49.
186. Balsac and Mayaud 1962, pp. 72-4.
187. Safriel 1980, pp. 82-8.
188. Cramp and Simmons 1977, p. 344.
189. *Ibid.*, p. 344.
190. Goodman and Storer 1985.
191. For references, see Gardiner 1957, p. 474, Sign-list H3.
192. Moreau 1930, pp. 65-6, does not agree with the identification of this figure as a European Spoonbill, but suggests that it is an egret. We believe that the bird is indeed a spoonbill, as many writers have also stated. See, e.g., Newberry 1900, p. 3; Loret 1901, pp. 230-1; Boussac 1910a, pp. 50-2.
193. For the entire scene, see Newberry 1893a, pl. XXXIV.
194. For the bird in color, see Newberry 1900, pl. X.
195. E.g., Mackay *et al.* 1929, pl. XXVI; Varille 1938, p. 12, fig. 4; Moussa and Altenmüller 1977, pls. 4-5 and figs. 5-6; Simpson 1980, pl. XLIV and fig. 30.
196. E.g., Murray 1905, pl. XI; Capart 1907, pl. LXXXV; Wreszinski 1923, pl. 214; Simpson 1980, pl. III(d) and fig. 4.
197. See Scott 1940, pp. 163-4; Hayes 1959, p. 215, fig. 127.
198. See Werbrouck 1934a, pl. 33 (here the block is attributed to Dynasty XVIII, but it is now thought to date from about 500 B.C.). Also see a fantastic creature with the head of a spoonbill, in Sauneron 1969, pl. VI(a) and fig. 3.
199. Meinertzhagen 1930, p. 453. Meinertzhagen states that he examined Greater Flamingo eggs taken from Lake Menzaleh in 1894.
200. Whymper 1909, p. 166.
201. For other Greater Flamingo hieroglyphs, see Smith 1946, pl. B; Davies 1958, pl. IV, no. 4; Fischer 1979, p. 27.
202. For the entire fragment, see Smith 1946, pl. 34(b).
203. For the bird in color, see Petrie 1892, frontispiece, no. 6; Moreau 1930, pl. IV, fig. 3.
204. Forbes 1909-1910, p. 38; Dechambre 1951, pp. 105-6; Vandier 1952, pp. 342-3.
205. For some other good examples of the birds on these pots, see Petrie 1921, pls. XXXIV-XXXV; Hayes 1953, p. 23, fig. 14; British Museum 1975, p. 194, fig. 72; Bourriau 1981, p. 26, cat. no. 30 and p. 40, cat. no. 58.
206. For example, Wreszinski 1936, p. 246; Lauer 1976, p. 57.
207. For the entire papyrus, see Faulkner 1972; Dondelinger 1979; Rossiter 1979.
208. Bleeker 1958, pp. 1-17; Griffiths 1966, pp. 28-9; Otto 1968, p. 29.
209. See Werbrouck 1938, p. 141, fig. 14, no. 7.

210. Cramp and Simmons 1980, p. 31. Also see the remarks of Adams 1870, pp. 21-2.
211. Gurney 1876, p. 140; Brooksbank 1925, p. 22.
212. Caminos 1954, p. 384.
213. For other Egyptian Vulture hieroglyphs, see Griffith 1896, pl. II, fig. 13; Griffith 1898, pl. I, fig. 4; Capart 1931, pl. 35; Davies 1958, pl. IV, no. 1.
214. For the restoration of the scene in which this fragment occurred, see Smith 1937, pl. IV; Smith 1946, p. 154, fig. 61.
215. For the bird in color, see Anonymous 1944, p. 34; Smith 1946, pl. B.
216. E.g., Murray 1905, pls. I and II.
217. Cramp and Simmons 1980, pp. 65-7.
218. There are many descriptions, but none as graphic as Hasselquist 1766, pp. 194-6.
219. Wreszinski 1923, pl. 343.
220. It should be noted here, that Brunner-Traut 1977b, p. 514, states that the Egyptian Vulture figured in the mythology of the goddesses Nekhbet and Mut. However, our findings do not bear this out. We agree with Wilkinson 1878, Vol. 3, p. 313: "The vulture Percnopterus was probably regarded with great indulgence by the Egyptians; but though frequently represented in the sculptures, there is no evidence of it having been worshipped, or even considered the peculiar emblem of any deity."
221. Meinertzhagen 1930, pp. 424-5; Etchécopar and Hüe 1967, p. 112. It should be noted that this distribution is based on old information and there is no recent evidence of this species breeding in Egypt.
222. Keimer 1927, p. 228, n. 5; Moreau 1930, pl. II.
223. Capart 1940, pp. 30-7.
224. For the entire scene, see Naville 1897, pl. XXXVI.
225. For the bird in color, see Naville 1897, pl. XXXVIII; Wilkinson 1983, p. 6.
226. Petrie 1953, pl. E; Spencer 1980, pl. 64, cat. no. 576.
227. E.g., Keimer 1927, pp. 226-31; Gardiner 1957, p. 469, Sign-list G14.
228. See Terrace 1967, pl. XXXVIII (note white speckled upper parts). Also Davies 1900, p. 19, figs. 116-17 ("the body spotted").
229. For some examples of the hieroglyph, see Duell 1938, pl. 215(b); Smith 1946, pls. 37 and B; Hornung 1971, pl. 13(b); Brack and Brack 1977, pl. 4(b).
230. E.g., Davis 1908a, 4th pl.; University of Chicago, Oriental Institute 1940, pls. 207-8, 220 and 222; Piankoff 1954, pls. 145, 160, 172 and 177; Calverley 1958, pls. 1, 17, and 35; Thausing and Goedicke 1971, pls. 31 and 135.
231. Carter 1927, pp. 111 and 124; Schüz and König 1983, p. 463.
232. For the front side of the pectoral, and a more detailed discussion of the subject, see Aldred 1971, pl. 103; Edwards 1976a, pl. 14 and p. 133.
233. For an illustration of an actual Lappet-faced Vulture displaying this same type of posture, see Heinzel *et al.* 1977, p. 83; Cramp and Simmons 1980, p. 86, fig. (c).
234. See Murray 1905, pl. XXXVII, no. 18. In referring to this hieroglyph from the mastaba of Ptahhotep I (D 62) on p. 41, Murray remarks that this is a large vulture with a a naked neck and throat, and "the repulsive appearance of the folds of skin on the neck is well shown in an otherwise greatly conventionalized representation." This can only be the Lappet-faced Vulture. For examples of the 𓅐 hieroglyph from Dynasty XII which also show a strong influence from the Lappet-faced Vulture, see Lacau and Chevrier 1969, pl. VII. During the New Kingdom, the species likewise influenced the sign 𓅐 , see Guilmant 1907, pl. LXVI; Vandier 1954, pl. VI.
235. See Chevrier 1930, pl. III; Lacau and Chevrier 1969, pl. XXXI.
236. Carter 1927, pl. LXXVI(a); Capart 1940, p. 32, fig. 3; Montet 1942, pl. XVIII; Winlock 1948, pl. 25; Aldred 1971, pls. 72, 92, and 111; Edwards 1976a, pls. 12 and 13.
237. For references, see under bird No. 21, with n. 230.
238. Grossman and Hamlet 1964, p. 333.
239. Meinertzhagen 1930, pp. 395-6. It should be noted that this distribution is based on old information and there is no recent evidence of this species breeding in Egypt.
240. For other Long-legged Buzzard hieroglyphs, see Davies

1900, pl. VII, fig. 88; Anonymous 1944, p. 34; Davies 1958, pl. IV, no. 3; Brack and Brack 1977, pl. 31.

241. For the bird in color, see Griffith 1898, pl. I, fig. 1.
242. This is based upon the coloring of the sign in the mastaba of Nefermaat and Atet at Meidum, see Smith 1946, p. 376, G4.
243. Gardiner 1957, p. 467, Sign-list G4; Fischer 1979, p. 26.
244. Heuglin 1869, p. 43. The author states that the Lesser Kestrel breeds near Alexandria. However, we know of no evidence to support such a claim.
245. The Egyptian breeding population is augmented by northern migrants during the winter months.
246. For the entire scene, see Bruyère 1959, pl. XXXII.
247. Meinertzhagen 1930, p. 381.
248. Gaillard and Daressy 1905, p. 54; Hanzák 1977, p. 87.
249. E.g., Bruyère 1928, p. 83, fig. 56; Vandier 1935, pls. XX-XXI; Hornung 1982, p. 115; Saleh 1984, p. 15, figs. 11-12.
250. E.g., Rossiter 1979, pp. 86-7.
251. See Davies 1936, pl. XCIII; Thausing and Goedicke 1971, pls. 19, 22, and 133.
252. Walter 1979, pp. 272-7 and pp. 285-9; Cramp and Simmons 1980, p. 328.
253. The subspecies of the Peregrine Falcon that breeds in Egypt (*F. p. pelegrinoides*) has a pale reddish plumage. During the nonbreeding season, the Egyptian population is augmented by the migration of two extralimital subspecies of Peregrine Falcons (*F. p. peregrinus* and *F. p. calidus*). The migrant adult birds have a dark blue back and a white underside, which is more like the coloring of the "Horus Falcon" than the Egyptian subspecies.
254. For other "Horus Falcon" hieroglyphs, see Petrie 1927, pl. XII; Davies 1958, pl. III, no. 2; Terrace 1967, pl. XL; Hornung 1971, pl. 11 (b).
255. For the bird in color, see Loret 1903, pl. I.
256. In general, see Mercer 1942.
257. Černý 1952, p. 23; Edwards 1976a, p. 138.
258. Altenmüller 1977, p. 94.
259. E.g., Griffith 1898, p. 20.
260. Gaillard and Daressy 1905, pp. 47-50, review a few of these identifications.
261. E.g., Loret 1903, pp. 1-24; Bénédite 1909, pp. 5-28.
262. This view was apparently also held by Ludwig Keimer, see Gardiner 1957, p. 467, Sign-list G5.
263. See Smith 1946, p. 114, fig. 30; Petrie 1953, pls. A, fig. 3, E, and G, fig. 17.
264. See Smith 1946, pl. 29 (b); Petrie 1953, pl. J.
265. E.g., Davies 1927, pl. XIV; Lhote and Hassia 1954, pl. III.
266. E.g., Aldred 1971, pls. 7, 11, 33, 37-8, 65, 73-4, 104; Fazzini 1975, p. 126, cat. no. 112.
267. E.g., Reisner 1907, pl. XX, nos. 12516, 12525-7; Petrie 1914, pl. XLI, fig. 245.
268. E.g., Steindorff 1946, pls. XCIX-CI; Roeder 1956, pl. 56 (e and f); Fazzini 1975, p. 116, cat. no. 99.
269. Herodotus II, 65.
270. For references, see Altenmüller 1977, p. 95.
271. Gaillard and Daressy 1905, pls. XLIII-XLV and LX-LXIII; Diener 1973, pp. 60-5; Smith 1974, p. 45.
272. See under bird No. 40, with n. 448.
273. The major works dealing with falcon mummies and their identification are: Lortet and Gaillard 1903, pp. 146-58; Gaillard and Daressy 1905.
274. See Capart 1930, p. 222; Keimer 1950, p. 52.
275. In many cases it is not possible to determine whether the breeding birds at certain localities are native or from feral domestic stock.
276. Flower 1933, p. 41; Bodenham 1945, p. 19.
277. Boessneck 1953, p. 35; Vandier d'Abbadie 1973, pp. 35-49. Both of these authors state that Mute Swans occur elsewhere in Egyptian art. However, their identifications do not stand up to close scrutiny.
278. de Morgan 1903, p. 74.
279. Vandier d'Abbadie 1973, p. 38, n. 3, gives the dimensions of this sculpture as 42.5 cm in height and 53 cm in length.
280. *Ibid.*, p. 38.
281. E.g., Davis 1912, p. 105; de Rachewiltz 1960, pl. 86.
282. de Morgan 1903, pp. 65-76.
283. Jéquier 1918, p. 163; Jéquier 1921, p. 331; van de Walle 1984, p. 756.
284. Schrader 1892, p. 52; El Negumi 1949, pp. 20-1; Cramp and Simmons 1977, p. 386.
285. For the entire scene, see Quibell *et al.* 1898, pl. XXXI; Wreszinski 1936, pl. 17.
286. Vandier d'Abbadie 1973, p. 37, suggests that the bird depicted in the tomb of Ptahhotep II should be identified as a Mute Swan, because it is shown with a curved neck. This is a very poor characteristic on which alone to base identification.
287. Boessneck 1953, pl. 16, fig. 34; Vandier d'Abbadie 1973, p. 43, fig. 7. Both authors publish a scene from the Dynasty XVIII tomb of Amenemhab (No. 85) at Thebes, and each describes it as illustrating the trapping of swans in a marsh. This scene, as Vandier d'Abbadie notes, was never completed and the birds lack such details as heads. We believe that if the scene had been finished, the birds would have represented ducks, not swans. Indeed, when the entire scene is viewed, see Wreszinski 1923, pl. 24, a man who is walking away from the net is carrying four of the birds which have been painted with details, and they are ducks. Had the scene been completed, a trapping scene in the Dynasty XVIII tomb of Wah (No. 22) at Thebes, see Wreszinski 1923, pl. 121 (a), may have been a near parallel to it.
288. Delacour 1954, pp. 74-5, 87.
289. Simon 1952, p. 602; Fitzgibbon 1976, p. 463.
290. E.g., Quibell *et al.* 1898, p. 30; Wreszinski 1936, p. 27, n. 5; Moreau 1930, p. 64.
291. See Engelbach 1915, pl. XXIII; Jéquier 1921, p. 331.
292. See Carter and Newberry 1904, p. 15, no. 46068.
293. See Carter 1927, pl. LII (a).
294. Abitz 1979, p. 93, with n. 96 (from Carter's unpublished notes).
295. E.g., Daressy 1902, p. 283, no. 24914; Davis 1912, p. 105, no. 25; Jéquier 1921, p. 331; Hermann 1932, p. 91, n. 3; Keimer 1957b, p. 150; Vandier d'Abbadie 1973, pp. 41-2.
296. Bonnet 1952, pp. 689-90; Abitz 1979, pp. 92-3.
297. Balsac and Mayaud 1962, p. 81. Here a record of the Greylag Goose breeding at Lake Fezara, Algeria is reported. This is the only record that we are aware of for this species breeding in North Africa, and it should be regarded as quite exceptional.
298. El Negumi *et al.* 1950, p. 225. Their identification was made certain as they were able to collect one individual out of the six they observed. It should also be noted that domestic Greylag Geese are common as poutlry stock throughout most of Egypt.
299. Boessneck 1953, pp. 33-4; Boessneck 1960, pp. 192-206; Boessneck 1962, pp. 356-7. Boessneck, at great length, identifies the Greylag Goose occurring in a number of places in Egyptian art. We entirely disagree with his findings. Not one of the birds he refers to displays features that could lead to a specific identification of it as a Greylag Goose. He further speculates that a few geese which are shown white (or left uncolored) are the domestic descendants of the Greylag Goose, because the modern domestic forms of this species are white. This slender evidence cannot be used to identify the bird, as the derived domestic stock of other *Anser* geese could also be white. This view has been uncritically accepted in the literature. E.g., Zeuner 1963, pp. 468-9; Störk 1977c, p. 374. Amusing is the identification of a Greylag Goose in Boussac 1904, p. 209, fig. 1. It is, in fact, an Ostrich from the Dynasty XI tomb of Baket III (No. 15) at Beni Hasan.
300. Frankfort 1929, pp. 58-71.
301. For the scene, see Frankfort 1929, pl. X.
302. See Frankfort 1929, pl. XI.
303. Delacour 1954, pp. 94-5.
304. Boessneck and von den Driesch 1982, pp. 121, 124-5.
305. Lortet and Gaillard 1908, pp. 147-8.
306. E.g., Newberry 1895, pl. XXII; Bissing 1905, pls. X and XII; Capart 1907, pls. LXXXV, LXXXVII-LXXXVIII; Duell 1938, pl. 52.
307. E.g., Newberry 1893b, pl. XIV; Davies and Davies 1933, pls. XIII and XV; Junker 1943, fig. 16; Badawy 1976, fig. 20 and pls. 20-1.
308. E.g., Macramallah 1935, pl. XXVII; Duell 1938, pls. 57-8, 60 (a) and 65; Smith 1946, frontispiece; Wild 1966, pls. CXLVIII (b), CLXI-CLXII and CLXXIX.

179

309. Vandier 1969, pp. 400-1.
310. For the entire fragment in color, see Davies 1936, pl. I; Vandersleyen 1975, pl. XVIII; National Geographic Society 1978, pp. 40-1; Wilkinson 1983, pp. 8-9.
311. For the restoration of the scene in which the fragment occurred, see Smith 1937, pl. IV; Smith 1946, p. 154, fig. 61.
312. For the birds in color, see n. 310.
313. Moreau 1930, p. 63; Riddell 1943, p. 152.
314. For the entire scene, see Junker 1940, pl. VII.
315. For the scene in which the goose appears, see Newberry 1893a, pl. XXX (third register from bottom, left).
316. Delacour 1954, pp. 105-6.
317. Boessneck and von den Driesch 1982, pp. 121, 124-5.
318. Gaillard and Daressy 1905, pp. 63, 115-6; Lortet and Gaillard 1908, p. 149.
319. Winlock 1941, p. 17.
320. Gardiner 1957, p. 471, Sign-list G38.
321. For some examples of the sign, see Griffith 1896, pl. II, fig. 6; Davies 1936, pl. VI; Smith 1946, pl. B.
322. Meinertzhagen 1930, p. 460.
323. For the other Bean Goose on the fragment, see references in n. 310.
324. Gaillard 1907, pp. 214-15, believes that the goose we show here is a Bean Goose, but that the bird on the other end of the panel is a Greylag Goose, not a Bean Goose, while Lortet and Gaillard 1907, pp. 95-7, think that both geese are Greylag Geese, an opinion shared by Boessneck 1960, p. 199. Both geese, however, are surely Bean Geese, as a number of ornithologists have also pointed out over the years. E.g., Barrett-Hamilton 1897, p. 486; Whymper 1909, p. 176; Moreau 1930, p. 63; Schüz 1966, p. 264. It is also the opinion of Davies 1936, p. 5 and Goelet 1983, p. 45, n. 11.
325. For the Bean Goose in color, see n. 310.
326. Instructive is the group of *Anser* geese in Moussa and Altenmüller 1971, pl. 24, which by their hieroglyphic names consist of two kinds, and are clearly not white-fronted geese. But it is not possible to identify them beyond that.
327. Winlock 1941, p. 17.
328. Meinertzhagen 1930, p. 461.
329. Schrader 1892, p. 52.
330. For the geese in color, see n. 310.
331. Already noted by Goelet 1983, pp. 45-6.
332. Winlock 1941, p. 17.
333. For some interesting remarks on the changes in the migration pattern of the Red-breasted Goose as evinced from art, see Sterbetz 1978, pp. 73-8.
334. Hudson 1975, p. 36; Cramp and Simmons 1977, p. 443.
335. Although the vernacular name of the species implies that it is a goose, this is a misnomer, as the bird is not a true goose (*Anser* and *Branta*), but rather is a member of the sheld-geese and shelducks group (often referred to as the tribe Tadornini).
336. Cramp and Simmons 1977, pp. 447-8. Egyptian Geese were introduced into this area sometime in the eighteenth century, and they continue to thrive in some parts. Populations introduced at the same time in central Europe are now extinct.
337. The species was formerly a breeding resident in Syria and Israel, see Cramp and Simmons 1977, p. 447.
338. Meininger *et al.* 1979, p. 12.
339. Horváth 1959, p. 456; Meininger *et al.* 1979, p. 12.
340. Wilkinson 1878, Vol. II, p. 105; Kuentz 1926, p. 44; Vandier 1971, p. 28.
341. Derchain 1975, p. 63; Baines and Málek 1980, p. 206.
342. E.g., Wreszinski 1923, pl. 77(a); Davies 1936, pl. XLVII (but here the bird has been expunged); Müller 1940, pl. V(a); Säve-Söderbergh 1957, pl. XIV; Seele 1959, pl. 4.
343. E.g., Wilkinson 1983, p. 150.
344. For the bird in color, see Davies 1936, pls. LXV-LXVI; Vandersleyen 1975, pl. XXXIII; Baines and Málek 1980, pp. 206-7.
345. Delacour 1954, pp. 237-8.
346. Etchécopar and Hüe 1967, p. 82; Cramp and Simmons 1977, p. 449.
347. Caminos 1954, pp. 381-2.
348. E.g., Macramallah 1935, frontispiece and pls. VI-VII; Duell 1938, pl. 19; Wild 1953, pl. CXIX.
349. Kuentz 1926, pp. 3-7.
350. *Ibid.*, pp. 39-41. The Egyptian Goose has been known to be kept in modern Egypt as well. See Russell 1835, p. 341; Kuentz 1926, p. 29.
351. Kuentz 1926, p. 42.
352. *Ibid.*, pp. 48-50; Vandier 1971, pp. 5-41.
353. E.g., Davies 1941, p. 15, n. 1; Davies 1943, p. 31, n. 72; Vandier 1971, pp. 27-8.
354. E.g., Kuentz 1926, p. 8, fig. 6; p. 9, figs. 8-9; p. 11, fig. 10.
355. E.g., *ibid.*, p. 13, fig. 11 and pl. I, fig. 1.
356. E.g., *ibid.*, p. 16, fig. 14; p. 18, fig. 15; p. 20, fig. 16; p. 21, fig. 17; p. 32, fig. 19.
357. Kayser 1958, p. 193.
358. See n. 347.
359. Kuentz 1926, p. 42, and see p. 51, fig. 27.
360. Simon 1952, p. 567; Delacour 1954, p. 237.
361. Delacour 1954, pp. 237-8.
362. This is also basically the view of Boessneck 1960, pp. 201-3.
363. Lortet and Gaillard 1908, pp. 154-8; Kuentz 1926, pp. 1-2, and 53. The actual deposit consisted of "8 geese" and "some dishes filled with goose-eggs", but only five of the birds were identified; probably all eight were Egyptian Geese. See Weigall 1906, pp. 125-6.
364. Etchécopar and Hüe 1967, p. 86. Here a possible breeding record for this species is mentioned from the Eastern Desert south of Suez. We are not aware of the basis for this record, and until further evidence is available, the Ruddy Shelduck should be considered only a migrant to Egypt.
365. Other writers have wished to see this species occurring elsewhere in Egyptian art. Their identifications, however, do not stand up to close scrutiny. E.g., Newberry 1900, p. 4, pl. XII; Wrezsinski 1936, p. 27, n. 6; Boessneck 1953, p. 35.
366. Some examples of Ruddy Shelducks from the mastaba of Mehu can be seen in color in Lange and Hirmer 1968, pl. VIII.
367. Simon 1952, p. 557.
368. Shelley 1872, p. 282.
369. For the entire scene, see Newberry 1895, pls. XX-XXI.
370. The basic workings of the clap-net are given by Dunham 1937, pp. 50-4.
371. Morris 1895, p. 71; Simon 1952, p. 557.
372. Gurney 1876, p. 224; Meininger *et al.* 1979, p. 28.
373. For the entire scene, see Davies 1930a, pls. XXVI-XXXII.
374. For the birds in color, see Davies 1930a, pl. XXXI.
375. Several writers have identified Green-winged Teal as occurring in Old Kingdom art, e.g., Wreszinski 1936, p. 172; Moussa and Altenmüller 1977, p. 161. However, none of these birds, nor any others from the Old Kingdom with which we are familiar, display the necessary detail for the identification of them as Green-winged Teal.
376. For this scene in color, see Yoyotte 1968, p. 60; Scott 1973, fig. 45; Vandersleyen 1975, pl. XXVIII.
377. See Rosellini 1834, pl. XIII.
378. Simon 1952, p. 603; Fitzgibbon 1976, p. 472.
379. Lortet and Gaillard 1908, pp. 152-4; Churcher 1972, p. 35.
380. Boessneck and von den Driesch 1982, pp. 121 and 125.
381. Winlock 1941, p. 17.
382. Brooksbank 1925, p. 42; Meininger *et al.* 1979, p. 28.
383. This distribution is based upon Meinertzhagen 1930, p. 470.
384. For the bird in color, see Griffith 1896, pl. II, fig. 11; Anonymous 1944, p. 32.
385. For other wigeon hieroglyphs, see Newberry 1893a, pl. XXVII; Michalowski 1968, fig. 87.
386. The duck identified as a European Wigeon in Wreszinski 1936, p. 174, can only be called one on the evidence of its accompanying hieroglyphic name. See too Gardiner 1957, p. 472, Sign-list G42, n. 1.
387. Simon 1952, pp. 611-12; Fitzgibbon 1976, p. 513.
388. Hasselquist 1766, p. 209; Shelley 1872, p. 288; Gurney 1876, pp. 93-4 and 227-8; Meininger *et al.* 1979, p. 28.
389. For a more detailed discussion of this piece, see Cooney 1965, pp. 17-18; Aldred 1973, p. 187.
390. Cooney 1965, p. 17.
391. See Smith 1965a, pl. 14; Vandersleyen 1975, pl. 239.
392. E.g., Newberry 1895, pl. XXII; Bissing 1905, pl. IX; Éperon *et al.* 1939, pl. VII.

393. Delacour 1956, pp. 131-2.
394. E.g., Murray 1905, pl. XI; Capart 1907, pls. XXXVIII-XXXIX; Naville 1908, pl. CLXIII; Wreszinski 1923, pl. 184; Wild 1953, pl. CXXII.
395. E.g., Blackman 1914, pl. II; Wreszinski 1923, pls. 117 and 183; Davies 1936, pl. LIV; Smith 1965a, pl. 141 (b); Brack and Brack 1980, pls. 1, 22, and 67.
396. E.g., Newberry 1893a, pl. X; Davies 1901, pls. XVI-XVII and XXV-XXVII; Capart 1907, pls. XLV, XLVII, LII, LX-LXI; Williams 1932, pls. IX-X; Wild 1953, pls. LXXXVIII (b) and CXXI; Wild 1966, pls. CXLVIII, CLXII, CLXXIX-CLXXXI.
397. E.g., Davies 1901, pls. XXIV and XXXIV; Duell 1938, pls. 63-4; Wild 1966, pl. CLXI.
398. E.g., Mogensen 1921, p. 22, fig. 17 and pl. VII; Junker 1943, fig. 16 and pl. XI; Moussa and Altenmüller 1977, pls. 82-5; Martin 1979, pl. 17.
399. Junker 1940, pl. VII.
400. Simon 1952, pp. 590-1; Fitzgibbon 1976, p. 342.
401. Boessneck and von den Driesch 1982, pp. 121, 124-5.
402. Lortet and Gaillard 1908, pp. 150-1.
403. Meininger et al. 1979, p. 28. This is also based on our observations in the markets of Cairo.
404. Hermann 1932, pp. 86-105; Cooney 1965, p. 108.
405. Werbrouck 1934b, pp. 21-5; Bissing 1941.
406. Derchain 1975, pp. 62-3; Derchain 1976, p. 8.
407. Moreau 1930, p. 64.
408. For the entire scene, see Wild 1953, pl. CXXII.
409. Morris 1895, p. 146; Simon 1952, pp. 558-9.
410. Meininger et al. 1979, p. 28.
411. Hubbard and Seymour 1968, p. 576.
412. For Common Quail hieroglyphs, see Griffith 1896, pl. II, fig. 15; Davies 1958, pl. IV, no. 8; Lacau and Chevrier 1969, pls. IX-X.
413. For the entire scene, see Duell 1938, pls. 168-170.
414. Hasselquist 1766, p. 209.
415. Klebs 1934, pp. 83-4; Hornell 1937, pp. 72-3; Day 1938, p. 118.
416. See Petrie 1927, pl. XIV.
417. For more on the identification of the ᚦ sign as a young Common Quail, see Keimer 1930a, p. 6 and n. 3.
418. For the bird in color, see Smith 1946, pl. B.
419. See Blackman 1924, pl. XIV; Simpson 1980, pl. IV (c) and fig. 4.
420. See Davies 1917a, pls. XVIII, XIX (a) and XX.
421. See Capart and Werbrouck 1926, p. 190, fig. 112.
422. Wreszinski 1923, pl. 198; Davies and Davies 1933, pls. XXX (a) and XLV; Davies 1963, pl. II. Although not directly related, see also Cooney 1965, pp. 106-7; Lefebvre 1924, pl. XLIX.
423. Herodotus II, 77.
424. See Vandier 1969, pp. 441-445.
425. Klebs 1934, p. 80; Forbes 1955, pp. 186-7; Lucas 1962, p. 269; Vandier 1969, p. 445.
426. Athenaeus IX, 393.
427. Simon 1952, p. 594; Fitzgibbon 1976, p. 374.
428. It should be noted that several writers have mentioned that Common Quail remains have been found in tombs, where they had been placed as food offerings. It is not known whether these identifications were made by qualified persons or not. E.g., Hayes 1959, pp. 52 and 86; Emery 1962, p. 6.
429. For a review of this interesting migration, see Moreau 1927-1928, pp. 6-13.
430. Ibid., p. 9.
431. Diodorus I, 60. Also see Jarvis 1932, pp. 258-64.
432. Darwin 1898, p. 258, n. 33; Delacour 1951, p. 108.
433. Carter 1923, p. 1.
434. E.g., Keimer 1956a, p. 7; Brunner-Traut 1980, p. 70.
435. Coltherd 1966, p. 220.
436. Salonen 1973, p. 154; Heimpel and Calmeyer 1972-1975, pp. 487-8.
437. Haller 1954, pl. 29, fig. 161; Smith 1965b, fig. 40.
438. Cottevieille-Giraudet 1931, pl. VIII, no. 42 and correction on p. 74. This is not the only instance of someone wishing to see the Red Junglefowl occurring in Egyptian art before the Ramesside era. Also see Stubbs and Rowe 1912, pp. 7-10; Hornblower 1935, p. 82.
439. Sethe 1916, pp. 109-116.
440. E.g., Carter 1923, pp. 3-4; Klebs 1934, p. 85; Capart 1941, p. 210; Posener 1959, p. 31; Brunner-Traut 1980, p. 70.
441. Keimer 1926, p. 287, n. 4.
442. It has often been stated that a rhyton which appears amongst the tribute from Crete figured in a scene in the Dynasty XVIII tomb of Rekhmire (No. 100) at Thebes is in the shape of a Red Junglefowl. This identification is very doubtful, see Davies 1943, p. 21, n. 27; Vercoutter 1956, p. 314 and n. 3.
443. For a full discussion, see Simpson 1959, p. 38.
444. See Dunham 1955, p. 37, fig. 22 (b and e).
445. Darby et al. 1977, p. 304, figs. 6.32-6.33. The authors publish skeletal remains and eggs from the Egyptian Agricultural Museum, Dokki, and they refer to them as being the earliest known remains and eggs of the domestic fowl in Egypt. They give the date of this material as "New Kingdom; date uncertain." On p. 301, they use the remains and eggs (here they are said to come from Dynasty XVIII) to infer that the bird was consumed during Dynastic times. Until properly identified, dated, and a complete account given of the context in which they were found, this material cannot be accepted.
446. Capart 1931, pp. 90-2.
447. E.g., Strzygowski 1904, pl. XIX, nos 8882-3; Mogensen 1930, pl. LII, no. A381; Capart 1941, p. 208, fig. 1; Gabra 1941, pl. XLIV; Aldred et al. 1980, p. 198, fig. 190.
448. Martin 1981, p. 27.
449. Diodorus I, 74. Also see Burton 1972, p. 217.
450. Lane 1860, p. 311.
451. A good description of this method is given, for example, by Clarke 1817, pp. 314-17; Lane 1860, pp. 309-11; Wilkinson 1878, Vol. 2, pp. 449-52.
452. Anonymous 1959, pp. 29-33.
453. For example, we have seen Helmeted Guineafowl for sale in pet stores in Cairo. Also Hasselquist 1766, pp. 202-3 notes that in his day guineafowl were imported by merchants from Nubia, who sold them in the markets of Cairo.
454. Vaurie 1965, p. 328.
455. For other Helmeted Guineafowl hieroglyphs, see Davies 1940, pls. XIV-XV; Lacau and Chevrier 1969, pl. VIII, no. 24.
456. Fischer 1979, p. 26.
457. E.g., Keimer 1942, p. 329, fig. 66; Moorey 1970, p. 15, pl. 4.
458. See Müller 1959b, pl. III (a); Müller 1964, pp. 12-13, A3.
459. Legge 1909, p. 299.
460. Stubbs and Rowe 1912, pp. 9-10.
461. Vandier 1952, p. 585.
462. Müller 1959b, p. 68, n. 4.
463. Keimer 1938, pp. 258-60.
464. Hartert 1919-1920, p. 2006; Balsac and Mayaud 1962, p. 99.
465. Etchécopar and Hüe 1967, p. 180.
466. Rice 1983, pp. 19, 94-5.
467. For the entire fragment see Wreszinski 1923, pl. 27; Wreszinski 1936, pl. 83 (c).
468. See Mogensen 1930, pl. XCI, no. A656; Vandersleyen 1975, pl. 242.
469. E.g., Newberry 1893a, pl. XXX; Newberry 1893b, pl. XIV; Wreszinski 1923, pls. 157 and 345 (b); Junker 1943, fig. 16; Smith 1946, pl. 59 (b).
470. Boessneck 1981, pp. 18-19 and pl. 13 (a), wishes to see a third species of crane in Egyptian art, namely the Siberian Crane (Grus leucogeranus), from a much damaged figure of a long-legged bird in the Dynasty XII tomb of Antefoker (No. 60) at Thebes. The bird cannot be accurately identified, but our guess is that it is a European Spoonbill, as is the bird standing next to it. See Davies 1920, pls. V-V (a). Nor can we accept the proposed identification of the Crowned Crane (Balearica pavonina) on the Dynasty I Libya Palette. See Keimer 1954b, pp. 135-6.
471. E.g., Newberry 1895, pl. XXII; Davies 1902, Vol. 1, pl. XVI; Capart 1907, pl. LXXXIX; Wreszinski 1936, pl. 77; Duell 1938, pl. 52; Éperon et al. 1939, pls. VIII, XXXIII-XXXIV; Kees 1939, pl. IV (b).
472. E.g., Davies 1920, pl. XIII; Junker 1938, p. 139, fig. 18 and pl. VII (b); Vandier 1954, pl. VIII; Wild 1966, pl. CLXII.
473. Archibald 1974, pp. 147-55; Archibald and Viess 1979, pp. 51-73.

474. Altenmüller 1974, pp. 13-18, offers a somewhat different view than our own. Because cranes do not breed very well in captivity, we do not think that the Egyptians bred them domestically on a large scale.

475. As already noted by Moreau 1930, pp. 67-8.

476. See Emery 1938, pl. 12, cat. no. 310; Altenmüller 1974, p. 13, fig. 1.

477. Vandier 1952, p. 804; Altenmüller 1974, pp. 13-18.

478. E.g., Pegge 1773, pp. 171-6; Toynbee 1973, pp. 243-4.

479. Simon 1952, p. 548.

480. Blanford 1898, p. 187.

481. Darby et al. 1977, p. 291.

482. There are no recent records of the species breeding in Morocco, and this popultaion may now be extinct. See Balsac and Mayaud 1962, pp. 101-2.

483. For the entire scene, see Naville 1901, pls. CVIII-CX.

484. For other examples, see Davies 1923, pl. LVI; Davies 1930a, pl. XXVII; Kuhlmann and Schenkel 1983, pl. 53.

485. Whymper 1909, pp. 138-9.

486. E.g., Capart 1907, pl. LVIII; Blackman 1924, pl. IX.

487. At one time the Purple Gallinule bred in the Faiyum. See Meinertzhagen 1930, p. 642.

488. For the entire block, see n. 108.

489. See Petrie 1892, pl. XXII; Baines and Málek 1980, p. 56.

490. E.g., Junker 1940, fig. 8; Wild 1953, pl. CXIX; Moussa and Altenmüller 1971, pl. 5; Simpson 1976, pls. VI and C; Simpson 1980, pl. XLIV and fig. 30.

491. See Hassan 1943, p. 135, fig. 77 and pl. XXXVII.

492. See Moussa and Altenmüller 1977, pls. 5, 74-5 and fig. 6.

493. See Davies 1902, Vol. II, pl. IV and p. 5.

494. Meinertzhagen 1930, p. 642.

495. Taylor 1896, p. 481; Meininger et al. 1979, p. 28.

496. For the bird in color, see Rosellini 1834, pl. IX, fig. 8.

497. Compare with the living bird shown in Heinzel et al. 1977, p. 117.

498. Some have wished to see the coot appearing in Old Kingdom art. See Wreszinski 1936, p. 173.

499. See Winlock 1955, frontispiece and pls. 51 and 53.

500. Ibid., p. 66.

501. See Davies 1917a, pls. XXIII(b) and XXVI; Davies 1936, pl. XLVII.

502. See Wreszinski 1923, pl. 249; Brack and Brack 1980, pls. 19 and 73(a).

503. Simon 1952, p. 546; Fitzgibbon 1976, p. 110.

504. Gurney 1876, p. 95; Whymper 1909, p. 173; Meininger et al. 1979, p. 28.

505. Meinertzhagen 1930, p. 586.

506. See already Newberry 1900, p. 3, pl. XIII.

507. For the bird in color, see Rosellini 1834, pl. X, fig. 6; Newberry 1900, pl. XIII, fig. 1 (here the white underside and the "shoulder stripe" are shown pinkish, which is an error on the part of the copyist).

508. Boussac 1908, p. 285, has suggested that the bird is a Ringed Plover. We think that it is too general for specific identification.

509. Shelley 1872, p. 231, states that the Lapwing breeds in Egypt south of Cairo. However, we know of no evidence to support this.

510. For Lapwing hieroglyphs, see Davies 1900, pl. XVIII, fig. 410; Murray 1905, pl. XXXVII, nos 15-16; Davies 1958, pl. III, no. 5; Lacau and Chevrier 1969, pl. VIII.

511. For the entire scene, see Moussa and Altenmüller 1971, pl. 1.

512. We know of only one other example, see Mastaba of Ptah-shepses 1976, fig. 33. Sometimes the king is shown holding a Lapwing, but these are surely not pets. E.g., Calverley 1958, pl. 22; National Geographic Society 1978, p. 26.

513. See Petrie 1953, pl. B, fig. 4.

514. Gunn 1926, pp. 186-7; Gardiner 1947, pp. 101-6; Gardiner 1961, p. 403.

515. Hayes 1937, p. 31; Desroches-Noblecourt 1976, p. 280.

516. E.g., Firth and Quibell 1935, pl. 58; Hayes 1937, p. 31, n. 127; Vandersleyen 1975, pl. 186.

517. E.g., Randall-MacIver and Woolley 1911, pl. 19; Davies and Gardiner 1926, pls. XX and XXII; University of Chicago, Oriental Institute 1980, pls. 24-6; Smith and Redford 1976, pl. 77.

518. E.g., Vandersleyen 1975, pl. 384; Brack and Brack 1980, pls. 6(d), 39 and 86.

519. E.g., Davies 1905, pl. VI; Hölscher 1951, pl. 5; Smith and Redford 1976, p. 129, fig. 21 and pl. 61.

520. Gunn 1926, p. 186, with n. 2.

521. E.g., Petrie 1892, pl. XXII.

522. For the bird in color, see Gaillard 1934, pl. I, figs. 1-2.

523. J. G. Wilkinson was the only copyist to have correctly noted the presence of a crest on this representation. See Wilkinson 1878, Vol. II, p. 112, no. 368, fig. 12.

524. In discussing the spurs on the legs of this bird, Gaillard 1934, pp. 10-12, has suggested that this feature may have disappeared from the living Spur-winged Plover since the time of Dynasty XI. This, however, is totally unfounded, as such a major change could not have taken place in this species' bone structure over a mere four thousand years.

525. Moreau 1930, p. 69. See Wild 1953, pl. CXIX.

526. Shelley 1872, p. 232; Brooksbank 1925, p. 77.

527. E.g., Macramallah 1935, frontispiece and pl. XXVIII (c 9).

528. Herodotus II, 68.

529. For a discussion on the identity of this bird, see Adams 1870, pp. 53-4; Gaillard 1934, pp. 7-8; Thompson 1966, pp. 288-9; Lloyd 1976, p. 307; and especially Howell 1979, pp. 3-5.

530. For the entire scene, see Wild 1953, pl. CXIX.

531. See ibid.

532. See Holwerda et al. 1908, pl. XIV; Wreszinski 1923, pl. 106.

533. Meinertzhagen 1930, p. 576; Etchécopar and Hüe 1967, p. 258. This distribution is based on older information and there are no recent records of this species breeding in Egypt.

534. Paran 1980, pp. 3-4. Here the author mentions that 15,000 Avocets were observed during January 1972 near Bur Fuad.

535. For the bird in color, see Rosellini 1834, pl. X, fig. 8.

536. See Wild 1953, pl. CXIX.

537. For the other scene, see Newberry 1895, pl. XVIII.

538. See ibid., pl. XXI.

539. Moreau 1930, p. 69; Meininger et al. 1979, p. 28.

540. Fitzgibbon 1976, p. 25.

541. Kaiser 1890, p. 521; Baker 1921, p. 283; Etchécopar and Hüe 1967, p. 312.

542. It is interesting to note that Wilkinson also believed that this bird was a sandgrouse. See Davies 1949, p. 20, no. 29.

543. For the bird in color, see Rosellini 1834, pl. X, fig. 5.

544. The vernacular name of this species is generally given as the Rock Dove. However, to avoid confusion, we prefer to call the members of the genus Columba pigeons, and the members of the genus Streptopelia doves.

545. For the entire scene, see Frankfort 1929, pls. II-VI.

546. For the bird in color, see ibid., pl. V.

547. See Glanville 1926, pl. XII, figs. 1-3; Vandier 1952, p. 312, fig. 219.

548. It should be noted that pigeon remains are said to have been found in a tomb and in a foundation deposit, where they had been placed as food offerings. However, it is not known whether these identifications were made by qualified persons or not. See Hayes 1959, p. 104; Emery 1962, p. 6.

549. Darwin 1898, p. 167; Goodwin 1967, p. 54.

550. Hornell 1947, pp. 182-5; Keimer 1956b, pp. 24-9; Anonymous 1960, pp. 22-8.

551. Keimer 1956b, pp. 26-7.

552. Husselman 1953, pp. 81-91.

553. For the entire coffin and a discussion of the technique employed in the painting of this dove, see Dunham and Smith 1949, pp. 261-8; Terrace 1967.

554. For the bird in color, see Müller 1959a, pl. 14; Terrace 1967, pl. VII.

555. Dunham and Smith 1949, p. 267; Terrace 1967, p. 39.

556. E.g., Mogensen 1930, pl. XCII, A664; Wreszinski 1936, pl. 83(b); Moussa and Altenmüller 1977, pl. 83.

557. Duell 1938, pl. 52.

558. Goodwin 1955, pp. 72-3.

559. Boussac 1909, pp. 264-7; Moreau 1930, p. 70; Keimer 1956b, p. 28.

560. Junker 1940, pl. VII.

561. Duell 1938, pls. 127-8.

562. E.g., Wreszinski 1936, pls. 17, 76-7, 81, and 83(c).

563. See Lhote and Hassia 1954, pls. 60-1; Forman and Kischkewitz 1972, pls. 10-11; Peck and Ross 1978, pls. XI and 120.

564. E.g., Davies 1901, pls. XXVI-XXVII and XXXII-XXXIII; Murray 1905, pls. IX-X; Macramallah 1935, pl. XVII.
565. Newberry 1893a, pl. XXX.
566. Wild 1966, pl. CLXXI.
567. Boessneck and von den Driesch 1982, pp. 121, 124-5.
568. Sonnini 1800, p. 200; Baker 1913, p. 194.
569. Meininger *et al.* 1979, p. 19.
570. This distribution is based upon Vaurie 1965, pp. 574-5, but Etchécopar and Hüe 1967, p. 333, give the bird's range in Egypt as occurring throughout most of the country east of the Nile, except along the Red Sea coast. This distribution cannot, however, be substantiated by published records.
571. Wreszinski 1935, pl. 27, fig. o, refers to this bird as a "*Sporenkuckuck?*", that is, a Senegal Coucal (*Centropus senegalensis*), a cuckoo without a crest. As the bird is shown with a crest, the Great Spotted Cuckoo is certainly the more likely identification.
572. Friedmann 1964a, pp. 24-47.
573. Shelley 1872, p. 163.
574. Friedmann 1964b, pp. 283-5.
575. For other Barn Owl hieroglyphs, see Davies 1900, pls. VII, figs 81-2, 92 and XVIII, fig. 409; Terrace 1967, pls. XXXIII, XXXV-XXXVII and XXXIX-XLII; Lacau and Chevrier 1969, pl. XII.
576. One need only be referred to any field guide book of birds.
577. The species' heart-shaped face is sometimes even more pronounced than it is here. E.g., Vandier 1954, pl. VI; Peck and Ross 1978, pl. X.
578. Fischer 1979, p. 10.
579. It should be noted that Ludwig Keimer does not regard these as being feather tufts. See Keimer 1951, pp. 78-9. However, we are not alone in interpreting them as "ears". E.g., Brooklyn Museum 1956, p. 32; Brunner-Traut 1979, p. 65; Page 1983, p. 45, no. 64.
580. See Spencer 1980, pls. 8-9, cat. no. 16; James 1982, p. 113, fig. 49.
581. E.g., Petrie 1892, frontispiece, no. 2; Smith 1946, pl. A.
582. For the other example, see Davies 1927, pl. XXX.
583. For the entire scene, see Keimer 1940, pl. I; Vandier 1973, pl. XVIII.
584. Osborn and Helmy 1980, p. 422.
585. Newberry 1951, p. 72, refers to this owl as being figured three-quarter face. He further states that there is another owl in this scene, but this cannot be confirmed from the fragment.
586. E.g., Edgar 1906, pls. XXXVI-XXXVII; Capart 1931, pl. 94; Steindorff 1946, pl. LXIII, cat. no. 356(a).
587. E.g., Capart 1927, pl. 87; Steindorff 1946, pls. XLVII, cat. no. 289 and LIV, cat. nos. 274-5; Kueny and Yoyotte 1979, front cover and pp. 107-8.
588. Stricker 1957, pp. 1-14; Kaplony 1977, pp. 39-40.
589. For the entire palette, and a more detailed discussion of it, see Vandier 1952, pp. 590-2; Petrie 1953, pl. G, figs. 19-20; Terrace and Fischer 1970, pp. 21-4.
590. E.g., Keimer 1951, p. 81; Newberry 1951, p. 73.
591. See n. 580.
592. E.g., Petrie 1927, pl. XIII; Smith 1946, pl. 35; Keimer 1951, fig. 8 (a-f); Smith 1965a, pl. 13.
593. Newberry 1951, p. 72.
594. E.g., Davies 1936, pl. VI.
595. Meinertzhagen 1930, p. 333, states that Rollers are rare during the spring migration, but common during the autumn migration.
596. For the entire scene, see Newberry 1893b, pl. VI.
597. Gaillard 1929, p. 27; Witherby 1938, p. 270.
598. Bannerman 1971, p. 123.
599. This is based upon our own observations in the tomb.
600. See Newberry 1893b, pl. XVI; Gaillard 1929, pl. II, fig. 4 (in color).
601. For the bird in color, see Gaillard 1929, pl. II, fig. 5.
602. This whole class of scene is discussed by Keel 1977, pp. 103-42.
603. Whymper 1909, pp. 49-50; Nicoll 1919, p. 43. Both authors state that the Kingfisher in the not too distant past bred in Egypt. However, we know of no satisfactory evidence for such a claim.
604. For the entire block, see n. 108.
605. See Hassan 1943, p. 135, fig. 77 and pl. XXXVII.
606. E.g., Junker 1940, fig. 8; Wild 1953, pl. CXIX; Smith 1964, p. 145.
607. The Pied Kingfisher has not been recorded in the Faiyum since 1957. See Horváth 1959, p. 467.
608. For the entire scene, see n. 545.
609. E.g., Macramallah 1935, frontispiece and pls. VI-VIII; Duell 1938, pls. 10 and 19; Wild 1953, pl. CXIX; Müller 1959a, pl. 8; Moussa and Altenmüller 1977, pl. 5 and fig. 6.
610. See Bissing 1956, pl. IX; Edel 1963, p. 190, fig. 14.
611. Gaillard 1931, pp. 260-70, suggests that the Pied Kingfisher may have changed its nesting habits since antiquity, because it is so often rendered in Egyptian art nesting in papyrus swamps. This *absolutely* cannot be accepted.
612. Brooksbank 1925, pp. 37-9; Etchécopar and Hüe 1967, p. 360.
613. Shelley 1872, p. 169, states that the Bee-eater occasionally breeds in Egypt. However, we know of no supporting evidence.
614. Other writers have wished to see the bee-eater elsewhere in Egyptian art, but their identifications do not stand up to close scrutiny. E.g., Dawson 1925, pp. 590-3; Wreszinski 1936, p. 242.
615. For a reconstruction of the Puntite scene, see Smith 1965b, figs. 173-4.
616. On the location of Punt, see Kitchen 1971, pp. 184-207.
617. Whymper 1909, p. 56, also noted that this bird is a bee-eater.
618. For the bee-eaters of East Africa, see Dresser 1884-1886; Mackworth-Praed and Grant 1952, pp. 584-604.
619. For references, see Gardiner 1957, p. 469, Sign-list G22.
620. Frankfort 1929, p. 23.
621. Smith 1965a, p. 110.
622. For the bird in color, see Newberry 1900, pl. VI; Davies 1936, pl. IX; Yoyotte 1968, p. 61.
623. See Hassan 1943, p. 135, fig. 77 and pl. XXXVII.
624. E.g., Blackman 1914, pl. II; Macramallah 1935, pls. VI-VIII; Wild 1953, pl. CXIX; Simpson 1976, pls. VI and C; Moussa and Altenmüller 1977, pls. 4-5 and figs. 5-6.
625. Cott 1947, p. 464.
626. Cecil 1904, p. 35; Meininger *et al.* 1979, p. 28.
627. Cecil 1904, p. 35.
628. Keimer 1930b, pp. 310-11 and 317.
629. See Wreszinski 1936, pp. 42-3 and pl. 22; Duell 1938, pl. 162.
630. Keimer 1930b, pp. 310-11 and 317.
631. Dawson 1925, p. 594; Keimer 1930b, pp. 315-17.
632. Hayes 1959, p. 388; Piankoff and Jacquet-Gordon 1974, p. 69 and pls. 23 and 38.
633. See Keimer 1930b, pp. 314-15, figs. 5-6 and pl. IV.
634. Other writers have identified crag martins occurring elsewhere in Egyptian art. However, their identifications do not stand up to close scrutiny. E.g., Boussac 1905a, p. 662; Moreau 1930, p. 60.
635. See Daressy 1902.
636. It should be noted that the family Hirundinidae, to which crag martins belong, is composed of both swallows and martins. When referring to the members of this family in a collective sense, they are often called swallows. Hence, our use of the word "swallow" does not refer to the Swallow (*Hirundo rustica*), but rather to swallows collectively.
637. This is based upon our personal observation.
638. For the entire papyrus, see Piankoff 1957, pl. 25.
639. *Ibid.*, p. 187.
640. *Ibid.*, p. 187.
641. This is based upon our personal observation.
642. See Mariette 1876, pl. 17; Boussac 1905a, p. 661, fig. 1.
643. E.g., Piankoff 1957, pls. 2, 6, 9, 11 and 21; Bruyère 1959, pl. XXVII; Rossiter 1979, pp. 36 and 52.
644. te Velde 1972, pp. 26-31; Wassermann 1984, p. 754.
645. te Velde 1972, p. 27.
646. See Carter 1927, pl. LXXXII (a); Edwards 1976b, p. 24, no. 19.
647. E.g., Boussac 1905a, p. 661, fig. 1, p. 662, fig. 3, p. 665, fig. 6; Speleers 1917, pl. XXII; Bruyère 1933, pl. XIV; Piankoff 1957, pls. 15 and 18.
648. te Velde 1972, pp. 28-9.
649. Bruyère 1952, pp. 105-14; Wassermann 1984, p. 754.
650. For the entire stela, see Tosi and Roccati 1972, p. 285, no. 50056.
651. te Velde 1972, p. 29.
652. te Velde 1972, p. 31; Wassermann 1984, p. 754 with n. 14.

653. For the bird in color, see Vandersleyen 1975, pl. XXVI.
654. Smith 1946, p. 373, G36.
655. E.g., Petrie 1892, frontispiece, no. 4; Griffith 1896, pl. II, fig. 9; Smith 1946, pl. A.
656. E.g., Griffith 1896, pl. II, fig. 14; Davies 1958, pl. III, no. 3; Thausing and Goedicke 1971, pls. 138, 140, 152, 154.
657. See Griffith 1898, pl. I, fig. 3.
658. Gardiner 1957, p. 471, Sign-list G36.
659. See Smith 1946, p. 373, G36. For another outstanding picture of the House Martin hieroglyph, see Terrace 1967, pl. XL.
660. The European subspecies of this species (*M. alba alba*) that visits Egypt in the winter is called the White Wagtail, while the breeding Egyptian subspecies (*M. alba vidua*) is called the Pied Wagtail. It is inappropriate to assign this representation to either one or the other subspecies.
661. Meinertzhagen 1930, p. 170.
662. Davies 1936, p. 126.
663. See Wild 1953, pls. LXXXIII (a) and CXIX.
664. Meinertzhagen 1930, p. 183. He states that Red-backed Shrikes are rare in Egypt during the spring migration, but are common during the autumn migration.
665. Moussa and Altenmüller 1977, p. 60, the authors wish to see a Red-backed Shrike in an Old Kingdom swamp scene. We disagree with their suggestion.
666. Moreau 1930, p. 60.
667. For the bird in color, see Newberry 1900, pl. VII; Davies 1936, pl. IX; Yoyotte 1968, p. 61.
668. Nicoll 1919, p. 27 states that the Masked Shrike sometimes breeds in Upper Egypt. However, we know of no evidence to support this.
669. For the bird in color, see Davies 1936, pl. IX; Yoyotte 1968, p. 61.
670. For the entire scene, see Newberry 1893b, pl. VI.
671. See *ibid.*, pl. XVI.
672. See Duell 1938, pl. 162; Grdseloff 1938, p. 137, fig. 2.
673. For the bird in color, see Gaillard 1929, pl. II, fig. 2.
674. Vandier 1969, pp. 313-18.
675. E.g., Mohr 1943, p. 50, fig. 20; Smith 1965a, p. 70, fig. 31 and pl. 50(a); Wild 1966, pls. CXLV(b) and CLXX; Moussa and Altenmüller 1977, pl. 22 and fig. 9; van de Walle 1978, pl. 9.
676. Gaillard 1929, p. 36.
677. See Moussa and Altenmüller 1977, pl. 22 and fig. 9.
678. Macpherson 1897, p. 17; Cott 1947, p. 464.
679. Sonnini 1800, p. 703; Ghabbour 1976, pp. 19-20; and our own personal observations in Egypt.
680. Ghabbour 1976, pp. 19-20.
681. Ticehurst 1912, p. 45; Goodman and Ames 1983.
682. Ghabbour 1976, pp. 19-20; Woldhek 1979, p. 51; Goodman and Ames 1983.
683. E.g., Blackman and Apted 1953a, pl. XXVIII; Fischer 1978, pp. 44-5.
684. Meininger *et al.* 1980, pp. 245-50. The authors document the recent spread of the House Crow into modern Egypt. It is extremely doubtful, therefore, that the species occurred in ancient Egypt.
685. Meinertzhagen 1930, p. 95.
686. *Ibid.*, p. 90.
687. Davies 1917b, p. 239, offers a much different interpretation of the drawing of the two crows than ours.
688. E.g., Vandier d'Abbadie 1936b, pls. IV-VIII; Peterson 1973, pl. 55, no. 104; Brunner-Traut 1979, pl. XVIII, no. 23; Hodjash and Berlev 1982, no. 96.
689. Vandier d'Abbadie 1946, pp. 16-21.
690. *Ibid.*, pp. 12-16; Brunner-Traut 1975, p. 83.
691. E.g., Vandier d'Abbadie 1936b, pls. I-III; Vandier d'Abbadie 1959, pls. XCVI-XCVII; Peterson 1973, pl. 56, no. 105; Peck and Ross 1978, pl. 105.
692. E.g., Vandier d'Abbadie 1936b, pl. III, no. 2006; Vandier d'Abbadie 1946, p. 11 and n. 1.
693. Meinertzhagen 1954, p. 77; Tregenza 1958, pp. 108-9.
694. See Petrie 1953, pl. E; Spencer 1980, pl. 64, no. 576.
695. Winlock 1945, pp. 18-19.
696. E.g., Vandier d'Abbadie 1946, p. 64; Omlin 1973, p. 30.
697. This scene seems to be related to one on an ostracon which shows a Hippopotamus in a sycamore fig tree and a crow eating figs. See Vandier d'Abbadie 1937, pl. XCII, no. 2717.
698. Wilber 1960, pp. 265-6.
699. In general, see Brunner-Traut 1955, pp. 12-32; Brunner-Traut 1977a.
700. See Davies 1936, pl. L.
701. See Petrie 1890, pl. XVIII and p. 38.
702. Burlington Fine Arts Club 1922, p. 17; Aldred 1971, pp. 213-14.
703. Shelley 1872, p. 82.
704. For the bird in color, see Davies 1936, pl. IX; Yoyotte 1968, p. 61.
705. See Newberry 1900, frontispiece.
706. The House Sparrow populations south of the Sahara Desert have been introduced, see Halland and Moreau 1970, p. 313.
707. For references, see Gardiner 1957, p. 471, Sign-list G37.
708. For the entire scene, see Davies 1927, frontispiece and pl. IX; Davies 1936, pl. LXXXVII.
709. Davies 1927, p. 17; Davies 1936, p. 169; Mekhitarian 1954, p. 134.
710. E.g., Murray 1905, pl. XXXVII, no. 19. For another example of this sign, see Smith 1946, pl. B.
711. Fischer 1979, pp. 28-9.
712. Ghabbour 1976, pp. 17-29; Ali and Hafez 1976, pp. 277-8.
713. Caminos 1954, pp. 247 and 315.
714. For the bats of modern Egypt, see Flower 1932, pp. 376-86; Sandborn and Hoogstraal 1955, pp. 103-19; Hoogstraal 1962, pp. 143-62; Gaisler *et al.* 1972, pp. 1-40.
715. See Sandborn and Hoogstraal 1955, pp. 106, 110-11; Hoogstraal 1962, pp. 152, 154-5.
716. Vandier d'Abbadie 1936a, p. 120, fig. 3 and pl. I, no. 2. The author publishes a small amulet from the New Kingdom which she says depicts a bat. While in our view it is possible that it is indeed a bat, it is not unmistakably so.
717. For line drawings of the bats, see Vandier d'Abbadie 1936a, p. 118, fig. 1; Davies 1949, pl. III.
718. Anderson 1902, p. 92.
719. Boussac 1907, pp. 211-12; Allen 1939, p. 10, fig. 2; Madkour 1977, pp. 167-8.
720. Wilkinson 1878, Vol. III, p. 270; Störk 1977b, p. 263.
721. Leviticus XI, 19 and Deuteronomy XIV, 18.
722. E.g., Aldrovandi 1599, pp. 571-80; Yapp 1981, p. 40, fig. 26.
723. Fischer 1968, pp. 6-7.
724. Vandier d'Abbadie 1936a, p. 120; Roeder 1956, p. 384, no. 514.
725. Störk 1977b, p. 263, with n. 15.
726. Adams 1870, p. 73; Gurney 1876, p. 101; Gaisler *et al.* 1972, p. 11.

184

NOTES TO THE CHECKLIST

1. Meinertzhagen 1930.
2. El Negumi *et al.* 1950.
3. Al Hussaini 1938a, 1938b, 1939.
4. Al Hussaini 1954.
5. Horváth 1959.
6. Mayr and Cottrell 1979.
7. Delacour 1954, 1956, 1959.
8. Vaurie 1959, 1965.
9. Voous 1973, 1977.
10. Al Hussaini 1954; Anonymous 1941, reprinted almost in its entirety by Hafez 1978; El Negumi *et al.* 1950; Etchécopar and Hüe 1964; Kamil and Sallamah 1967; Meinertzhagen 1930, p. 681; Muraad 1967, translation of Whymper 1909; our own unpublished notes.
11. Meinertzhagen 1930.
12. Goodman *et al.* 1984.
13. Horváth 1959, p. 452; Meininger and Mullié 1981b, p. 65.
14. Goodman and Watson 1983, p. 101.
15. Hartert 1920, 2, p. 1449; Witherby *et al.* 1940, 4, p. 94; Cramp and Simmons 1977, p. 90; Short and Horne 1981, p. 43.
16. El Negumi *et al.* 1950, p. 214.
17. Borman 1929, p. 646; Jourdain and Lynes 1936, p. 46; Maclaren 1949, p. 545; Goodman and Storer 1985.
18. Meinertzhagen 1930, p. 486.
19. Also reported by Koenig 1932, p. 210.
20. Kumerloeve 1962, p. 221.
21. Flower 1933, p. 42; Horváth 1959, p. 453.
22. Bijlsma and de Roder 1982; Goodman and Storer 1985.
23. Goodman and Storer 1985.
24. Baha el Din and Saleh 1983, p. 6.
25. Horváth 1959, p. 456.
26. Flower 1933, p. 41.
27. Gurney 1876, p. 298, post-publication note.
28. Mr. Michael Walters, personal communication.
29. Goodman and Storer 1985.
30. Placed after the ANSERIFORMES in some other works.
31. Goodman and Watson 1983, p. 101.
32. Moreau 1928, p. 475; El Negumi *et al.* 1950, p. 314; Bijlsma 1982, pp. 144-5.
33. El Negumi *et al.* 1950, p. 304.
34. Goodman 1984a, p. 42.
35. Tregenza 1951, pp. 9-10; Goodman and Mowla Atta 1985.
36. Meinertzhagen 1930, p. 427.
37. Goodman 1984a, p. 43.
38. Meinertzhagen 1930, pp. 406-7; Ticehurst 1931, p. 576; Horváth 1959, pp. 459-60.
39. Previously reported by Meinertzhagen 1930, pp. 387-8.
40. *Ibid.*, p. 391.
41. Flower 1933, pp. 38-9.
42. See Thomson 1976 for comments on the type citation.
43. Moreau 1934, pp. 603-4; Bulman 1944, p. 483; Goodwin 1949, p. 63; Tregenza 1951, pp. 12-13; Galal el Din 1959; Booth 1961, pp. 129-30; Anonymous 1981, p. 12; Goodman and Mowla Atta 1985.
44. Meinertzhagen 1930, p. 457; Flower 1933, p. 41; Bodenham 1945, p. 19.
45. Schrader 1892, p. 52; El Negumi *et al.* 1950, p. 566; Short and Horne 1981, p. 46.
46. El Negumi *et al.* 1950, p. 225.
47. Also reported by Meinertzhagen 1930, p. 460.
48. Jourdain and Lynes 1936, p. 45.
49. Schrader 1892, p. 52; Meinertzhagen 1930, p. 461.
50. Ripley 1963, p. 108.
51. Cholmley 1897, p. 200.
52. Wimpfheimer *et al.* 1983, p. 59.
53. Also reported by Meinertzhagen 1930, p. 481.
54. Heuglin 1873, 2, pt. 2, p. 1353; Meinertzhagen 1954, p. 427.
55. Thomson 1965.
56. Also reported by Meinertzhagen 1930, p. 624.
57. Goodman and Watson 1983, p. 101.
58. Meiklejohn 1944, p. 18; Anonymous 1981, p. 12.
59. Flower 1933, p. 45; Koenig 1928, p. 250.
60. Wimpfheimer *et al.* 1983, p. 62.
61. Meinertzhagen 1930, p. 562.
62. Elliott and Monk 1952, p. 529; Anonymous 1981, p. 12; Wimpfheimer *et al.* 1983, p. 63.
63. El Negumi *et al.* 1950, p. 135.
64. Taylor 1896, p. 481; Ticehurst 1912, p. 58; Moreau 1928, p. 462; Wimpfheimer *et al.* 1983, p. 62.
65. Jourdain and Lynes 1936, p. 47; Horváth 1959, p. 464.
66. Wimpfheimer *et al.* 1983, p. 63.
67. El Negumi *et al.* 1950, pp. 154-5.
68. Meinertzhagen 1930, p. 590; Meiklejohn 1944, p. 18; Fischer 1963, p. 101; Goodman and Mowla Atta 1985.
69. Mörzer Bruyns and Voous 1965.
70. Goodman and Storer 1985; Meininger and Sørensen 1985.
71. El Negumi *et al.* 1950, p. 175.
72. Goodman and Storer 1985; Meininger and Sørensen 1985.
73. *Ibid.*
74. *Bull. Zoological Nomenclature*, 1970, 26, p. 225.
75. Anonymous 1981, p. 12.
76. *Contra* Etchécopar and Hüe 1967, p. 302.
77. Goodman and Storer 1985.
78. Short and Horne 1981, p. 52.
79. Wimpfheimer *et al.* 1983, p. 65.
80. Ticehurst 1912, p. 59.
81. Sometimes this order is given family or subordinal status in the COLUMBIFORMES or CHARADRIFORMES.
82. Goodman 1984a, p. 45.
83. Mr. Hesham Sabry, personal communication.
84. *Contra* Etchécopar and Hüe 1967, p. 312.
85. Goodman and Watson 1983, pp. 101-2; Goodman and Mowla Atta 1985.
86. Goodman 1984a, p. 45.
87. Greaves in Marchant 1941, p. 289.
88. Goodman and Houlihan 1981.
89. Meininger and Mullié 1981a, p. 2; Anonymous 1981, p. 12; Wimpfheimer *et al.* 1983, p. 65.
90. El Negumi 1949; Goodman and Watson 1983, p. 102; Goodman 1984a, p. 46.
91. Goodman 1982.
92. Meinertzhagen 1930, p. 364.
93. Goodman and Sabry 1984.
94. Horváth 1959, p. 470.
95. Date verified by Dr. Horváth.
96. Goodman and Watson 1983, p. 102.
97. *Ibid.*, p. 102.
98. Meinertzhagen 1930, p. 317; Marietti 1933, p. 168; Rowntree 1943, p. 25; Hutson 1944, p. 10; Elliott and Monk 1952, p. 530; Haensel 1980, p. 23.
99. Goodman and Watson 1983, p. 102.
100. Schrader 1892, p. 43; Meinertzhagen 1930, p. 316; Marietti 1933, p. 168; Hutson 1944, p. 10; Meininger and Mullié 1981a, p. 2; Short and Horne 1981, p. 54; Wimpfheimer *et al.* 1983, p. 66.
101. Misonne 1974, p. 62.
102. Wimpfheimer *et al.* 1983, p. 66.
103. Goodman and Watson 1983, p. 103.
104. Meinertzhagen 1930, p. 312.
105. El Negumi 1949; Goodman 1984a, p. 47.
106. Moreau 1934, p. 602.
107. Meinertzhagen 1930, p. 135.
108. Goodman 1984a, pp. 47-8.
109. Meinertzhagen 1930, p. 136.
110. *Ibid.*, p. 133.
111. Goodman and Watson 1983, p. 103.
112. Meinertzhagen 1930, p. 132; Jourdain and Lynes 1936, p. 40.
113. Meinertzhagen 1930, p. 184.

114. Moreau 1934, p. 602; Horváth 1959, p. 478.
115. Horváth 1959, p. 478; Goodman 1984a, p. 48.
116. Also reported by Meinertzhagen 1930, p. 179.
117. Goodman 1984a, p. 48.
118. Meinertzhagen 1930, p. 101.
119. Wimpfheimer *et al.* 1983, p. 71.
120. Horváth 1959, p. 479.
121. Meininger and Dielissen 1979, pp. 85-6; Meininger *et al.* 1980.
122. Meinertzhagen 1930, p. 95.
123. Greaves 1939, pp. 50-1; El Negumi 1949; Goodman 1984a. p. 49.
124. Wimpfheimer *et al.* 1983, p. 68.
125. Goodman and Watson 1983, p. 103.
126. Hubbard and Seymour 1968, p. 576.
127. In some other works the families (as used here) SYL-VIIDAE, MUSICAPIDAE, TURDIDAE, and TIMALIIDAE are given subfamily status in the MUSCI-CAPIDAE.
128. Wimpfheimer *et al.* 1983, p. 69.
129. Meinertzhagen 1930, p. 203.
130. Hubbard and Seymour 1968, pp. 576-7; Goodman and Watson 1983, p. 103.
131. Goodman and Watson 1983, p. 103.
132. *Ibid.*, pp. 103-4.
133. Also reported by Meinertzhagen 1930, p. 222.
134. Nicoll 1911, p. 91; Meinertzhagen 1930, p. 226; Goodman and Mowla Atta 1985.
135. Hubbard and Seymour 1968, pp. 576-7; Goodman and Watson 1983, p. 104.
136. Goodman and Tewfik 1983.
137. Meinertzhagen 1930, p. 237.
138. Goodman 1984b.
139. In some other works the wheatear portion of the common name for *Oenanthe* spp. is replaced by chat, e.g., Pied Wheatear becomes Pied Chat.
140. Meinertzhagen 1930, p. 273.
141. Sluys and van den Berg 1982.
142. Meinertzhagen 1930, p. 266.
143. Goodman and Ames 1983, p. 92.
144. Meinertzhagen 1930, p. 277; Tregenza 1951, p. 4; Misonne 1974, p. 66; Meininger and Mullié 1981a, p. 3; Short and Horne 1981, p. 56; Goodman and Mowla Atta 1985.
145. Meinertzhagen 1930, pp. 279-80.
146. Goodman 1984a, p. 49.
147. Misonne 1974, pp. 66-7.
148. See Goodman and Watson 1984 for a review of records of *Turdus* spp. in Egypt.
149. Goodman and Ames 1983, p. 92.
150. Goodman 1984a, pp. 49-50.
151. Wimpfheimer *et al.* 1983, p. 70.
152. Meinertzhagen 1930, p. 171.
153. Williams 1955, p. 251; Goodman 1984a, p. 50.
154. Safriel 1975, p. 79; Anonymous 1981, p. 12; Wimpfheimer *et al.* 1983, p. 71.
155. Goodman 1984a, p. 50.
156. *Ibid.*
157. Wimpfheimer *et al.* 1983, p. 71.
158. Misonne 1974, p. 68.
159. Meininger and Sørensen 1984.
160. Hubbard and Seymour 1968, pp. 576-7.
161. Goodman and Watson 1983, p. 104.
162. Hubbard and Seymour 1968, p. 577; Goodman and Watson 1983, p. 105.
163. Also reported by Meinertzhagen 1930, p. 125.
164. Schrader 1892, p. 47.
165. Previously reported by Meinertzhagen 1930, p. 128.
166. Goodman 1984a, p. 51.
167. Misonne 1974, p. 68.
168. Goodman and Watson 1983, p. 105.
169. Wimpfheimer *et al.* 1983, p. 72.
170. Meinertzhagen 1930, p. 129.

CHRONOLOGICAL TABLE

All dates are B.C. unless otherwise indicated, and before Dynasty XXVI are not necessarily exact. The individual monarchs listed are only those who are mentioned in this book.

PREDYNASTIC PERIOD
Badarian	4500-4000
Amratian (Naqada I)	4000-3500
Gerzean (Naqada II)	3500-3000
Late Predynastic	3100-3000
King "Scorpion"	

EARLY DYNASTIC PERIOD
Dynasty I	3000-2770
Narmer (Menes?)	
Djet (Uadji)	
Dynasty II	2770-2649

OLD KINGDOM
Dynasty III	2649-2575
Dynasty IV	2575-2465
Dynasty V	2465-2323
Userkaf	2465-2458
Niuserre	2416-2392
Dynasty VI	2323-2150

FIRST INTERMEDIATE PERIOD
Dynasties VII-X	2150-2040

MIDDLE KINGDOM
Dynasty XI	2040-1991
Dynasty XII	1991-1783
Sesostris I	1971-1926
Amenemhat III	1844-1797
Dynasty XIII	1783-1640

SECOND INTERMEDIATE PERIOD
Dynasties XIV-XVII	1640-1532

NEW KINGDOM
Dynasty XVIII	1550-1307
Hatshepsut	1479-1458
Tuthmosis III	1479-1425
Tuthmosis IV	1401-1391
Amenhotep III	1391-1353
Akhenaten (Amenhotep IV)	1353-1335
Tutankhamun	1333-1323
Haremhab	1319-1307
Dynasty XIX	1307-1196
Seti II	1214-1204
Dynasty XX (Ramesside Period)	1196-1070
Ramesses III	1194-1163
Ramesses IX	1131-1112

THIRD INTERMEDIATE PERIOD
Dynasties XXI-XXIV	1070-712

LATE DYNASTIC PERIOD
Dynasty XXV	712-657
Dynasty XXVI	664-525
Dynasty XXVII (Persian)	525-404
Dynasty XXVIII	404-399
Dynasty XXIX	399-380
Dynasty XXX	380-343
Second Persian Period	343-332

GRECO-ROMAN PERIOD
Macedonian Kings	332-304
Philip Arrhidaeus	323-316
Ptolemaic Period	304-30
Ptolemy II	285-246
Roman Period	30-A.D. 395

BYZANTINE OR COPTIC PERIOD
A.D. 395-640

ARAB CONQUEST OF EGYPT
A.D. 640

INDEX: ENGLISH NAMES

189

INDEX: SCIENTIFIC NAMES

191